DATE DUE FOR RETURN

This book may be recalled before the above date.

THE RELIGION OF THE HINDUS

THE RELIGION
of
THE HINDUS

Edited by

KENNETH W. MORGAN

CONTRIBUTORS

D. S. SARMA

R. N. DANDEKAR

JITENDRA NATH BANERJEA

SIVAPRASAD BHATTACHARYYA

RADHAGOVINDA BASAK

SATIS CHANDRA CHATTERJEE

V. RAGHAVAN

MOTILAL BANARSIDASS
Delhi Varanasi Patna
Bangalore Madras

First Published, 1953
Reprinted in Delhi, 1987

MOTILAL BANARSIDASS
Bungalow Road, Jawahar Nagar, Delhi 110 007

Branches
Chowk, Varanasi 221 001
Ashok Rajpath, Patna 800 004
24, Race Course Road, Bangalore 560 001
120, Royapettah High Road, Mylapore, Madras 600 004

ISBN: 81-208-0387-6

PRINTED IN INDIA
BY JAINENDRA PRAKASH JAIN AT SHRI JAINENDRA PRESS, A-45 NARAINA INDUSTRIAL AREA, PHASE I, NEW DELHI 110 028 AND PUBLISHED BY NARENDRA PRAKASH JAIN FOR MOTILAL BANARSIDASS, DELHI 110 007.

PREFACE

Recognition of the need for this book grew out of conversations with Fellows of The National Council on Religion in Higher Education. We agreed that a study of the religion of the Hindus is necessary if one is to understand the people and culture of India, and that such a study should be based on materials written by Hindus themselves.

We realized that our Western cultural patterns and habits of thought have been shaped both consciously and unconsciously by the Greek-Hebrew-Christian tradition, and that many of the misunderstandings which arise between East and West come from our inevitable tendency to describe and judge the people of India by our own standards. The religious, social, and speculative patterns of India have been built on assumptions and beliefs so different from ours that it is difficult for a Westerner to describe them without distortion.

We decided that there is need for a book which sets forth the beliefs and practices of the Hindus, written by devout Hindus and designed for the Western reader who seeks a sympathetic understanding of Hinduism. Such a book, we agreed, would be useful for all people interested in a better understanding between East and West: the government official, the businessman, the casual visitor, and especially those who are concerned with college teaching in courses in religion, in area studies, or in general education programs.

Aided by a grant from The Edward W. Hazen Foundation, I spent six months in India visiting all the major cities, the chief university centers, and many places of holy pilgrimage, interviewing Hindus prominent in political and cultural activities, college professors, swamis, and holy men. I showed them an outline of the material which we in America agreed was necessary for an understanding of Hinduism and asked if they considered it to be fair and representative, frequently modifying the outline in the light of their carefully considered suggestions. I also asked them to suggest the men who, in their opinion, would be best qualified to write the different sections, men who are recognized as competent students and devout followers of Hinduism. As a result of their recommendations, I was brought in touch with the distinguished scholars who have contributed to this book.

My function as editor has been to provide the general outline for the book and to make such editorial changes as seemed necessary to avoid duplication and to meet the needs of the Western reader. Such variations in interpretation as may be found in the different chapters have been allowed to remain only when they are judged to be representative of differing interpretations in contemporary Hinduism. Although each chapter is given in the words of the author, it has been necessary to condense each section, to rearrange the material in some cases, and to eliminate many technical and Sanskrit words which would be used in India but would be confusing to Western readers. Each new term is defined when it first appears and may be found in the glossary or index in case the definition is forgotten.

The seven men who have contributed to this book come from different sections of India, have lived all their lives in India, and are known for their competence as scholars and their devotion to Hinduism. Each writer has been conscious of friends and colleagues looking over his shoulder as he wrote, checking him as to accuracy in citing facts, caution in generalizations, and justice to his religious faith.

Professor D. S. Sarma, now retired after serving as Principal of Vivekananda College, Madras, is the author of many books on Hinduism, and has former students all over India who refer to him with admiration and affection.

Professor Jitendra Nath Banerjea, Carmichael Professor and Head of the Department of Ancient Indian History and Culture, The University of Calcutta, is recognized as one of the leading iconographers in India, has traveled extensively visiting the sacred places of Hinduism, and has given his life to the devoted study of the subject which he discusses in this book.

Professor Radhagovinda Basak, now retired, was Professor of Sanskrit and Head of the Department of Sanskrit and Sanskritic Languages at Presidency College, Calcutta. He brings to his writings great competence in Sanskrit studies, a thorough knowledge of the literature, and skill in exposition gained through a lifetime of teaching and research.

Professor R. N. Dandekar, Professor of Sanskrit and Head of the Department of Sanskrit and Prakrit Languages, University of Poona, is well known throughout India and among scholars in the West for his writings. His discussion of the role of man in Hinduism is based on a broad background of linguistic study and philosophical insight.

Professor Sivaprasad Bhattacharyya, Emeritus Senior Professor of Sanskrit at Presidency College, Calcutta, is especially competent to deal with the religious practices of the Hindus because in addition to being a Sanskrit scholar he has long been regarded in his section of India as an authority on the religious practices of the home and the temple, frequently serving as a guru for devout Hindus.

Dr. Satis Chandra Chatterjee, Premchand Roychand Scholar and Lecturer in Philosophy, The University of Calcutta, is well known for his able writings in philosophy, highly regarded for the insights and clarity of exposition in his teaching, and honored by his friends for the quiet sincerity of his religious faith.

Professor V. Raghavan, Head of the Department of Sanskrit, Madras University, is known throughout India as a Sanskrit scholar, as well as an authority on Indian music and dancing. His selections and translations from the sacred writings of Hinduism are based on a full knowledge of the Hindu scriptures, years of experience in translation, and a deep devotion to the materials with which he works.

It should be borne in mind that each of these writers has been compelled to limit himself to a few pages when a volume would not suffice for a full treatment of his subject. The complexity of Hinduism with its many levels of development and the variations in different parts of the country make it especially difficult to write a concise, introductory account of the religion of the Hindus without erroneous generalizations, or distortions through what is included or omitted. As editor, I wish to pay my tribute to these men who have so ably and patiently applied themselves to this extremely difficult task which we asked them to add to their busy lives.

As supplementary materials for those who wish to go further in their study of contemporary Hinduism, and especially for teachers in the field of religion, I brought back some recordings of Hindu religious music, and colored slides showing the chief temples, pilgrimage places, and religious ceremonies of the Hindus. The Hindu religious music was recorded by Professor Alain Danielou of Banaras Hindu University, and has been published in this country by Folkways Records, Incorporated, in New York. The colored slides have been duplicated by, and may be purchased from, Professor Paul Vieth of The Divinity School, Yale University.

I am indebted to Professor D. S. Sarma and to the Madras Law Journal Press for permission to print selections from the translation of the *Bhagavad Gita* made by Professor Sarma. I am especially indebted to Professor Haridas Bhattacharyya of Calcutta for his wise counsel and for reading the first draft of the manuscripts. In gathering these materials, I have been helped in many ways by Mr. K. S. Krishnaswamy of Bangalore, and by his wife and their many friends. Many of the swamis of the Ramakrishna Mission have helped me, not only with their advice, but often by opening doors for me which might otherwise have remained closed.

At every step in the gathering of these materials I have been aided and encouraged by The Edward W. Hazen Foundation, and by the Fellows of The National Council on Religion in Higher Education.

KENNETH W. MORGAN

Hamilton, New York
August, 1953

CONTENTS

PART II

Selections from Hindu Sacred Writings

APPENDIX

GUIDE TO PRONUNCIATION

Those who are unacquainted with Sanskrit may approximate correct pronunciation by referring to the following table. Letters for which examples are not given here may be pronounced as they are pronounced in English, even when diacritical marks are used.

a	as the vowel sound in *gun*
ā	as in *father*
i	as in *pin*
ī	as in *pique*
u	as in *pull*
ū	as in *rule*
e	as the *a* in *cake*
ai	as in *aisle*
o	as in *note*
au	as in the vowel sound in *house*
g	as in *go*
s	as in *sea*
ś	as in *shop*
ḥ	as in *hah*
h	The letter *h* is always sounded separately in pronouncing Sanskrit words: *th* as in anthill, *dh* as in mudhen, *bh* as in abhor, *ph* as in haphazard. In this book there are two exceptions: since *c* has been transliterated as *ch, ch* is pronounced as in *church;* and since *ṣ* has been transliterated as *sh, sh* is pronounced as in *shop.*
ṛ	has been transliterated *ṛi* throughout this book; it may be pronounced as in *rich.*

PART I

Beliefs and Practices

Chapter 1

THE NATURE AND HISTORY OF HINDUISM

by D. S. SARMA

Hinduism, the oldest of the world's living religions, has now about three hundred million followers, most of whom live in India. This religion has no founder. It is ethnic, not creedal, with a history contemporaneous with the history of the races with which it is associated. Hence it is closely connected with the mythology, the folklore, and the customs and manners of Hindus, making it rather difficult to distinguish its essentials from its nonessentials.

Hinduism is not simply a system of ethics, though it includes in its teachings a code of ethics as comprehensive as any that has ever been devised by man. It is not simply a system of theology, though it includes within its scope more than one theology as consolatory as the heart of man could desire. It is essentially a school of metaphysics, for its aim is not merely to make man a perfect human being on earth or a happy denizen of heaven singing for all time the glories of god, but to make him one with the ultimate Reality, the eternal, universal Spirit in which there are no distinctions—no cause and effect, no time and space, no good and evil, no pairs of opposites, and no categories of thought. This goal cannot be reached by merely improving human conduct or reforming human character; it can only be attained by transforming human consciousness. Accordingly the Hindu sages, by the ethical and religious disciplines they prescribe, contemplate nothing less than that release (*moksha*) which comes to man through the opening up of a new realm of consciousness.

The Hindu scriptures, therefore, teach that the ultimate end of human life is liberation (*moksha*) from that finite human consciousness of ours which makes us see all things as separate from one another and not as part of a whole. When a higher consciousness dawns upon us, we see the individual parts of the universe as deriving their true significance from the central unity of spirit. It is the beginning of this experience which the Hindu scriptures call the second birth, or the opening of the third eye or the eye of wisdom. The consummation of this experience is the more or less permanent establishment of the transcendent consciousness which is the ultimate goal of man.

Our political and social institutions, our arts and sciences, our creeds and rituals are not ends in themselves, but only means to this goal of liberation. When this goal is reached, man is lifted above his mortal plane and becomes one with that ocean of pure Being, Consciousness, and Bliss, called Brahman in Hindu scriptures. Men who have attained liberation have only contempt for the pleasures of this world; they have no attachments and are untouched by sorrow. They see the whole world of things and beings centered in one indivisible spirit, and the bliss they enjoy is inexpressible in human speech.

Since, however, this transformation of human consciousness into divine consciousness (which is the high destiny to which men are called) is not possible in the course of a single life, Hinduism believes in a series of lives for each individual and the continuity of the self in all of them, either here on earth or elsewhere. Otherwise there would be no meaning in millions of human beings dying even before they are in sight of the goal, and there could be no explanation for the glaring fact that some men are, even from birth, far better equipped than others for reaching the goal.

Recognizing thus that the present life is only one in a series of lives, and that men are in different stages of their journey, Hinduism prescribes the kind of discipline which will suit their condition and will enable them to pass on to the next stage. If the metaphysical ideal is too advanced and abstract for a man, a theological ideal is set before him. At this stage the impersonal Absolute, Brahman, becomes a personal God, the perfect becomes the good, manifestation becomes creation, liberation becomes life in heaven, and love takes the place of knowledge. If he is not fit even for this stage, a course of ritualistic and moral action is prescribed for him. At this level the personal God is represented by an image in a temple, ritual and prayer take the place of meditation, and righteous conduct takes the place of love.

These three stages are only illustrative, not exhaustive. There are, in fact, as many stages as there are levels of culture in a vast community, and there are as many kinds of discipline. Hinduism provides for all classes of men from the highest to the lowest. In its hospitable mansions there is room for all sorts and conditions of men, from the mystic, who is very near the goal, to the illiterate peasant, who has not yet set his foot on the path. It does not thrust all men into the pigeonhole of a single unalterable creed.

This religious hospitality is shown by two characteristic Hindu doctrines called the doctrine of spiritual competence (*adhikāra*) and the doctrine of the chosen deity (*ishṭa-devatā*). The doctrine of spiritual competence requires that the religious discipline prescribed for a man should correspond to his spiritual competence. It is worse than useless to teach abstract metaphysics to a man whose heart hungers for concrete gods. A laborer requires a different type of religion from a scholar—so instruction should be carefully graded.

The doctrine of the chosen deity means that, out of the numerous forms of the Supreme Being conceived by the heart of man in the past and recorded in the scriptures, the worshiper should be taught to choose that which satisfies his spiritual longing and to make it the object of his love and adoration. It may be any one of the gods and goddesses of the Hindu pantheon, or it may be even a tribal deity, rendered concrete to the eye of the flesh by means of an image.

Naturally there is, as a result of the wide catholicity indicated by these two doctrines, a great complexity of worship and belief within the Hindu fold. The greatest difficulty about the study of Hinduism, therefore, is that one is apt to miss the wood for the trees. One often fails to see the underlying unity amid the bewildering variety of castes and subcastes with their own customs and manners, and of sects and subsects with their own cults and symbols and forms of worship, and amid the many schools of philosophy and systems of theology with their different texts and scriptures and their commentaries, and commentaries on commentaries, and glosses on commentaries, and glosses on glosses—all within the fold of Hinduism.

There are, for instance, three main sects in the Hindu fold: the Vaishṇavas, the Śaivas, and the Śāktas. The Vaishṇava sect has about twenty subsects, the Śaiva about ten, and the Śākta about five. In addition to these there are at least fifteen miscellaneous sects. The same is true of castes. According to tradition, there are four main castes: the *Brāhmans,* the scholarly or priestly caste; the *Kshatriyas,* the warrior and ruling caste; the *Vaiśyas,* the commercial and agricultural caste; and the *Śūdras,* the laboring caste. But there are innumerable subcastes. Among the Brāhmans there are traditionally ten classes, five northern and five southern, but every province has its own divisions and subdivisions. The subdivisions among the other castes cannot be counted. As might be expected where there is such great diversity, the rituals, forms of worship, customs, and manners vary among all these divisions and subdivisions of the people.

UNITY WITHIN DIVERSITY

At the same time there is an underlying unity in the religious life of India. The soul of Hinduism has ever been the same even though it has had different embodiments in different ages and among different levels of the people. There are five elements which contribute to this unity of Hinduism: common scriptures, common deities, common ideals, common beliefs, and common practices.

Common Scriptures

The most important common scriptures are the Vedas, the Epics (the Rāmāyaṇa and the Mahābhārata), and the Bhāgavata Purāṇa; though the Bhāgavata Purāṇa may not be held sacred by some Śaiva sects. The rest of the Hindu scriptures are more or less sectional or sectarian. The Vedas are called *Śruti* (that which is heard), while the rest of the sacred writings are known as *Smṛiti* (that which is remembered). Great sages and seers are said to have heard the eternal truths of religion and to have left a record of them for the benefit of others. The Vedas are therefore said to be eternal, their composers being only the channels through which the revelations of the Supreme have come. Accordingly, the Śruti forms the supreme authority for Hinduism. All the other scriptures, which form the Smṛiti, are secondary, deriving their authority from the Vedas, and accepted as authoritative only in so far as they follow the teachings of the primary scriptures. These secondary scriptures, which are elaborations of the truths revealed in the Vedas, include the epics, the codes of law, the sacred romances (*Purāṇas*), the manuals of philosophy (*Darśanas*), and the sectarian scriptures (*Āgamas*).

There are four Vedas, the Ṛigveda, the Sāmaveda, the Yajurveda, and the Atharvaveda, each one consisting of four parts: the *Mantras,* which are the basic verses; the *Brāhmaṇas,* the explanations of those verses or hymns and of the related rituals; the *Āraṇyakas,* meditations on their meanings; and the *Upanishads,* mystical utterances revealing profound spiritual truths. As the Upanishads come at the end of the Veda, the teaching based on them is called *Vedānta,* for *anta* in Sanskrit means the end. The Upanishads are thus the Himālayan springs from which have flowed the rivers of the Spirit which have watered the Indian Peninsula for the last twenty-five centuries.

The Upanishads were later systematized in the Vedānta Sūtras. The *sūtra* is a literary form peculiar to India; it is a mnemonic formula from which all unnecessary words have been removed, leaving a highly elliptical structure which requires the use of commentaries for understanding the full meaning of the writing. The Vedānta Sūtras, based on the teachings of the Upanishads, became authoritative for almost all schools of Hindu thought.

The teachings of the Upanishads were summarized in another and more attractive literary form in the Bhagavad Gītā, which forms part of the Mahābhārata. The Gītā is a dialogue between Arjuna, the hero of the Epic, and Kṛishṇa, who is believed to be an *avatāra,* or incarnation of God. There is a well-known Sanskrit verse which compares the Upanishads to cows, the Gītā to milk, Kṛishṇa to a milkman, Arjuna to a calf, and the wise men to those who drink the milk. The Bhagavad Gītā has come to be looked upon as the layman's Upanishad, for it presents the great teachings of the Upanishads in such a simple and beautiful form that the common people can understand them.

What the Vedas are for the learned, the Rāmāyaṇa, the Mahābhārata, and the Bhāgavata Purāṇa are for the common man. They are accepted as sacred books by all Hindus. The Rāmāyaṇa story of Rāma's exile and his search for Sītā, the Mahābhārata story of the struggle of the sons of Pāṇdu to regain their kingdom, and the wonderful stories of the childhood of Kṛishṇa told in the Bhāgavata Purāṇa are, as it were, part of the mother's milk which every Hindu child draws in his infancy. For most Hindus these epics and romantic narratives are far more historical than sober history, for they give them the higher truth of poetry. For countless generations the lives of the people of India have been molded by the ideals set for them in these epics. These two poems describe in concrete historical terms the eternal struggle between the forces of good and evil.

Thus it is that with the Vedas, accepted as the final authority by all Hindus, the Rāmāyaṇa, the Mahābhārata, and the Bhāgavata Purāṇa, revered as sacred books throughout the land, and the other sacred writings deriving their authority from the Vedas, the scriptures of Hinduism are a strong force making for unity within all the diversity of beliefs and practices.[1]

Common Deities

The common deities are derived from the common scriptures. Though the Vedic hymns are addressed to many gods, the Vedic seers in their search after truth very soon discovered that there is one Supreme Spirit of which the various gods worshiped by men are only partial manifestations. There is a Vedic passage which is often quoted in support of this statement, "Reality is one; sages speak of it in different ways." This idea that every god whom men worship is the embodiment of a limited ideal, that he is the symbol of one aspect of the Absolute, has persisted down the ages and is, in fact, one of the most fundamental characteristics of Hinduism. It is this idea which makes Hinduism the most tolerant of religions and averse to proselytization through religious propaganda. It is also this idea which is responsible for the continued existence of a host of gods in the imagination of the people, even when they believe in one Supreme Spirit.

The common people have generally hungered for some concrete embodiments of the Divine, while the learned, who knew better, were tolerant of—and even encouraged—all popular forms of worship. Thus, in the course of time, through many steps which have been lost to us, the three important functions

[1] The Scriptures of Hinduism are discussed at greater length in Part II. Those who are unfamiliar with the sacred writings of the Hindus may find it helpful to read portions of Part II as they are referred to in Part I, especially the Epics, the Bhāgavata Purāṇa, and excerpts from the Upanishads.

of the Supreme, that is, creation, protection, and destruction, came to be established in the imagination of the people as the three great gods Brahmā, Vishṇu, and Śiva, known as the Hindu Triad, or Trinity. The power that was associated with each of these great gods was also later personified and represented as his consort. The consort of Brahmā the creator was called Sarasvatī (the goddess of speech and learning), that of Vishṇu the protector was called Lakshmī (the goddess of wealth and prosperity), and that of Śiva the destroyer was called Śakti (the goddess of power and destruction). Also, as Vishṇu is the protector of creation, He is represented as coming down as an avatāra, taking human form whenever the world order is disturbed by some colossal form of evil. Rāma and Kṛishṇa are regarded as such avatāras or incarnations of Vishṇu and are objects of worship for all Hindus.

Popular imagination that revels in the concrete has not stopped there. It has provided the great gods with their own appropriate heavens, their own attendants, their own vehicles, and even their own progeny. The more intelligent among the people understand the meaning of all this symbolism, but to the masses the symbols are ends in themselves. The point to be noticed here, however, is that this symbolism is common to all Hindus and that the exclusive emphasis on a particular god or goddess in this scheme at a later time gave rise to sectarian theisms in the fold of Hinduism, such as the Vaishṇavism of the worshipers of Vishṇu, the Śaivism of the worshipers of Śiva, and the Śāktism of the worshipers of Śakti or Power, a name exclusively given to the consort of Śiva. A fourth sect, called Smārtas, is made up of worshipers who do not belong to these three sects nor follow their sectarian scriptures (Āgamas), but who go by the ancient traditions (Smṛitis) and worship all the gods without any exclusive preference.

The sectarian worshipers in Hinduism are like the exclusive political parties, each with its own policies, shibboleths, and programs. And, just as a large and overwhelming majority of the people in a country do not belong to any party, but vote conservative or liberal according to the needs of the hour, so an overwhelming majority of Hindus are nonsectarian. They are neither exclusively Vaishṇavas, nor Śaivas, nor Śāktas. This is possible because the people are taught that the particular name and form of any deity are limitations which we in our weakness impose on the all-pervading Spirit, which is really nameless and formless. Also, even the common people are taught that the worship of a personal god is only a halfway house in man's journey to the Ultimate Reality.

We represent the Supreme Spirit as a person because personality is the most intelligible and attractive concept of which our minds are capable. The Supreme Being is a person only in relation to ourselves and our needs. In Himself He is something above personality. When the sun blazing in the sky cannot be looked at by us, we use a smoked glass and then see it as a round, red disk. Similarly, when the Supreme Being in His glory cannot be perceived as He is, we perceive Him through our human spectacles and apprehend only some aspects of Him and think of Him as a person. Thus even the highest theism is only a sort of glorified anthropomorphism, but we cannot do without it.

The heart of man hungers for a god of love, grace, and mercy. These sublime qualities may exist in the Supreme Spirit in some transcendent forms unknown to us but we can lay hold of them only in their human forms and raise them to their highest potential, and by assimilating them rise to the transcendence of the Spirit. Accordingly, Hinduism at its highest neither rejects theism nor accepts it as the last word in religious philosophy. "Reality is one; sages speak of it in different ways," and Hinduism achieves unity in diversity by cherishing the many ways in which men have represented and worshiped the various aspects of the Supreme Spirit.

Common Ideals

All the sects and offshoots of Hinduism have the same moral ideals. The cardinal virtues of Hinduism are purity, self-control, detachment, truth, and nonviolence; it is these ideals which have given the people of India a common idea of a good life.

Purity means both ceremonial purity and moral purity; the former is considered to be preliminary to the latter. All purificatory baths and ceremonials and all the elaborate rules regarding food and drink prescribed in the Hindu scriptures are meant to lead to purity of mind and spirit.

Similarly, self-control implies both the control of the flesh and the control of the mind. When this virtue is pushed to an extreme it becomes asceticism, and it must be admitted that India generally loves an ascetic. All her great moral and religious teachers from Buddha to Śrī Rāmakṛishṇa have been ascetics. But Hinduism, at its best, does not glorify asceticism. It does not call upon its followers to suppress the flesh altogether. On the contrary, it teaches that the body is an instrument of righteousness and seeks to regulate its appetites and cravings, teaching the flesh its place. Hinduism takes into account all the factors of human personality, the body, mind, soul, and spirit, and prescribes a graded discipline for all. It advocates a complete and integrated life in which the claims of all parts of man's nature are reconciled and harmonized.

The higher phase of self-control is detachment. We have not only to overcome what is evil in life but also to become independent of what is good. For instance, our domestic affections, our family ties, our love of home and friends are all good in themselves. But as long as we are passionately attached to these earthly things we are only on the lower rungs of the spiritual ladder. Love, affection, and friendship are indeed divine qualities, and the more we cherish them the nearer we are to the Supreme Spirit. But the way to cherish them is not to be blindly attached to the particular objects of these feelings. Complete liberation from this world and union with the Divine are not possible so long as one clings either to the evil or to the good in this existence.

The positive side of detachment from the changing world is attachment to the Reality which endures forever. Truth as a cardinal virtue in Hinduism means far more than mere truthfulness; it means the eternal reality. Mahātmā Gāndhi described Hinduism as a quest for truth through nonviolence. The Hindu scriptures say that the pursuit of truth, wherever it may lead and whatever sacrifices it may involve, is indispensable to the progress of man. Hence Hinduism has never opposed scientific progress nor speculations in metaphysics or ethics.

Truth is always associated with nonviolence (*ahiṁsā*) in the Hindu scriptures. The two together are considered to be the highest virtues. The greatest exponent of nonviolence in modern times was, of course, Mahātmā Gāndhi, who taught that nonviolence must be practiced not only by individuals but also by communities and nations—in all spheres of life. The influence of this ideal is seen in all aspects of Hindu life: their mildness, their hospitality, their horror of bloodshed, their gentleness, their toleration, and their kindness to animals—especially the cow—all are due to the ideal of nonviolence which they have cherished through the ages. The pacific character of Hindu civilization is due to this great moral ideal.

Common Beliefs

Underlying all schools of religious thought in Hinduism there are some fundamental beliefs which every system-builder takes for granted, as they form part of the authoritative religious tradition. These may be described in modern terms as beliefs concerning: (*a*) the evolution of the world; (*b*) the organization of society; (*c*) the progress of the individual; (*d*) the fourfold end of human life; and (*e*) the law of karma and rebirth.

The evolution of the world, according to the teaching given in one of the Upanishads, came about through successive stages beginning with matter and going on through life, consciousness, and intelligence to spiritual bliss or perfection. At one end of the cosmic scale there is pure matter in which spirit lies dormant, and at the other end pure spirit in which matter lies dormant. Between these two extremes there are various orders of dual beings composed partly of matter and partly of spirit. Spirit becomes richer as it ascends the scale, and matter becomes poorer. The spirit appears as life in vegetables, as consciousness in animals, as intelligence in men, and as bliss in the Supreme Spirit. So there is a gradual ascent from matter to life, from life to consciousness, from consciousness to reason, and from reason to spiritual perfection.

A man is nearer to the Supreme Spirit than an animal is; an animal is nearer to Him than a plant, and a plant is nearer to Him than a lifeless stone. Similarly, a good man is nearer to the Supreme Spirit than a bad man, a saint is nearer than a sinner. The more of such spiritual qualities as goodness, justice, mercy, love, and kindness a man has, the nearer he is to the Supreme Being who is the source and perfection of all spiritual qualities. And the more he has of qualities such as cruelty, selfishness, greed, and lust, the nearer he is to the animal. Thus the universe is a vast amphitheater in which there is a colossal struggle going on between spirit and matter, giving rise to various orders of beings ranging from the lifeless stone to the omniscient Supreme Spirit.

The Upanishads thus reveal to us the law of spiritual progression underlying creation. But, of course, we see only the intermediate stages of this cosmic process. As the Bhagavad Gītā says, "Unmanifest is the origin of beings, manifest their midmost stage, and unmanifest again their end." We do not know how the Primal Spirit came to divide itself into subject and object and started the process of evolution, nor how the sundered spirit will finally be restored to its original wholeness in the Absolute. For the beginning and the end of the cosmic process are beyond time, which is a narrow bridge between two eternities. All that we humans located in time and space can know is that there is a process of spiritual progression on a vast scale going on in the universe and that it should be our guiding principle in all our plans and schemes.

Any scheme or plan designed by us for enhancing the spiritual values in the world would therefore be in accordance with the cosmic purpose. And any scheme which reverses the order and places the lower biological or material values above the higher spiritual values goes contrary to the divine plan. Thus the law of spiritual progression is an unerring standard for us. It decrees that spiritual values such as truth, beauty, love, and righteousness are of the highest importance; next come intellectual values, such as clarity, cogency, subtlety, and skill; then come such biological values as health, strength, and vitality; and last, at the lowest level, come such material values as riches, possessions, and pleasures.

It is very necessary for us to keep this formula of spiritual progression ever before our minds. It is the master key which opens every room in the mansion of Hindu civilization. Let us, for instance, take the Hindu view of history. Though the Hindus have not produced great historians, their sages had a correct view of historical progress and decline, a correct standard for judging civilizations. In their view the golden age in the history of man is the period in which all moral and spiritual values are well established and universally recognized and acted upon. They picturesquely described it as a time when the "cow of righteousness" (dharma) walked on all its four legs. And all the ages which fell away from the standard of that golden age—ages in which the cow of righteousness limped on three legs or two legs, or stood precariously on one leg—were ages of inferior civilization, whatever their achievements might be in other directions.

Thus the Hindu sages judged the greatness of nations not

by the empires they possessed, nor by the wealth they accumulated, nor by the scientific progress they achieved, but by the degree of righteousness and justice they cultivated. Their teaching is that man's true progress is to be judged by moral and spiritual standards, and not by material and scientific standards. This teaching has been in our own day underlined and emphasized by Mahātmā Gāndhi.

The second of the common beliefs of Hinduism, concerning the organization of society, grows from the first, the principle of spiritual progression. In accordance with that principle which they had observed in nature and the history of races and nations, the Hindu lawgivers tried to construct an ideal society in which men should be ranked, not according to their numerical strength or wealth or power, but according to their spiritual progress and culture. In their view, numbers, wealth, and power should be subordinated to learning, virtue, and character.

A social system which embodies this ideal is called varṇa-dharma. *Varṇa* literally means color, and *dharma,* which is a difficult word to translate literally, here means duty which results from the particular abilities with which a man is born. In very early times Hindu society consisted of two races, the fair-skinned Aryans and the dark-skinned pre-Aryans. The contrast of color between the two gave rise to the concept of varṇa, which later came to mean caste. As the Aryan conquerors became partially assimilated, society became stratified; the priestly and military classes were distinguished from the common people who, together with the conquered tribes, tilled the soil and carried on trade. Thus there came into existence even in the early prehistoric times the four castes: the Brāhmans (the teaching class), the Kshatriyas (the military class), the Vaiśyas (the mercantile and agricultural class), and the Śūdras (the laboring class).

The earliest reference to the four castes is found in a late book of the Ṛigveda, where they are represented as forming parts of the body of the Creator. Obviously it is only a poetic image indicating the organic nature of the society of the time. In later ages the Hindu lawgivers, epic poets, and authors of popular religious works persistently maintained this theocratic ideal so that, in spite of all the transformations which the society was undergoing before their very eyes, people looked on the fourfold caste system as a divine institution to which they should conform if they would save their souls. Not only were the four castes conceived as the creation of God but also they were said to conform to the cosmic law of spiritual progression, the most spiritual class occupying the top and the least spiritual the bottom.

Also, according to the science of the time, nature had three fundamental qualities of purity (*sattva*), energy (*rajas*), and inertia (*tamas*). It was supposed that those in whom purity predominated formed the first caste, those in whom energy predominated formed the second caste, and those in whom inertia predominated in varying degrees formed the third and fourth castes. According to this theory, each caste should perform its own duties, follow its own hereditary occupations, and all should cooperate with one another in working for the common welfare. The theory also provided that the good actions of a man in this life earned for him promotion to a higher caste in the next life.

The dream of the Hindu sages and lawgivers was evidently to organize the Hindu society into a cooperative hierarchy like the Hindu joint family, where the elder members had greater freedom and responsibility and the younger ones had greater shelter and protection. The system thus advocated had its own merits and defects. It arranged for division of labor, it cut short competition, and gave full weight to the principle of heredity. But it gave no scope for individual genius, it made too much of the accident of birth, and it killed all initiative. In a word, it made for order and not for progress.

But we should not forget that all this was only a theory and an ideal. At no time in the history of India did the actual facts ever correspond to it. At no time of which we have any reliable history were there the four simple homogeneous castes postulated by the varṇadharma theory. The normal civic life of the people in their daily occupations often cut across all racial and class divisions and in the course of centuries produced innumerable hereditary occupational castes.

Again, in religious schisms and the formation of religious sects is found another force cutting across class divisions and eventually producing new groups which, in their turn, through exclusive marriage laws, developed into subsects. There were also numerous other influences, such as excommunications, mixed marriages, distant migrations, and colonizations which contributed their own share to the complexities of the caste system. It is upon this very complex and, we may say, recalcitrant material that the Hindu sages and nation-builders tried to impose through the ages their ideal scheme of varṇadharma. Although they were never completely successful, the diagram of the four castes was so indelibly impressed on the national imagination that, during all those centuries when a strong central government was either nonexistent in the country or was frequently changing hands, it was the theocratic ideal of the caste system that saved the Hindu society from disruption.

What the Hindu governing class failed to do the teaching class did after its own fashion. The Hindu kings failed to build an enduring state capable of dissolving all class jealousies and antagonisms and warding off foreign invaders. The Hindu teachers established instead the ideal of varṇadharma, which for a long time mitigated class antagonisms and harmonized communities occupying various levels of culture into a single society with common moral and spiritual ideals. They could not, of course, ward off foreign conquest, but they neutralized its effects. It is no exaggeration to say that it is the caste system with its ideal of varṇadharma that has saved the Hindu civilization from the fate of many ancient civilizations which have passed away.

However, it must be admitted that in the very act of saving Hindu society the system became far too rigid and exclusive and lost all its old elasticity. In the name of the caste system the Hindus have developed too much of class hatred and too little of the spirit of cooperation. The caste system with its rigid walls of separation is bound to pass away, as it has become completely out of place in modern world conditions. But the underlying principle of varṇadharma is valid for all time, for in the ideal society wealth, numbers, and power should be subordinate to character and culture; cooperation should take the place of competition; and there should be an organic relation between men's aptitudes and their occupations. In any ideal society built upon the Upanishad principle of spiritual progression the most responsible positions should be occupied by the men spiritually most advanced, irrespective of the caste into which they may have been born. This ideal continues to be a unifying belief in the religion of the Hindus.

The third unifying belief of the Hindus is that the individual life should be built upon the same concept of spiritual progression which should control community life. The Hindu sages divided the ideal life of an individual into four successive stages, called *āśramas:* the student, the householder, the recluse who withdraws from the world, and finally the *sannyāsin* (religious mendicant) who renounces the world. These stages indicate the path of progress for the ideally ordered life of an individual.

The first stage is devoted entirely to study and discipline. The student should have no other responsibilities and no distractions of any kind. He should not indulge in any pleasures but should subject himself to a rigorous discipline. He should look upon his teacher as his spiritual parent, and by his habits of attention, obedience, and reverence should please him and humbly receive what he has to impart. This is a stage of preparation and probation, and not of action.

After the period of preparation is over, the student should marry and settle down as a householder and faithfully discharge his duties to his community and country. By glorifying the householder's stage and by sanctioning his pursuit of wealth and pleasure within the bounds of the moral law, Hinduism does justice to the flesh as well as the spirit of man. It lays down no impossible rules of asceticism for normal human beings, but recommends a gradual and progressive conquest of spirit over flesh.

When this period of active life and citizenship is over, and after all the duties that fall to his lot are discharged, the householder should retire to a quiet place in the country and meditate on the higher things of the spirit. He is now free from all social bonds and can take a detached view of all problems of human life. This is, as it were, his second period of probation. Just as the student's life is a preparation for the householder's life, the retired life of the recluse is a preparation for the renunciation of all earthly ties in the final stage of life.

After this second probation is over, the recluse becomes a *sannyāsin,* one who has renounced all earthly possessions and ties. In this final stage one need not observe any distinctions of caste, or perform any rites and ceremonies, or attach one's self to any particular country, nation, or religion. Looking upon all beings as so many forms of the Universal Spirit, the sannyāsin wanders from place to place, feels at home everywhere, and gives himself up entirely to the service of the Supreme Spirit. According to Hinduism, renunciation is the crown of human life, and therefore all Hindus bow before a sannyāsin and think it is a privilege to serve him.

Here again, this scheme of the four stages of life is only an ideal. In practice, not even one in a thousand traverses the entire path and goes regularly through all the stages. Though technically the scheme is supposed to hold good only for the first three castes, it is an ideal accepted by all Hindus. There are now sannyāsins from all castes, and they are revered by all without distinction. This ideal of the four stages of life, which is cherished by all Hindus, once again emphasizes the unity in diversity characteristic of Hinduism.

The fourth of the common beliefs of Hinduism is the belief in the fourfold end of human life. It is based on the principle of the progressive realization of the spirit, as was the case with the four castes and the four stages of life. The goal of life for a man is called dharma-artha-kāma-moksha. In this formula *dharma* means righteousness, *artha* means worldly prosperity, *kāma* means enjoyment, and *moksha* means liberation.

The ultimate aim of man is liberation—liberation not only from the bondage of the flesh but also from the limitations of a finite being. In other words, *moksha* means becoming a perfect spirit like the Supreme Spirit—but on his way to this final goal man has to satisfy the animal wants of his body and the economic and other demands of his family and community.

The wants of his body are indicated by the word *kāma,* which stands for all the appetites of the flesh. The demands of the social environment are indicated by the word *artha,* which means wealth. That is, man has to acquire wealth so that he may maintain his family and help his dependents; but all this should be done within the limits of the moral law indicated by the word *dharma* in this formula.

The Sanskrit word *dharma* is difficult to translate. It is translated into English as law, righteousness, duty, morality. Dharma is moksha in the making. If moksha is complete divinity, dharma is divinity under human conditions. Dharma is half divine and half human. It is divine because it is the call of the spirit, and it is human because it changes according to the conditions of time and place. As man progresses, the code of laws also progresses—but at every stage there is a divine element in it and so it has to be obeyed as a divine commandment until it is abrogated.

The Hindu formula regarding the fourfold end of life thus lays down that the pursuit of pleasure and the acquisition of wealth should always be subject to the moral law. This means that one should be temperate in one's habits and never run to excess in indulgence in animal pleasures. Similarly, in acquiring wealth and property one should not use any unfair means or accumulate big fortunes, disregarding the poverty of others. But, within the limits of moral law, a man may satisfy the legitimate demands of his body and the needs of his family and dependents. Thus this famous formula of dharma-artha-kāma-moksha, which expresses one of the beliefs common to all Hindus, is a complete chart of life giving proper directions to all our needs—physical, social, moral, and spiritual.

The fifth of the common beliefs of Hinduism is the belief in the law of *karma,* or the law of moral causation, which is a unique characteristic of the religious thought of India. The law of karma is a moral law corresponding to the physical law of causation. Just as the law of cause and effect works in the physical world, the law of karma works in the moral world. When we put our fingers into a fire, they are burned, and similarly, whenever a man steals, his moral nature is injured. The more often he steals, the more thievish he becomes. On the other hand, whenever a man helps his neighbor his moral nature is improved. The more often he helps, the more beneficent he becomes.

The law of karma is only an extension beyond the present life of this invariable sequence that we see in this life—for the law of karma postulates that every individual has to pass through a series of lives, either on earth again or somewhere else, before he obtains moksha or liberation, and it further explains that what we are at present is the result of what we thought and did in the past life and that what we shall be in a future life will be the result of what we think and do now. We carry with us our own past. The mental and moral tendencies that the soul acquires in a particular life as a result of its motives and actions work themselves out in suitable surroundings in the next. New sets of tendencies are acquired which again seek a suitable environment in which they work themselves out. This process goes on through several lives, the individual sliding upward or downward in the moral scale until his soul obtains liberation.

Hinduism teaches that all creatures, as long as they are creatures, are involved in this time process which is called *saṁsāra,* the state of each creature in any particular life depending upon the good or evil it has done in the preceding lives. Thus our characters and destinies shape themselves from life to life, not according to the arbitrary decrees of an external and whimsical god, but according to an organic law which is wrought into our very nature. According to Hindu belief, god is not a judge sitting in a remote heaven meting out punishments, but an indwelling Spirit whose will works in us through the moral law here and now.

Common Practices

Four of the common elements in Hinduism have so far been discussed—the common scriptures, deities, ideals, and beliefs—of which there were five main ones. Common practices make up the fifth element contributing to the unity of Hinduism. Under these we may include not only certain rituals common to large sections of Hindu society but also certain forms of mental discipline common to all Hindu sects. Hinduism is a highly practical as well as a highly philosophical religion. Therefore, side by side with its great philosophical systems it has elaborate schemes of religious ritual for bringing the worshiper into intimate contact with the deity he worships.

Every religious Hindu is advised to have his own chosen deity or ishṭa-devatā, on whose form, features, and qualities he should concentrate his mind and whose image he should worship every day with flowers and incense. At the same time he is taught to recognize that the deity is only a means to the realization of the Supreme Spirit. Herein lies the strength of Hinduism—strength which consists not in mere unity, but in unity in diversity. It is a grand federal structure that exists here.

The Hindu view of ritualism is that all men need the help of rituals, but in varying degrees and kinds, until the end which the ritual is designed to secure is gained. When the end is gained there is no longer any need for the means. In the final stage of religious life there is no need for any ritual. A sannyāsin accordingly performs no rites nor ceremonies. Since the ritual employed at every stage should be suitable to the disposition and level of culture of the worshiper, the uneducated people require grosser forms of ritual than the educated.

According to Hinduism, the ultimate purpose of ritualistic worship is the realization of the Supreme. It is to be achieved by the gradual transformation of the worshiper into the form of the deity who is worshiped. The first step in this direction is taken when the mind is made to dwell on some concrete form of the deity—an image, or an emblem, or a diagram—and thus to overcome its inherent tendency to distraction. The worship that accompanies this may be external or internal. In the external worship the deity is treated as a king or an honored guest. He or she is formally invoked, then served with various ritual acts, such as the offering of flowers or the burning of incense, and finally bidden farewell.

Internal worship consists of prayer and meditation. The meditation is often strengthened by japa, mudrā, and nyāsa. *Japa* is the repetition of a group of mystic syllables technically called a *mantra*. A *mantra* is not a mere formula or a magic spell or a prayer; it is an embodiment in sound of a particular deity. It is the deity itself. And so, when a mantra is repeated a hundred times, or a thousand times, or even more, and the worshiper makes an effort to identify himself with the worshiped, the power of the deity comes to his help. Human power is thus supplemented by the divine power. A prayer is different from the repetition of a mantra, for it is a purely human effort. One may pray in any language and in any form, but a mantra, being an embodiment of a deity in sound, has to be repeated in that form alone in which it first revealed itself to the mind of a Seer, a *Ṛishi.* It is not to be learned from books, but from the living voice of a teacher, a *guru,* who gives the initiation, and it has for its object the gradual transformation of the personality of the worshiper into that of the worshiped. Therefore the more a worshiper advances in his japa or the repetition of the sacred mantra, the more does he partake of the nature of the deity he worships, and the less he is himself.

This process of deification through worship is strengthened by mudrā and nyāsa. *Mudrā* is a gesture of the hands and fingers calculated to visualize and emphasize the intention of the mind, and *nyāsa* consists in placing the hands of the worshiper on different parts of his body—the forehead, arms, and chest, for instance, in token of the identification of himself with the deity or the deities he worships. Continued thought and repetition of the mantra and the engagement of the body in cooperation with the mind are calculated to produce the desired change in the worshiper. This is the general procedure that is adopted in private worship.

In big public temples, however, the deity is treated as the King of Kings. There are seven or eight services held in the course of the day in the larger temples. The god as king is formally roused from sleep with music early in the morning and sent to bed with music at night. The intervening services represent such royal acts as holding a court, giving audience to the faithful, and going out in state. This mystery play of everyday life reaches its climax in the royal wedding, which is an annual function attended by thousands of worshipers.

Lastly, mention might also be made of the pilgrimages which all devout Hindus undertake to places made sacred by the birth of a holy person or by association with one of the deities they worship. Such pilgrimages, together with the ceremonial baths in sacred rivers or temple tanks, are considered symbolic of the individual self's pilgrimage to the Supreme Spirit and of its purification from all sins.

Unlike most of the rites and ceremonies, the processes of mental discipline indicated by the word *yoga* are common to all Hindu sects. The word *yoga* is used in several different senses in the Hindu scriptures. It is cognate with the English word *yoke* and literally means yoking together, or union. It is in this sense that the word is most often used in the Bhagavad Gītā, which indicates three paths leading to the goal of union with God: *karma yoga* or union through disinterested service, *bhakti yoga* or union through self-forgetting love and devotion, and *jñāna yoga* or union through transcendent divine knowledge. A man may choose, like Mahātmā Gāndhi, to lead an active life in the world and make every one of his actions an offering unto God, or he may devote his whole life, like Śrī Rāmakṛishṇa, to the loving worship of God, or he may, like Śaṅkara, seek to realize God through philosophical inquiry. Which of these three well-known paths a man chooses will depend on his own temperament and the accumulated experience of his past lives.

In addition to these three, there is another path which is indicated in the Gītā and which was developed later by Patañjali (ca. second century B.C.) in great detail. Patañjali, the author of the Yoga Sūtras, defines *yoga* as the method of restraining the functions of the mind. He was the first to systematize the practices of this technical yoga, but the practices themselves had been in vogue in India from time immemorial. They are mentioned in the Upanishads and all later Hindu scriptures accept them as legitimate means of concentrating one's mind on the Supreme Being. Thus there is a practical unanimity on the part of all Indian teachers of religion on the question of the utility of yoga practices. Patañjali's yoga, which is called *rāja yoga,* is described as consisting of eight stages of discipline culminating in rapt contemplation of the Reality, a state called *samādhi.*

It should, however, be admitted that these elements of unity, the common scriptures, deities, ideals, beliefs, and practices are often obscured by many a wild growth of sectarian belief and ritual and many a survival of primitive custom and superstition. The proverbial Hindu toleration has had its own disadvantages as well as advantages. There has never been a single central authority in Hinduism charged with the duty of maintaining purity of doctrine and ritual; if there has been no heresy-hunting in Hinduism, there has been no restraining influence either. The Brāhmans have been the custodians of religion, but they never have had, as a class, any political or ecclesiastical power. Moreover, for some centuries India has been under alien rulers and Hinduism has had to fight with its back to the wall for mere survival. Within the past century, however, there have been stirrings of a new life full of hope, a renaissance of Hinduism. Before describing this recent development, the history of Hinduism which preceded it should be sketched briefly.

THE HISTORY OF HINDUISM

The history of the religion of the Hindus does not closely follow the political history of India. The political history is generally divided into three periods—the Hindu, the Muslim, and the British. In the long history of Hinduism, covering about forty centuries (2000 B.C. to A.D. 1950), the Muslim rule (or misrule) of India for less than six centuries (A.D. 1200 to 1750)—with large pockets of resistance in the country throughout the time—and the British rule which operated effectively for only about a century and a half (1800 to 1947), are only brief though painful episodes. Therefore, division of the history of Hinduism into convenient periods must be guided more by the internal developments in the religion itself than by the external changes in the political fortunes of the Indian people.

Following this principle and admitting that there is no hard and fast line between one period and another, one may say that there are three periods in the history of Hinduism, the ancient, the medieval, and the modern. The ancient period ends with the establishment of Śaṅkara's system of Advaita philosophy and the final triumph of Hinduism over Buddhism and Jainism in the ninth century. The medieval period opens with the consolidation of the *bhakti* (devotional) systems in the teachings of Rāmānuja and Madhva and comes to a close when the bhakti movement exhausts itself about the middle of the eighteenth century. The modern period begins with the new reform movements in Hinduism, such as the Brāhmo Samāj founded by Rām Mohun Roy in 1830.

ANCIENT HINDUISM

The Vedic Period (2000 B.C.-500 B.C.)

It is not, of course, possible to give the exact chronological limits of the Vedic period. The later limit may be taken as 500 B.C., since the Vedas, including the chief Upanishads, are far anterior to Buddha—who died about 483 B.C. It is more difficult to fix the earlier limit, but modern scholars are inclined to believe that the earliest hymns in the Ṛigveda were composed between 2500 and 2000 B.C. So it will not be far wrong to consider that the Vedic period extends from 2000 to 500 B.C.

The literature of this period shows three successive stages in which were recorded the Mantras, the Brāhmaṇas, and the Āraṇyakas, together with the Upanishads.

In the Mantras of the Vedas is a most astonishing march of the human mind from the worship of the half-personified forces of nature, such as fire, wind, and rain, to the conception of the Absolute, the One. At first there was no clear demarcation between one Vedic deity and another, since all were phenomena of nature only. The same name was used to describe more than one deity, the same power was attributed to a number of gods, and this led to the belief that they were all one in essence and that, while one was being praised and worshiped, the others might be ignored. In this way, two of the gods rose into prominence for a time, Indra the god of power and Varuṇa the god of righteousness, but neither of them rose to the supreme rank. On the contrary, in later times both of them receded, Indra becoming the ruler of a celestial region and Varuṇa becoming the god of the sea.

For a time, a striking quality common to some of the gods—for instance, the creative power—was personified and raised to the supreme state. Thus arose a series of supreme deities such as Prajāpati (Lord of Creatures), Aditi (the Infinite), Prāṇa (Life), and Kāla (Time). The Vedic seers thus groped their way, and gradually, discarding all anthropomorphism, arrived at a single primordial Reality which unfolds itself as the universe. The farthest reach of the religious quest in the Mantra period was the tendency toward monism, which was later strongly developed in the Upanishads.

Another important development in the Vedic mantras was the conception of *ṛita,* or cosmic order, from which were derived in later times the characteristic Hindu ideas of dharma and the law of karma. Ṛita was originally the order of natural events, such as the movements of heavenly bodies and the succession of the seasons, but soon it came to mean moral as well as natural order. The gods were considered guardians of both and so they had to be propitiated by means of sacrifice. Thus, in the course of time, the punctilious performance of sacrifices came to be considered very necessary for the maintenance of the world and its natural and moral laws.

This belief gave rise to a professional class of priests who were required to conduct the sacrifices correctly and efficiently, and since the sacrifices were conducted with the chanting of the Vedic texts, the texts gradually became more important than the gods themselves. This belief in the importance of the priesthood had a tremendous influence on the evolution of

Hindu society, and the worship of the letter of the Vedas led later to the important doctrine that the Vedas were uncreated and eternal.

The age of the Mantras was succeeded by the age of the Brāhmaṇas. We are justified in looking upon the age of the Brāhmaṇas as one of extreme conservatism, if not stagnation; ritualism of a very soulless and mechanical type was its marked feature. Characteristically enough, it was during this age that the doctrine of caste and the four stages of life, varṇa-āśrama-dharma, was formulated; Prajāpati was looked upon as the chief god and creator, Vishṇu rose in importance and became the deity presiding over sacrifices, and Śiva, a pre-Aryan god, became identified with the Vedic god Rudra. But the most important feature of the age is that the priesthood became all-powerful and supreme, and the priests conducted congregational sacrifices on a large scale.

The age of the Brāhmaṇas was followed by the age of the Āraṇyakas and the Upanishads. If the former age was one of priests, the latter was one of prophets. The Upanishads are the finest flower of the Vedic thought. We may unhesitatingly say that it was in the Upanishadic period that the foundations of Hinduism were well and truly laid. The later ages but built a superstructure on them. All orthodox schools of Hinduism look upon the Upanishads as their supreme authority.

The Upanishadic Seers turned the searchlight inward. They discovered that at the center of man's being, beyond the senses, beyond the mind, and beyond the understanding, there is the same divine spirit as there is in the starry heavens above. That is the meaning of their famous identification of Brahman with *ātman,* the self. Brahman is the universal spirit approached from the objective side; the self, ātman, is the same universal spirit approached from the subjective side. In man the self, ātman, is imprisoned in a particular body, mind, and understanding, all of which foster in him a congenital ignorance of his own infinitude and of his oneness with all beings. Moksha is liberation from this prison house of individuality. That is the true end of man, the true goal of human life; not earthly riches nor the temporary bliss of heaven to which all the sacrifices to the gods were believed to lead.

In the age of the Upanishads, moksha became the end, and transcendent knowledge, jñāna, became the means. The gods receded into the background and so did the sacrifices. Even the knowledge of the Vedas was considered to be inferior knowledge. The supreme knowledge was the knowledge of the self, the ātman. All efforts were made to secure this highest knowledge. Thus the sacrificial religion of the age of the Brāhmaṇas based on caste and the four stages of life gave place to the intensely personal religion based on the higher consciousness of the unity of all things in the world. In this new religion, liberation took the place of heaven, higher knowledge of sacrifice, and the Absolute of the gods (*devas*). Another remarkable development in the age of the Upanishads was that the law of karma and rebirth, already explained, became one of the fundamental tenets of Hindu philosophy and religion.

It should be noted that the Upanishadic teaching about the self was a kind of secret doctrine imparted only to advanced souls. The moral and spiritual competence of these men was well tested before the teaching was imparted. Therefore, from its very nature, the religion of the Upanishads could be the religion only of the few.

The Sūtra Period (500 B.C.-200 B.C.)

The second period of ancient Hinduism may be called the Sūtra Period from the point of view of the religion of the Hindus; it was also the period of the greatest rise of Buddhism in India. The rule of the Buddhist emperor Aśoka (273-236 B.C.) was one of the most glorious epochs in the history of India; but it is a mistake to suppose that Buddhism was at any time the prevailing religion of India as a whole. From time to time, either Buddhism or Jainism may have flourished in some of the kingdoms, but neither of them ever superseded the orthodox Vedic religion. Hinduism has been the dominant religion of India from the earliest times to the present day.

The age of the sūtras was the period to which the manuals of ritualism, the Kalpa Sūtras, belong. From these sūtras we see that the conditions of popular religion at the time were similar to those of the age of the Brāhmaṇas. There were the same sacrifices, the same rites and ceremonies, the same belief in a host of gods, but a more rigorous insistence on caste and the four stages of man, as if the great Seers of the Upanishads had never lived and taught. The only trace of the Upanishadic teaching remaining is that the goal of life is defined as liberation, moksha, rather than heavenly happiness. The orthodoxy of the priests remained practically the same; they were steeped in their ritualism and sacrifices and their narrow codes of law.

It was in these circumstances that Buddhism and Jainism arose as reforming sects. They retained the philosophical and ethical ideals of the older religion, but repudiated the authority of the Vedas and the ascendancy of the priests and turned away from all sacrifices and speculations. Buddha was something of a belated Upanishadic seer protesting against the soulless ritualism of the priests. He never broke away entirely from the religious tradition of his country; he lived and died a Hindu. Buddhism finally died out in the land of its birth because of its negative doctrines, its overemphasis on monastic life, the substitution of individual reason for the authority of the Vedas as a guide in religious matters, and the absence of any object of worship which could satisfy the longings of the human heart.

In contrast to the Buddhist system of cold, atheistic self-culture there arose in the fifth century B.C., in the northwest, a strongly theistic cult which was destined to play a very important part in the history of Hinduism. This was the bhāgavata cult which had its center in the city of Mathurā and whose object of worship was Kṛishṇa. It is believed by some scholars that Kṛishṇa was at first a renowned teacher of this bhāgavata religion, the cult of passionate devotion to God, that later he himself became the object of worship and, finally, as a result of a long process, emerged as an avatāra of Vishṇu (as Vishṇu living among men in a human form).

The Epic Period (200 B.C.-A.D. 300)

During this period there was no single paramount power in India, but it was a time when Indians went abroad and colonized Sumatra, Java, Borneo, Malaya, and Indochina and established kingdoms, some of which were ruled by Indian princes and remained Hindu or Buddhist until they were overthrown by Muslims in the sixteenth century. In this period of expansion it was felt that India, in spite of all its complexity of races, kingdoms, and creeds, was really one.

To this period belong the two great epics in their final form, the Rāmāyaṇa and the Mahābhārata with that superb masterpiece, the Bhagavad Gītā; and the Laws of Manu, the Code of Yājñavalkya, the minor Upanishads, and some of the earliest Purāṇas and philosophical sūtras. In the epics the ancient stories and legends of the people were made the instruments of a great religious revival. The old ballads were so expanded and interspersed with didactic matter that they became the Vedas for the multitude. Thus the teaching of the Upanishads was brought home to the common people in a concrete form which they could understand and the knowledge which had hitherto been the exclusive possession of a few was made available to all.

As a result of this popularization of religion through the epics there came a remarkable development in the traditional religion. It was no longer predominantly sacrificial as in the Brāhmaṇas, nor predominantly metaphysical as in the Upanishads, but it became predominantly theistic in the epics. The abstract metaphysics of the Upanishads was kept in the background and the concrete theistic elements in them were developed around the great gods Vishṇu and Śiva. Śiva, originally a pre-Aryan deity, was identified with the Vedic deity Rudra, a principle of identification which was fully exploited in this age. All the gods and goddesses which belonged to the religion of the people in various parts of the land were easily incorporated into the Hindu pantheon and represented as different aspects of the Supreme Spirit. The three most important functions of that Spirit, the creation, preservation, and destruction of the world, were associated with the great gods Brahmā, Vishṇu, and Śiva. Thus arose the doctrine of the Hindu Trinity, the Trimūrti.

The next step in the development of theism during this age was the doctrine of avatāras, the belief that whenever the evil in the world requires it God takes the form of a human being to set the world right. It was first formulated in the Bhagavad Gītā. Theism was further developed through the use of images, temples, pilgrimages to sacred places associated with the deities, and festivals. The organization of temple worship was one of the characteristic features of the religious development during these centuries, so that the public temple became as important as the old sacrificial altar.

As a result of all these far-reaching changes in the Epic Age, Brahmanism expanded into Hinduism. By this time, Hinduism had already developed almost all the main features with which we are acquainted today: (1) the conception of the impersonal Absolute (Brahman) and the personal God (Īśvara); (2) the supreme authority of the Vedas; (3) the law of karma and rebirth; (4) the systems of caste, the four stages of life, and the four ends of life; (5) the threefold path of karma, bhakti, and jñāna yoga; (6) the doctrines of the Hindu Trinity and repeated incarnations of the Supreme (avatāras); (7) the doctrines of the chosen deity (ishṭa-devatā) and different levels of spiritual ability (adhikāra); (8) the rituals of image worship; (9) the sectarian beliefs and practices of the Vaishṇavas, Śaivas, and Śāktas; (10) faith in pilgrimages to holy shrines, rivers, and mountains.

THE PURĀṆIC AGE (A.D. 300-750)

The first two centuries of this period are considered to be the golden age in the history of the Hindu rule in India. The expansion of Hinduism which was so remarkable in the Epic Age continued its progress in the Purāṇic Age.

In this period there were three great developments in the process of popularization and systematization of Hinduism: the composition of the sectarian Purāṇas, the organization of the worship of the Mother Goddess (Śaktism), and the production of the philosophical sūtras of the six orthodox schools of Hindu thought.

The sectarian spirit, of which we see the beginnings in the epics, became more and more aggressive in the Purāṇas. There is not much advance in religious thought in them, except the probable extension of the doctrines of incarnations (avatāras). The Purāṇas are full of fantastic stories, wild exaggerations, and incredible legends, but behind all these we have the same teachings of Hindu dharma and philosophy that we find in the epics. The interest of the authors is not in the history or geography or cosmogony they give, or even in the adventures of the gods and demons they describe. Their interest is in the inculcation of what may be called the Hindu view of life. The Purāṇas were meant to be instruments of mass education bringing Hindu philosophy, Hindu ideals, and Hindu codes of manners to the minds of the illiterate peasantry of the land. They provided both entertainment and instruction when the stories contained in them were read and explained to the people at public gatherings or when plays based on them were enacted during festivals.

Of the same class as the Purāṇas are the Tantras, the sectarian scriptures of the Śāktas who are the worshipers of Śakti, the Divine Power personified as a goddess. This sect had a remarkable development during this period. There is no doubt that Śāktism was the result of the fusion of the Aryan and the pre-Aryan elements in Hinduism to which we have referred above. In the early literature of this sect we clearly see the process by which the non-Aryan cults of the Mother Goddess were taken up, purified, united, and incorporated into the Vedic religion. A host of tribal deities were brought under one supreme goddess, here called Durgā, and she was spiritualized and brought under the influence of Vedānta philosophy. This process was continued in later literature and the goddess became the center of a great cult and the object of worship on the part of a sect as important as the Vaishṇava and Śaiva sects. In the literature of this Śākta sect, the goddess was identified with the Absolute, as Vishṇu and Śiva were in the sects named after them, and a whole system of philosophy, theology, and ritual came into existence.

While the popular religion was developing along the lines of the Purāṇas and the Tantras and their complicated rituals and theologies, the religion of the learned classes began to be systematized into the philosophical sūtras of the six schools of Hindu thought: Nyāya, Vaiśeshika, Sāṅkhya, Yoga, Mīmāṁsā, and Vedānta. Each school is called a *Darśana,* which means a view of life. The very form of these sūtras shows that a long course of development of the subject matter must have preceded such a terse formulation. However, it was only when the classical commentaries on these sūtras were written that the various schools of philosophy became well established. That is why we have called the next period the Later Darśana Period.

The Later Darśana Period (a.d. 750-1000)

During this period Buddhism was defeated and absorbed in India through the activities of two groups of mystical poets and two philosophers.

In southern India in the seventh and eighth centuries there were twelve mystical poets, known as Ālvārs, who were wandering singers intensely absorbed in Vishṇu. Some of their poems and hymns of devotion reach the high-water mark of devotional poetry in the world. There was a similar devotional movement in Śaivism, also in the south, led by mystical poets known as the Nāyanārs. Their traditional number is sixty-three, and images of the most important of them are to be seen in all Śiva temples in south India. It was these mystical poets of the Vaishṇavas and Śaivas who made the position of Buddhism and Jainism untenable in southern India. Beside their flaming devotion to God, their utter humility and self-surrender, and the joyousness of their religious experience, the atheistic creeds of Buddhism and Jainism shrank into cold and repulsive systems of self-torture. It has been truly said that the Ālvārs and Nāyanārs sang Buddhism and Jainism out of southern India.

While the mystic poets fought Buddhism and Jainism on the ground of devotion, the philosopher Kumārila fought them on the ground of ritual. Kumārila was the founder of the school of Mīmāṁsā [Vedic interpretation]. He took his stand on the doctrine of the infallibility and eternity of the Vedas and the necessity of performing the rites and ceremonies enjoined in the Vedas.

More important than Kumārila was Śaṅkara, who was the greatest exponent of Advaita Vedānta. Śaṅkara was a Brāhman of southern India, born about A.D. 788 in North Travancore. He renounced the world at an early age, became a religious teacher, wandered all over India, and established four monasteries which continue to the present time—one in the Himālayas at Badarīnāth, a second at Dwārakā on the west coast, a third at Pūri on the east coast, and a fourth at Śringeri in Mysore State. His Advaita system of philosophy, based on the Upanishads, the Vedānta Sūtras, and the Bhagavad Gītā, is a monument of spiritual insight and intellectual subtlety. In establishing this system he refuted not only the unorthodox Buddhist school of philosophy but also the semiorthodox schools of Sāṅkhya and Yoga, the orthodox but soulless ritualism of Mīmāṁsā, and what he considered to be erroneous interpretations of Vedānta. Śaṅkara was not only the champion of the orthodox Vedic faith, he was also a great reformer who put down some of the gross and repulsive forms of Śaivism and Śāktism. He was not only one of the greatest philosophers that the world has ever seen, but also an ardent devotee who composed passionate hymns in praise of the deities he worshiped.

In the history of Hinduism the establishment of Śaṅkara's Advaita system of philosophy is a great landmark. A large body of literature has grown around it and a majority of Hindus are Śaṅkara's followers. The Advaita system also influenced some of the sectarian theologies of Śaṅkara's time. For instance, the theistic systems of the Śāktas and the Bhāgavatas have a distinctly advaitic background. This is especially noticeable in the Bhāgavata Purāṇa.

An unknown poet of great imagination, having assimilated the teachings of the Bhagavad Gītā, the Vishṇu Purāṇa, and the Harivaṁśa (which is an appendix to the Mahābhārata), produced at the beginning of the tenth century the Bhāgavata Purāṇa, a religious romance of marvelous beauty which made a profound impression on the mind of India. The account he gives of the early pastoral life of Kṛishṇa in the woods of Vrindāban and on the sandy banks of the Jumna river has held captive the imagination of the Hindus from the tenth century down to the present day. No wonder that this Purāṇa has been raised to the rank of the great epics, the Rāmāyaṇa and the Mahābhārata!

Out of this wonderful book there arose in the next period five schools of theology, in all of which Kṛishṇa, the eternal Lover of Souls, occupies the center of worship. And, apart from these, the Bhāgavata Purāṇa has given rise to innumerable songs, dramas, romances, pictures, and dances, all connected with the boyhood and youth of Kṛishṇa. The teaching of Kṛishṇa in the Bhagavad Gītā is comparatively for the few, but the ravishing beauty of Kṛishṇa in the Bhāgavata Purāṇa is for all. The latter is enshrined in the hearts of millions of men and women in India.

MEDIEVAL HINDUISM

The Rise of the Devotional Movement in South India (A.D. 1000-1400)

The medieval period in Hinduism is characterized by the expansion of the devotional (bhakti) movement throughout India, first in the southern and then in the northern part of the country.

This was the period of the Muslim conquest of parts of India, the greatest disaster that overtook Hinduism in the course of its history. Other invaders had been assimilated, but the Muslims came with a crusading religion and an alien culture which could not be assimilated or overcome. There is no doubt that the Hindus suffered terribly on account of the religious fanaticism of the Muslim conquerors. There were forcible conversions, destruction of temples, and desecration of holy places. During this time the Hindu teachers resolutely clung to their own ideals and their own religion and became more and more conservative in their social philosophy and customs and manners.

Even before the time of Śaṅkara there had been some theistic interpretations of the Vedānta. These continued in spite of the popularity of Śaṅkara's teachings, were strengthened by the passionate devotional hymns of the Ālvārs, and culminated in the philosophy of Rāmānuja. Rāmānuja, who died in 1137, was a Brāhman of southern India who taught for a long time at the sacred shrine of Śrīraṅgam, near modern Tiruchirāppalli. He tried to reconcile the teachings of the Veda with those of the mystic poets, the Ālvārs. According to him, devotion (bhakti) was the central teaching of the Vedānta. His system is called Viśishṭādvaita (qualified monism). Unlike Śaṅkara, Rāmānuja gave a higher place to love of god than to knowledge (jñāna) and taught that absolute self-surrender was the quickest way to salvation. In addition to his systematization of theistic Vedānta, Rāmānuja did much for the religious uplift of the lower classes in his day, bringing many of them into the Vaishṇava fold without in any way violating the social restrictions of the higher castes.

The early years of the thirteenth century witnessed the rise of two philosophical systems which have continued to the present time, the dualistic (*dvaita*) system of Madhva and the Śaiva-Siddhānta system of Meykaṇḍār. Madhva, not satisfied with the strict monism of Śaṅkara or the qualified monism of Rāmānuja, developed a strictly dualistic system of philosophy. Meykaṇḍār's religious teachings, elaborated by his followers, became the basis of a theism centered in the Lord Śiva. It was in this period that there arose another Śaiva sect which worships Śiva and no other god; they are called Liṅgāyats because they worship the Śiva-liṅgam, a symbolic representation of Śiva. A Liṅgāyat always carries with him a small liṅga in a reliquary suspended from his neck.

The Rise of the Devotional Movement in North India (A.D. 1400-1800)

The devotional (bhakti) movement in northern India came during the fifteenth and sixteenth centuries as a purely Vaishṇavite movement centering around the two incarnations (avatāras) of Vishṇu, Rāma, and Kṛishṇa.

Rāmānanda was the leader of the movement centering around Rāma. He discouraged caste distinctions and wrote his hymns, like the Ālvārs, in the language of the people. He taught that Rāma was the Supreme Lord and that salvation could be gained only by devotion to Him and by repeating His sacred name. The order of ascetics founded by him was known as Rāmānandis, and to this order belonged Tulsī Dās, the author of the famous Hindi version of the Rāmāyaṇa.

Two of the men who owed their inspiration to Rāmānanda

showed Muslim leanings also. These were Kabīr, a genuine mystic, and Nānak, the founder of the religion of Sikhism. Kabīr was a Muslim weaver of Banaras who came under the influence of Rāmānanda and became his disciple. He accepted the Hindu doctrine of the law of karma and the ideal of release, shared the Hindu faith in the efficacy of repeating the Holy Name, and called his God Rāma. But he rejected the doctrine of avatāras, denounced idol worship and caste distinctions, and rejected the authority of the Vedas as well as of the Koran. He was denounced as a heretic by both Hindus and Muslims, but because of his genuine religious experience his poems became very popular, and he was later looked upon as a saint by all.

Nānak, the founder of Sikhism, stands in a closer relation to Hinduism. He, too, denounced caste distinctions and idol worship, and insisted on faith and purity of life. He also accepted the Hindu doctrines of karma and release (moksha), believed in the mystic value of the name of Rāma, and insisted on extreme reverence to the spiritual preceptor (*guru*). Unlike Kabīr, he accepted the gods of the Hindu pantheon and tolerated ritualism as a lower form of worship. His work was more lasting than Kabīr's because his followers soon created a center of authority for their religion by collecting the hymns of their gurus in a Holy Book—called the Granth Sahib—and making it an object of worship.

The devotion that centers around Kṛishṇa is of two types. Some worship Kṛishṇa of the legendary history, the husband of Rukmiṇī and the friend of the Pāṇḍavas. Others worship Kṛishṇa of the allegorical romance, as the lover of Rādhā, who symbolizes the human soul. Naturally, the devotion of the former class is pure and serene, while that of the latter is highly erotic, passionate, and tempestuous.

The Rādhā-Kṛishṇa cult appears as a rounded philosophical system in the teaching of Nimbārka, who wrote in the twelfth century. The cult expanded considerably in the thirteenth century, and in the fourteenth and fifteenth centuries was made widely popular by a number of brilliant Vaishṇava poets who wrote exquisite songs about Rādhā and Kṛishṇa. Perhaps the best known of these poets are Chaṇḍīdās of Bengal and Mīrā Bāi of Rajputana. And finally, in the first quarter of the sixteenth century two great teachers arose who founded their systems on the Rādhā-Kṛishṇa cult, Vallabha (1479-1531) and Chaitanya (1486-1533).

In Vallabha's system Kṛishṇa becomes the eternal Brahman and Rādhā is His eternal spouse with whom He plays eternally in the celestial Vrindāban together with their devotees. Chaitanya, who was a contemporary of Vallabha, was at first only a scholar and a hair-splitting logician but later, under the influence of the song writers of the Rādhā-Kṛishṇa cult, he became a devotee of the most passionate kind. He renounced the world and settled down at Pūri near the temple of Jagannāth. By his ecstatic devotion to Kṛishṇa, which expressed itself in singing, dancing, and teaching, he brought about a great religious revival in Bengal, where he is still highly revered.

The bhakti movement continued to advance in the various parts of the country during the rest of this period, producing innumerable sects and a mass of devotional poetry in several languages of the people; but it had practically exhausted itself by the middle of the eighteenth century.

MODERN HINDUISM

The modern period in the history of Hinduism begins about 1800. At the beginning of the nineteenth century the fortunes of Hinduism may be said to have been at their lowest ebb. In fact, we may say that after the bhakti movement exhausted itself about the middle of the eighteenth century, there is nothing great or noteworthy in Hindu religion, art, or literature until we come to Rām Mohun Roy, the morning star of the present Hindu renaissance. And even after him the darkness continued for another fifty years.

The British rule in India, which lasted about a century and a half, was quite unlike the Muslim conquest. The Muslims had little effect on the development of Hinduism, but the British, by breaking the isolation of India and bringing Hindus into contact with European history, science, and literature, and European political and social institutions and customs and manners, widened their outlook and made them scrape away many of the crude notions which had encrusted their religion during the medieval period. For a time, Hindus were thrown off their balance and began to ape English ways of life, but this stage did not last long. The inherent vitality of Hinduism soon asserted itself.

The herald of the coming change was Rām Mohun Roy (1772-1833), the founder of the Brāhmo Samāj. He fought in defense of what he considered true Hinduism against both the orthodox Hindu paṇḍits (religious teachers) and the Christian missionaries of his day. He brought about the abolition of the cruel custom of *sati* (burning the widow on the funeral pyre of her husband), encouraged scientific education, denounced idol worship and the caste system, and founded the Brāhmo Samāj, which is a school of rational theism on the basis of the Upanishads. Rām Mohun Roy never contemplated any separation from the parent religion; after his death, however, under the leadership of Devendranāth Tagore, the Brāhmo Samāj became more rationalistic and later, under the leadership of Keshub Chander Sen, it became more Christian than Hindu. On account of these developments and the schisms within, the Samāj split up into three groups and lost a considerable part of its influence.

The Ārya Samāj founded by Swāmī Dayānanda (1824-1883) is a better representative of Hinduism than the Brāhmo Samāj. It has become the spearhead of a dynamic type of Hinduism trying to unify all sections of Hindu society, reclaiming those who have gone out of the fold, making new converts, and fighting all enemies who make inroads into the Vedic religion.

It takes its stand on the Vedas and the Vedas alone, and ignores all the later developments; thus it denounces idol worship and the caste system. Curiously enough, it takes little account of the philosophy of the Upanishads, and consequently cuts itself off from the perennial sources of Hindu religious thought. Therefore the Samāj has become more a school of nationalism than of religion proper.

The part played in the modern Hindu renaissance by Mrs. Annie Besant (1847-1933) was certainly very great. At a time when Hinduism was being unjustly attacked on all sides, the eloquent defense and adoption of it by an Englishwoman of genius, who had once been a freethinker, had a tremendous influence. Mrs. Besant not only delivered numberless lectures on Hinduism but also translated and popularized the Gītā and started a Hindu College in Banaras, which has grown into the present Banaras Hindu University. Her Hinduism was too much colored, however, especially in later years, by a very pretentious type of occultism and the teachings of the Theosophical Society.

The true renaissance of Hinduism in this period begins with the teachings of Śrī Rāmakṛishṇa (1836-1886). His marvelous discourses are recorded in the *Gospel of Śrī Rāmakṛishṇa,* which is one of the greatest books in the Hindu religious tradition. He spoke with authority because he had firsthand religious experience. The religion that he lived and taught was not mere absolutism or theism, not mere jñāna, or bhakti, or yoga, not mere Vedism or Vedāntism or Śāktism or Purāṇic Hinduism, not even entire Hinduism, but the universal religion of which all the historical religions of the world are only certain aspects. He was a living synthesis of all religions. And yet he never cut himself off from the Hindu tradition and authority. Far from doing so, he lived and taught in the precincts of a temple, and it was through the worship of the image of Kālī that he attained to the realization of the Absolute.

Śrī Rāmakṛishṇa was not a scholar; he had no book learning.

All his knowledge was derived from oral tradition and his own bold experiments in religion. Hence he was able to infuse into his followers a spirit of renunciation and of zeal for true religion and service of humanity. He handed on the torch to his favorite disciple Swāmī Vivekānanda (1863-1902) who, after his visits to America and Europe, founded the famous Rāmakṛishṇa Mission which has now more than a hundred centers in all parts of the world. Vivekānanda's originality lay in applying his Master's teachings to the problems of national life and in making the Hindu order of sannyāsins set an example to the lay public not only in religious practice but also in social service and relief work. His lectures and talks made clear to the students of Hinduism for the first time the essentials and nonessentials of that religion. He pointed out in a thousand ways how Vedānta was the steel frame within that vast structure which goes by the name of Hinduism. His work in elucidating the essential principles of Hinduism to students of religion, both inside and outside India, is now being very ably continued by Professor Rādhākṛishṇan.

The present renaissance has reached its zenith in the work of three great men who have achieved world-wide reputation in this generation, Śrī Aurobindo Ghose, Rabīndranāth Tagore, and Mahātmā Gāndhi.

Śrī Aurobindo Ghose (1872-1950), in his magnum opus, *The Divine Life,* and other works, has reinterpreted in impressive language the Hindu concepts of moksha, yoga, and *jīvanmukti* (the state of the self which has realized Brahman while still in its human body). As explained in an earlier section, *moksha* means the liberation of man from his finite human consciousness and the realization of the divine consciousness. Śrī Aurobindo calls this higher consciousness the Life Divine or the Supermind. He taught that by means of a new type of integral yoga the higher consciousness might not only be realized but also brought down to irradiate the mind and the body of the individual. A man who succeeded in doing this would be a spiritual superman, who would correspond exactly to the jīvanmukta described in the ancient Vedānta literature. Śrī Aurobindo believed that all the political, social, and economic problems which plague humanity at the present time could finally be solved only by the society producing individuals of this higher type; so he gave up all active life and settled down in Pondicherry, in southern India, in 1910 and built up an *āśrama* (hermitage), like the Seers of old, for that purpose. He practiced his yoga and taught it for about forty years to those who came from all parts of the world to seek his help.

Rabīndranāth Tagore (1861-1941) is one of the greatest mystical poets of the world. Though he once belonged to the Brāhmo Samāj, his religion always transcended the limitations of his group. He drew his inspiration from the Upanishads and the Vaishṇava poets of Bengal who sang about the loves of Rādhā and Kṛishṇa. His discourses in *Sādhana* may be considered a modern commentary on the Upanishadic texts. His songs in *Gītānjali* and other collections may be described as the modernized and universalized versions of the old Vaishṇava mystical poetry, but the nature-mysticism with which much of his poetry is suffused is his own. Tagore was not only a great religious poet but also a great prophet of humanity. In his later life he traveled all over the world, calling upon all nations to give up wars and exploitation and denouncing the aggressive nationalism of the West as a crime against humanity.

Mahātmā Gāndhi (1869-1948) is generally considered to be one of the greatest saints that ever lived. He was the architect of India's freedom, but will be remembered by future generations as the great prophet of nonviolence. His originality lay in his application of the principle of nonviolence to national and international affairs. Nonviolence had occupied the highest place among the Hindu cardinal virtues from time immemorial, but it had been applied only to individual action. Gāndhiji extended it to communities and nations and developed a suitable technique of action for it, called satyāgraha, which is nonviolent defense of what one considers to be truth. His message was not meant simply for Hindus or India, but for the whole world. Though his activities were confined to the political sphere, he repeatedly declared that they were only a means to the realization of Truth, moksha. According to him, Truth is God and nonviolence the means of reaching it. Perfect nonviolence is perfect self-realization. Mahātmā Gāndhi confessed that he was only an erring mortal, but most of his countrymen venerate him almost as an avatāra. There is no doubt that he is the greatest man that India has produced since Buddha.

It will be seen from this short outline of the history of Hinduism that the religion of the Hindus is as vigorous today as it was in any of its past periods of expansion. At the beginning of the modern period, Hindu society was stagnant, fettered with a thousand restrictions and customs which were looked upon as the Laws of God. Now, child marriages are illegal, intermarriage between castes is becoming frequent. The cruel custom of sati is gone; women are now educated, have the franchise, and have been serving as Ministers of State and as ambassadors. Untouchability is prohibited by law, and the ban on foreign travel has been removed. There is now a greater knowledge of the essentials of Hinduism among the people; the Bhagavad Gītā is being widely read; many good books on the religion of the Hindus have been published within the past fifty years in all the languages of India.

India is now free. She is conducting a huge experiment in democracy over a vast subcontinent. It is not too much to hope that the religion of the Hindus will soon be recognized by all as one of the great spiritualizing forces in the world, a force leading humanity to its goal.

Chapter 2

THE HINDU CONCEPT OF GOD

by JITENDRA NATH BANERJEA

THE SUPREME BEING

THE IMPERSONAL BRAHMAN

Faith in the existence of one spiritual reality, generally conceived as a personal god, and belief in the law of karma and the transmigration of souls, are the most important elements in the religious thought of a Hindu. An intelligent Hindu thinks of god as residing within himself, controlling all his actions as the "Inner Controller," and at the same time god is outside him, manifest in innumerable ways, known and unknown.

The Supreme Being is described as "beyond the measure of all attributes," as the resting place of the Power which creates and sustains everything, and to which the created things return upon dissolution. The earlier Upanishads, referring to the three principal activities of the Supreme Being, creation, preservation, and dissolution, say, "everything is born in Him [in the beginning], is absorbed in Him [in the end], and breathes or is sustained in Him [in the period of its existence]."

The Hindu belief that the divine is both immanent and transcendant is beautifully expressed in the Ṛigvedic verse, "Thousand-headed was the Supreme Being, thousand-eyed and thousand-footed. Covering the world all around, He yet exceeded it by a span. All this is the Supreme Being, what is past and what is in the future; He is the Lord of immortality as well as of that which grows by food [mortal creatures]" (X.90.1-2). This mantra appealed so much to the mind of the Hindu that he selected it as specially suited for recitation at the time of the ceremonial washing of his image. The mantra constitutes the first two couplets of the famous Hymn to the Supreme Being (Purusha-sūkta) which summarizes the Vedic concept of God.

The Personal God

This Supreme Being, the neutral and impersonal Brahman of the earlier Upanishads, is also known as a personal god. In the Śvetāśvatara Upanishad (IV.11;VI.7), Brahman is described as "superintending all natural causes, from whom all this rises and to whom it returns," and He is also known as "the great Lord of lords, the great God of gods, the Master of masters, greater than the great, the adorable Lord of the world." Here the cosmic, transcendent character of the Supreme Reality is not ignored, but the personal and immanent relationship comes to the fore. Here the Supreme Being is known as the Inner Controller, as described in the last chapter of the Bhagavad Gītā, "God resides in the heart of all beings, and by His *māyā* [creative energy] moves them from within as if they were turned by a machine."

The concept of "the adorable Lord of the world," the God "who resides in the heart of all beings," plays a most important part in the spiritual life of the Hindu. The feeling of deep loving adoration which he has for his God in his heart is called *bhakti*. There are different types of bhakti, of inferior and superior order. The highest type is that which does not seek for the fulfilment of any desire, and which is not determined by any conditions. This ideal type of devotion is characterized with unusual charm in the Bhāgavata Purāṇa. The God says, "As the waters of the Ganges flow incessantly towards the ocean, so do the minds of those [devotees having the ideal type of bhakti for their god] move constantly towards Me, the Supreme Person residing in every heart, immediately they hear about My qualities. They have no desire for the fruits of their actions, and [they know] that there is no real barrier between them and Me. This is the characteristic sign of the way of the unqualified bhakta. These persons would not accept even such [gifts] as life in the same heaven with Me, creative power similar to Mine, nearness to Me, the same form as Mine, or the state of union with Me; they would always prefer My service to them all" (III.11-13).

This mental attitude towards one's own god is the ideal type of loving adoration. There is room in it for the imagination of different kinds of personal relationships with god, such as that of a father and son, a husband and wife, or a master and servant, and at the same time there is in it the deep undercurrent of the idea that the Lord and His devotee are essentially one in nature. In this way the ideal type of theism advocated by the highest devotee is monistic in character and thus there is no real difference between the strictly monistic thought of the Upanishadic Seers and the concept of the personal relationship between God and His devotees in some of the theistic schools of India.

Thus, through the worship and adoration of the devotee, the cosmic character of the Supreme Reality as conceived in the Upanishads was easily and consistently transferred to the chief cult deities of later times. Side by side with his belief in the existence of one and only one Supreme Being, a Hindu would appear to an uncritical observer to have faith in the existence of many deities. But even from a very early period a Hindu was conscious of the fact that the multitudinous deities of his pantheon really illustrate the various ways of describing one single God, the eternally existent One Being with his manifold attributes and manifestations. As early as the Ṛigveda, this idea was expressed in what has become a favorite mantra of the Hindus, "They call Him Indra, Mitra, Varuṇa, Agni, and even the fleet-winged celestial bird Garuḍa. The One Reality, the learned speak of in many ways" (I.64). While this particular hymn is sung in honor of the Sun God, who is here described as the one divinity, this concept of giving many names to one god is the important thing to be noted here.

THE HINDU DEITIES

An attempt is made in many of the early and late Vedic texts to fix the number of the members of the pantheon at thirty-three. These thirty-three gods were divided into three groups of eleven each, one group associated with heaven, the second group with earth, and the third with the waters and atmosphere. Such listings usually centered around the three deities governing the natural phenomena, the sun (Sūrya) for heaven, fire (Agni) for earth, and the wind god (Vāyu) or Indra for the atmospheric region. In the common parlance of the Hindus of much later days, the number thirty-three for the gods and goddesses was enlarged to as many as thirty-three *crores*—and a crore is ten million. But underlying this very multiplicity lay the sense of unity. To the discerning Hindu mind this numerousness of his deities really is just a way of expressing the immense and uncountable manifestations of the One Supreme Being.

This fluid multiplicity served also a very important purpose from the historical point of view. It provided a workable method for absorbing the gods of other races, nationalities, and creeds into the Hindu fold. The belief in many divine incarnations was also useful for this purpose. Thus, this so-called concept of many deities was expressive in a unique manner of the catholicity of the Hindu mind. This is not polytheism, but a recognition that the Supreme Being is known in many ways and worshiped in many forms.

Major Cults

The development of the bhakti movement in Hinduism played a most important part in the evolution of the different religious sects which became established in India. Five deities came to prominence as the objects of devotion, Śiva, Vishṇu, Śakti, Sūrya (the sun god), and Gaṇeśa or Gaṇapati (the elephant-headed god). Around these five deities grew up the five chief cults found in India today. For the duly initiated follower of a sect, his chosen deity is his exclusive object of worship and all the other gods and goddesses are subsidiary manifestations of his Supreme God.

The Śaiva and Śākta cults seem to have been the oldest among these religious systems, their origins going back to pre-Vedic times. Vaishṇavism evolved in the post-Vedic age. The worship of the sun god (Sūrya) is also very old; one aspect of the cult, however, was introduced to northern India from Iran about two thousand years ago. There is no clear literary reference to the exclusive worshipers of Gaṇeśa before the time of the great monist philosopher Śaṅkara (eighth century A.D.), though his images of a much earlier date are known. Of these five sects, the first three are the most important in modern times. Although the Sun is worshiped, and there are many shrines dedicated to Gaṇeśa, and they are honored in the pantheons of the other deities, there are very few persons today who would consider Sūrya or Gaṇeśa to be their chosen deity, or would consider themselves to be members of a sect devoted to either of these gods.

In addition to the Śaivas, the Vaishṇavas, and the Śāktas, there is one other eclectic sectarian group which is known in India today as the Smārtas. They are guided principally by the rules laid down in the Smṛitis, such as the Laws of Manu and the Yājñavalkya Smṛiti, since the different sectaries chiefly follow their own Purāṇas. The Smārtas worship the five principal divinities: Śiva, Vishṇu, Śakti, Sūrya and Gaṇeśa. In their ritualistic worship, veneration is first offered to them with the mantra, "Salutation to the five divinities with Gaṇeśa at the beginning." Gaṇeśa is mentioned first, not because of higher rank, but because he is the remover of obstacles, and his blessing is invoked at the outset so that the ceremony may not come to any grief. The initiated Smārtas may have a chosen deity, but worship equally all five deities and their subordinate forms.

Deities Without Cults

The major deities worshiped in contemporary Hinduism may be classified according to their individual cult affiliations, Vishṇu, Śiva, and Śakti, with Gaṇeśa and Sūrya associated with them. There are also deities in the Hindu pantheon which do not have a clear-cut cult affiliation; most of these had their origin in the Vedic age before sectarian religions were developed, though some of them are more recent. Deities without clear sectarian affiliations include Brahmā the Creator, Vāyu the wind god, Agni the god of fire, Hanumān the monkey god, Yama the god of death, Varuṇa the god of waters, Indra the god of the heavens, Kāma the god of love, and others. Finally, there are the demons (Asuras), and the semidivine beings such as the snake deities (Nāgas) and the divine damsels (Apsaras).

Vehicles of the Gods

Associated with each of the major deities of Hinduism is an animal known as the god's vehicle. The word *vehicle* is a translation of the Sanskrit word *vāhana* which literally means *carrier* or *that on which one rides*. In some cases the animals might well have been mythological carriers of the god, as in the case of the lion for Pārvatī; in other cases clear proofs can be given to show that the mounts of the gods are nothing but their animal forms. In many others, however, this cannot be clearly demonstrated and the association of a particular animal with a deity may be ascribed to other factors.

Vishṇu—One of the Three Chief Gods of the Hindus

Vishṇu, the protector and sustainer of the world, is one of the most highly venerated of the Hindu gods, sharing popularity with Śiva and Śakti. He is an important member of the Hindu Triad, or Trinity, made up of Brahmā, Vishṇu, and Śiva, and is the central figure of worship in the major cult of Vaishṇavism, which is followed all over India. Vishṇu, around whom the great Vaishṇava cult has developed, is really an amalgam of various god concepts. The central and most important basis for the concept of Vishṇu was the man Vāsudeva, an ancient hero who was deified by his kinsmen and followers. That concept was strengthened by merging it with the solar deity, Vishṇu, and the cosmic god, Nārāyaṇa, of the Vedas and Brāhmaṇas, developing into one of the greatest and most lovable gods of India.

The most important trait of Vāsudeva's character which is emphasized in the earlier tales about him was his love of righteousness (dharma) and of the performance of one's duties without any desire for rewards. The part he played among his contemporaries seems to have inspired in the hearts of many of them a feeling of loving admiration and adoration for him. Early inscriptions show that soon he was identified with the Vedic god Vishṇu and had as his vehicle the sun-bird Garuḍa—really the sun conceived as a bird because of his apparent flight through the sky. Nārāyaṇa, the cosmic god, is portrayed as the Supreme God, lying on the coils of Śesha the serpent, floating on the primeval waters, the resting place of all worlds.

The concept of Vishṇu as blending the characteristics of Vasudeva, Vishṇu, and Nārāyaṇa was complete in very early times. More than two thousand years ago the Vaishṇava cult is known to have made much progress. The only major development after that time was the rise of the worship of Vishṇu in the form of Kṛishṇa, which came at the time of the bhakti movement in the medieval period.

The medieval images of Vishṇu illustrate the fourfold form of Vishṇu, showing how this composite cult god has many aspects. They are four-faced and four-armed (sometimes eight); the peaceful central face is human, representing Vasudeva, while the other three represent in a mystic and esoteric manner the ideal qualities which emanate from Vishṇu's creative power: knowledge, strength, lordship, virility, ability, and splendor.

Different Forms of Vishṇu. The avatāra forms of Vishṇu are numerous. *Avatāra* means "the descent of the Lord into the world of men and animals," and may be translated as *incarnation* if it is remembered that the word is used in this special sense. A secondary indication of the word is that in this world the best and most excellent things that were, are, and will be, are so many forms of the Lord. This idea is beautifully expressed in the Bhagavad Gītā by Kṛishṇa when he tells Arjuna that he becomes incarnate in age after age for the deliverance of the righteous, the chastisement of the wicked, and for the establishment of virtue and righteousness in the world whenever good decays and the evil becomes triumphant (IV.7-8).

Thus, the exact number of avatāras is immaterial, and the Bhāgavata Purāṇa rightly says that the "incarnations [of the Lord] are uncountable." Of the many lists of varying numbers, the number ten is usually accepted by the Hindus for the sake of convenience. These ten incarnations of Vishṇu are: Fish, Tortoise, Boar, Man-Lion, Dwarf, Paraśurāma, Rāma, Balarāma, Buddha, and Kalkin.

The first three avatāras were so many forms of Prajāpati according to the Brāhmaṇas, but they were later transferred to Vishṇu when his cult came into prominence. Myths tell us that the Lord incarnated himself as a Fish to deliver the Vedas from the demons, as a Tortoise to sustain the world on his back, and as a Boar to raise the earth when it was dragged down to the nether regions by a demon. In his Man-Lion incarnation he killed a great demon planning to kill his own son; this demon's son had shown great devotion to Hari (Vishṇu), and it was necessary to take this form since the demon could be killed neither by a man nor a beast.

In his Dwarf incarnation, Vishṇu assumed the form of a young student, dwarfish in stature; his elder brothers, the gods Indra and others, had been deprived of all their possessions by the demons and were sulking in misery. The demon king was then performing the horse sacrifice (*Aśvamedha*) and granting whatever was being asked from him, so the Dwarf went to his court and asked for just that space in which he could take three steps. This was granted, and lo! the Dwarf suddenly assumed a gigantic form. By the first step he covered the heavens, his second step filled the earth, and with the third placed on the head of the king, who was also one of his great admirers and devotees, he sent the latter to the nether regions. Thus were recovered the heavens and the earth for the gods. This Dwarf form of Vishṇu, as well as the Boar and Man-Lion, were and are today very popular with the Hindus. The mythological themes have been variously worked out in the epics and Purāṇas, and numerous sculptures illustrating them are found in many early and late Vaishṇava shrines throughout India.

Paraśurāma was a human incarnation of the Lord. He is the symbol of militant Brāhmanism and is said to have destroyed the Kshatriyas of the earth several times because of their arrogant and unrighteous acts. He is depicted as a bearded sage with a battle-axe in his hand.

The Rāma incarnation represents the noblest ideal of Kshatriya manhood; it was at Rāma's hands that the pride of Paraśurāma as the destroyer of the Kshatriyas was curbed. The story of Rāma appealed so much to the ancient Hindus that it was put into epic form in the Rāmāyaṇa for their delight. The life incidents of this great hero who stands for all that is noble and virtuous in man were not only told in some of the finest literature of India, but they were also chiseled beautifully on the walls of many early and late temples of India and Indonesia. Part of the Vaishṇava sect known as the Rāmāites also came to worship Rāma exclusively. Many temples in different parts of India enshrine beautiful images of Rāma. He is two-armed, holding a bow and arrow in his hands, almost invariably attended by his faithful wife Sītā, his dear brother Lakshmaṇa, and his devoted servant Hanumān, the monkey-god. Such is the feeling of deep love and adoration for this hero god in many Hindu hearts that even his monkey servant, Hanumān, is worshiped as The Great Hero (*Mahāvīra*) in wayside and village shrines in many parts of India.

The Balarāma incarnation seems to have some association with the primitive snake (Nāga) cult of India; he has also some agricultural and bucolic traits. His two-armed figure holding a ploughshare and a drinking vessel in the hands invariably stands under a canopy of snake hoods.

Buddha, the founder of a religious order which is heterodox from the Brāhmaṇical Hindu point of view, is given a place in the ten incarnations. In the Purāṇas, Vishṇu is said to have been born as "the Deluder" in the Śākya race in order to delude the demons with false doctrines and thus work for their undoing. They accepted his teachings, gave up Vedic rites and practices, and as a consequence were defeated by the gods. This is a peculiar way of acknowledging the greatness and sanctity of the heretical teacher and decrying the doctrines attributed to him.

The tenth incarnation, as Kalkin, is yet to come.

Although these aspects of Vishṇu discussed above are held in highest veneration by the Hindus in general and the Vaishṇavas among them in particular, except for the Rāma shrines very few of those aspects have temples dedicated to them at present. Most of the innumerable modern Vaishṇava temples of India enshrine Vishṇu in his Nārāyaṇa aspect, or as Kṛishṇa. Four-handed Vishṇu-Nārāyaṇa is shown lying on the coils of the Śesha (serpent), attended by some of his companions, the chief among them being his consort, Śrī or Lakshmī. Brahmā is seated on a lotus issuing from Vishṇu's navel, and the whole image is floating on the primeval waters. This image portrays Vishṇu as one Supreme God, the resting place of all the worlds. This is one of the most highly venerated types of Vishṇu images in south India, where the god is placed in the main sanctum and worshiped with great veneration. The most sacred of such

Vaishṇava shrines in southern India is at Śrīraṅgam, near Tiruchirāppalli, where Rāmānuja taught. Another very sacred temple enshrining this type of image is that of Paḍmanābha at Trivandrum in the extreme south of India.

Vishṇu as Kṛishṇa. The Kṛishṇa aspect of Vishṇu is another very important unit in the Vaishṇava pantheon. In some lists of the ten incarnations he comes after Balarāma instead of Buddha, but he is usually regarded as the God Himself and not as one of His avatāras. The life history of Kṛishṇa as narrated in the Mahābhārata (especially in the supplement called Harivaṁśa) and in the Bhāgvata Purāṇa is the basis for the various ways of meditating on him and for the variety of images which are enshrined in the many Vaishṇava temples in different parts of India.

The most cherished forms of Kṛishṇa are associated with his early life and, in the scenes often depicted on temple walls, the child god's exploits are favorite themes. The main image in the temples dedicated to him often shows him as the divine infant on all fours holding a sweet cake in one of his two hands, or the divine child dancing in glee for having got a lump of butter to eat, or the divine youth playing on a flute and thus ravishing the hearts of his companions, the cowherd boys, the cowherd lasses, and even the cows. He is shown as the chastiser of the serpent Kāliya, who used to kill the inhabitants of Mathurā with his poison, or as the champion cowherd holding the mountain over his village to shelter it from the rains sent down in wrath by Indra. Again, he is depicted as the youthful and ardent lover of Rādhā and her many companions, the cowherdesses (*gopīs*); or he may be pictured as the charioteer of Arjuna in the war with the Kurus. The images enshrined in many temples, especially in eastern and northern parts of India, generally show Kṛishṇa standing in a graceful pose (the three-bend pose, his body showing three bends), playing on a rustic flute accompanied by Rādhā, his most beloved among the gopīs.

The theme of the divine act of love was worked out in manifold ways by the pious devotees of the god into one of the highly mystical bhakti cults of India. The apparently erotic elements in some of its phases were nothing but ways of expressing the deepest and sweetest love of a devotee for his or her god, just as a person feels for his or her most cherished lover. Some of the sincerest and noblest religious poetry of India owes its origin to this feeling of mystic love and adoration, and some of the finest images enshrined in medieval and modern Vaishṇava temples characterize it in a sublime manner. Awe and veneration are not the keynotes in this type of mental attitude toward the god; here are found the sweetest and most lovable feelings of intimate companionship between the worshiper and the worshiped.

There are several festivals which are particularly associated with Kṛishṇa and have a special sanctity for the Vaishṇavas, though they are shared by Hindus in general. The car festival, held in the month which in the Hindu calendar overlaps June-July, is the time for placing the portable images on wooden chariots and dragging them in procession through the streets. In August-September a festival celebrates Kṛishṇa's birth in the prison of his uncle on the eighth day of the dark fortnight, and his transference to the cowherd village. In July-August, images of Kṛishṇa and Rādhā are swung in decorated swings. In October-November, beautifully decorated images of Kṛishṇa and Rādhā and their eight female companions are worshiped with great pomp. In February-March colored water and powder are ceremonially offered to the images of Kṛishṇa and Rādhā, and it is at this time that Hindus go through the streets throwing colored water and powder on each other.

Thousands of shrines dedicated to Kṛishṇa are scattered across the length and breadth of India, testifying to the great feeling of love and adoration in which he is held by his untold millions of votaries throughout the country. Only a few of them may be mentioned here: the beautiful temples at Mathurā and Vrindāban are especially sacred. The temples of Govindajī at Jaipur and of Nāthaji at Nathdwāra near Udaipur are both in the Rajasthan Union. The temples in west Bengal, associated with Śrī Chaitanya and revered by his followers, are at Nabadwīp, Sāntipur, and Ambicā Kālnā. The temple of Jagannāth at Pūri and the Gopāla temple not far from it are in Orissa on the east coast, and the Kṛishṇa temple at Dwārakā on the Kathiawar Peninsula is on the west coast. In the south are the temples at Tirupati, at Conjeevaram, and in Madras at Triplicane, all in Madras State.

Vishṇu is not only an object of worship in temples generally open to the public, but small stones known as *sālagrāmas* which represent him are also the objects of daily worship in millions of Hindu homes in India. Sālagrāmas are usually small, flintified ammonite shells, river-worn and thus smoothly rounded. They are small stones of different colors, with black predominating, and with one or more holes in the side in which are seen several spiral grooves resembling the wheel emblem of Vishṇu. These stones are generally recovered from the bed of the river Gaṇḍakī in north Bihar, one of the tributaries of the Ganges. The Purāṇas say that the river goddess prayed to Vishṇu to be born in her womb; the god heard her prayer and appeared in the river bed as sālagrāma stones. The loving veneration of the orthodox Vaishṇava householder for these nonrepresentational symbols of their principal god is a noteworthy feature of their religious faith. The god thus symbolized has his living presence, as it were, in the household, and the women of the family spend much of their time every day in preparation of the different materials for his ritual worship, which is usually performed by the head of the family or the family priest. The sālagrāmas are also worshiped in Vaishṇava shrines along with the images of the god.

Śiva—One of the Three Chief Hindu Deities

Śiva is the god of destruction or absorption in the concept of the Hindu Triad made up of Brahmā, Vishṇu, and Śiva. He, however, not only destroys, but also creates, sustains, obscures by his power of illusion (*māyā*), and offers grace to the suffering world. These are his fivefold activities, according to a devout Śaiva. Śiva was known as the father-god, the lord of animals, and the great ascetic from very ancient, pre-Vedic times. Later developments show him in his terrifying and his gracious aspects; many myths and shrines have grown up around these two aspects of his character.

Phallic emblems and the figure of a deity seated in a peculiar yogic posture surrounded by a man and several animals, found in the Indus valley archeological excavations, indicate that the concept of a father-god who was at the same time a lord of animals and a great ascetic was well established in pre-Vedic times. It is probable, if not certain, that the principal deity of the Śaiva cult is the result of the amalgamation of such pre-Vedic god-concepts with Rudra of the Ṛigveda, who has his terrifying and gracious aspects—and with other god-concepts of later times. However, "Śiva" as his proper name was somewhat late in making its appearance in literature; the word was first used in the sense of "auspicious," but from the time that it was used as the proper name of the god it was the favorite.

The first tangible references to the exclusive worshipers of Śiva are found in grammatical texts of the fifth century B.C. About eighteen hundred years ago Lakulīśa seems to have organized the cult of Śiva devotees which became known by his name. Lakulīśa was deified by posterity and he occupies an honored place in the Śaiva pantheon. Some of his immediate disciples also seem to have founded other subsects allied to the system, which were of an extreme type. Some of their religious rites and practices were of an unsocial character and not generally approved by other members of the Hindu society.

There grew up popular as well as highly philosophical systems devoted to Śiva, both of which contained some of the highest and purest ideas about god. Unsophisticated villagers look upon him as their familiar friend, the father of a family consisting of his wife Durgā and his two sons Kārttikeya and Gaṇeśa (his favorite son), and his two daughters, Lakshmī the goddess of fortune and Sarasvatī the goddess of learning. Durgā is the daughter of the personified Himālaya mountain. At their annual festival on the concluding day of the year, many villagers work out this homely idea about their lovable companion god who looks after their well-being and is easily pleased with their festive rites and ceremonies. Side by side with this popular aspect of the god can be placed the highly philosophical ideas current about him in the monistic, dualistic, and pluralistic schools of Śaivism. The Pratyabhijñā system of the Kashmir school of Śaivism, for instance, idealizes him in the highest and most abstruse manner.

The great god has been represented by many different images, animal, anthropomorphic, and phallic. The sacred bull is the god in his animal form, transformed by the Śaiva devotees centuries ago into his vehicle, to accompany the deity represented in human or phallic form. In every Śiva temple may be seen an image of this sacred bull, called Nandi, placed on a high pedestal facing the shrine, its eyes riveted on the emblem of the god in the main sanctum.

There are numerous human images of Śiva, showing him in his terrifying and his gracious aspects, most of them illustrating the innumerable tales that are told about him. Śiva is said to have destroyed various demons, such as the Elephant-Demon and others. He also punished such gods as Brahmā for telling lies, and Yama, the god of death, for his audacity in attempting to take away the life of one of the devotees of Śiva. Kāma, the god of love, was punished for daring to hit him with his flowery arrows in order that his meditation, into which he had entered after the tragic death of his first wife Satī, might be disturbed and he would have feelings of love for Umā (Pārvatī, the daughter of the Himālaya), whom he afterward married.

Śiva is also said to have conferred grace on gods, men, and

even demons on various occasions; thus at one time he was pleased with the great devotion of Vishṇu and presented him with the wheel or discus (*chakra*), one of the principal attributes of Vishṇu. While in exile, Arjuna, hero of the Mahabhārata epic, practiced severe penance to please Śiva and get some invincible weapons from him, and Śiva, after testing his strength, gave him the great weapon which stood the Pāṇḍava brothers in good stead in the war with the Kurus. Rāvaṇa, the demon king of Laṅkā in the Rāmāyaṇa epic, was a great devotee of Śiva and once attempted to uplift bodily Śiva's favorite section of the Himālaya mountain and take it, along with Śiva and Pārvatī, to Laṅkā to establish them there. Śiva at first punished his devotee for his audacity, but later, satisfied with his extreme devotion, favored him by agreeing to accompany him to his country. The rock-cut temple at Ellora illustrates the story of Rāvaṇa's punishment. The divine river Ganges condescended to come down to the earth after being assured that Śiva, the great God of the Himālaya mountains, had been pleased, as a result of a devotee's penance, to bear the forceful impact of the falling torrents of the river on the matted locks of his head.

The forms of Śiva which do not portray any particular mythology are also numerous. In his gracious character he is shown sometimes as the loving husband of Umā (also called Durgā) and the father of a family. Others show him as master in various arts, learning, and yogic attainments. Thus he is a great dancer, the king among dancers, Naṭarāja, who dances in the sheer playful joy of creation, and the forms which the Indian artists give to this aspect of the god are some of the most beautiful and sublime creations in the world of art. One of the holiest Śaiva shrines of southern India is that at Chidambaram, said by its devotees to be the center of the universe, and there the principal object of worship is Śiva as Naṭarāja, the Dancing Śiva. As a great performer of instrumental music he is shown as playing on a lute; again, he is depicted as the greatest expounder of the scriptures; as the great meditator, he is presented to his devotees in his yoga state.

It is a fact, however, that the anthropomorphic forms of Śiva are not usually the principal objects of worship in Śaiva shrines. They are indeed highly venerated, and many such anthropomorphic images are to be found in the Śaiva temples, but the main sanctum there almost invariably contains the supreme emblem of the father-god, the Śiva liṅga. That is the chief object of veneration, and it is necessary to say something about its original character, antiquity, and gradual acceptance as the noblest symbol of his god by a Śaiva and by Hindus in general.

The main idea underlying the Śiva liṅga in its most primitive aspect was undoubtedly phallic. The liṅga seems to have been one of the cult objects of the ancient people, and it is presumable that the Vedic Aryans did not approve of it. The Vedic sages revile in no uncertain terms those who worship a phallic emblem, and invoke their chief god Indra to destroy them. It is also true that no clear reference to the worship of the phallic emblem as forming a part of the ritualistic religion of the early Indo-Aryans is found in the older sections of their literature, nor is there any clear reference in the earlier post-Vedic literature. The first explicit mention of it is found in the Mahābhārata, showing that it was already well established in the Hindu fold by the first or second century A.D.

The reason for this early nonacceptance of the emblem by the orthodox section of the Hindus can be traced without doubt to the very realistic representation of the male generative organ in earlier times. The ancient idea about it as a symbol of the virile father-god was too strong among the people to be brushed aside and ignored, however, and the intellectuals among them made a compromise. They accepted the emblem as the holiest symbol of Śiva, but conventionalized it in such a way that its original realism was thoroughly lost. This transformation began in the Gupta period, the age of cultural renaissance in ancient India. So great was the change in the manner of its representation that some uninformed modern scholars thought that it originated from the Buddhist votive stūpas or reliquary mounds.

It also should not be supposed that in its early phase it symbolized in any way the union of male and female. Even in its conventionalized shape, though its base and the horizontal projecting piece are sometimes regarded as representing the female principle, these features of the emblem really serve the very useful purpose of putting it firmly in position and draining off to some distance from its base the water profusely poured on its top.

The conventionalized emblems are of different sizes and their shapes sometimes vary; in general they resemble a short post, rounded at the top. Great sanctity is attached to all of them. Purest and most easily procurable things, fresh flowers, pure water, young sprouts of grass, fruit, leaves, and sun-dried rice are ordinarily used in the ritual part of their worship. The god symbolized by the Śiva liṅga is meditated upon by the worshiper in his anthropomorphic form. The mantra for meditation on the god describes him as having a beautiful four-armed and five-faced form; two of the four hands hold a battle-axe and a deer, while the other two are shown in assurance and boon-conferring poses. The five faces stand for his fivefold aspects. He is thought of as the source of the world. The name used to describe the Śiva liṅga in inscriptions, past and present, is almost invariably Mahādeva (The Great God).

Śiva is worshiped throughout all India. The most important Śaiva shrines in the north are Amarnāth in Kashmir, Kedārnāth in the Himālayas, Ekliṅgaji near Udaipur, Biśveśvar in Banaras, Tārakeśvar in West Bengal, Bhuvaneśwar in Orissa, and Somnath on the Kathiawar Peninsula. The most important shrines in the south are at Conjeevaram, Jambukeśvara near Śrīraṅgam, Tiruvaṇṇāmalai and Kālahasti in Madras State, and Chidambaram.

Small elliptical stones of a special kind with a natural polish resulting from the action of river water are known as bāṇaliṅgas. They are very sacred objects of worship to the Hindus and are the Śaiva counterparts of the Vaishṇava sālagrāmas. They are most frequently picked up from the bed of the river Narmadā, one of the seven most sacred rivers of the Hindus.

Śakti—One of the Three Most Widely Worshiped Deities

Śakti, the Mother Goddess, conceived as power both destructive and creative, has also been an object of worship in India from ancient times. Ring stones of a peculiar shape and many rude female figurines found by archeologists in the Indus Valley have been identified by scholars as pre-Vedic symbols of the Mother Goddess. There are few references to female deities in the Rigveda, but the Hymn to the Goddess (Devī-sūkta, X.125) holds special sanctity among Śāktas and Hindus in general for the striking way in which it emphasizes the concept of power and energy and divine grace in the goddess of speech, here called Vāk. But such well-known names of the goddess as Ambikā, Umā, Durgā, and Kālī do not occur in the Ṛigvedic hymns; they are found in the later Āraṇyakas and Upanishads. Ambikā is at first described as the sister and then as the spouse of Rudra, the Vedic counterpart of Śiva. Umā, the daughter of the Himālaya mountain, is the personified knowledge about the Brahman, and Kālī is first mentioned as the name of one of the seven tongues or flames of Agni, the sacrificial fire.

Such evidence leads to the conclusion that worship of the Mother Goddess was influenced by pre-Vedic customs, and was present in Vedic times, though not in a highly developed form. There is also evidence that the goddess was worshiped in her virgin aspect as the daughter-virgin (Kanyā-Kumārī). An Egyptian Greek author of the first century A.D. refers to the southern tip of India as the region where the goddess had been worshiped as a virgin from the remote past. Cape Comorin, the southern point of the Indian subcontinent, is today a sacred pilgrimage place for Hindus, where they worship Kanyā-Kumārī, the virgin goddess.

The chief references to the Mother Goddess are found in the Tāntric literature, the two Durgā hymns in the Mahābhārata, the Harivaṁśa supplement to the Mahābhārata, and in the Purāṇas. There the pre-Vedic concepts are blended with Vedic and later beliefs concerning the Mother Goddess. The one great goddess, the Divine Mother, became the object of worship of a special section of Hindus known as Śāktas, and the object of special veneration for Hindus in general. The one goddess is said to have come down to the world in many forms in times past for the destruction of evil and strengthening of the good. As a result she has many names, all referring to the one goddess who is an aspect of the one divinity: Mahamāyā the great goddess of illusion, Mahāśakti the goddess of supreme power, Lalitā, Durgā, Kālī, Pārvatī, Umā, Lakshmī, Sarasvatī, are only a few of the names applied to the female aspect of the divine.

Durgā. The goddess is worshiped in her terrifying and in her gracious forms. Durgā slaying the buffalo demon is shown as eight- or ten-armed, riding on her vehicle the lion, engaged in mortal combat with the demon emerging in human form from the decapitated trunk of the buffalo. This is the form in which she is worshiped in the autumn in Hindu households and public places. The Hindus of Bengal have mellowed down the dire form of this fighting goddess by showing her in company with her two sons, Kārttikeya and Gaṇeśa, and her two daughters, Lakshmī and Sarasvatī. This annual autumnal festival of goddess worship, Durgā-pūjā, is a great occasion in the life of a Bengali Hindu and is a time for his family reunion and social gatherings.

Kālī. Another characteristic form in which the goddess is worshiped is Kālī, the four-armed goddess standing on the prostrate body of Śiva, holding in her hands a shield, a sword, the severed head of one of the demons, and with the fourth hand in the assurance pose, assuring her devotees of her protection. She is without any clothing but wears a garland of skulls; the severed hands of the demons killed by her are strung together and used as a skirt. She has bared her teeth, and her tongue is out. All these features emphasize Kālī in her terrifying aspect. Śiva as Mahākāla is "The Great Time Eternal"; time destroys, and thus time is death. Kālī in this aspect as Śiva's consort, standing on Śiva's body, is a goddess of destruction, but she is chiefly shown as the destroyer of evil. The Tāntric group of Śakti worshipers make her the special object of worship under various titles such as "Kālī worshiped in a cremation ground," "Kālī ensuring protection," "Kālī offering grace." Thus the goddess Kālī is worshiped as power, power which is gracious and destructive, as inexorable as time which creates and destroys.

The goddess Kālī is also associated with the Vaishṇava cult in the story of the birth of Kṛishṇa. When Kṛishṇa was born and the baby was exchanged for the daughter of Yaśodā in the cowherd village, the demon uncle Kaṁsa came to the prison to kill the child; she slipped from his hands and flew into the sky, revealing herself as the divine Mahākālī. Thus she is regarded as Kṛishṇa's sister and there are Vaishṇava shrines where her image is placed between those of Kṛishṇa and Balarāma. In that aspect she is called Subhadrā. In the great Jagannāth temple in Pūri hers is one of the three images in the central shrine.

Lakshmī. Lakshmī and Sarasvatī, the two consorts of the composite cult god Vishṇu, portray the great goddess in her gracious form. Lakshmī, also called Śrī, symbolizing prosperity and good fortune, has been an object of great veneration to countless generations of Hindus. She is now ceremonially worshiped several times throughout the year in Hindu households, two of her principal days of worship falling on the full moon night following the Durgā-pūjā and the new moon night when ceremonial worship is also offered to the goddess Kālī.

Lakshmī is shown standing or seated on a lotus, holding a full-blown lotus in one of her hands, the other hand being shown in the boon-conferring pose. There is another form of her, known from early times, showing her as described above with two elephants (the elephants of the quarters, the bringers of rain) bathing her with two jars of water held in their upraised trunks. This form is one of the most ancient motifs in Indian art.

In the seasonal worship of Lakshmī, her images are rarely used. Instead it is customary to have an earthen bowl full of rice and rice heaped on a small wooden stool with cowrie shells and miniature wooden boxes of various shapes (one with an old gold or silver coin inside it) neatly arranged on the rice. These symbolize the goddess of good luck, abundance, and prosperity.

Sarasvatī. Sarasvatī owes her origin to the personification of the river Sarasvatī, now flowing through the northern part of Uttar Pradesh and losing itself in the desert of Rajputana. On its banks the Indian sages of the remote past preached and practiced Vedic ideals. The land near the river is described in the Smṛiti as equal to the heavens in sanctity. The goddess Sarasvatī has a swan for her vehicle and holds in her two hands a lute and a manuscript. She is the goddess of learning, wisdom, and song, fittingly associated with the sage Brahmā as his consort. Her seasonal worship occurs at the advent of spring in January-February, for it is held that the worship of the goddess of learning and fine arts ushers in the season of spring, full of joy and merriment. Being the presiding deity of knowledge, she is enthusiastically worshiped by all persons interested in education, teachers and students alike.

Popular Forms of Śakti. There are other popular elements in the worship of the goddess. As the universal mother and protector of all children she is called Shashṭhī, the mother of the divine child Skanda-Kumāra. In this aspect she is worshiped several times a year by the women of Hindu households, her worship consisting of ceremonial observances by the chief woman of the family with no image being used. Diseases such as smallpox are also personified by the simple folk as Śītalā and as others, and are propitiated with offerings in times of their seasonal outbreak. The worship of Śītalā is very old. Her southern India counterpart is Jyeshṭhā, whose worship was once very popular there. Such was her popularity that one of the Ālvārs, the medieval mystic poets of the South, complained in some of his songs that misguided people worshiped such deities as Jyeshṭhā when they should have been worshipers of one god, Vishṇu. This statement of the great Vaishṇava saint sums up the mental attitude of a rational Hindu regarding such animistic beliefs and practices of the unenlightened and uninformed in the Hindu fold.

Hindus generally and Śāktas in particular believe in the existence of numerous sacred places of Śakti worship, usually agreed to be fifty-one; most are scattered throughout northern India. The fifty-one places are associated with the story of Satī, who chose Śiva as her husband against the wishes of her parents. Śiva was not liked by them because of his peculiar habits and outlandish behavior in wandering around cremation grounds, or spending his time in yogic exercises, his body covered with dust and ashes. When her father was performing a great sacrifice he did not invite Śiva and Satī, but Satī attended uninvited. She was cut to the quick by her father's reviling her husband, and died on the spot. When Śiva heard of her death he came there with his followers and destroyed the sacrifice and severely punished her father for his blasphemies against the great god.

Śiva was so afflicted with grief that he roamed over the world unmindful of his divine duties, with the body of his beloved wife on his shoulder. Vishṇu, in order to bring him back to an orderly life, cut the dead body to pieces with his wheel (chakra), scattering it over various parts of India. The places where the severed parts of Satī fell became the fifty-one sacred Śakti shrines. Śiva was thus brought back to his divine work. Later, his meditation was disturbed by Kāma, the god of love, and he was induced to marry Umā, the daughter of the Himālayas, so that she might be the mother of a god who would be commander of the divine troops against the demons.

The Śakti cult is not so widely spread over India as are the other two cults of Vaishṇavas and Śaivas. Its best-known shrines are in the northern parts of India in Bengal, Rajputana, and the Kathiawar Peninsula. Some of the famous shrines are Kālighāt near Calcutta, Kāmākhyā near Gauhaṭi in Assam, Jvālāmukhī in east Punjab, Virajā in Orissa, and Vindhyavāsinī near Mirzapur in Uttar Pradesh.

Other Deities

Of the other gods in the Hindu pantheon, mention may be made here of Gaṇeśa and Kārttikeya. Gaṇeśa, or Gaṇapati, has a cult of his own known as the Gāṇapatya, with a small following in modern times, while Kārttikeya has none. Mythologically the two are the sons of Śiva and Pārvatī. Gaṇapati means "the leader of the impish attendants" of Śiva. He is characterized by an elephant head, potbelly, two or four arms holding such emblems as a pot of sweetmeats, a hatchet, a radish, or one of his broken tusks, and a string of prayer beads in his hands. His vehicle is a mouse. The worship of this god is not as old as that of the other cult deities, having come into prominence in medieval times. Though the god has very few exclusive worshipers now, he is honored by Hindus in general because of his being a remover of obstacles.

The name of his brother Kārttikeya is derived from the myth that the Pleiades asterisms (Krittikā) were his foster mothers. Kārttikeya, the leader of the divine soldiers, is characterized by his peacock vehicle and by a bow and an arrow in his two hands. In ancient times his worship was popular among some of the martial tribes, but now he is worshiped chiefly by persons who desire good and sturdy sons. He is well known in southern India as Subrahmaṇya, honored in many folk songs in the Tamil language.

Sūrya, the sun, is highly venerated by the Hindus. They also pay homage to some other units in the solar constellation, including the planets Mars, Mercury, Jupiter, Venus, and Saturn. The moon, the satellite of the earth, finds a place in the list of the Nine Planets, probably because the earth is separately venerated as the "container of wealth." Two other so-called planets, Rāhu and Ketu, the ascending and descending nodes of the moon, go to make up the total of the Nine Planets. The worship of the planets is resorted to by Hindus in times of disease and natural calamities. It is commonly believed that the vicissitudes in a man's life are to a great extent due to the anger of these astral bodies; if they are properly propitiated by their ceremonial worship they will bring peace and immunity from natural calamities to the households of their worshipers. Sacred verses in honor of the Sun God and the Nine Planets, culled from the epic and Purāṇic literature, are daily recited by many devout Hindus early in the morning before they commence their day's work.

Tradition says, and archaeology confirms, that a form of sun worship was introduced into India from eastern Iran about two thousand years ago. The Magas of India are the same as the Magi, the priestly class in ancient Iran in charge of the ceremonial worship of the sun and fire. Their descendants are still to be found here and there, especially in eastern parts of India, where many of their community follow the professions of astrology and soothsaying. The Sun God is not ceremonially worshiped now in separate images and shrines. Veneration is offered to him in association with the eight other planets also not represented by images.

The Vedic Gods

The prominent Vedic gods, Indra, Varuṇa, Vāyu, Agni, Yama and the others are not forgotten altogether. They have found a place in the ritualistic worship of the different sects, but most of them are assigned to the position of guardians of the quarters of the compass, and a Hindu affiliated with one of the sects is enjoined to pay his homage to them. In the beginning of his religious ceremonies he says the mantra, "Salutation to the guardians of the ten quarters, Indra and others." The eight prominent guardians of the quarters are: Indra (east), Agni (southeast), Yama (south), Nirṛiti (southwest), Varuṇa (west), Vāyu (northwest), Kubera (north), and Īśāna (northeast). The first six among them are well-known members of the Vedic pantheon; Kubera and Īśāna were recruited from the folk cults of earlier times.

In later mythology, Indra is shorn of all greatness. He rides on an elephant and holds a thunderbolt in one of his two hands. The elephant and thunderbolt indicate his original nature as a god of rain, for they represent the thunder clouds which bring rain. Agni, the god of fire, has a ram for his vehicle and is bearded and potbellied. Yama, the god of death, rides a buffalo and holds a mace in his hand. Nirṛiti, remembered only as a god of darkness and evil, has a man for his vehicle. Varuṇa is regarded as the presiding deity of the ocean; he has a mythical alligator-like animal as his vehicle and holds a noose in his hands. Vāyu, the wind god, is obscured by the importance given to his son Hanumān, the monkey god; Vāyu's vehicle is a fleet-footed stag and he carries a flag in his hand. Kubera, the lord of treasures, is known as the treasurer of Lakshmī, the goddess of good fortune and prosperity; his vehicle is a man, sometimes a horse. Īśāna is completely merged in Śiva and is regarded as one of his aspects; he rides a bull and holds a trident in his hands.

Kāma, not one of the gods of the quarters, is the great god of love and eroticism. He is known as "one who is born in one's mind" and "one who disturbs mental equilibrium," and has two wives, Trishā (passionate desire) and Rati (pleasure arising out of the satisfaction of desire). He holds a flowery bow with flowery arrows with which he smites people, bringing upon them the pangs of love.

Brahmā (also called Prajāpati), the most prominent deity of late Vedic times, could not, however, be brushed aside by the sectarians, as were Indra and the others, and he is now given the first place in the Hindu concept of the Triad or Trinity. The three gods of the Triad, Brahmā, Vishṇu, and Śiva, are associated respectively with the cosmic functions of creation, preservation, and destruction, but Brahmā could never rival the other two cult gods in position and influence and was allowed to occupy the first place in the list of the three gods only by sufferance. There are many mythological stories in the literature of the Vaishṇavas and Śaivas which illustrate this point. Orthodox Brāhmans seem to have attempted in the remote past to transform him into a cult deity, but they were never successful. There is in India today only one prominent temple dedicated to him, at Pushkara, near Ajmer, in Rajputana; there Hindu pilgrims of different sects from all parts of India pay their homage, the veneration offered by them to Brahmā being of a general character.

Brahmā the creator should not be confused with Brahman the Supreme Being of the Upanishads, for there is very little relation between them. Brahmā undoubtedly is a later development of the creator and protector god Prajāpati so frequently mentioned in the late Vedic texts. Brahmā is usually conceived as four-faced and four-armed, a bearded deity, holding in two of his hands the sacrificial implements, with a string of prayer beads and a manuscript in the other two. He is usually gracefully seated on a lotus seat below which is placed a swan, his vehicle. The four faces represent the four Vedas, the sacrificial implements indicate that he is the god of sacrifice; his beard and the prayer beads and manuscript of the Vedas portray him as a venerable, wise sage.

Sāvitrī is supposed to be the consort of the sage god. Her name is derived from one of the names of the Sun God extolled in the Vedic mantra entitled Gāyatrī. This holiest of the holy mantras, which every Brāhman is enjoined to recite daily from the time of his initiation until his death, stands for Vedic learning. It is fittingly personified as the chaste wife of Brahmā who himself symbolizes Vedic ritualism and wisdom. Sarasvatī, the Hindu goddess of learning and fine arts, is sometimes regarded as the second wife of Brahmā, though she is also associated with Vishṇu as his consort.

Most of the stories associated with Brahmā owe their origin to the other sectarians who assign him a secondary position. Although the first member of the Triad, and the creator of the world, he himself was created by Vishṇu. He evolved from a lotus issuing from the navel of Vishṇu, which is the origin of his designation as "the Lotus-born." He was saved from the attacks of demons by the intervention of Vishṇu. The gods, when defeated at the hands of the demons, resort to Brahmā for advice, but he himself is powerless to do anything for them and seeks the assistance of the prominent cult gods, usually Vishṇu, sometimes Śiva. He is the grandfather of gods and men, and thus venerably old.

But the sectarians did not hesitate to impute dishonorable acts to him and there are stories in the epic and Purāṇic literature illustrating these phases of his character. There can be no doubt that these sectarians, zealous about the greatness of their gods, gave unfavorable twists to allegories current about Brahmā. In one Śaiva myth, he is presented as a liar. The lie uttered by him on that occasion brought upon him the curse of Śiva that he was never to have a cult of his own. This myth tries to explain in a naïve way why Brahmā is not worshiped exclusively by any group of Hindus.

One of the comparatively new entrants into the Hindu pantheon is Satya-Nārāyaṇa, or Satyapīr. *Pīr* ordinarily means a Muslim saint, but in this context the word designates the one God (Allah or Rahim) of Islam. An attempt was undoubtedly made some centuries ago to absorb him into the Hindu fold and it was laid down that there is no real difference between Rāma and Rahim, that Rāma and Rahim have really one soul, although their bodies are different. His worship is very popular in some parts of eastern India, but it is done only occasionally when the story about the introduction of the worship of Satya-pīr is narrated by the priest, and no image is used in the ceremony.

Demons

The demons or undivine beings frequently referred to in Hindu mythology can be divided into two general classifications. The first group includes the Asuras and Rākshasas or man-eaters. They are characterized by hypocrisy, pride, self-conceit, wrath, insolence, and ignorance. Kaṁsa, for instance, the uncle who sought to kill the baby Kṛishṇa, was such a devil incarnate; so was Rāvaṇa, who stole Sītā from Rāma. According to Vaishṇava tradition, some of the demons are successive reincarnations of attendants of Vishṇu, cursed to take repeated births as demons and to have Hari (Vishṇu) in one of his many forms as their enemy, their approach to the great god to be one of hate and not of love. This sort of approach would, however, work indirectly for their salvation, since their obsession about their great enemy would bring them nearer to him. Thus, the Hindu mind does not conceive anything wholly evil in this context and emphasizes that whatever evil is present is necessary for the manifestation of the divine grace in redeeming it. A similar concept underlies the stories of the destructive acts of the Divine Mother, for although she kills the demons in battle, their destruction is necessary not only for the good of the world but also for their own salvation.

Semidivine Beings

The second group of undivine or semidivine beings includes the Yakshas, Nāgas, and Apsaras. Yakshas really stand for the primitive animistic objects of worship, still worshiped by a section of the people in remote, unenlightened corners of the country. Big trees such as the banyan, woods and forests, were and still are regarded by unenlightened folk of somewhat primitive bent of mind as abodes of these Yakshas, or evil spirits. The worship of Nāgas, or snakes, was once a common trait of a large section of the Indian people. One of the questions put to a candidate seeking admission to the Buddhist order in ancient times was whether or not he was a Nāga worshiper. The story of Kṛishṇa's overpowering the serpent Kāliya is sometimes interpreted as an allusion to the subjugation of a primitive animistic cult by the nobler cult of bhakti centering around Kṛishṇa. But Nāga worship had taken a root in the religion of many Indians so deep that it could not be eradicated. The worship still persists in homage to Manasā, the snake goddess, shown as a lady seated with a child on her lap under a canopy of snake hoods. Naïve stories are told of the way in which the merchant Chand, a great devotee of Śiva, was compelled to accept Manasā as a goddess and thus to permit the continued worship of the Nāgas.

The Apsaras are divine damsels, dancers in the heavenly court, whose principal function according to the current mythology is to test the strength of mind of the men engaged in austerities and to try by blandishment to entice them away from their path of austerity. It is Indra, the king of the gods, who sets the courtesans of the heavens to this task lest he should be ousted from his heavenly throne by one practicing austerities greater than those which had made Indra king of heaven. They are not objects of worship, but beautiful lyric poetry has been composed about them by some of the foremost poets of ancient and medieval India.

IMAGES IN HINDU WORSHIP

A few observations need to be made here concerning the images and the symbols which represent the Hindu deities. The symbolic forms consist of the liṅgas and sālagrāmas already described, and the yantras and paṭṭas. *Yantras* are usually metal plaques of different shapes and sizes with intricate diagrams and "seed-letters" (one-syllabled mantras of esoteric significance) inscribed on their surface. They are chiefly used by the Śakti worshipers in their religious rites. The *paṭṭas* are usually Vishṇu paṭṭas, stone or metal plaques with miniature figures of Vishṇu and his ten incarnations engraved on them. The images are mainly anthropomorphic, much less frequently animal or hybrid.

In the anthropomorphic images of the gods, exaggeration is often found in the number of arms and heads. By this the Hindus were trying to emphasize the limitless attributes and the superhuman power of their deity. For the Hindu a deep and esoteric symbolism underlies most of these iconic representations. To the devotees of the different sects, the images and emblems of their respective deities are necessary for the outward manifestations of their wholehearted devotion. An image serves the same purpose in the modern Hindu worship as was served by fire in the sacrificial religion of the Vedic age. Fire was the bearer of the oblations of the sacrificer to the god; in a similar manner, the image serves as the holy medium through which the worshiper can transfer his devotion to the god of his choice.

A Vaishṇava, for instance, worships his god by various acts, called pūjā. These are: going to the temple of the deity with one's speech, body, and mind centered on him, collecting such materials of worship as flowers, incense, and offerings, the very act of worshiping the auspicious body of the god, the repetition of the mantra specially chosen for his god, and finally meditative union of the adorer and the adored. In the case of a Vaishṇava the principal mantra repeated is the sacred twelve-syllabled *OM namo bhagavate Vāsudevāya* (OM, salutation to the worshipful Lord Vāsudeva).

The true significance and purpose of the worship of images by the Hindus should be understood in the light of their importance in meditation. Many teachers of the yogic art of meditation have said that images are necessary for the full success of meditation and blissful union with god. The gods themselves are often shown in the pose of meditation, immersed in meditation, thus helping the devotee to concentrate his mind on the deity and in an indirect way on the unknowable principle behind it, that something beyond the images and the gods themselves which is "minute or atomic, unknowable, beyond description."

Yet it must be admitted that the practice of image worship has not received the universal sanction of the Hindu intellectuals. In earlier times, many Indian thinkers criticized and derided the efforts of those who sought to attain salvation through images. The Jābāla Upanishad says, "Yogis should find god within their own selves, and not in images; the latter are meant only as aids to meditation for the ignorant." One of the Tantras says that the efforts of persons to attain salvation through the worship of images made of stone, metal, clay, or wood are as unreal as the possession of kingdoms by persons in their dreams. The authors of these texts, however, were firm believers in the worship of the highest principle without the aid of any medium. They followed the early Upanishadic dictum, "There does not exist the form of this [Supreme Principle] in anything to be seen, nor can one see it with his eyes."

But there is another side of the picture. Of the Hindu sectarians, the bhāgavatas, Vaishṇava devotees, who were perhaps most responsible for the wide diffusion of image worship in India, attached a great deal of importance to the images of their god and his various aspects. A bhāgavata who took delight in establishing a close personal bond in his mind between his god and his own self found such an image indispensable for the practice of the several modes of bhakti for his lord. Some of the most devout saints of the Vaishṇavas, such as Rāmānuja, were highly cultured and supremely intellectual men, yet they worshiped images of their god, recognizing in them many of his "auspicious bodies." There are countless persons in the Hindu community, many of them possessing high education and culture, who accept the usefulness of images for their religious uplift and the realization of the presence of their chosen personal god.

It should be noted, however, that these images and symbols of the deities become sacred objects of worship to the devotee only after they have been duly and ceremonially consecrated and the very life principle, as it were, has been infused into them by the worshiper himself or the priest officiating on his behalf. Even then the scriptures enjoin that the worshiper should purify his own mind first, and see his god not only residing in his own heart but also in the hearts of all beings (mere ceremony of image worship without this preliminary preparation is useless). This is the ideal type of image worship advocated by a bhāgavata.

THE HINDU BELIEF IN ONE SUPREME REALITY

As is to be expected, the Hindu mind never accepted with any complacency even a moderate multiplicity in the number of its gods. From the time of the Vedas, the search after unity continued unabated. While the philosophically inclined tried to conceive of the gods as many forms, manifestations, aspects, or attributes of one Primal Being, the devotionally inclined tended to integrate them in other ways. In the Vedas many of the gods were credited with identical attributes and functions; the many names for a single deity were meant to emphasize the different functions of the same god. The same invocation would serve to welcome a number of different gods for, except rarely, the gods are of the same mind and are in perfect accord with one another. When acute sectarianism served at a much later time to import rivalry and enmity into divine relations and attempted to lower the power and prestige of all rival gods in relation to one's chosen deity, a healthy instinct asserted itself and quickly ended all divine jealousies and quarrels.

Synthesis was effected in a number of ways. There was first a grouping of the gods with the obvious idea of allocating different cosmic functions to different deities in order to coordinate their activities. The Triad concept belongs to this category, the world process in its three aspects of origination, maintenance, and destruction being assigned to Brahmā, Vishṇu, and Śiva. In the Śaiva sectarian form, the Triad was viewed as the emanation of two subordinate forms out of the principal one, Śiva. When functional assimilation was imperfect, a modified monolatry sometimes developed, as in the combined worship of the five cult gods, Vishṇu, Śiva, Śakti, Gaṇeśa, and Sūrya, with the image of the chosen deity in the middle and the others ranged around it in the four corners of a square. To this class also belongs the panel of such gods as the Nine Planets and the Ten Incarnations of Vishṇu.

Alliance of creeds is effected also by importing family relationship among the gods, as when Śiva and Pārvatī are married, or seated together as a divine pair, or seated in close embrace, or shown with their children. Further intimacy is indicated by identifying one god with another, as for example in the well-known expressions, Vishṇu is Śiva, Śiva is Vishṇu, Śakti is Śiva, Śiva is Śakti. It is also shown by fusing their figures in a composite deity, of which the most famous is the androgynous Śiva in which one half of the image is Śiva and the other is Śakti. There are similar fused images of Hari (Vishṇu) and Hara (Śiva), and even of Kṛishṇa and Kālī in popular Bengali Vaishṇava forms. Needless to say, all these overtures to other creeds were prompted by a spirit of liberation and toleration designed to establish social amity, concord, and understanding.

The Hindu's belief in one god, the supreme reality beyond the measure of name and form, and unrealizable by the sensory organs, has been persistent in India from time immemorial. But his deep and innate desire for the outward expression of his profound devotion for his god has led him to endow the object of his meditation and worship with various names and forms. These are really the external manifestations of one great principle as he has conceived them. Various mythologies have been composed from time to time to explain and emphasize the different aspects of his god, and underlying all these stories is the idea of one divine dispenser of justice, the destroyer of evil and benefactor of the good, the one creator, sustainer, and absorber of the world.

A single-minded devotee striving for the realization of this god must pass through many stages of progress in his effort. When he reaches his goal, he is blessed with the vision of the Greatest of the great gods, of Him who is the essence of and present in all gods, the Supreme Being.

Chapter 3

THE HINDU CONCEPT OF THE NATURAL WORLD

by RADHAGOVINDA BASAK

THE ULTIMATE NATURE OF THE UNIVERSE

Since the dawn of reason man has applied himself to the formulation and interpretation of the three famous concepts of God, Nature, and Man—of the Supreme Being, the Universe, and the Individual Self. In India today most enlightened Hindus base their theological and philosophical ideas concerning the Supreme Being, the Universe, and the Individual Self on the teachings of the Upanishads, the great speculative treatises of ancient India. Their minds are saturated with the wholesome and heart-solacing high ideas of Vedāntic truth revealed in those writings.

Basic to the Hindu concept of the natural world is the belief in the Ultimate Absolute Reality, the Supreme Self or Soul, which is described as Existence-Consciousness-Bliss. The Hindu scriptures identify God with the Universe, the natural world of multiplicity and differentiations, believing that Brahman transforms Himself into the ever blossoming and developing form of the external world. Even the individual souls of men are thought of as identical with the Highest Soul. The Supreme Being is the whole universe, animate and inanimate. He is the origin of it, the place of its preservation, and of its dissolution at the end of the long cycle of existence. In thus believing in the identity of the Supreme Being and Nature, the Hindus see Him in everything, and everything in Him, and worship Him as abiding in all kinds of created things.

At the same time most Hindus, while acknowledging the immanence of Ultimate Reality in all objects of nature, do not fail to reflect on His transcendence of the created world. They remember the description of creation in the Ṛigveda, of how the Supreme Being transcended the limits of the Universe—"covering the world all around, He yet exceeded it by a span." In this bold conception of the omniscient and blissful yet omnipotent God, the Hindus worship Him as being both immanent and transcendent, accepting the words of the Bhagavad Gītā, "I stand pervading this whole universe with a single fragment of myself" (X.42).

Although most Hindu philosophers have accepted this interpretation of the Brahman as both immanent and transcendent, there have been some thinkers who, holding to a strictly humanistic and rationalistic system of thought, have either denied or ignored the existence of a Supreme Being and have held that the universe is made up only of undifferentiated matter and individual souls which have coexisted eternally, combining to form the natural world. Others, accepting the belief in the Supreme Being, have held that only the Supreme Being exists and all that we call the natural world is illusion, a phantasm of the human mind having no real existence of its own.

Prakṛiti and Purusha

Philosophers may differ as to whether the ultimate nature of the universe is monistic, dualistic, or pluralistic, but most of them use the concept of *prakṛiti* and the three guṇas in explaining their point of view. *Prakṛiti* is the ultimate cosmic energy, primal matter which exists eternally. It is the uncaused first cause of the universe, that out of which the universe is formed, latent matter of the finest form. This prakṛiti, the primal cause of all that is created, is made up of the three guṇas held together in a state of equilibrium. The *guṇas* are the subtle essence of prakṛiti, the attributes or qualities or properties of primal matter. The first guṇa, *sattva,* is harmony, balance, of the nature of wisdom, purity, or pleasure when found in its created form. The second guṇa, *rajas,* is activity, motion, of the nature of pain, stimulating and restless and energetic in its created form. The third guṇa, *tamas,* is inertia, heavy, of the nature of indifference, laziness, dullness, when found in its created form.

These three guṇas, strandlike constituents of the rope of prakṛiti, produce in man virtues and vices depending upon the different proportions in which they are mixed in the individual. The scriptures often mention human tendencies which result from the mixtures of the guṇas in men: wisdom in a man who is predominantly sattva; greed and passion in men controlled by rajas; and sloth and delusion in those subject to tamas.

Prakṛiti, the primal matter, coexists eternally with *purusha,* the conscious principle of creation, the plurality of selves in the universe. Both are by themselves eternal, beginningless, undetermined, and inactive, devoid of characteristics, and formless; but prakṛiti is unintelligent, and liable to transformations through variations in the three guṇas, while purusha is intelligent and unchangeable, and unaffected by the guṇas. Prakṛiti in its transformations becomes a perceivable object, while purusha, the self, remains the perceiving subject.

Creation

Creation occurs through the union of prakṛiti and purusha. Philosophers differ as to whether that union comes about through the will of a creator or is a result of the combination of the two without the active intervention of any divine agent, but the natural world as known by men is a result of that union. Though prakṛiti is nonintelligent, rather blind, so to speak, and purusha is inactive, crippled, as it were, if united they can accomplish their mission just as a crippled man who is able to see can reach his destination by mounting on the shoulders of a blind man who can walk. The union, however, between primal matter and spirit or individual souls is not permanent. When the individual self, purusha, attains the knowledge of the truth that it is absolutely different from matter, prakṛiti, it ceases to be affected any more by the attraction of matter's creative power.

It is māyā which brings about the union of the individual soul and primal matter. In some philosophies, *māyā* is defined as illusion or ignorance: the illusion that the self and matter are the same, that one must be associated with the other; or ignorance of the true nature of the self, which binds it to this material existence. In other philosophies, māyā is thought of as cosmic energy by which the creator brings the world into being, the power of the Supreme Being with which it sports in the illusive universe produced from itself and by which it makes all beings do what they do. It is by the divine māyā that the incarnations, avatāras, are brought into being. People are playing on the stage of life only through the power of illusion of the Lord, according to the Bhagavad Gītā. The veil of magic can be removed only by the magician himself; god's mercy toward those who take refuge in him can alone dispel the illusion and save the deluded man from all bondage in this natural world.

Thus, although there are various interpretations among the philosophers, most Hindus would agree that the natural world in which we live as human beings was created out of a combination of primal matter, prakṛiti, and cosmic spirit, purusha, by means of the action of māyā, the illusive cosmic energy of the creator.

The myths of the creation of the world, of its nature, and the relations of the parts which make up this universe are narrated in almost identical terms in the chief Purāṇas. In these myths, prakriti and purusha are parts of the same Supreme Being, the ultimate regulator of the universe in whose mind all objects existed before creation. It is the guiding and controlling will of the eternal Brahman, the substratum of the universe, which gave the first impetus to primal matter to shake off its equilibrium and start its work of evolution into the various subtle and gross manifestations which make up our world.

According to the sage Manu, the universe prior to its creation was enveloped in primordial gloom, in an imperceptible, undefinable, inexpressible, and unknowable state in which it remained, as it were, lulled in sleep. The cosmos was not dead then, but it lay thus, bearing in itself all the potentialities carried over from its life in the previous aeon, awaiting a new manifestation in diverse forms. After the end of the universal deluge, the self-born Supreme Being, the director of cosmic primal matter, with his power of creation unobstructed, became manifest in subtle forms as intelligence, I-ness or my-ness, organs of the senses, and the mind, and became manifest in gross forms perceivable by the senses.

Brahman, the Supreme Being, having desired to create the world of beings, by a mere act of will first created water into which he cast his seed; this turned into an egg of golden color, resplendent like the light of the sun. In this egg was born Brahmā, the earliest progenitor of all creatures. This Brahmā having dwelt in the egg for one celestial year, split it into two parts by his meditations and made the heaven out of one part, the earth out of the other, and placed the sky between them. Then, beginning with the most subtle and going on to the most gross, Brahmā created all that exists on the earth. He created the host of gods, the demigods, fire, air, the sun, stars, planets, time, rivers, seas, mountains, and the hilly and level ground. He created asceticism, speech, desires, anger, pleasure, and all beings which dwell on earth. Brahmā, the creator, used names and functions for different created objects which he got from the Vedas themselves, for the Vedas lay dormant in subtle form in the Supreme Self at the time of universal dissolution and manifested themselves again at the time of the new creation.

Brahmā created the Brāhmans, the priestly caste, from his mouth; the Kshatriyas, warriors, from his arms; the Vaiśyas, the commercial and agricultural caste, from his thighs; and the Śūdras, the laborers, from his legs—perhaps to represent the four human functions of cogitation, protection, sustenance, and service. Brahmā then divided his own body into halves and, having become male in one half and female in the other, begat Virāj, the first illustrious descendant. From Virāj, by the practicing of austerities, came Manu, and by the same process were created the ten Lords of Beings. They then created all forms of living things, all gods, demigods, demons, men, Nāgas, serpents, the forefathers existing in other worlds, clouds, thunderbolts, lightning, rainbows, meteors, birds, worms, beasts, insects, and the plants which burst out of the earth. Thus are all forms of life, from Brahmā at the top all the way down to the grasses of the earth, subject to the ever changing transmigration of birth and death.

Time

Brahmā brings about the time of universal dissolution and destruction by vanishing into Himself. When He is awake, the universe is animated and in operation, and when He with reposeful mind sleeps, the universe is dormant and becomes unmanifest. This is partial dissolution, in which the world is only withdrawn into its cause, Brahmā, without undergoing any change in its form or content; but when Brahmā has completed His hundredth divine year there will come the great universal dissolution, in which the universe together with Brahmā Himself is withdrawn into the unmanifest prakṛiti of the Supreme Being, Brahman, and having lost its cosmic form it will remain there in that subtle condition until the will of that Supreme Being is moved to create anew.

According to the Vaishṇava scriptures, which identify Vishṇu with Brahman, the universe upon dissolution assumes the appearance of an ocean on which Vishṇu rests after withdrawing from all manifest activities and remains only in meditative sleep, resting on the great serpent Śesha. When after having enjoyed this meditative sleep he awakes, the universe once more comes into being.

In order to comprehend the length of time that each created

universe endures, the Hindu religious treatises have given an account of time measurement in accordance with the motion in space of the sun and moon. One lunar month of thirty days, as counted by human beings, is equal to a day and a night of the forefathers who dwell in other worlds for a while. The fifteen days following the full moon make up their day for action, and the fifteen days following the new moon are their night for sleep. Each human year of three hundred and sixty days is equal to a day and a night of the gods. Each human year is divided into two periods of six months, the period of the northward journey of the sun being the day of the gods, and the six months of the southward journey being the night. Thus a year of the gods lasts three hundred and sixty human years.

According to the scriptures, we are now living in the fourth aeon, the Iron Age. The first aeon was the Golden Age and lasted 4,800 divine years, or 1,728,000 human years. The second aeon was a fourth shorter, darker, and lasted 3,600 divine years or 1,296,000 human years; the third was a fourth shorter, darker, lasting 2,400 divine years, or 864,000 human years. The present age, which is the darkest and briefest of all, will last 1,200 divine years, or 432,000 human years. The total of these four aeons, 12,000 divine years, that is 4,320,000 human years, makes one divine aeon of the gods. One thousand of those, or 4,320,000,000 human years, make one day for Brahmā, and a similar length of time is his night. Each such daytime of Brahmā is the period of existence of the universe, and each such nighttime is the period of its dissolution. This state of creation and dissolution of the world goes on until Brahmā completes his hundredth year, and then he is to return to the Supreme Being from which he came. Such is the method of time measurement used for computing the duration of the universe.

Space

Having always been conscious of the infinite vastness of time and space, the Hindus could easily conceive of the possibility of the existence of worlds other than this one or the sun or moon. Their strong belief in the doctrine of karma and a revolving cycle of existences determined by good and bad actions in this life has led them to conceive of many other worlds where men might be born after death to experience the fruits of their moral and immoral deeds. The Upanishads clearly state that a man's acquired knowledge, his faculty of impression, and his karma (which is made up of the results of actions in life), follow him at death and cause his rebirth. The combination of those factors causes him, in strict justice, to be born in one of the other worlds, either the world of the forefathers, the world of the demigods, the world of the gods, the world of Brahmā the creator, or the world of Brahman the Highest Being.

The Upanishads say that a man becomes after death just what he deserves to be as a result of his works in this life. For the experiencing of the results of actions of merit and demerit done in this world, he is first led to other worlds; after the destruction of those consequences of his actions he has to return again to this world. The Chāndogya Upanishad also states that men, after enjoying the results of their good or bad actions in life by a stay for some time in other worlds, are reborn in good and high families of Brāhmans, Kshatriyas, or Vaiśyas, or in bad and low species such as dogs or boars, or the outcastes of the cremation grounds. Thus, from the metaphysical point of view, the belief in other worlds may be justified.

The number of worlds is conveniently counted as three or fourteen, but they are only representative of the innumerable worlds in space as part of the vast universe. The conventional three worlds are known as the earth, the sky in which the luminaries move about, and the heavens; in post-Vedic times the three were often referred to as the heavens, the land of mortals, and the nether world. The fourteen worlds are usually counted as seven rising from the earth and seven descending into the nether regions.

The nether regions are described in some Purāṇas as having lands of various colors where dwell many a demon, Yaksha, and Nāga. After visiting these nether worlds the sage Nārada is said once to have returned to heaven and reported to the gods that those places were more beautiful than the heavenly ones. Even the recluses are attracted, he said, by the beautiful appearance of the daughters of the denizens of those regions. The sun's rays, though shining there, do not heat the people and the moon's rays, though giving light, do not make them cold. The demons enjoy excellent food and drink, and time glides imperceptibly for them. The great serpent Śesha resides there, holding the earth on his thousand heads and causing earthquakes when he yawns.

The Purāṇas give an account, though not scientifically correct, of the distances from the earth to the planets and the worlds of the heavens. The sun's position is given as 800,000 miles from the earth, and the planets are above one another, equal distances between them. In these upper worlds the people enjoy the fruits of the sacrifices offered by them while they were on earth.

The fourth world, 88,000,000 miles above the earth, is the residence of the sages who deserve to stay for an aeon. Above the fourth world is the world of the sons of Brahmā; above that is the world of the companions of Brahmā, and finally in the seventh heaven, which is 1,848,000,000 miles above the earth, is the world where the immortal beings live. The demigods and ascetics live in the space between the earth and the sun. All these worlds re-enter the body of the first originator at the time of the universal dissolution.

A clear idea of Vishṇu's own world can be obtained from its description in the Bhāgavata Purāṇa (II.9.8-14). In this shining world there is a complete absence of suffering and misery, of fear and infatuation. This world is attained only by the knowers of Brahman and in it the residents are free from the influence of the three guṇas and time. In this world, all the people are attendants of Hari, the Lord, and there Lakshmī Herself sings in praise of Her husband, Vishṇu, the Lord of the Universe, and there She worships Him.

The Sun

Ever since Vedic times, the Sun has been looked upon as a form of fire placed by the gods in space. This god, Sūrya, the Sun, who is the remover of all darkness and gloom, is also known in his other aspects as the stimulator and the nourisher of men. The Hindus were conscious from a very early period of the beneficent nature of solar energy. This god has the power not only of dispelling darkness, but also of curing such diseases as blindness and leprosy, of removing poverty, and of heating and illuminating the world. He is invoked as the all-seeing eye of the world, witnessing all the good and bad activities of mortals whose daily work starts along with his rise in the morning. He is also thought of as the guardian of all objects, movable and immovable. It is the beneficent power of the Sun which conducts the dead on the far path to the forefathers and to the abodes of bliss in the next world.

In order that they may receive stimulation from the Sun God, orthodox Brāhmans repeat the Gāyatrī mantra each day at morning, noon, and evening, saying three times the most sacred Ṛigvedic verse, "We meditate upon that adorable effulgence of the Resplendent Vivifier, Savitar; may He stimulate our intellects." The Sun is praised as assuming the form of Brahmā in the morning, Vishṇu at midday, and Śiva in the evening. Hindus in general worship the Sun every year on the seventh day after the new moon in the month which corresponds to January-February.

Varāhamihira, in the sixth century A.D., discourses on the spots on the Sun which indicate blessings in the form of good rainfall, or plentiful crops, and also foretell such evils as famine, disease, death, war, or the loss of a king. Since he is surrounded in many positions by the revolving planets, the Sun, the sole supporter of universal space, is believed to shed his influence on the destinies of human beings on earth.

Fire

The celestial fire in the Sun is manifest as lightning in the atmosphere, and as the household fire on earth. Known by the Vedic name, Agni, Fire is supposed to be the carrier of offerings to gods in heaven, thus playing an important role in both Śrauta and Smārta ceremonials, in which fire oblations are essential. Agni is a personification of the sacrificial fire. Devouring the dry wood from which it is born, Agni is described as a child devouring its parents. He is a powerful benefactor of his worshipers, conferring on them the boons of domestic welfare, healthy offspring, and prosperity, and consuming their enemies and overcoming the malevolent. He is said to grant immortality to his votaries. It is speculated mystically that he has the power to conduct the corpse to the other worlds where the gods and the forefathers dwell. It is a Vedic idea that Fire was born of the waters and bore the first germ of all life. Strictly speaking, every Brāhman householder should at all times maintain the sacred fire in his house and offer oblations to it three times a day along with his usual three chantings of the Gāyatrī, for the fire in the household is the counterpart on earth of the Sun God.

The Moon

The moon is represented mythologically as having been produced from the ocean at the time of its churning when the gods and demons sought the nectar which would give them immortality. The twenty-seven lunar mansions, that is the groups of stars indicating the parts of the heavens into which the moon's course is divided, one for each day, are represented as the granddaughters of Brahmā and described as the wives of the Moon. In priestly speculation the Vedic deity Soma, originally presiding over the soma plant from which an intoxicating drink was obtained in ancient times, became identified with the celestial moon. By the time of the Upanishads, the identification of Soma with the moon was a commonplace idea. The waning of the moon is caused by the gods consuming, in regular rotation, the intoxicating ambrosia of which it consists; then they must wait until the moon is filled again by the sun. Another explanation of the waning of the moon comes from the myth that because of his special fascination and partiality for Rohiṇī, one of his wives, his father-in-law, a famous Seer, caused him to be consumptive, but at the intercession of his other wives, Rohiṇī's sisters, the sentence was commuted to one of periodical consumption and renewal.

The potent effect of the moon's rays on vegetation is popularly imagined and gives the moon the name of the Lord of Plants. In some of the older Upanishads it is said that a man who has performed good deeds on earth, but has not attained saving knowledge, goes to the world of the moon where he resides until the fruit of his deeds is exhausted; then he takes rebirth on earth. It is interesting to note that many Purāṇic and other mythological legends trace the descent of royal families from either the sun or the moon.

Astrologically the moon, revolving around the earth which revolves around the sun, is thought of as influencing, in conjunction with the stars, the destiny of men living on the earth. When moving toward certain constellations, the moon can produce auspicious or inauspicious results on the different parts of the earth. Abundance or scarcity of crops, death, disease, and other distresses of the people, prosperity or adversity of kings, war or peace in a country—all are often indicated by the appearance of different shapes of the point of the crescent moon. It is said that a brilliant moon, white as frost or a lily or a crystal, confers great benefits on the earth.

Eclipses of the sun or the moon are times of great importance in the life of the Hindus. Mythologically it is said that the eclipses are caused by the demon Rāhu. At the time of the churning of the ocean to make the nectar which would give immortality, Rāhu tasted the nectar without permission. When the Sun and Moon called this to the attention of Vishṇu the god immediately cut off Rāhu's head, but since he had drunk the nectar, his head became immortal. The head was placed in the heavens and Rāhu was allowed as a means of revenge on the Sun and the Moon to approach them at certain times and thus render them unclean so that their bodies at those times would become thin and black. The duration of an eclipse is therefore regarded as a time of uncleanness, and orthodox Hindus purify themselves at that time by bathing in the holy rivers of India. During the eclipse conch shells are sounded, devotional songs are sung, and the women bathers utter shrill cries, all of which are considered to be auspicious and to help drive Rāhu away from the sun or moon.

The Calendar

The lunar calendar, based on the daily rising and setting of the moon, and on its waxing and waning, provides the exact time measure of the lunar days, important in Hindu almanacs for ascertaining the date and time for the performance of auspicious domestic ceremonies such as initiation and the investiture with the sacred thread, commencement of schooling for children, marriage, entry into newly built houses, sowing seeds and reaping crops, establishment of temples, construction of lakes and pools, and for the worship of gods and goddesses in different seasons.

The days of the week are named after the seven planets: the Sun, Sunday; the Moon, Monday; Mars, Tuesday; Mercury, Wednesday; Jupiter, Thursday; Venus, Friday; and Saturn, Saturday. Thirty days make a lunar month, with the month divided into halves according to the waxing and waning of the moon. Beginning with the new moon day, the next fifteen days are known as the bright fortnight; the fifteen days following the full moon are called the dark fortnight. Twelve months of thirty days each make up the year of three hundred and sixty days, with an additional month once in five years to correct the difference between the lunar and the solar year. The thirteenth month is considered to be a profane month.

The months of the Hindu calendar overlap those of the calendar used in the western countries. The year begins about the middle of March (Chaitra) in southern India and the middle of October (Kārttika) in the north, but the names of the months are the same: Chaitra (March-April), Vaiśākha (April-May), Jyeshṭha (May-June), Āshāḍha (June-July), Śrāvaṇa (July-August), Bhādrapada (August-September), Āśvina (September-October), Kārttika (October-November), Agrahāyaṇa (November-December), Pausha (December-January), Māgha (January-February), Phālguna (February-March).

The year is divided into six seasons of two months each, beginning with Vaiśākha and Jyeshṭha, known as Summer, Rainy, Autumn, Winter, Dewy, and Spring. The year is also divided into two periods of six months each, one covering the northward progress of the sun and the other its southward journey.

The fixed times for the annual ceremonies and festivals for the worship of the different deities are determined by the lunar calendar. For instance, the worship of the goddess of the Ganges (Daśarā) comes on the tenth lunar day of the bright fortnight of Jyeshṭha (May-June); the car festival of Jagannāth (Rathayātrā) is the second day of the bright fortnight in Āshāḍha (June-July). The ceremony of swinging the Lord Kṛishṇa (Jhulanayātrā) is held from the eleventh to the fifteenth days of the bright fortnight of Śrāvaṇa (July-August), and the birthday of Kṛishṇa (Janmāshṭamī) is celebrated on the eighth day of the dark fortnight of Bhādrapada (August-September). The great Durgā-pūjā festival at which the goddess of power is worshiped is held from the seventh to the tenth days of the bright fortnight of Āśvina (September-October), and the next full moon day is the Lakshmī-pūjā for the worship of the goddess of wealth and prosperity. The next new moon day after the Lakshmī-pūjā is devoted to the worship of the goddess Kālī. The last day of the month of Kārttika, the middle of November, is the day for the worship of Kārttikeya, the god of war. The full moon day of Kārttika (October-November) is the ceremony of the circular dance of Kṛishṇa with the gopīs of Vrindāban (Rāsayātrā). The fifth day of the bright fortnight of Māgha (January-February), just before the advent of spring, is the time for the worship of the goddess of learning, the Sarasvatī-pūjā. The great festival to Śiva (Śivarātri) is held on the fourteenth day of the dark fortnight of Phālguna (February-March), and the full moon day of the same month is the festival at which colored water and powders are offered to Kṛishṇa and Rādhā (Dolayātrā), popularly known as Holi, when people joyously celebrate the advent of spring by throwing colored water and powders on each other.

The Stars

The early Indians regarded the science of astronomy as one of the six auxiliary sciences of the Vedas, since astronomy was intended to provide the rules for calculating and fixing the days and hours for the performance of various sacrifices. Early astronomers, such as Varāhamihira in the sixth century A.D., seem to have known something of the astronomy of China, Arabia, Babylonia, and Greece, but they produced in their own works the results of their independent observations and investigations of the natural phenomena of the earth's revolution around the sun, its rotation on its own axis, the equation of the orbits of the planets and the variations in their motion, the eclipses of the sun and moon and their duration, and the approximately correct time for the length of the solar year. They knew of the ascending and descending nodes of the moon, but unscientifically thought of them as two planets, called Rāhu and Ketu, which caused eclipses.

Astrology grew out of the early studies of astronomy, becoming known as applied astronomy, that is, a study of the planetary movements which give results both good and bad. Some of the early astronomical works discussed the idea of signs of the zodiac, and the fixed point on the eastern horizon which serves in astrology as the basis for comparing the positions of the planets. The astronomer's studies of the motions of the planets of the solar system and of the conjunctions of the moon with the lunar mansions paved the way for astrology, which, however, could not be elevated to the level of such a science as astronomy.

The early astrologers must have observed the influence of the waxing and waning moon on the human body, bringing about appreciable changes in it on certain lunar days, and they undoubtedly observed the influence of the moon on the tides of the ocean. Since all things of the world are regarded as interlinked and exerting their influence on one another, astrologers were led to believe that the rotation of the planets around the central luminary, the sun, singly or in conjunction with their comrades in different signs of the zodiac, might also exert influence on the physiological and psychological characteristics of human and other beings in the world. Depending on such a belief, they must have collected observations of the happenings in the lives of particular men and correlated them with the positions of the planets. As these correlations became established, predictions could be made on the basis of the position of the planets at the time of birth, and auspicious times could be predicted on the basis of the relations of the planets at a given time.

Astrology became a believable study when people came to recognize the general coincidence of predictions with actual happenings, though, of course, not all results foretold could be obtained in one's life. Having based their belief on the probable influence of the planets on human destiny, the Hindus, prone as they are to the worship of Śakti or the power of the Divinity in all the glorious forces of Nature, began to personify and deify the planets too, and to introduce the worship of the nine planets into their social life so that the planets might abate their inauspicious tendencies and show good will towards their devotees.

According to the Hindu astrologers, the zodiac is assumed to be a belt of the horizon outside which the sun and moon and major planets do not pass; that area of the heavens is divided crosswise into twelve equal areas called signs. Each of these areas or signs is imagined to be presided over by a particular planet. The particular sign in which the moon is situated at the time of a man's birth is called his own sign. Astrological calculations are based on the location of the fixed point on the eastern horizon at the time of birth; the locations of all the planets are defined in relation to it by most astrologers, although some use the sign in which the moon was present at birth as the starting point.

The exact knowledge of the time of birth and of the position of the different planets in the different signs or areas at that moment is essential for the astrologer to make his predictions concerning a man's probable future. Some astrologers accept one hundred and eight years as the normal span of a man's life; others use one hundred and twenty years as the basis of their calculations. Those who work on the basis of one hundred and eight years compute the duration of the influence of the sun on a man's life as six years; the moon's influence is fifteen years; for Mars it is eight years; seventeen for Mercury; ten for Saturn; nineteen for Jupiter; twelve for Rāhu; and twenty-one for Venus.

Beginning either with the fixed point or with the position of the moon (depending upon the astrologer), the following twelve aspects of a man's life are considered serially by their assignment to the twelve signs or areas of the heavens. The first sign is concerned with a man's health, the second his wealth and prosperity, the third his brothers and sisters, the fourth his parents and friends, the fifth his children and learning, the sixth his enemies, the seventh his wife, the eighth his length of life, the ninth his good fortune and piety, the tenth his works, his career, the eleventh his income, and the twelfth his expenditure. On the basis of the position of the planets in each of the signs at the time of birth, the astrologers thus predict the future for men.

Astrology could not claim to have reached the status of a perfect science in earlier periods for want of patronage from the State and because of some aversion to it by men of intellect, who never have liked to be haunted by the predictions of the astrologers, especially the unfavorable ones. Even now many of the enlightened people of India do not depend on astrology for guidance in new undertakings and they tend to regard it as a sort of superstition to consult astrologers. But the generality of men in society consult astrological almanacs for finding the auspicious days and moments for commencing any important work.

In addition to the auspicious and inauspicious times which are determined by the relations between men and the stars, there are certain fixed times which are generally regarded as auspicious or inauspicious. For instance, there is a period of roughly an hour and a half each day which many persons consider to be inauspicious for starting a trip or for undertaking a new project, for performing a ceremony, or for social gatherings. The specific time may vary in different parts of India, but it is a widespread custom to consider a certain period each day inauspicious. In northern India, from seven-thirty to nine o'clock in the morning on Tuesday is inauspicious, and from nine to ten-thirty o'clock on Friday, from ten-thirty to noon on Sunday, from noon to one-thirty on Wednesday, from one-thirty to three on Saturday, from three to four-thirty on Monday, and from four-thirty to six in the afternoon on Thursday.

Men by their nature want to know beforehand the possibility of ups and downs in their lives, their chances for success or failure, for prosperity or adversity, for good fortune or misfortune; they want to know the chances for profit or loss in business, the probable results of lawsuits, the prospects for good marital and love connections, and all such matters in the different stages of their lives. The astrologers skillfully exploit human weakness and by their predictions often lead men to the path of mental stagnation and make them almost forget that they should exert their own free will without depending fully on fate. Probably for this reason, in later times, the astrologers were socially relegated to the rank of lower-class Brāhmans. The lower status of the astrologers also resulted because a large section of the worshipers of the Sun, who specialized in astrology, came originally from Iran; as descendents of the Magi of Iran, they were known as Magas, or Śākadvīpī Brāhmans, retaining their separate status among Brāhmans. Even today no orthodox Hindu will take water from their hands.

This degradation of the astrologers was in all likelihood one of the reasons that astrology did not attain the perfection of a natural science. Kauṭilya, in the fourth century B.C., was a severe critic of astrologers. He did not approve of a king's desire to enquire into the auspiciousness of particular days and constellations before starting on a military campaign and remarked pungently, "Success eludes the fool who consults too much the constellations. Purpose is to be regarded as [the stimulating] star for [the success of] the object in view. Of what avail are the stars?"

But the great Varāhamihira has praised good astrologers who, according to him, should be consulted and honored by kings, just as the bad ones should be shunned because they by their imperfect knowledge of astrology lead kings to utter ruin. He says, moreover, that "like a night without a lamp, and the sky without sunlight, a king without a good astrologer stalks on the path [of duty] like a blind man."

Animals and Birds

In addition to the worlds in the heavens, and all the planets and stars, and the sun and the moon, the Creator made this earth with its animals, birds, trees, flowers, rivers, mountains, and, of course, man. The role of man in Hindu thought will be discussed later; here we shall consider some of the attitudes which characterize the thinking of the Hindus concerning the natural world around us.

Because of its geographical and climatic features, India is a unique country in the variety of flora and fauna which it possesses. The Hindu concept of the divinity of nature may be reminiscent of a form of worship which came down from an early age. From the studies of relics recently discovered by archaeologists at Mohenjodaro in northwest India, scholars are still attempting to establish the view that some form of animal worship was common among the people of the Indus Valley civilization. At any rate, the Hindu belief that all that exists has been created by the Supreme Being, comes from the Supreme Being, and will return to the Supreme Being, is adequate basis for the veneration of the natural world in which man finds himself.

Among the animals of special concern to the Hindus the first is the cow, for the sanctity of this animal has been maintained in India since the times of the Ṛigveda. In later times the cow has been regarded as a goddess, being an embodiment of several of the deities in the Hindu pantheon. This is entirely due to the extreme usefulness of the cow as a source of milk, an important food material both for secular purposes and for religious ceremonies. Gifts of cows to Brāhmans have always been meritorious acts. The cow was the favorite animal of Lord Kṛishṇa and his associates, the gopīs and cowherds of Vrindāban.

The monkey god, Hanumān, famous in the story of the Rāmāyaṇa, is still worshiped in many parts of India. Everyone knows the great and laudable part played by Hanumān in getting Sītā, Rāma's consort, released from the hands of the demon Rāvaṇa. Out of deference to this king of the monkeys, the mischief done by this species is treated with much forbearance by the Hindus and the killing of monkeys is generally regarded as an impious act. Hanumān in medieval Hinduism was worshiped as a great devotee of Rāma, thought of as an avatāra of Vishṇu. He is also taken to be a fertility god, granting barren women the blessing of children, and he is popularly considered to be a helper in need and a remover of obstacles.

Serpent worship is a primitive form of devotion still prevalent in Indian villages. Nāgas or serpent deities are often represented as demons or semidivine beings with human faces and serpent tails, dwelling in waters or in subterranean regions. Kṛishṇa's exploit in conquering Kāliya, the snake king of the Jumna River, is a well-known Hindu legend. Vishṇu is mythologically described as lying down on a couch formed by the snake Śesha, after the dissolution of the universe. Many royal families have Nāga as a part of their names. Worship of snakes may be attributed to their deadliness and the belief still persists that a man will be saved from the injury of snake bite if he remembers to utter the name of the sage Āstika, at whose intercession the famous snake Takshaka was saved from death. Manasā, the mother of Āstika, is widely worshiped as the serpent goddess, especially in snake-infested areas.

Many animals are held in special regard because they are associated with the gods as their vehicles, called *vāhanas* (those which carry, or those on which they ride). They are probably associated with the gods because of their beneficent nature, or because they should be kept under control by those particular deities so that they may not follow their natural propensity to do evil. During the worship of the gods and goddesses, the vehicles also receive salutations and sometimes worship from the devotees.

The Garuḍa is a half-mythical bird, described variously as a gigantic crane, a vulture, or an eagle, and treated mythologically as the chief of the feathered race. This half-human bird is Vishṇu's vehicle and it carries the god on its outstretched wings. The Garuḍa is generally believed to be an implacable enemy of serpents.

The lion, the lord of beasts, is the vehicle for Durgā (Pārvatī), the goddess of the Śakti cult who is known as the "Mother Goddess riding on the lion." Since the goddess is Power incarnate, the lion, the most powerful of beasts, is fittingly considered to be her vehicle. The fight between the forces of good and evil in the world is shown in images and art as the battle between Durgā, with her lion fighting fiercely by her side, and the buffalo demon whose head has been severed and from whose trunk the demon is emerging.

The tiger is the vehicle of the goddess Kātyāyanī in southern India, and his skin is used as a seat by Śiva worshipers and by sannyāsins, men who have renounced the world.

The elephant is the vehicle for the eight deities who guard the quarters of the compass in the heavens; Śiva is said to wear an elephant hide, and it is used to adorn some Śiva images. This ponderous but majestic animal, so important a factor in ancient Indian warfare, is fittingly thought of as the best vehicle for the superintending deities of the cardinal points in their constant watch over their jurisdictions.

The white humped bull is the vehicle of the white god, Śiva, who is called the bull-bannered god. In Vedic times Indra was often conceived in the form of a bull; later the bull represented dharma symbolically, its four legs standing for truth, purity, kindness, and charity. Whiteness is the symbol of the sattva guṇa without which dharma cannot be acquired. Śiva's attendant, Nandi, is often represented in sculpture by a recumbent bull placed in Śiva shrines.

Seven horses representing perhaps the seven constituent colors of the sun's rays draw the chariot of the Sun God, and the moon is often represented as riding in a chariot pulled by ten horses. The great Horse Sacrifice which was performed in early times by powerful monarchs was one of the greatest sacrifices of the Vedas.

The buffalo is the vehicle of Yama, the god of death. The fierceness of this animal symbolizes the spirit of the god of death in taking away the breath of life from mortal beings, which is always done before the full span of one hundred and eight years.

The ass is the vehicle of the village goddess, Śītalā, who presides over smallpox; one remedy for smallpox is ass's milk.

The dog is the vehicle for the terrible-looking god Bhairava, born of Śiva's blood. Although loyal to its master, this animal often assumes a very frightening attitude toward men and other animals.

The deer is the vehicle of Vāyu the wind god, fittingly chosen because of its swiftness. The antelope is sometimes used as a symbol in the hands of Śaiva images.

The mouse is the vehicle for the elephant-headed god Gaṇeśa, the god of wisdom, giver of success, and remover of obstacles. Hindus invoke and worship this god at the beginning of every important ceremony. The Sanskrit verbal root for mouse is derived from the word meaning *to steal,* and the theologians figuratively explain that the mouse is one who pilfers all results of actions, for unless the results of actions are discarded one cannot be successful in realizing God. In this sense it is associated with Gaṇeśa, the remover of obstacles, as a beneficial animal. It should also be remembered in this connection, however, that among the six classes of natural disasters from which the agricultural people of India suffer, mice form one class—the other five being excessive rain, drought, locusts, parrots, and nearness to aggressive foreign kings. In this sense Gaṇeśa as the remover of obstacles keeps the mouse in check and prevents him from doing mischief.

The owl has been chosen as the vehicle for Lakshmī, the goddess of beauty, wealth, and prosperity. This bird appears to have been made the companion of the goddess of prosperity because it aids agricultural prosperity by feeding on rats, mice, and squirrels which damage crops.

The peacock, known to be a slayer of snakes, is the vehicle of the war god, Kārttikeya, who according to mythology slew the demon Tāraka in battle. It may be that the peacock was chosen as the vehicle for this god to be a warrior against snakes. It is a curious fact that the other name for Kārttikeya, Subrahmaṇya, in its contracted form is a synonym for snake, and in southern India the same day is held sacred for the serpent god and for Subrahmaṇya.

The swan is the vehicle for Brahmā, the Creator; and Sarasvatī the goddess of learning, wisdom, and speech is also shown as having the swan for her vehicle. The swan symbolizes the whiteness or purity of learning and the power of discrimination, which is the essential quality for the acquisition of saving knowledge. In southern India the peacock sometimes replaces the swan as Sarasvatī's vehicle.

The Makara is a mythological water animal often identified with the crocodile. It is the emblem of the god of love, Kāma. It is an amphibious animal, proverbially very hypocritical, and so is a fit emblem for the god of love. In later Hinduism Gaṅgā, the presiding deity of the Ganges, is supposed to ride a Makara, which is spoken of as the most glorified creature among fishes.

Trees, Plants, Grasses, and Flowers

Trees, plants, grasses, and flowers also play a prominent part in the lives of the Hindus. A scientific truth was long ago expressed by Manu when he said, "All trees and plants are full of consciousness within themselves and are endowed with the feeling of pleasure and pain." The Hindus regard all life as valuable and sacred. It is no wonder then that they cherish a sentiment of adoration for particular species of trees, plants, and grasses, and are fond of selecting particular varieties of flowers to offer to their deities. In the Bṛihatsaṁhitā (LIX), it is required that before taking from particular trees wood which must be used for making images of gods and goddesses, the people of the four castes should invoke those trees after worship at night with a prayer in these words: "O tree! you are intended for the making of an image of such-and-such a deity. I salute you. Please accept my worship offered according to injunctions. May those beings who reside here arrange for their residence elsewhere after accepting the oblations offered according to injunctions! Let them forgive me. Salutation to them all." Such was the concern of the Hindus for the life of the trees, thought of as being presided over by deities.

Another chapter in the same ancient book discourses on the various methods of medical treatment of trees when they suffer from withered branches or their sap is running from wounds. The people believe with the author of that book that trees, planted by them with worship after purification with bath and unction, grow with thick foliage and bear fruits and flowers in abundance. Experts in the science of the medical treatment of trees published their observations on the influence of the conjunctions of certain heavenly bodies on the productivity of trees. They were also aware of certain chemical processes used in the preparation of seeds which produced immediate germination and earlier prolific growth of fruits and flowers.

The pipal tree appears to have been associated with the Mother Goddess in the Indus Valley civilization. This sacred fig tree is mentioned in the Ṛigveda, and in the Vedic age its wood was used for fire vessels and for the drill for producing the sacred fire. In later mythology it is regarded as a representation of the god Vishṇu. It is sprinkled with water accompanied by prayer for the removal of certain ills, such as throbbing of the eyes and arms, dreadful dreams, and the rise of enemies.

The banyan tree with its chief and secondary trunks and prop roots, its big dome of foliage and innumerable branches offering roosting quarters to the feathery race, has also been held in great adoration since Vedic times. The Buddha attained his enlightenment while seated under this tree.

The silk-cotton tree (*Bombax Malabaricum*) with its scarlet flowers blooming in early spring is also an object of adoration to Hindu eyes. The tamāla tree with its dark bark and leaves is associated with the dark god Kṛishṇa and receives worship from Vaishṇava devotees.

The worship of Śiva and other gods and goddesses of the Śaivas cannot be contemplated without the offering of the leaves of the sacred vilva tree. It is forbidden to break its branches. At the great Durgā-pūjā festival in the autumn, Durgā is invoked on a twig of this tree.

The śamī tree is held sacred because of its being pregnant inside with fire. Sometimes five particular trees are planted in a group to make a spot of special sanctity and it was under such a group of trees that Rāmakṛishṇa Paramahaṁsa attained true knowledge of the Absolute Reality at Dakshiṇeśwar temple near Calcutta.

Various trees of the evergreen type, cereals such as rice and wheat, oilseed plants, fiber crops, spices, grapes, oranges, pears, apples, bananas, mangoes, pineapples, and such other growing things as are found to be nutritious and useful are offered to the deities. The Hindu devotees think with the author of the Bhagavad Gītā that "those who enjoy the objects [of food] given to us by the gods without offering them in return [in sacrifice and worship] are veritable thieves." In the worship of some gods and the forefathers, and on ceremonial and festive occasions, rice, barley, and sesame seeds with sandal paste are important requisites. The food value of these grains and seeds for the staple diets of the Hindus is very great and that probably led to the recognition of their value in worship.

Medicinal herbs are thought to partake of the ambrosia of the moon and thus owe their healing properties to the moon. That is why the moon is also called the presiding deity of herbs.

The tulasī plant is a very holy plant among the Hindus, especially the worshipers of Vishṇu, for without its leaves no ceremonial worship of Vishṇu is possible. It is praised as destroying all the evils of the present aeon and it is considered sinful to break its branches. The curative effect of the juice of tulasī leaves is acknowledged by the Āyurvedic system of medicine, based on the Atharvaveda.

Of the grasses, the dūrvā, called bent or panic grass, is treated as a sacred article of worship and is offered to the deities. It is regarded as a very auspicious grass because of its long life. Kuśa is another holy grass, an essential requisite in religious sacrifices and domestic ceremonies, especially in the rites performed for the forefathers.

Throughout all ages and countries, flowers, regarded as the glorious creations of the Divinity, whose very sight produces joy and wonder in the human mind, have been used in worship and adoration. No Hindu worship of gods and goddesses can be thought of without the offering of flowers. It is, however, curious that particular flowers are associated with particular deities. For example, in worshiping Śiva red China roses are essential; for Vishṇu, white flowers; for Lakshmī, lotuses; for Sarasvatī, yellow flowers; for Kāma, mango blossoms; for the Sun, red lotuses; for the planet Saturn, blue flowers. It seems clear that seasonal flowers have been selected to be the special varieties to be offered to the deities at their major festivals. The sanctity of lotuses may be traced to the mythological stories that Brahmā, the Creator, was born of the lotus issuing from the navel of Vishṇu.

At a later period in Hinduism, there grew up the convention that certain flowers are prohibited for particular deities and others are favored. Śiva's favorite flowers are banned in worship of the Sun, for instance, and tulasī leaves are prohibited in the worship of Gaṇeśa.

It is a curious fact of nature known to the Hindus from early times that the excessive growth of certain flowers predicts the prospective abundance of certain crops and articles of domestic use, and also provides a warning of certain distresses which will befall mankind.

Food

The intimate relationship between man and the natural world around him determines the attitude of the Hindus toward the food which they eat. The Hindus seek to avoid a diet which hampers the development of their bodily and mental strength. Bad food habits must be avoided lest through them a man should fail to acquire mental purity and should be kept from ecstatic communion with God. It is believed that the mental tranquillity necessary for the worship of the Supreme Being is difficult to achieve by men who are accustomed to eat food in which rajas and tamas predominate, such as fish, flesh, eggs, and liquor. Even in eating food which is predominantly sattva, moderation is commended lest excess should increase bodily lethargy and consequent mental deterioration. Chastity of life may be hard hit by the choice of objectionable and prohibited foods.

The Bhagavad Gītā (XVII.8) has defined the three types of food in very clear terms, stating that the eatables for sāttvika people, those who are pure and wise, are those things which augment longevity, energy, vigor, health, joy, and zest, and which are delicious, bland, substantial, and agreeable; rājasika people, those energetic souls who are swayed by passions, tend to eat foods that are bitter, sour, saline, overhot, pungent, astringent, and burning and which produce pain, affliction, and disease; while tāmasika people, those who are lethargic, lazy, and ignorant, eat foods which are cold, flat, putrid, and stale, and are the leavings of others' dishes and plates, and are unclean.

The partaking of unwholesome and prohibited foods is considered by the ancient writings to be one of the main causes of death destroying the Brāhmans. The religious scriptures prescribe a healthy diet for human beings and prohibit those foods, both animal and vegetable, which may unbalance the physical system and cause distractions of the mind and disturbances to worship and the meditative mood essential to worship. Hence certain varieties of foods, cereal and noncereal, vegetables, rice, wheat, fish, meat, milk, and fruits have been commended as proper diet and certain other foods have been prohibited. The Laws of Manu give the general dictum that "no sin is attached to eating flesh or drinking wine, or gratifying the sexual urge, for these are the natural propensities of men; but abstinence from these bears greater fruits." Manu also teaches that "by living on pure fruit, roots, or food grains used by the sages, a man does not acquire the same religious merit as he does by forswearing the use of meat." He gives us the high religious view that the person who does not wish to inflict on any animal the pain of death or even of captivity will enjoy perfect felicity and will easily obtain whatever he contemplates, strives for, and seeks with all his heart.

The cow, regarded in the Ṛigveda as an animal not to be killed, is a sacred and valued possession which may not be slaughtered and eaten. The chief sacrificial victims are the sheep, the ox, and the goat, and in modern times it is primarily the goat, and that mostly in Bengal. In modern times, fish and meat are not usually eaten by Brāhmans outside Bengal; but in Bengal, in accordance with the rulings of certain authoritative lawgivers, Brāhmans are allowed to eat the flesh of goats and deer and to eat certain varieties of fish which are white and have scales. The eating of meat, but not of beef, is more widespread among the lower castes and the outcaste communities.

Fish which have ugly forms or the heads of snakes are forbidden. Snails, crabs, fowl, cranes, ducks, water crows, camels, and boars are forbidden. No fish or meat should be eaten until it has been sanctified by the repetition of mantras offering it to the gods.

In the case of students who are studying the Vedas, the merit of a vegetarian diet is fully recognized; they must avoid irritating and exciting foods in the interest of celibacy. Honey, for instance, is taboo for students and for women under certain circumstances, since it is an excitant. Unfit for tne consumption of the twice-born are garlic, turnip, onion, and mushrooms. Brāhmans who wilfully eat a mushroom, a pig, garlic, a village cock, an onion, or a turnip lose the privileges of their order. They must fast and perform penances of certain kinds to atone for eating forbidden foods. Spirituous liquors, too, are forbidden.

The milk of cows and buffaloes—and a variety of milk products—are popular in the diet of Hindus, but the milk of a newly parturient cow and of a she-camel are banned. Rice, barley, wheat, beans, mustard seed, coconut, milk, curds, clarified butter, and the numerous fruits and nuts of India have all along been the wholesome and staple articles of food for the Hindu.

Rivers

Rivers have always played an important part in the lives of the Indian people, who have regarded them as deities since Vedic times. Countries fed by river waters are said to have rivers as their nourishing mothers because their agriculture depends entirely on the irrigation made possible by the waters of their rivers. The rivers of India are invoked as deities capable of bestowing wealth, plenty, nourishment, and offspring on their worshipers. Bathing in sacred rivers, or in tanks made sacred by the addition of water from such rivers, is a part of the religious duties required of all Hindus. Such bathing purifies the devotees of uncleanness, and when done with the proper mantras washes away many sins. Bathing is especially commended at the time of the new moon, on certain festival days, and at the time of an eclipse when the darkening of the sun or moon creates an unclean period on earth requiring a purificatory bath by the devotees. At such times, countless thousands of Hindus bathe in the sacred rivers of India.

While all rivers in India are sacred, there are seven which are regarded as the most sacred: the Ganges, Jumna, Godāvarī, Sarasvatī, Narmadā, Indus, and Kāverī.

Of all Indian rivers, the Ganges with its many tributaries is regarded by the Hindus as the holiest. The personified deity of the river, the goddess Gaṅgā, is worshiped every year in the Daśarā festival. She is described in mythology as coming out of the feet of Vishṇu and descending to the earth by falling on the head of Śiva. Believers in the sacredness of the Ganges chant a mantra while they bathe in any pond, lake, or ordinary river, or use water for any ceremony, praying for the presence of the famous holy rivers as purifying agents in these words, "O you, Gaṅgā, Yamunā, Godāvarī, Sarasvatī, Narmadā, Sindhu, and Kāverī—be pleased to be present here in this water." It is popularly believed that a bath in the Ganges on certain ceremonial and festive occasions or on particular conjunctions of the heavenly bodies washes away a man's blackest sins. Crematory ashes and pieces of the burnt bones of dead persons are ceremoniously thrown into this holy river, especially at Hardwar, Banaras, or Allahabad, in the belief that the spirit of the cremated person will be wafted to higher worlds. Mahātmā Gāndhi's cremation ashes were thrown into the waters of the Ganges and the other holy rivers of India.

The Indus which carried to the Arabian Sea the largest volume of water and flowed the swiftest, "rushing onward like a bellowing bull," received the greatest attention in Vedic times. It is the River *Sindhu* (which word also means a river) which gave the name *India* to the subcontinent; the land of the Indus became the land of the Hindus in the language of the early Persians. The fertile valley, which easily produced wheat and other crops, and the facility of communication by boats along this river, may have been the basis for the praise and worship of the river by the Vedic poets.

The Sarasvatī river was referred to frequently in the Ṛigveda as one of the most sacred in India, probably because on its banks the Vedic sacrifices were held and there the Vedic sages chanted their mantras. It is generally identified with the river of that name lost in ancient times in the desert of Rajputana;

hence it is called the "lost river." The name of the goddess of learning, Sarasvatī, was probably connected with the river because of the association with the Vedic Seers who first repeated there the mantras which were revealed to them.

The Brahmaputra, descending from the Tibetan Himālayas, is an uncontrollable river which often causes devastating floods during the rainy season. Probably to assuage the fury of the river the people worshiped the attending deity of the river, especially during the months of April and May. It is popularly believed that a bath in the river at that time will destroy all sins and make one fit for attaining the path of union with Brahman.

The famous rivers of southern India, the Godāvarī, the Kṛishṇa, the Kāverī, the Narmadā, and the Tāpī are holy objects of worship. The Godāvarī is associated with the story of Rāma, just as the Jumna in the north is associated with the story of the Supreme Person Kṛishṇa who played on its banks with the gopīs.

On the river banks at Hardwar, Vrindāban, Banaras, and Allahabad are especially sacred pilgrimage places where the people are enjoined to take their baths and perform their austerities, sacrifices, almsgiving, and ceremonies in honor of their forefathers, and to contemplate on God.

Mountains

Mountains, as well as rivers, have always excited the imaginations and received the devoted worship of the Hindus. It is recognized that the greatest contributions to the wealth, health, and prosperity of a country are made by its rivers and mountains. The agricultural productivity of northern India owes its origin to the summer monsoon which beats against the Himālayan range extending almost fifteen hundred miles from east to west. The mysterious and solitary grandeur of the mountains has made such an impression on the minds of the Hindus that they could not but think of their personification and glorification, and have from ancient times offered worship to the deities presiding over them. Kṛishṇa, in the Bhagavad Gītā, says, "Whatever thing is glorious, beautiful, and mighty, you should understand that to be born of a fragment of My splendor."

The real Indian mind spoke when the great poet Bhāravi described the Himālaya mountains in these lofty words, "This lord of mountains, which is as if rending the sky into a thousand parts by its snow-white peaks, is perforce competent to destroy the series of sins of people by its very appearance," and he continued "thoughts of shaking off worldly ties arise [in the minds] of those who desire to attain oneness with the excellent and pure Brahman by their residence on this [mountain] which, like the study of scriptures, is capable of removing all darkness [of ignorance.]" It is well known that hermits and ascetics resort to the solitude of mountains for meditation and the cultivation of mental purity and also for the performance of austerities. Some shrines of gods and goddesses are situated in the lofty heights of hills and mountains to draw devotees up there and to teach them that the way to attain salvation is difficult and full of perils. Hard to climb is the abode of Divinity.

The highest and largest mountain range in the world, the Himālaya, inspires strength in the minds of men by its august and solid appearance. This lofty mountain, clasped by the black clouds on its slopes, inlaid with green valleys, and pushing into space its high peaks enveloped in snow, forms a wall against nature's depredations. As a source of the waters that stream into the three big rivers of northern India, the Indus, the Brahmaputra, and the Ganges, the Himālaya mountains make a great contribution to the welfare of India. It is no wonder that the Hindus regard this king of mountains as being imbued with the spirit of a superintending deity. The snow-clad mount Kailāsa was conceived by the mythologists as a place fit for the residence of the god Śiva, who is probably the White God because of his intimate association with the snowy peaks of this mountain. Śiva's wife, Pārvatī, is the daughter of the Himālayas. Another part of the mountain is sacred as the spot where Arjuna performed severe penances in order to win from Śiva the weapons used in the war with the Kurus. Also sacred is the mountain of herbs which Hanumān took to Ceylon to save the life of Lakshmaṇa, Rāma's brother, in the battle with Rāvaṇa. The most famous shrines in the Himālayas are Badarīnāth and Kedārnāth, some distance above Hardwar.

The southern mountain range, the Vindhya, was not known to the Vedic Aryans, but has long been a source of inspiration and devotion in the south. This range formed a great natural defense for a long time against the Aryan invasion from the north. Mythologically it is said that the sage Agastya humbled this mountain by making it prostrate before him when it was trying to obstruct the path of the sun by its ever growing height. The mountain remained in a bending posture out of reverence for the sage and agreed to remain thus until he returned from the south. But the sage never returned, and the range remained bent in reverence. This story is the basis of the popular superstition that anyone starting on a journey on the first day of an Indian month, as Agastya did, may not return at all. These southern ranges of mountains and hills are held in reverence in the south just as the Himālayas are revered in the north, with many sacred pilgrimage places located on the heights of the southern mountains.

In this brief description of the role of the natural world in the thinking and worship of the Hindus, we have tried to make clear the way in which the Hindus, believing in the identity of the Supreme Being and Nature, see Him in everything, everything in Him, and worship Him as abiding in all created things.

Chapter 4

THE ROLE OF MAN IN HINDUISM

by R. N. Dandekar

MAN IN RELATION TO THE SUPREME BEING

The most distinctive feature of the speculative wisdom of the Indians is its essential cosmic character. According to Indian thinkers, from the philosophical point of view man cannot be regarded as standing apart from the universe in any way, much less can he be said to enjoy any place of special privilege in it. Their speculations have never, therefore, tended to become anthropocentric. They look upon man as just one of the many forms in which the Supreme Being is manifested in this universe.

The Upanishads express this point of view in a telling manner when they say, "The essential self or the vital essence in man is the same as that in an ant, the same as that in a gnat, the same as that in an elephant, the same as that in these three worlds, indeed the same as that in the whole universe." A proper understanding of this ancient cosmic outlook would serve as an adequate background for a correct estimate of the role of man in Hinduism, for that outlook has deeply influenced the Hindu concepts of man's relations with himself, with god, and with the world in which he lives.

The Essential or Real Self

One of the main teachings of the Upanishads is: Know thyself. The philosophical implication of this teaching is that the essential or real self (ātman) is different from the empirical self (jīva), and that true philosophical knowledge consists in not confusing the one with the other.

This is the teaching of the famous parable in the eighth book of the Chāndogya Upanishad. Once upon a time the god Indra and the demon Virocana came to the great creator and teacher Prajāpati and asked him to teach them the nature of the self "which is free from sin, free from old age, free from death and grief, free from hunger and thirst, which desires nothing, and imagines nothing." They both lived with Prajāpati as his pupils for thirty-two years, since such a long apprenticeship was a necessary precondition for the great spiritual truth being imparted to them. But even after their long apprenticeship Prajāpati tested their capacity to understand and their critical acumen by telling them that the essential self was nothing different from "the image seen in the eye," that is, the essential self is the same as the embodied self when awake and conscious of external objects.

Thereupon Virocana became complacent in the belief that he understood the true nature of the essential self and hurried back to the demons and proclaimed that he had obtained the ultimate knowledge of the self from Prajāpati. At this stage, the Upanishad slyly adds that those who believe in the identity of the essential self with their bodily consciousness have learned only the "gospel of demons." Indra, however, was too clever and critical to be satisfied with this teaching. He thought to himself, if the body is identical with the essential self, then it will be subject to fear, sin, old age, and death, but that is false for the essential self is subject to none of these. Indra therefore concluded that there was no glory in possessing that knowledge. Since his thirst for true knowledge was not quenched, he went back to Prajāpati.

At the end of the second apprenticeship of thirty-two years, Prajāpati told Indra that the essential self is identical with the self when it is dreaming, for then the self is not affected by the limitations of the body and the mind is active so that the self is conscious only of internal objects and the enjoyment of subtle things. This teaching certainly represented an advance over the earlier one, but even so it could not satisfy Indra. For, he thought, in a dream the self may not be affected by the limitations of the body, but it is still influenced by the limitations and characteristics of the mind. We are struck and chased and shed tears in our dreams, and how can this be reconciled with the fearless and painless nature of the self? So, undaunted in his spiritual quest, for the third time Indra went to Prajāpati.

Prajāpati must indeed have been satisfied that Indra was a worthy pupil, so, after the usual term of studentship of thirty-two years, he led Indra a step further in the knowledge of the self. He told him that the essential self is identical with the self in the condition of deep sleep, when neither the body nor the mind affects the self and it "desires no desires and dreams no dreams." Indra thought, this deep sleep is indeed free from fear and pain, but it could not be identified with the essential self for in deep sleep we are conscious of nothing, neither of ourselves nor of external objects. Such repose and rest would be the same as the repose and rest of a log of wood.

Indra then proved himself worthy of receiving the highest wisdom by going back to Prajāpati and again questioning him about the true nature of the essential self. So Prajāpati asked him to live a student's life with him for five more years and at the completion of that period he imparted to Indra the highest knowledge about the self. The essential self must not be mistaken for bodily consciousness, nor must it be confused with the consciousness of dreams. It transcends even the condition of deep sleep, though some intimations of its nature are available in that condition. The essential self is indeed of the nature of pure self-consciousness, which is beyond all bodily and mental conditions.

Through this very suggestive analysis of human consciousness, some characteristic features of the nature of the essential self are clearly brought out. The essential self is not identical with either the body or the mind and is, therefore, free from all the limitations, changes, and experiences to which the body and the mind are subjected. It is eternal and immutable existence (*sat*). The self is neither the subject, nor the object, nor the act—neither the knower nor the known nor the knowing. In the expression "I know," for instance, the essential self is not represented by the "I," nor is it represented by the act of knowing. But, at the same time, the "I" and "knowing" become impossible without the essential self.

The parable of Indra and Prajāpati also points out that the essential self does not imply the absence of consciousness as in the condition of deep sleep. It is certainly conscious, but of nothing else but itself—it is purely and exclusively consciousness as such (*chit*). The essential self is realizable through self-intuition as pure self-consciousness when it is in a state which transcends wakefulness, dreaming, and deep sleep and when the body and the senses, mind, intellect, and ego cease to function.

The essential self is described as being something more than pure existence as such (sat) and pure consciousness as such (chit). That something more is understandable through the doctrine of the five sheaths. The second book of the Taittirīya Upanishad analyses man by proceeding from the grosser forms of man to the subtler forms—of course on the assumption that the subtler the form the more real it is. First of all there is the physical body which is said to be made of food or matter. But this cannot be the ultimate or real essence of man because, the Upanishad tells us, there is within the physical body "another body which is made up of vital air; the former is filled with the latter, which is also like unto the shape of man." More internal, and therefore subtler and more real than the body made of vital air, is another body made up of mind. More internal still than the mental body is another body which is made of intelligence or consciousness. Within this body of intelligence or consciousness is the most internal and central of all bodies, the body of bliss. This is the subtlest and therefore more real than the other four bodies.

It is needless to add that this description is not to be understood in a literal sense. This doctrine of the five sheaths represents a sort of symbolic attempt to analyse man into his five basic elements, the physical body, vital breath, mind, intellect or consciousness, and pure bliss. As a result of this analysis we arrive at the conclusion that the essential self in man transcends the physical, vital, mental, and intellectual forms and must be identified with the innermost and subtlest form, the beatific form. In other words, man realizes his essential self in an ecstatic, mystical state in which the only experience is that of pure bliss. The ultimate nature of the real or essential self is, therefore, pure existence (sat), pure consciousness (chit) and pure bliss (*ānanda*).

As has been discussed in other chapters in this book, the Upanishads record the analysis of the cosmos which shows that the Supreme Reality is existence-consciousness-bliss (sat-chit-ānanda). It naturally follows that the essential self in man (ātman) and the ultimate Cosmic Reality (Brahman) are the same. This grand philosophical doctrine emphasizes the fact that neither the empirical self nor the tangible phenomenal world, with which the empirical self seems to come into contact, possesses any reality from the ultimate point of view.

Thus we come to the conclusion that the true philosophical knowledge concerning the nature of man clearly realizes the distinction between the essential self and the empirical self. This should not be misunderstood to mean that man possesses two selves. The real self is actually one, but under certain conditions it assumes an individuality characterized by a body, mind, and intellect, and that empirical self is then mistaken for the real self. The real self is neither the doer nor the experiencer, and is in no way involved in the changes of the phenomenal world, nor governed by the laws of time, space, and causality. It is of the nature of existence-consciousness-bliss, and thus identified with the Supreme Reality. The true nature of the essential self, and its identity with the cosmic self, can be realized only in an ecstatic, mystical state which transcends the normal states of human consciousness.

This is the most representative view in Hinduism about the nature of the essential self in man, but it is by no means the only view. There are, for instance, some thinkers who regard the self as, in a sense, finite and atomic. There are others who believe that the essential self in man is identical with the cosmic self or the Supreme Being only in essence, but not in form. There are still others who assert that the essential self is distinct from the Supreme Being both in form and essence. It is not necessary to examine all these different views at length. It may be pointed out, though, that in spite of fundamental differences most of them agree in the assumption that the real self is distinct from the body-mind complex.

The Empirical Self

The empirical self, the self which has experience in this changing world of the senses, comes into being, according to the Hindu view, when through the operation of original ignorance (*avidyā*) the essential self falls from its serene aloofness, thereby forgetting, so to say, its identity with the Supreme Being. It becomes then a part of the phenomenal world which is also a creation of original ignorance, sometimes described as the illusive power of the Creator. The question as to how or why the original ignorance becomes operative is by its very nature philosophically inadmissible. Thinking can take place only after the creation of minds, which come into being through the operation of original ignorance. When before the operation of original ignorance there existed only one Ultimate Reality, who could have been the thinker and what could have been thought?

Some aspects of the nature of the individual or the empirical self have already become evident in the discussion of the nature of the essential self. The most distinctive characteristic of an individual is his assumption of a body. In Hindu thought, body is understood in a very comprehensive sense and is made to denote all kinds of limitations that are produced by original ignorance of the nature of the true self. That is why the empirical self is often called the embodied self.

According to the most representative Hindu view, the body to which the essential self is supposed to be attached as a result of the action of original ignorance is of three kinds: physical, subtle, and causal. The physical body is said to have been produced out of the five elements of earth, water, light, wind, and ether. It serves as the abode of all the experiences relating to the external world, and as the basis of consciousness in the state of wakefulness. At the death of the individual, only the physical body perishes, that is, dissolves into the five elements out of which it is produced. According to the Hindu view, death can affect only the physical body and nothing else.

The second body is known as the subtle body because it is made up of elements far subtler than the five elements of the physical body. There are seventeen subtle elements in the subtle body: mind, intellect, five vital breaths, five organs of action, and five organs of knowledge. The five vital breaths are located in different parts of the body: prāṇa in the heart, apāna in the anus, samāna in the navel, udāna in the throat, and vyāna diffused through the whole body. The five organs of action are speech, hands, feet, anus, and the organ of generation. The five organs of knowledge are ear, skin, eye, tongue, and nose. Consequently the subtle body becomes equivalent to the vital, mental, and intellectual functions together. It serves as the basis of dream consciousness. These functions are possible only because of the presence and direct awareness of the essential self and thus the subtle body serves as the indicatory mark (liṅga) of the presence of the self.

The most important role of the subtle body is played in connection with the transmigration of the self from one body to another, for it is believed that the subtle body serves as the medium through which the eternal and inexorable law of karma operates. Although the physical body perishes at death, individuality does not end. Individuality ends only through moksha, release into final identity with the Supreme Reality. Death is only a junction where the self changes the body and perhaps the route of the journey. The subtle body serves as the repository for the moral consequences of a man's life, both the direct and the indirect consequences, until they have their effect in the individual's rebirth. The direct moral consequences determine the kind of physical body to be taken at rebirth and the environmental conditions in which the individual will live; the indirect moral consequences produce in the individual innate tendencies which prompt him to act one way or another. The subtle body is the medium by which the individual changes from one physical body to another.

The third body which the empirical self is believed to assume is called the causal body. The presence of the causal body is indicated in the condition of deep sleep when both the physical and the subtle bodies cease to function temporarily. Furthermore, the physical and subtle bodies seem to rise from the causal body, and to dissolve into it.

Thus it is seen that it is the empirical self with his three bodies who is involved in this world of experience; he is the doer and the experiencer, subject to all the changes of phenomenal existence. It is indeed only in reference to him that we can speak of the role of man.

The actions of man in this world of experience are said to be mainly of three kinds: bodily, vocal, and mental; and they produce inevitable moral consequences. The nature of these actions is further said to be dependent on the makeup of the empirical self, which is characterized by the varying proportions of the three guṇas in it. The individual in whom sattva (knowledge, balance, light) predominates is characterized by knowledge, passionless detachment, and glory. The individual in whom rajas (passion, energy, action) predominates is absorbed in actions and impelled by desires, passions, and impulses. The individual in whom tamas (ignorance, passivity) predominates is characterized by ignorance, vice, infatuation, and greed.

Belief in Rebirth

Belief in rebirth is common to several ancient religions of the world, but the distinctive contribution of Hinduism to the doctrine of transmigration is that it has attempted to give a metaphysical and ethical interpretation of that belief. The essential self is believed to exist in all serenity and aloofness, mystically united with the Supreme Being, until as a result of the operation of original ignorance the self seems to enter the stage of individuality. There it is conditioned by the body-mind complex and is involved in the world of human experience. At that point there are two possibilities: either the individual through true knowledge returns at once to the original state of the essential self, that is, attains liberation, moksha; or the individual continues his pilgrimage through various rebirths until he finally reaches that goal of liberation.

There are four main principles involved in the Hindu theory of rebirths or transmigration: the permanence of the essential self, the operation of original ignorance, the possibility of union with the Supreme Being, and the doctrine of karma. The fundamental principle is, of course, the Hindu concept of the permanence of the essential self for, without the assumption of a permanent entity, the talk of rebirth would be meaningless. That is why the materialists, who do not believe in a permanent entity like the ātman, do not accept the possibility of rebirth.

The second principle is also essential for the whole process of rebirth is made possible by the operation of original ignorance, avidyā, in causing the essential self to assume an individuality. It is interesting to note that in the Hindu view of the creation of man the original cause of birth is not a moral error;

original ignorance is a metaphysical rather than a moral concept and moral concepts have relevance only after the process of human experience has started.

The third principle which is basic to the belief in rebirths is the concept of the possibility of liberation, moksha. For the Hindu, human existence is not a futile and unmotivated journey nor a wild goose chase; the concept of moksha represents the answer to the eternal question: Whither Mankind? Although in common parlance we speak of attaining moksha, it should be remembered that the state of liberation is not something different from the real nature of the self. Hindu thinkers claim that moksha is not to be reached, nor to be created, nor to be got as the result of some modification or change, nor to be got as the result of attempts to gain refinement or perfection. Liberation does not imply that the self acquires something which it does not have, or becomes something which it is not. Liberation means realizing one's own true self which is already there but not realized because of the influence of original ignorance. It is only through the accident of ignorance that man feels divested of his true nature of identity with the Supreme Being. The concept of liberation is indeed morally very significant for it elevates man by denying all creatureliness in him.

Since liberation is native to man, the Hindus believe that it follows as a corollary that it is the birthright of every individual; man himself, and not any extraneous power, is responsible for his own emancipation. This view is the very antithesis of the doctrine of God's grace. For the Hindu, man's life is the soul's pilgrimage to be terminated by liberation, release from original ignorance to man's natural state, mystical union with the Supreme. Even if liberation is not realized in one life, man is sustained through all the stages of transmigration by this message of faith and hope that he cannot be deprived of his birthright, moksha.

While ordinarily liberation, also called *mukti,* is thought of as escape from the shackles of individuality and attaining the mystic state of spiritual union with the Supreme Being, the Bhagavad Gītā glorifies as the highest ideal of man the state of liberation while still living in the human body, called jīvanmukti. In that state the individual develops a universality of outlook, a freedom from all attachments, a discernment of the truth which could come only to the liberated soul, but retains the physical body as a basis for action in this world. This is the ideal of the yogi and the bhakta.

The fourth principle on which the theory of rebirths rests is the law of karma. Original ignorance, the cause of the birth of the individual, is a metaphysical principle; the law of karma, causing the rebirths of the individual, is an ethical principle. The doctrine of karma, one of the most distinctive features of Hinduism, is an essential element of Hindu ethical theory and of the popular faiths of India. The popular sectarian beliefs of Hinduism may differ widely, at some points being poles apart, but all of them, orthodox as well as heterodox (with the exception of the materialists), accept the doctrine of karma as one of their firmest beliefs.

The doctrine of karma is the solution offered by Hinduism to the great riddle of the origin of suffering and the inequalities which exist among men in this world. According to the Hindus, the law of causation operates in the moral world in as invariable and inviolable a manner as it does in the physical world. Every action of an individual inevitably leads to some results, good or bad, and the life of the individual who acts becomes conditioned by the consequences of those acts. We cannot think of any acts which fizzle out without producing results, nor of any results which have no antecedents in the form of acts. This is the inexorable law of karma, the law of actions and their retribution.

This retribution which comes through the inexorable workings of the law of karma is not merely a mechanical causality, however, for it operates in such a way that morally good acts necessarily produce good results and morally bad acts produce bad results. It can be proved empirically that there is perfect justice in the functioning of this law. But if that is the case, we may wonder what happens when all the acts, both good and bad, do not fructify within the span of an individual's life. What becomes of those acts? According to the law of karma, no actions end lamely. It becomes necessary, therefore, to postulate another life for that individual during which he may experience the results of his actions in the preceding life. As a matter of fact, we have to assume a series of lives for the individual in order that all results of actions may be worked out. Thus the theory of rebirths becomes a necessary corollary to the law of karma.

The present life of an individual is conditioned by the consequences of those acts done by him in his previous life which did not produce their results during that lifetime. The moral consequences of his past conduct are conserved and have their effect in the present life. His past acts, for instance, determine the kind of body which he assumes, the family, society, and position in which he may be born, and the acts which he may do in the present life. Every creature is the creation of his own past deeds. Nothing in this world, either physical or moral, happens as the result of mere caprice or blind chance. Everything which exists has come into being by the operation of an immutable law. Thus the otherwise inexplicable vicissitudes of life and the inequalities among human beings are explained by the doctrine of karma.

If, then, whatever we are and do is preordained, is not karma just another name for fate? Is not all freedom lost and man reduced to the unenviable position of a helpless victim of a mechanical law? These and similar questions betray an inadequate understanding of some of the essential features of the doctrine of karma. This doctrine, it should be clearly understood, does not imply the operation in man's life of any extraneous factors or external power, such as fate or destiny. The doctrine of karma teaches that man himself is the architect of his life. What he did in the past life is entirely responsible for what he is in the present life. This is the very opposite of fatalism. It eliminates caprice or chance and discountenances the working of an overriding providence. The causes of an individual's present condition are to be traced back ultimately to the individual himself. The individual is the product of countless preceding births and in this series of rebirths his own actions condition each succeeding birth.

One objection which is likely to be raised against the doctrine of karma is that if each existence is the result of the actions in the previous existence, then how could there be a first birth in the series of rebirths? Such a question is philosophically inadmissible, according to Hindu thought, for the world of existence is beginningless. It is impossible to visualize an individual without antecedents. If the essential self were unaffected by any antecedents, it would not be born at all and thus would not assume individuality.

A second objection is perhaps more pertinent. We may accept the belief that the series of births is beginningless, and that the individual's past actions condition his present life, and that the individual himself is accountable for what he is in his present life—but do not the individual's past deeds now become, in a sense, extraneous forces so far as his present is concerned? The past, even though it is his past, is already determined, and it determines his present, thereby leaving him no freedom to shape it as he would like. He cannot say that he will see that his actions are such that they will lead to a better life next time for the simple reason that his actions in this life are not really his, they are predetermined. Such an objection is met by the Hindu thinkers by postulating a twofold consummation of all actions. First, every action produces its direct results which determine our present body and the conditions directly relating to and consequent upon our birth. Concerning these we have no choice; we must accept them as they are ordained. But our past deeds also produce indirect results in the form of innate tendencies which prompt us to act one way or another. It is necessary to emphasize that these innate tendencies prompt but do not compel us to act in a particular manner, thus affording ample scope for initiative and self-determination on the part of the individual. Therefore, although the individual's birth and initial environment are predetermined, he has before him the gratifying prospect of being able to master his innate tendencies which are the mainsprings of all his actions.

Thus we see that the doctrine of karma includes within itself the possibility of moral progress. In spite of the initial conditioning of our present life, we can employ every moment in it to make ourselves whatever we wish to be. And when it is realized that the present life represents not the whole term allotted to an individual but only a stage in the soul's progress towards its goal, even that partial predetermination does not matter much. Teaching as it does that in the ultimate analysis the individual is himself the architect of his own life, this doctrine of karma does not preclude free will, which is the very basis of ethical conduct, nor does it countenance such a thing as cruel fate or an unjust god. Though apparently a blind mechanical force, karma, it must be remembered, essentially represents the cosmic power of righteousness which forever encourages man on his march toward a higher spiritual goal.

One final difficulty arises concerning the law of karma. How can karma be reconciled with the spiritual goal of liberation, moksha? Do not even good actions produce their results and thus keep the individual involved in life? The Bhagavad Gītā has shown a satisfactory way out of this difficulty. It teaches that man's actions attain their consummation in the form of direct results and innate tendencies only if he performs those actions with a feeling of attachment for their results. If, however, he acts, as he must by the force of the law of karma, but at the same time acts in a spirit of passionless detachment toward the fruits of his actions, he will be leaving the road open for the soul's progress toward ultimate release, moksha.

The God-consciousness of Hinduism

The consideration of the role of man in relation to god is relevant to our discussion of the Hindu concept of man. Just as the philosophical approach to the problem of the role of man gives rise to the dualism between the essential self and the empirical self, so the religious or theistic approach presupposes the dualism between man and god. Philosophically, this dualism between man and god is inadmissible for, as shown above, essentially man is god. The very concepts of man and god cannot be said to possess absolute reality; they belong to the realm of the world of experience. That is why many philosophical systems in India are essentially nontheistic or supertheistic. They are not required to posit the existence of a personal god in order to answer the various cosmological, psychological, metaphysical, and even ethical questions which they have raised in the course of their spiritual quest. This does not, however, mean that Hinduism has nothing to do with god. On the contrary, Hinduism, particularly popular Hinduism, is crowded with gods. Hinduism is certainly god-conscious, indeed very much so.

It redounds to the glory of Hinduism that in it absolute monistic idealism and passionate devotionalism should abide side by side and without any conflict. What is still more creditable is that Hinduism has achieved this marvelous feat in a more or less rational manner through the assumption of the possibility of two points of view in philosophical matters, the absolute point of view and the relative point of view, the one not spurning the other, each possessing reality in its own way, and each independently leading to the final goal. The proverbial catholicity of the Hindu mind is also, in no small measure, responsible for what would appear to a casual observer to be the paradoxes of Hinduism. Indeed, one of the most beautiful of such paradoxes is to be seen in the fact that a staunch monistic idealist like Śaṅkara has composed some of the sweetest and most stirring hymns in praise of personal divinities.

To put it in broad but philosophically not quite precise terms, god stands in the same relation to the Supreme Being as an individual does to the essential self. Thus the relation between god and man is in many ways influenced by the relation between the Supreme Being and the essential self. Theistically, the goal sought by man is either to live in the same world as god, or to be nearest to god, or to assume the same form as god, or, finally, to achieve intimate union with god. It will be seen that, while the first three goals more or less represent the stages leading to the last goal, the last goal is but a reflection of the philosophical goal of the mystic union of the essential self with the Supreme Being. The philosophically accepted identity between the Supreme Being and the essential self is sometimes qualified in theism by suggesting that god and man are identical in essence but different in form. What sparks are in relation to fire, men are in relation to god. A further development of this partial separateness of man from god is that god is described as being not really external to man, but as being the inner controller in man. Theism describes god as the efficient directive cause in man's life.

This theistic approach conceives of god as the creator and moral governor of man and the universe, the dispenser of the law of karma. It is interesting to note, in this connection, that even though he accepts the complete separateness and the awe-inspiring distance between man and god, the Hindu seeks to achieve a direct personal communion with god through a complete surrender of his whole being to god. This is the ideal of a Hindu devotee. Devotion, bhakti, according to the Hindu view, implies dedicating all one's actions to god, rendering service to him, and meditating on him in single-pointed concentration; devotion requires that man rid himself of all consciousness of "I" and "my," and develop an attitude of being the same to all god's beings, whether friend or foe; and, paradoxical as it may seem, devotion requires that the devotee create in himself a peculiar mystic power through surrender, humility, and faith. Prayer, worship, ritual, and religious observances have places in the Hindu religious practice, but the doctrine of true devotion must be regarded as the most potent factor which governs the role of the Hindu in relation to god.

MAN IN RELATION TO THE WORLD

When we turn to the consideration of the role of man in relation to the world in general and his fellowmen in particular it should be remembered that according to the higher philosophical thought of the Hindus the essential self of man is never involved in the doings of this phenomenal world. From the ultimate point of view, therefore, the question of the role of man—the real man—in this world would have no relevance whatsoever. Even with reference to the empirical self the consideration of such a question would have but little intrinsic value, for the highest spiritual goal of a Hindu is to transcend the limitation of his individuality which binds him to this world and thus to realize his identity with the Supreme Being.

Life in this world is accordingly to be looked upon as a bridge over which one has, of necessity, to pass in order to reach one's destination, but on which it would be unwise to build one's house. Man's role in this world thus pertains to a lower stage of experience, and is generally treated as such by Hindu thinkers. The usual charge that in India ethics is regarded as merely a diversion from the serious business of philosophy, a concession, as it were, to the necessity of man's contact with the phenomenal world, is not altogether unjustified. It must be admitted that Indian philosophy transcends the merely ethical level as much as it does the merely intellectual level.

Dharma

This must not be misunderstood to mean that the Hindus have altogether neglected the role of man in this world. Hinduism does offer man expert guidance for a safe and speedy passage over the bridge of life. Its most significant contribution to this guidance is the concept of dharma. Dharma is indeed an elusive term which has meant different things in different contexts and has been translated in many ways. It may mean Vedic ritual, or religion and ethics in general, or caste rules, or civil and criminal law, but the underlying idea is everywhere the same. Dharma seeks to resolve the conflict between the spiritual and the material, the eternal and the temporal. It recognizes that, while striving after the ideal, man cannot afford to overlook the actual. Dharma, therefore, lays down a way of life which aims at securing the material and spiritual sustenance and growth of the individual and society. It is a unique joint product of the speculative and practical wisdom of the Hindus.

When we turn to the consideration of the role of man in society, the question at once arises as to how to reconcile the opposition between the individual good and the social good. The ultimate goal of the individual, liberation, presupposes that the individual will isolate himself from the world by resignation and actionless contemplation, while social stability and progress require that every individual play his part in this world with active interest and a sense of responsibility. There is often a tendency to regard the way of works and the way of renunciation as mutually exclusive and to praise one at the expense of the other. The Hindu view of life, however, is governed by an implicit faith in the efficacy and validity of both these ways and in the possibility of reconciling the claims of action and renunciation. This faith is indeed the very motive force of Hindu dharma.

It is fully realized in Hindu thought that the life of actionless contemplation is as much fraught with dangers as the life of attachment and bare activity. The ideal set forth in the scriptures is to synthesize these two ways of life in such a manner that one does not become an impediment to the other and that both together facilitate the realization of solidarity and progress for society and of liberation for the individual. It is not action as such which entangles man in the turmoil of this world, thereby making his chances of liberation remote, but the passion and attachment which accompany that action. Fruitful actionlessness, therefore, consists in the annihilation of such passion and attachment, of renunciation in action and not of action.

The Four Ends of Man

One of the typical results of this ideal of life is the Hindu doctrine of the four ends of man. Hindu thinkers have recognized that man possesses a complex personality which seeks expression through four channels: his instincts and natural desires, his craving for power and property, his social aims, and his spiritual urge. These are the four ends of man: the aesthetically beautiful expression of his desires and natural instincts (kāma), material prosperity (artha), the ethically sound life (dharma), and the spiritually free life (moksha). The first three ends are related to man's empirical life, while the fourth refers to his spiritual life. A truly integrated personality and an essentially full life are possible by the proper correlation of these four ends of man, by so regulating one's natural desires and one's material welfare by the righteous principles of dharma that these three are subordinated to the ultimate end of liberation. The Hindu theory and practice relating to the organization of man's individual life and his social existence can best be understood in the light of these four ends of man.

The Three Debts

Another factor which helped to shape the Hindu concept of the ideal pattern of life for man is the great ethical concept of the three debts which every individual is expected to repay during his life. First, there is the debt which he owes to the Supreme Being; this debt may be redeemed by dedicating his life to the service of the Supreme Being and by the proper promotion of the scheme of things as laid down by Him. The second debt is to the Seers, those Ṛishis who have been the See-ers of the truths revealed in the Vedas, and this debt can be repaid by preserving and enriching the cultural heritage handed down to him from age to age. Man owes his third debt to his ancestors, and this he repays by procreating good progeny and thereby ensuring the continuity of the human race.

The Four Stages of Life

The individual social life of the Hindu is so organized that the four ends of life may be realized and the three debts may be redeemed. The pattern for the individual life is known as the four stages of life, called *āśramadharma,* and the plan for the organization of society is the caste system, called *varṇadharma.* It must be pointed out, in this connection, that, since this twofold pattern of life pertains to the world of experience, its details vary in accordance with the varying characters and environments of the individuals. And in considering the variety of conditions under which men live, and the inequality of human character, it is necessary that the role of the law of karma in human affairs be constantly kept in mind.

According to Hindu thinkers, the life of an individual should be so organized into the four stages of life that he remains ever mindful of his sacred obligations and is given adequate opportunities to meet them. The four stages of life are: the life of a student, the life of a householder, the life of a hermit or recluse, and the life of an ascetic.

The Student. The life of a student starts after the rite of initiation, which ordinarily comes between the eighth and the twelfth year. He approaches his teacher with the sacred twig in hand as a gesture which symbolizes his willingness to obey and serve. For the next few years, normally twelve, the student has to live at the house of the teacher, devoting himself fully to the achievement of the three main goals of studentship: the acquisition of knowledge, the building of character, and the preparation for shouldering the responsibilities which will fall upon him in family and community life. This compulsory stay of the student in the teacher's house had the advantage of eliminating the possibility of conflict with the parents concerning the method and content of the education, and the constant personal contact between the teacher and student had great influence on the student's mind and character. This latter seems to be suggested by the symbolic rite whereby the teacher magically transferred his splendor to the pupil.

Normally a student was expected to live by begging and was not required to pay any fixed fees to the teacher. Begging implied that it was primarily the responsibility of the community to maintain the student, and it developed the habit of simple and self-reliant living and created a sense of equality among students. Since no fixed fees were charged, the education of an individual was not made dependent on his economic condition. The Hindu system of education was never commercialized and was scrupulously kept free from external control and influence. There was no prescribed course of study or method of teaching; the capacity of the student determined the nature of the instruction. It was constantly emphasized that learning is to be sought for its own sake and not for material gain. At the same time it was fully recognized that man has social responsibilities which his education must qualify him to shoulder adequately.

Although this ancient pattern of education is not followed in all its details in modern times, the ideals which it lays down and the stage of student life which it outlines are still the ideals of Indian education. During this first stage of life, the student is expected to apply himself diligently to his studies, to live a celibate life, and to honor his teachers as he would his parents. At the end of his student days there is a ceremonial bath which signifies his competence to assume the cares and responsibilities of the householder.

The Householder. The second stage of life, that of the householder, is frequently, and with full justification, glorified in Hindu literature as the sacred field for all achievements, and as offering the best scope for the realization of the first three ends of man, dharma, artha, and kāma. The starting point of the life of the householder is, of course, marriage. Hindu marriage is regarded as being essentially a sacrament, a religious duty and not a contract. The real significance of Hindu marriage is that it marks the beginning of a more responsible and purposeful life. The sacrament of marriage, and the various caste restrictions which normally govern every Hindu marriage, imply a perfect biological, psychological, moral, and spiritual union of husband and wife. The relationship between the two is governed by the sentiment of loyalty and devotion to each other until death.

Hindu thinkers have often emphasized that the social purpose of marriage is to create children and assure the continuation of the line, and to provide the basis for the most fundamental of all social institutions of the Hindus, the family. A Hindu family is normally a closely knit group based on the community of blood, held together by the remarkable affections, the bonds of mutual respect, devotion, and love which develop among the various members of a family. This characteristic of the Hindu family is rightly regarded as one of the most beautiful features of the social life of the Hindus.

A Hindu family has common residence, a common kitchen, common property, common worship, and consequently a common experience of the joys and sorrows of life. Such an arrangement has the advantage of encouraging a feeling of identity of interests and promotes in each individual a willingness to subordinate his own interests to those of the family. Sacrifice is the keynote of the harmony of the family. In practice, the family offers adequate protection and support to its weaker members such as widows, the aged and the infirm, and the unemployed. It is a school which prepares the individual for the larger communal life. Therefore, in spite of some of its disadvantages, such as that it encourages idleness and does not promote initiative and enterprise, the institution of the family has been a potent and valuable force in the social history of the Hindus.

The interest and capacities of a householder must not, however, be absorbed only by the ordinary family affairs. He is enjoined to look upon his home as a trust which has come down to him from his forefathers and which it is his duty to carry forward to posterity. The outward, visible symbol of this spiritual continuity is the sacred fire, which is kept burning in the house. Among all the duties of the householder, the greatest emphasis is put on the daily performance of the five great sacrifices. The first, Vedic study, is intended for the preservation by means of constant study of the sacred learning which was acquired during the stage of student life. This sacrifice consists of the daily recitation of the Vedas, actual in some cases, symbolic in others. The second sacrifice is the daily offering of waters to the forefathers, reminding one of one's part as a necessary link in the chain of historical and cultural continuity. The third sacrifice is made to the gods by the devotional offerings which may include a stick of fuel in the sacred fire. It is symbolic of the grateful and humble recognition that whatever man has really belongs to god. The fourth daily sacrifice consists of the offering of food to all beings. The great ethical significance of this sacrifice is that it emphatically deprecates the selfish tendencies in man and requires him to share his possessions with his needy fellow beings. The last daily sacrifice, the offerings to men, is only another name for the proverbial hospitality of the Hindus. These five great sacrifices represent the ideal of a householder's life. The spirit of sacrifice and service, which underlies all actions performed during the life of the householder, is indeed most elevating.

The role of woman in Hinduism is closely associated with the life of the family. In all the religious practices and social duties of a householder he can count on the willing cooperation and help of his wife. A man's religious life is considered to be essentially deficient without his wife's active participation in it; certain ceremonies cannot be performed by a Brāhman unless his wife is with him.

From the ultimate philosophical point of view there is no difference between man and woman, and what has been said about the distinction between the essential self and the empirical self of man, his karma and rebirths and his ultimate goal of liberation, is equally applicable to woman. Limitations are found primarily in religious and social fields, largely concerned with details rather than the spirit of religious practice. Some of the special sacraments do not apply to women and others are performed without the accompaniment of sacred mantras. A woman is not entitled to the rite of initiation at which the man is invested with the sacred thread and initiated into the responsibilities of his life as a student. The most important sacrament for a woman is marriage. After marriage a woman is generally considered to have no existence apart from her husband, especially so far as religious practices are concerned. Her husband is her proper spiritual preceptor, or guru, and in all spiritual matters she is dependent on him. The conscientious performance of household duties constitutes her proper ritual. In popular Hinduism, however, greater freedom is allowed women in the matter of worship and other religious practices.

Contradictory views have been expressed concerning the social status of a Hindu woman; on the one hand she is said to be deserving of worship and respect, and on the other we are told in the Laws of Manu that "Father protects her in childhood, husband in youth, and sons in old age; a woman does not deserve to remain free." That contradiction is more apparent than real, for the emphasis is not on the denial of woman's freedom, but on the duty of her near relatives to protect her at all costs, for woman is indeed too precious a treasure of mankind to be neglected or treated lightly. It must, however, be added that the legal implications of that passage have not been at all favorable to the woman.

If Hindus have anywhere succeeded in making a correct estimate of woman, it is in respect of her role in the family. It is indeed well and truly said that, for the Hindu, a home is not really a home unless a woman presides over it. In her role as the mistress of the house she is responsible for the solidarity and stability of the family. Without a wife, according to the scriptures, the psychological and moral personality of man remains imperfect. She is his constant companion in his religious life, preparing for him the sacred articles used in worship, accompanying him on pilgrimages, present at all ceremonies. Kālidāsa may be said to have epitomized beautifully the ideal of a Hindu wife when he characterized her as mistress of the home, counselor, friend of intimate moments, and beloved pupil in all the fine arts. And finally, in her role as the mother, woman is regarded as divine, respected many times more than the father and the teacher. Indeed there could not have been a higher compliment paid to a mother than the stirring words which are credited to Śaṅkara, "A bad son may be born, but there never is a bad mother."

The Hermit. After having lived a full and fruitful life as a householder, a man naturally begins to think of throwing off the ties of family and society. This is the stage of withdrawal from active life to live as a hermit in the forest. In this third stage a man may be accompanied by his wife, who is also expected to dissociate herself from all family and social ties. In the hermit stage a man no longer plays an active role through service and leadership but without imposing himself on the community he places at its disposal the rich experience which he has gathered during a long and busy life. It is also a time when a man can devote himself much more to the study of the scriptures and to the religious practices which were of necessity curtailed during his more active life as a householder.

The Sannyāsin. A man is not inclined to continue this partial and passive conduct with the affairs of the world for long, and soon he enters the last stage of complete renunciation and solitude, that of the sannyāsin. In this stage his only aim must be the realization of spiritual freedom, of mystic union with the divine. A sannyāsin must drown his consciousness of "I" and "my," must cut himself loose from the limitations of individuality, and thus prepare himself for the realization of the goal for which he has served a well-planned apprenticeship during the first three stages.

The Sacraments. In order to make the broad scheme of the four stages of life more tangible and definite, the Hindu thinkers have correlated it with their scheme of sacraments, religious rites intended to mark the creation in an individual of some inward spiritual grace. Among the various elements which make up these sacraments are the sacred fire, repetition of mantras, the bath, the sipping of water and the sprinkling of holy water, proper orientation to the points of the compass, particular symbols associated with each sacrament, taboos concerning inauspicious times or places or persons, and formulas which ward off evil spirits. The sacraments recognize all the important stages in the life of a man, beginning with the sacrament for conception, and going on through the sacraments for name-giving, tonsure, initiation and investiture with the sacred thread, the ceremonial bath at the end of studentship, marriage, and finally the funeral.

Apart from the popular and more or less superstitious purpose which the sacraments are supposed to serve by removing evil influences and attracting favorable ones, they serve a significant cultural purpose as landmarks in the process of the development of an individual into a full-fledged social being. It should also be noted that by prescribing the same sacraments for all classes of people—the only difference being that among the lower classes the sacraments are not accompanied by the recitation of sacred mantras—the Hindu thinkers have achieved a kind of unity and uniformity of their culture.

Thus it will be seen that a Hindu is provided with an outline of a well-defined plan of life complete with its four fixed stages, each stage having its own complex of duties. The main strength of the pattern of four stages of life lies in the fact that it lays down a graded discipline which is suitable to the physical and mental development of man at different ages, and in accordance with his capacities. This carefully worked out pattern shows indomitable faith in the possibility of progress for the individual and society through service and sacrifice, finally concentrating the attention of the individual on his own spiritual emancipation. True to the main trend of their thought, Hindu thinkers have taken care to emphasize that the four stages of life must not become ends in themselves. To use a classical metaphor, the stages merely constitute a four-runged ladder which an individual must climb in order to reach his ultimate goal.

The Caste System

The caste system of India represents the ethical organization of the social life of the Hindus, just as the four stages of life are the ethical organization of the personal life of the individual. It is much easier to describe caste than to define it. In broad outline, it is the division of society into four major caste groups, each with numerous subcastes within it: the Brāhmans, or the priestly, intellectual caste; the Kshatriyas, the warrior and ruling caste; the Vaiśyas, who are primarily commercial and agricultural; and the Śūdras, who form the laboring caste. In addition, there are the outcastes, the group below the Śūdras. The top three castes are known as the twice-born, those who have passed through the sacrament of initiation which is their second birth.

Although this general pattern of the four major castes continues today, there are actually more than three thousand castes in India forming a complex variety of real castes, subcastes, mixed castes, right-hand castes, left-hand castes, and exterior castes which form the society of the subcontinent. Membership in a caste is determined by birth, confirmed by initiation, and can be lost only by expulsion. The caste normally regulates diet, clothing, the language to be used in relation to other castes, religious practices, social life, marriage, and occupation. Restrictions on food include not merely the kind of food to be eaten, but they cover the persons who prepare it, and the persons with whom it may be eaten. Certain castes have special rights to wear certain clothes and certain ornaments. The kind of language to be used by one caste with reference to another is also sometimes determined by the status of those castes in the hierarchy. The right to perform, or even to observe certain religious ceremonies is determined by caste status, as is the obligation to perform certain rites. Even the normal social intercourse among members of the various castes is governed by set regulations. Members of a caste are forbidden to marry outside that caste, and within the caste the possible marriage combinations are defined. For most castes there are fixed occupations, with no freedom to shift to other types of work. And through the whole caste system there is the gradation which places the Brāhman at the top and the other castes in a descending order of privilege.

Each caste is essentially autonomous, making its own rules and establishing its own customs, and enforcing them through its council. The final basis for enforcement of these rules is expulsion from the caste, a contingency which a Hindu fears perhaps more than anything else in the world. In actual practice it is observed that the lower the castes in the social scale, the more efficient is the organization of its council. In this organization of society the role of the ruler is only to see that his laws are as far as possible compatible with the rules and customs of the castes, and so far as those caste rules are concerned his only responsibility is to see that they are fairly enforced..

In recent times, under modern social conditions, the place of a caste in the social scale is not always fixed. There is always the possibility, and there have actually been instances, of a caste rising in the social scale by means of its own efforts. A caste can, for instance, by changing and modifying its social and religious observances, so improve its way of life that its status in society is more or less automatically raised.

A subcaste sometimes develops within a large caste, through normal social processes, until it derives the character of a caste and is treated for all practical purposes as if it were a caste. Since it originates within a caste, and its status in the caste hierarchy is determined by the caste in which it originates, it is usually called a subcaste. Mixed castes are usually the result of the attempts of Hindu lawmakers to regularize the position of children born of marriages forbidden by dharma and discountenanced by custom. When regularizing such marriages, the lawmakers viewed with greater tolerance the marriage of men of higher castes with women of lower castes than the marriage of women of higher castes with men of lower status. But the children of such marriages belonged neither to the caste of the father nor of the mother; rather they belonged to a new caste, called mixed or intermediate.

The exterior castes, known also as outcastes or depressed castes, originated back in the times when certain groups were barred on purely magic-ritualistic grounds from participating in the communal ritual. Theirs is indeed an anomalous position for they are not altogether disowned by the Hindu society, but they are kept outside the caste system. They are condemned to suffer all legal, social, and religious disabilities to which a low caste Hindu is normally subjected, and at the same time they are denied the few advantages which would have accrued to them had they belonged to the regular caste system. They are casteless in the sense that they are excluded from the caste system, but they are called castes because among themselves they are divided into various smaller groups which observe the usual restrictions concerning marriage and social intercourse. Incidentally it may be added that the ignominious treatment meted out to these casteless people by the caste Hindus has been perhaps one of the most glaring inequities of the caste system.

The most complete and detailed picture of this social pattern with all its ramifications is to be found in the Laws of Manu, written about the second century B.C., which laid down that obedience to caste rules is the very essence of dharma. How did this system come into being? Many theories have been put forth concerning the origin and growth of castes, but no one of them seems to be adequate. Division of society into classes is a common feature all over the world but the caste system in India is peculiar in many respects and not comparable with analogous institutions existing elsewhere. One theory as to the origin of caste is that it is the result of the attempts of the culturally superior Aryan invaders to protect themselves from absorption by the barbarous aborigines. Another theory is that it is an artificial creation of the priesthood, an attempt by the Brāhmans to maintain the purity of the race of Aryan invaders. Another explanation is that the origin is due to occupation, built around the different guilds and the attempts of each professional and trade group to protect its secrets. It is also pointed out that the original four castes were set up on the basis of ritual, so that the various communal ritual duties might be performed by persons who were duly qualified by heredity, by purity preserved through taboos, and by knowledge to perform their special functions connected with ritual.

It is now almost impossible to mark out the various stages in the process of forming the castes as we have them today. Except on the assumption of a multiple origin, the extreme complexity of the modern caste system cannot be explained. Presumably, the pre-Aryan communities had certain distinctive concepts of taboo, pollution, and purification which were expressed in their religious rites. There is also sufficient evidence to assume that their social life was organized on the basis of graded functional guilds protecting the occupations of the members of their society. It may be further presumed, on the basis of Vedic evidence, that the social organization of the invading Aryans was based mainly on certain magic-ritualistic concepts. The impact of this social organization of the Aryans on the pattern of life of the indigenous Indian communities must have helped the growth of castes.

The further consolidation of these castes into a full-fledged system must have been aided by the geographical isolation of the Indian subcontinent, the enforcement of deliberate economic and administrative policies, the clash of cultures, the fusion of races, the shrewd application of the doctrine of karma, and the tendency toward religious and social exploitation. Such, then, was presumably the process of the origin and growth of castes.

Each caste is an independent social unit, guarding its members and customs, opposing other castes, but it is the peculiarity of the Hindu society that it integrates several such independent units into an organic whole. It is so organized that it can accommodate within itself, without difficulty, any new unit that comes into existence. Attempts have been made in the past to lessen the sense of inequality among castes and to rationalize the differences in privileges and prerogatives enjoyed by the members of different castes. It was suggested that the responsibility for the particular caste into which a person was born rested with the person himself since his actions in his preceding life determined his present existence. Caste was thus regarded as determined by the eternal and inexorable law of karma. It must be pointed out in this connection that the doctrine of karma not only justifies the present social status of an individual but it also offers a message of hope and sounds a note of warning. It emphatically lays down that an individual's rise or fall in the social scale in the next life depends entirely on the good or bad deeds which he performs in the present life.

In the Bhagavad Gītā there is an ethical idealization of the caste system which does not emphasize the differences and gradations among the castes, but stresses the important principle of the ethical interdependence involved in this system. Society as an integrated whole can be held together and progress only if its various units properly perform the functions assigned to them. The consideration of whether a function is high or low, to one's liking or not, is of no real importance. The feeling that, by observing your dharma in the position to which you have been born, you are actively promoting the solidarity, stability, and progress of society is in itself a reward greater than any other that can be sought after in this world.

It should be remembered that it is the institution of caste which has enabled the diverse elements of population in India to live together in a more or less organized form. The caste system, by evolving an organic whole out of diverse elements, minimized and in some cases entirely counteracted the serious consequences of the social upheaval which normally follows the invasions and encounters of various races and peoples. What is perhaps more significant is that, while doing so, it saw to it that the individual cultures of those races and peoples were not adversely affected. If, today, Hinduism is truly a federation of cultures, the credit for it must belong, in no small measure, to the caste system.

From the point of view of the individual, the caste to which he belongs affords him social and economic security from the very beginning; for his status, social connections, and occupation are already settled for him by his caste. The caste system not only provides for the various functions of social life but it puts a natural check on unemployment and has evolved a practicable scheme for division of labor. A caste serves as an efficient form of trade union. It is also the agency which has preserved several of the arts and crafts of India.

These are some of the items which can be shown to the credit of the caste system, but in the final accounting the debit side is likely to prove greater. However caste may have originated, there can be hardly any doubt that in the course of its consolidation it turned out to be the very antithesis of the principle of the essential equality of men. By accepting heredity as the only criterion which determines one's caste, the caste system completely blocked the way for individual progress. The doctrine of karma could be but a poor consolation under such circumstances. The security which the caste provides is purchased at a heavy price when men must completely subordinate themselves to it.

The caste system gave rise to still more serious social evils. It denied certain civil and religious rights to a large number of people and led to the oppression and exploitation of one class by another, which has proved a constant source of discontent and unrest. The extreme social segmentation naturally prevented the growth of the sentiment of national unity. Patriotism was often misunderstood as loyalty to one's caste and the interests of the caste rather than the community as a whole became the motive force in social life. True morality was superseded by the demands of caste observances, and sin came to mean nothing more than breach of caste rules.

In the course of history, voices were occasionally raised against the rigid social stratification created by the caste system, but without any tangible results. Neither Buddhism nor Islam can be said to have done much to exterminate or even change the caste system. Theoretically the British could not have had any sympathy for the caste system but as rulers they were too shrewd to interfere directly with any of the social institutions prevailing in India unless they hindered the stabilization of their power in the country. In many ways, the caste system actually proved helpful to their policies.

There are three main attitudes towards caste today. Some persons believe that the caste system is the creation of god, that it is governed by the inexorable law of karma, that it still has its uses, and that therefore it must not be, nay, cannot be supplanted under any circumstances. This view is too reactionary in the context of the conditions at present prevailing in India to deserve serious consideration. There are others who would like to see the present three thousand or more castes grouped together into the four basic social orders of Brāhmans, Kshatriyas, Vaiśyas, and Śūdras and to preserve the caste system in that form. It is easily seen that such a combination of castes is neither possible nor desirable.

The third attitude toward caste today is that of the social reformers who advocate a complete extermination of castes by all possible means. It is now realized that in spite of geographical, climatic, racial, religious, and linguistic diversity, India possesses a fundamental cultural unity. It is rightly pointed out that the gravest evil of the caste system is that it has rendered Indian society undemocratic and a sociological myth. One, therefore, feels inclined strongly to support the plea that an active nationwide campaign be launched against caste, both through governmental and private agencies.

Conditions are changing rapidly in modern India, both in the economic and the social spheres, bringing about many changes in the attitudes towards caste. The present economic pattern is slowly killing the occupational character of castes; new means of transportation and communication are breaking down the barriers against social intercourse; rigid observance of the rules regarding pollution through contact cannot be maintained. The belief in the divine origin of caste and its efficacy in preserving racial purity is now completely discountenanced. And the bhakti movement in religion has done much to unite the various castes in a sort of religious democracy.

The caste control of marriage, however, seems to die hard. Even an educated Hindu who claims freedom in the matter of food, social intercourse, occupation, and travel will observe scrupulously the matrimonial rules of caste. This aspect of caste will probably be the last to go. At any rate, it is most reassuring to find it laid down in the constitution of the Indian Republic, which indeed represents the collective will of the people of India, that "the State shall not discriminate against any citizen on the grounds only of religion, caste, sex, place of birth or any of them" and that "Untouchability is abolished and its practice in any form is forbidden."

The Ethics of Hinduism

The ethical writings of the Hindus have dealt not only with the way of righteous conduct (dharma) in the four ends of life, and the four stages of life, and the four castes, but have also dealt with the righteous conduct which is desirable in many specific circumstances. In spite of this concern for ethical conduct, general Hindu ethics cannot be said to have been reduced to any regular code. In ethics, as in metaphysics, the Hindu places greater emphasis on the inculcation of a proper attitude of mind than on the postulation of elaborate theories. For instance, the theoretical question as to whether the human will is free or determined does not seem to have particularly bothered a Hindu. All that he sought to do was to neutralize his will completely through mystic union with the Supreme Being.

The practical side of Hindu ethics is portrayed in the interesting parable in the Bṛihadāraṇyaka Upanishad (V.2) which outlines the three cardinal virtues. Gods, men, and demons are said once to have gone to their common father, Prajāpati, and requested him to instruct them. To the gods Prajāpati communicated the syllable "da," which they correctly understood to mean *dāmyata,* practice self control. To men Prajāpati communicated the syllable "da," which they understood to mean *datta,* practice charity. To demons, also, Prajāpati communicated the syllable "da," which they took to mean *dayadhvam,* practice compassion. The Upanishad further tells us that all beings are frequently reminded of this triple instruction of

Prajāpati to practice self control, charity, and compassion when they hear the thundering of the clouds which produces the sound "da-da-da."

The Bhagavad Gītā, in the sixteenth chapter especially, lists a large number of other virtues such as fearlessness, purity of mind, sacrifice, uprightness, nonviolence, truth, freedom from anger, renunciation, tranquillity, aversion to fault-finding, freedom from covetousness, gentleness, modesty, and steadiness. It also enjoins the avoidance of certain vices, particularly lust (kāma), anger, and greed, which represent the "triple gate of hell."

The Hindu concept of sin is indeed very comprehensive and includes several views which range all the way from the most primitive belief that sin is a disease to the most elevated one which holds that sin is a denial of the soul or a betrayal of the self. Other views describe sin as a debt, or a breach of caste rules, or a defiance of god, or absence of harmony with the spiritual environment, or lack of spiritual power.

It will thus be seen that the practical ethical theories of the Hindus are much the same as those of most civilized nations. But if the Hindus have anywhere distinguished themselves it is in their special emphasis on truth, nonviolence, sacrifice, and renunciation, which according to them are not merely passive virtues, but represent active social morality.

Very little need be said about truth. Attention may only be drawn to the parable in the fourth book of the Chāndogya Upaṇishad in which the student, when asked about his antecedents by his teacher, gave the forthright reply that he did not know from what family he had come, he knew only his mother's name; she had told him that she did not know from what father he was born since she had led a very wanton life in her youth. On account of this pure and straightforward truth told by the young man he was immediately accepted by the teacher as a worthy pupil for spiritual instruction—which emphasizes that truthfulness is to be recognized as the only criterion of an individual's character and position.

Nonviolence, ahiṁsā, is the cosmic outlook of the Hindus which teaches them to respect all life, indeed all god's creation. Closely allied with it is the teaching that man should see with equality everything in the image of one's own self and do good to all creatures. It is indeed well said that the doctrine of ahiṁsā, with its host of implications, is of far greater importance than the costliest philanthropic institutions.

The concept of sacrifice dominates the entire Hindu view of life. The form and extent of sacrifice may have varied from age to age, but its underlying spirit has endured through the ages—that spirit which is expressed in the words of the Bhagavad Gītā, "fostering each other you shall attain to the supreme good." The Bhagavad Gītā in the same passage in the third book also speaks of the whole universe as a "wheel of sacrifice," which works on the ethical principle of mutual interdependence among its constituents. One must not be remiss in playing his appointed part in that sacrifice lest the proper functioning of the world should be adversely affected.

The concept of renunciation in Hinduism has been very much misunderstood. It is often suggested that renunciation is a negative virtue, that it has no social value. It cannot be denied that the actual practice of renunciation in popular Hinduism has given sufficient ground for such a misunderstanding, but the true ideal in this respect is given in the Bhagavad Gītā, which reconciles renunciation with sacrifice and with the doctrine of the solidarity of society and the maintenance of the universe. A true sannyāsin, one who has renounced the world, practices renunciation in action, not renunciation of action.

The role of man in relation to the world is best described in the Bhagavad Gītā in the third chapter where it is said, "Therefore, without attachment perform always the work that has to be done, for man attains to the highest by doing work without attachment."

Chapter 5

RELIGIOUS PRACTICES OF THE HINDUS

by Sivaprasad Bhattacharyya

Although Hindu thought has been unambiguous in its recognition that spiritual values overshadow all earthly considerations, it has never been half-hearted in acknowledging the importance of worldly obligations. It has always held that whatever a man attempts and achieves in this life is nothing but a form of worship of the Divine in the world around us and in man. It is dharma which sustains and enlivens man, and if it is to be a live force in this world it must be expressed through a healthy network of practices which guide man in his everyday life.

Religion as mere sentiment or reverence cannot survive the test of time as well as religion based on ritualism which requires its devotees to practice the art and craft of religious worship. Religious practices are a means to an end and use the quickest and surest devices which have been discovered through common sense, custom, and intelligence. The religious practices discussed here embody the religious wisdom and experience of the Hindus through the ages.

The Vedic sacrifices of olden times have become pūjā, the worship of deities, in modern Hinduism, absorbing the old practices and adapting them to the needs of the settled life of a householder, aiming at peace and prosperity. The aim of pūjā, the modern form of sacrifice, is to give satisfaction to the Supreme Being as sacrifice did in the past. In this belief, the Lord is a cosmic person and His satisfaction is the final goal of religious experience. The offering of materials and the repetition of the liturgical prayers form the basis of the modern pūjā, retaining the pattern of the ancient sacrifice.

INDIVIDUAL RESPONSIBILITY IN HINDUISM

It is important to remember that for a Hindu worship is an individual experience. Communal and congregational worship are foreign to the fundamental idea of worship and the orthodox Hindu looks upon both as poses and artificial elaborations. The individual worship of the Hindu aims at the realization by the worshiper of the underlying unity with the deity. As the old Seers say, "Thou art veritably, I, O Omnipotent Deity, and I am Thou." Worship is thus a closed function, an individual's own affair. Even at the major festivals when large numbers of people gather, the individual aspect holds good, for the devotee must follow the rules and regulations himself and must participate with the proper mental attitude, which cannot be the responsibility of a proxy.

Diversity of Religious Practices

Any discussion of the religious practices of the Hindus must bear in mind the enormous diversity which is characteristic of the religious life of this subcontinent. We have the regularly performed worship in the home and the worship which is performed at special times and for special purposes. The followers of different cults, Śaivas, Vaishṇavas, Śāktas, and the Smārtas have their chosen deity or a group of deities as the object of their worship. There are variations in worship according to caste, and according to the Vedic and Tāntric forms of ritual; and there are many variations in practices in different parts of the country.

For instance, a Vaishṇava in southern India may accept Vishṇu as Nārāyaṇa as his chosen deity, with Lakshmī as the representation of Śakti for him; while a Vaishṇava in northern India, following Chaitanya, would worship Vishṇu as Kṛishṇa with Rādhā as the Mother Goddess. Another devotee might worship Rāma as his chosen deity, with Hanumān almost rivaling or even overshadowing him in certain circles; Sītā is equated with Śakti in this case. A worshiper of Śiva might have Umā or Durgā as the attendant deity, with Gaṇeśa also an object of devotion. A devotee of Śakti, Power, in her terrifying aspect might worship Kālī or Tārā as his chosen deity. In every case, the chosen deity is the primary object of devotion, but the images would be different and the practices would vary in many details.

Underlying Unity

Throughout all this diversity, however, there runs a common pattern, for in the practices as well as in the speculative thought of Hinduism there is an underlying unity. All twice-born Hindus recognize their five daily obligations: the offering to the gods, the offering to the Seers, the offering to the forefathers, the offering to lower animals, and the offering to humanity. These obligations are embodied in the daily religious practices in the home. Starting before sunrise, the religious Hindu purifies himself and performs his morning worship; at "midday," which may be anywhere from around ten o'clock until noon, he performs his worship before the image, and offers food to animals and to guests; at dusk, he once more worships according to a prescribed ritual, and after that he takes his evening meal.

In addition to the daily practices in the home, there are special religious practices which are common throughout all India. Of the sacraments, at least those of initiation, marriage, and burial would be practiced by all. If the father of the family is dead, the memorial rites for the forefathers, śrāddha, must be performed at regular intervals. Special vows and petitions are frequently observed, according to individual circumstances, and the major festivals of the gods are celebrated with varying practices according to the sectarian loyalties of the individual.

While the temples are dedicated to many different deities,

the daily practices in the temples follow a common pattern. They begin with the auspicious lamp ceremony at the last eighth of the night when the deity is awakened. Then the deity is bathed, and worshiped; at midday, cooked food is offered to the deity, followed by a lamp ceremony, after which the deity rests until late afternoon when there is the anointing and decorating ceremony. In the evening there is an elaborate lamp ceremony after which food is again offered to the deity, followed by the final ceremony at which the deity is retired for the night. In addition to these daily ceremonies, there are elaborate rites, often lasting several days, at the time of the important festivals. It should be born in mind that while the five daily offerings are an obligation for the Hindu, there is no obligation to participate in the ceremonies at the temple. Some very devout Hindus go to the temple rarely, if at all.

Pilgrimages, too, are a part of the religious practices of Hindus of all sects, and from all parts of the country. Long portions of the Purāṇas, and especially the Mahābhārata, are devoted to the description of the holy spots of India, and pilgrimages to such spots are regarded as being desirable for mental solace, the cultivation of piety, for spiritual uplift, and as a means of penance for sins. No Hindu life is complete without a pilgrimage to some of these holy places.

Also common to the religious practices of the Hindu is belief in the efficacy of the meditative disciplines of yoga as developed by the Seers and taught throughout the ages. Although the ordinary householder may not have the time or opportunity to gain great proficiency in the yogic disciplines, even in his daily practices he can follow them to some extent, and if he goes on to the fourth stage of life he will have the opportunity to practice them more fully.

Individuals Who Have Special Responsibilities

Before turning to a consideration of the religious practices followed in the household, in the temple, on pilgrimages, and in the yogic disciplines, a word should be said about the persons especially concerned with religious practices, the priest, guru, paṇḍit, astrologer, sannyāsin, sādhu, swāmī, and yogi. The technical part of temple worship is under the direction of the chief priest who is responsible for it, aided by competent assistants. The assistant priests take charge of the duties of the daily or periodical sprinkling ceremony, the sacred fire, the serving of cooked food, and the more advanced and scholarly among them give religious instruction. The assistant priests in some temples, including those under the Śaṅkara monastic order, are sannyāsins who have failed to attain the peak of renunciation marked out for the order, but are of pure character and of noble antecedents and lead self-controlled lives. The hired priests officiating for pilgrims and those in charge of technical duties tend to become greedy. In social rank they therefore hold an inferior position. The priests employed in temples, including their head, are regarded as having no inherent claim to spiritual enlightenment.

The priest who serves in the home never does the daily work in the temple; he may offer a sacrifice there for a pilgrim if given permission, but otherwise would participate only as a worshiper. These priests who serve in homes are never looked down upon as a class. In worship undertaken for a special purpose and in family performances, they discharge duties for the worshiper and receive fees for their services. Some families have a priest come to the home daily; others employ such a priest only for special events or when, as frequently happens, a family is under defilement through the death of a relative or some similar cause. Under those circumstances, the family deity may be worshiped at the home of the priest, especially if cooked food is to be offered to the deity. In all major ceremonies, both in the home and in the temple, priests come in as the indispensable agents as much because of the complications of the ceremony as the preoccupation of the householder with other duties. Like lawyers intervening for parties in law courts, priests know more about the technicalities, and in such major ceremonies as marriage or a big festival more than one priest would be employed.

The *guru* is the personal teacher, the spiritual preceptor who has himself gained spiritual insight; he is indispensable for spiritual betterment, and is a vital factor in the imparting of Vedic knowledge. Vedic knowledge is a precious treasure handed down from the elder to the younger, from the teacher to the pupil. The Upanishad says that "he who knows has a teacher." In later thought, the guru is the visible embodiment of truth, and is identified with god. Devotion and service to the teacher are cardinal virtues to this day. While the name *guru* stresses the static aspect, the name *āchārya* points to his dynamic phase; as a guru he is great and venerable in his knowledge and realization; while as an āchārya he is one who not only puts into practice his knowledge and himself walks the path, but puts the pupil also in the way and takes him along the path. No learned man attains completeness until he enriches his example and experience with propagation through teaching.

The family astrologer who warns of danger and determines the auspicious times for all new undertakings, and the *paṇḍit,* or learned man, who decides carefully the questions related to possible courses of action and correct conduct, are less important than the priest and the guru, but by no means unworthy.

The *sannyāsin* is a man who has renounced the worldly life and keeps himself away from it as much as possible, following a definite spiritual discipline designed to bring about union with god. He may be a man who has completed the first three stages of life, or a younger man who has adopted the ascetic path of the sannyāsin by choice. Ordinarily, a sannyāsin would be following a specific ascetic discipline laid down by his guru.

The *swāmī* is an initiated member of a religious order, subject to the usual vows of poverty, chastity, and obedience to the order, and following the pattern of religious and social practices of his order. Sometimes the title "swāmī" is restricted to the head of the order, but more commonly it applies to the senior members of the order who have attained spiritual insight.

Sādhu ordinarily means a holy man, not referring to any particular order or spiritual discipline. In common parlance, sannyāsin, swāmī, and sādhu are often used interchangeably without regard for special connotations, generally to denote persons leading—or, at any rate, professing to lead—a life of asceticism.

While anyone who follows a fixed path of yogic disciplines may be called a *yogi,* the name is usually applied to those who are following the path of meditation outlined in the Tāntric disciplines, especially the rules concerning posture, breathing, and mental control. In that sense, a guru, a sannyāsin, and a swāmī might also on occasion be referred to as a yogi.

MATERIALS USED IN WORSHIP

Some knowledge of the materials and techniques for worship is necessary in order to understand the practices which are such an important part of the religious life of the Hindu.

The Shrine and Symbols

In the home, the worship is performed in the pūjā room, either a room set aside for that purpose or a corner of another room, sometimes, though rarely, the kitchen. There on a small shrine will be placed the image of the god, or one of the abstract symbols commonly used. If an image is used in the home, it will usually be only a few inches high, sometimes several feet high in the temple, and usually made of such metal as gold, silver, copper, or an alloy of eight metals. Some images are made of stone, others of wood, and often an image is made of clay for ceremonial worship on an important occasion. Sometimes in a home or small shrine, a picture is used as the object of worship.

The abstract symbols used as the objects of worship include the *sālagrāma* for Vishṇu, a fossilized ammonite stone taken from the Gaṇḍakī River; the *bāṇaliṅga* for Śiva, a stone found in the Narmadā River; a stone found in the river Sone for Gaṇeśa; a round marble stone for Sūrya, the Sun. Some Vaishṇavas worship a *paṭṭa,* a stone or metallic plaque with figures of the Lord and his incarnations engraved on it. The Śiva *liṅga* is also included among the abstract symbols of the deity; it is shaped like a post with a rounded top, made of clay or stone, varying from a few inches to several feet in height. Worship may also be offered to books, as at the time of the festival devoted to Sarasvatī, the goddess of learning.

Those who have been initiated according to the Tāntric rites may worship a *yantra,* a mystic symbol often formed of a square with four openings, or doors, on its sides, enclosing a circle with eight spokes and a small circle at the center. The designs used in the yantras vary with different deities; another well-known mystic diagram is the *Śrī Yantra,* made up of complicated equilateral triangles, squares, and circles, representing the gates to the deities and their locations. These diagrams are inscribed on footstools, on birch leaves for Rāma, or on copper alloy plates; the designs may be cut into the metal, or made with saffron or turmeric paste or charcoal ashes of the lotus for Śakti; for Vishṇu, the designs may be made of sandal paste, and for Śiva holy gray ashes are used. Orthodox Śākta opinion does not allow a yantra near a sālagrāma or an image, nor does a strict Vaishṇava allow the touching of a yantra, especially in worship at night.

The *maṇḍala* is simpler than a yantra. It is a geometric design made on the ground with powders of five different colors, divided into circular, hexagonal, and square compartments. Near the maṇḍalas are the vessels to be consecrated for worship and sometimes there are cavities in the directions of the four quarters of the compass. Maṇḍalas can be for any deity, the god having been invoked in them in the midst of a closed room. Sometimes a maṇḍala is used in place of a sālagrāma, but only by those who have been initiated. Those who worship through a maṇḍala or a yantra hold that the symbol and the deity are as the body and the self, which indicates that this type of worship is only for the advanced worshiper.

Materials Used for Purification and Offering

A variety of material is used in the worship of the deity. Of great efficacy in worship is the use of fire, the purifier, the representation of the sun here on earth; it is through fire that the subtle body is released from the physical body at death. Earth as the sustainer of creatures in the form of clay, generally from sacred rivers, is used in the consecration of images, in the ceremonies for the forefathers, and in making a clay liṅga and idols. Bells and gongs are used to attract the attention of the gods and powers above who bear witness to the worship of the devotee.

Water is necessary for the ceremonial bath, for sipping and sprinkling in all ceremonies, for bathing the images, and as an offering in many ceremonies, especially those for deceased ancestors. Water must be touched before all forms of worship as a symbolic bath, and it is obligatory to sip water at every stage of worship as a sign of earnestness of intent. The importance of water is illustrated by a story narrated in the early literature of how three hundred millions of valiant, terrifying demons of evil intent, though of Lilliputian size, obstructed the sun's chariot and tried to gobble him up. The gods and sages simultaneously offered full water offerings, sanctified with the repetition of mantras, which acted like a thunderbolt on the demons and burned them up. The twice-born are enjoined to follow their example three times every day: early in the morning, before taking their main meal, and at dusk.

Foods of many kinds are used as offerings, sometimes grains and seeds such as barley, sesame, and rice, and sometimes cooked foods including an unending variety of sweets, vegetables, and rice. Clarified butter is often used to anoint the images and for purification of materials used in worship. Kuśa grass, which may be collected beforehand, is used as a seat for meditation, as the mat on which offerings are placed, and in the sacred fire; it is known as the purifier. Dūrvā grass, which should not be gathered and stored, is an ingredient of the offerings to the gods and the forefathers, and must be treated in different ways for the ceremonies for the forefathers and for the worship of Śiva. The leaves and branches of certain sacred trees are essential for many offerings and ceremonies. Sandalwood incense is regularly used in worship. Flowers and colored powders are used to decorate the images and in some of the larger temples there are elaborate jeweled costumes in which the deity is dressed for important festival occasions.

TIMES FOR RELIGIOUS OBSERVANCES

Time is an essential element in religious observances—as one ritualist puts it, it is better to have one offering at the proper time than to have many at unseasonable moments. The time for the morning worship is at sunrise, from twenty-four minutes before to twenty-four minutes after. A trangression of that time limitation requires expiation through the saying of ten Gāyatrīs. The midday worship is to be done in the morning before noon, and the evening worship must be done twenty-four minutes before or after sunset. An auspicious ceremony for one's forefathers must be done in the morning before noon. Similar injunctions set the proper time on holy days for the beginning and ending of fasts, taking ceremonial baths, and giving gifts. Auspicious times for fulfilling vows, going on pilgrimages, and for all ceremonies must be observed, taking into account the moment, the lunar mansion, the conjunction of the planets, the hour of the day, the day of the month, whether it is the bright or dark fortnight, the season, and the half year. The demands of the time schedule for worship may appear to be an unwarranted limitation on a man's freedom, but it is not a great worry to the devout Hindu who simply tries his level best to arrive at a golden mean between his obligations to the world and to his Creator.

PHYSICAL ACTS IN WORSHIP

Worship requires physical, verbal, and mental effort. The physical effort is concerned with the proper condition, posture, and use of the body; and with the proper arrangement and use of the materials involved in worship.

Bathing

The bath as an act of purification is a necessary preliminary to every religious performance. There are seven acknowledged varieties of bath, including what to the uninitiated may appear to be paradoxical, the fire bath with sacred ashes, and the air bath with the dust raised in the air from the hoofs of cows. There are times when baths are especially auspicious, such as at the time of an eclipse, or at the time of favorable conjunctions of the planets when special merit attaches to bathing. There are also particular lunar days for individual rivers and holy spots, as for instance at the time of the Daśarā festival when a dip in the Ganges is believed to cure a man of his burden of the ten sins of body, mind, and speech. At such times the river is worshiped in all solemnity, generally on the river bank.

Eating and Fasting

The food eaten is an important factor in the preparation of the body for the physical effort of worship; it must not be of the kind which excites the passions or hinders concentration, and it must not be taken before the morning or the midday worship, and in the evening it is taken after worship. Fasting for a long period is not encouraged, but fasting for a day is encouraged on the eleventh day of the month and required in certain months; sometimes it involves the regulation of the food eaten for longer periods of time. Fasting is also undertaken at times in the fulfilment of vows, and the preparation for special ceremonies. Sometimes a devout Śaiva fasts and worships on the fourteenth day of every month—for as long as fourteen years if he has a vow.

Clothing and Symbols on the Body

While worshiping and performing special rites, the man wears no upper garment, no sewed cotton garments, and no shoes. The sacred thread is worn over the left shoulder, going diagonally across the body to the right of the waist, but it is worn as a garland around the neck when making the water offering to saints, and worn over the right shoulder while performing the ceremonial rites for the forefathers. The devout Hindu also wears on his head the little lock of hair, the *śikhā,* sometimes knotted, sometimes merely a tuft of hair slightly longer than the rest, which the Tāntric devotee regards as the orifice of the spirit, the point at which the spirit entered at initiation (before initiation one is as good as dead) and leaves at death. The śikhā is the repository of spirit because all spiritual energy lies there. An old Vedic text runs, "Void is he if he is not covered and is cleanshaved; for him the śikhā is the cover (protection)." The śikhā is regarded as the symbol of a Hindu's resolve to face life unmoved.

At the time of worship, material must be available for putting the marks, called *tilaka* marks, on various parts of the body, particularly on the forehead. These tilaka marks, which are more common in southern India, are made in various ways, according to the cult of the worshiper, with sacred clay, ashes, sandal-paste, or simply water. Horizontal marks are Smārta or Śaiva; vertical marks are Vaishṇava.

Postures

In the matter of seats and postures, the Hindu ritualist is no less exacting. The approved seat is on purified ground which is covered with sacred kuśa grass, or a blanket of silk, or antelope skin, or tiger skin. This he cannot leave except on ritualistic necessity, which rarely occurs. The postures, which vary according to the adjustment of the legs, are known as the cross-legged position with eyes fixed on the tip of the nose, the appropriately happy posture, the posture of the tortoise, and the manly seat. The worshiper generally faces east or north, depending upon the deity being worshiped, but when making an offering to the forefathers he always faces south. When going around an image or sacred object, it must always be on the devotee's right.

The use of the hands is carefully regulated in worship. Only the right hand is used for touching the materials involved in worship, except in the case of the water offering, when the hands are joined in a designated way. There is a special sign language of the hands in which the different positions of the fingers are carefully regulated, each position known as a *mudrā* with a special name indicating its meaning. Some mudrās represent such animals as the fish, cow, or tortoise; others indicate the deity worshiped, such the conch shell, wheel, or lotus for Vishṇu; the monkey and bow and arrow for Rāma; the liṅga and trident for Śiva; licking incessantly, or beckoning, for Kālī. These mudrās, regularly used in worship and meditation, are the expression and support of the spiritual intent.

Breath control is an important part of the preparation for worship since, like correct posture, it helps to control the body and keep it from distracting the mind during meditation.

An important part of the act of worship is the placing of the deity in one's body, called *nyāsa,* by symbolically touching the forehead, the upper arms, the chest, and the thighs. Nyāsa may be done only once in a simple rite, or done many times in elaborate ceremonials. The sixfold touching of the body makes the touch of the Divine possible, for, to use the language of the poet Tagore, we need not merely His speech, but His touch in every limb.

Dancing

In former times, female dancers occupied an important position in temple worship and at festivals, but they are out of vogue now because of the temptations to immoral life which they held out. It is now becoming increasingly difficult to find such women who have dedicated themselves to the service of the deity and have adopted the profession of temple dancers.

Care of the Images

The personal care of the image is the one great concern of the worshiper, that which adds grace and grandeur to life. This includes the worry as to the proper maintenance and adjustment of the shrine. The arrangement of the materials used in the pūjā ceremony is governed by hard and fast rules; for instance, noncooked food and lamps are always placed on the image's left and cooked food on the image's right. Beautiful and graceful clothing should be provided for the image during the cold season, and in the hot season in the afternoon the image is immersed in showers of water and then offered seasonal fruits as refreshment. It is no mere poet's effusion in the Bhāgavata Purāṇa when it tells the classic story of the devout king Ambarīsha who led a god-centered life, employing his hands in cleansing the temple, his eyes in gazing at the Lord and His shrine, and his two nostrils in inhaling the fragrance of His lotus feet. Such is the devotion of the devout Hindu in caring for the shrine and image of the Lord.

Gifts

Gifts also play a prominent part in the religion of a devout Hindu as a means of expiating sins and acquiring merit and mental peace. They are the specific dharma assigned for the present aeon, and take the form of money, gold, land, food, and cows. The merit in giving a gift is heightened by considerations of time, place, the recipient, and the attitude of the donor, as well as the nature of the gift. At the time of an eclipse, for instance, it is especially auspicious to give gifts to beggars; certain rites are made more auspicious by giving gifts to Brāhmans; visits to certain important shrines and holy bathing places should also include the giving of gifts.

Consistent with the all-embracing character of religion, religious practices are made to include works of public utility such as the planting of trees on the roadside for wayfarers, the digging of wells and tanks, the erection of landing places on river banks for bathing, the building of shrines and temples and establishments for monks and for pilgrims, and the maintenance of asylums for the diseased. The erection and support of temples is as much a part of religion as is sacrifice, and is a necessary supplement to individual worship in the thought of the Hindus.

THE ROLE OF SOUND IN WORSHIP

Verbal effort in worship is more exacting than physical effort, especially from the point of view of ritualism. It is accomplished by the repetition of mantras.

THE MANTRA

A *mantra* is a mystic religious text which has been revealed to men by a Seer; it has the property of saving the soul of one who cherishes it. A mantra may be one syllable, as in the case of the mantra OM, or it is more likely to be a verse from the Vedic scriptures running to sixty or more syllables; in the Tāntric forms it may be a hundred and ten syllables, and sometimes even longer. It may be in prose or in poetry.

The effective power of correctly articulated sounds is an accepted belief in Hindu thought—they can create the world and sustain it. The sound itself is the basis for the efficacy of the mantra. The world was created by the utterance of the proper sounds, and it is maintained by the repetition of the proper sounds, just as the sun is kept in its proper position only because people worship it regularly with the proper mantras. The mantra has the same kind of creative power which was present at the creation of the universe. The power of the mantra is shown in the case of supernatural powers and miracles, for a mantra properly repeated by one who has been initiated into its mystic meaning and power helps him to get what is in his thoughts. In religious instruction the guru teaches a disciple a mantra and its inner, mystical meaning. To be efficacious, the mantra must be repeated by a person who believes in it and understands it; only then can worldly and spiritual ends be attained by the repetition of a mantra. To repeat a mantra incorrectly is a sin.

Not any and every sound has this mystic efficacy. Supermen, men who are all truth and have lived lives of perfect asceticism, can conceive and devise mantras. Lesser men have composed prayers and hymns which are used in worship but are regarded as of lesser value. Mantras are not created by men; they are recorded by those Seers capable of recognizing them.

Mantras form the vehicle of pūjā and are almost exclusively in Sanskrit, the speech of the gods. This has been the case all over the land except in some parts of southern and northwestern India where Tamil and Hindi, sometimes mixed with Sanskrit, have come to be used among certain groups under pressure of circumstances. The mantras repeated at the three daily services in the home generally come from the Vedic scriptures; Vedic mantras may be used only by twice-born men; women and Śūdras must use Purāṇic or Tāntric mantras. In the special pūjās, a number of mantras are in later Sanskrit, taken from or based on the Purāṇas. The Tantras have fundamental mystic prayers based on the Vedic mantras and have a host of monosyllabic essential, or crucial, mantras similar to the Vedic OM. In Tāntric worship there are mantras of six and twelve syllables, and specific syllabic mantras for specific tutelary deities, such as rām, kshaum, klīm, called seeds, and regarded as strictly secret.

Each individual syllable in the mantra should be pronounced neither slowly nor rapidly; it should be distinct, as they say, like the pearls falling off a broken pearl necklace. The process gains in effectiveness as it is more and more silently done, and the greatest efficacy attaches to meditation in which there is no muttering at all, where there is only silent meditation over the fundamental unity: I am He, He is I. From the conceptual standpoint, it is the realization of god in man, the ascent of the spirit toward the deity by means of the mantra. The division of mantras into male, female, and neuter, and into dormant and waking mantras, indicates their effectiveness in different operations as recognized by convention which has been shaped by the experiences of advanced worshipers.

The mantra OM and the Gāyatrī mantra have already been cited. Other representative mantras are given here:

"O waters, you are the veritable source of delight; as such do infuse strength into us to endow us with vision, at once great and gratifying. That favor of yours exceedingly beneficial, apportion it among us as do well-wishing mothers."

"That eye [the Sun] placed by the Lord and beneficial to the gods, which rises up blazing in the east—may we be seeing it for a hundred autumns, may we be hearing it for a hundred autumns, may we be discoursing on it for a hundred autumns, may we be enjoying it for a hundred autumns."

"May our donors prosper, let the Vedas and our children flourish. Let not our faith flicker. May we have much to offer as gifts. May our food multiply and may we be favored with guests. Let people come to beg of us but may we never be begging from another."[1]

"My obeisance to Śiva, the gentle, the one Cause of the three causes. To Thee I surrender myself. You are my resort, O Great and Lordly One."

"My salutation to Kṛishṇa, Govinda, the Lord who is related to the great Brahman, ever vigilant to the welfare of cows and Brāhmans, to him who guarantees welfare to the world."

"I bow to the forefathers, who are in heaven, the embodied partakers of the food offered in śrāddha in the context of the desire after fruit, competent to grant all desires. It is they who grant deliverance to them that are free from desires."

JAPA

The repetition, over and over again, of a mantra or one of the names of god is called *japa*. It serves the obvious purpose of centering the attention of the mind on a divine object, and also, when the mantra is properly understood and pronounced, creates the effect which the mantra is designed to produce. Repetition of the Gāyatrī ten, eighteen, twenty-eight, one hundred and eight, or one thousand times is an expiation for different sins. The repetition of the names of a deity eight, twelve, thirty-two, a hundred, a hundred and eight, or a thousand times, depending upon the requirements of the occasion, is held to be an armor of protection. Devout Hindus assign to particular names of a deity particular properties. For instance, Vishṇu is remembered as Vishṇu when one takes a medicine; he is remembered as Janāradana when taking food, and as Padmanābha when retiring at night. At all times of the day, at the beginning of every undertaking, the devout Hindu has one of the names of the Lord on his lips.

Prayer beads are used when a mantra or a name of a deity is

[1] This mantra is repeated during the ceremonial rites for the deceased forefathers.

to be repeated many times. The prayer beads are usually made of different woods for the different major deities, and additional beads or small earthen balls are used when there will be a large number of japas, running into the hundreds or thousands. The correct method for touching the beads while counting the japas is specifically outlined for the devotee.

In addition to the names of the Lord and mantras, the devout Hindu repeats each day prayers which are taken from the Vedic scriptures or from later compositions in the Purāṇas and the Tantras or even prayers written more recently, prayers which are evidences of the sincerity of "the heart in pilgrimage." The commonly used prayers include prayers to the nine planets, to the Sun, prayers based on the eight names of Vishṇu and Śiva, the prayer for Sarasvatī, and prayers to the chosen deity if it happens to be different from Vishṇu or Śiva.

Music

Music is an essential part of many public ceremonies, and plays a prominent role in popular religious practices as a means of retelling the Purāṇic and epic stories and as an expression of devotion among the bhaktas. Music is a necessary feature of all marriages, initiations, and other religious ceremonies. In order that the atmosphere may be purified by the auspicious sound of wind instruments and drums, a small orchestra is installed before the entrance of the house or temple where the ceremony is to be held and plays almost continuously. Such orchestras usually go before the processions of the deities when carried through the streets on festival occasions. Certain traditional musical themes, called *rāgas,* are recognized as creating a mood for meditation when played properly on stringed instruments.

The devout Hindu likes to gather with others, either in the home or temple or some public place, to hear competent musicians sing the hymns of devotion, many of which have come down from ancient and medieval times. Sometimes the hymns are sung by a soloist; sometimes a group of singers joins in the singing. One well-known form is the bhajana, a song of devotional love, based on traditional themes, and sung to the accompaniment of drums and stringed instruments. Another type of musical expression of devotion is the kīrtana, found chiefly in Bengal. It consists of the singing of a religious poem by a soloist, each verse being repeated by a chorus, with the singing occasionally giving place to recitation, dancing, and instrumental interludes. Kīrtanas often last several hours and usually create in the participants a state of religious exaltation.

PURITY IN WORSHIP

The place of worship and the worshiper must be scrupulously pure. In order to make sure that the heart and the shrine are fit to be the sanctuary of the Lord, the ritualists have insisted on five items of purity: purity of the body, purity of the image, purity of the things offered, purity or accuracy of the mantras, purity of the mind.

Purity of the body is insured by bathing, by sipping, and by cleaning the fingers and fingertips through the touch of a flower. It is negated by defilement both through birth and death of blood relatives. Those who follow strictly the orthodox regulations are not allowed to shave themselves. Sexual continence is invariably a prerequisite of the performance of religious rites.

Purity of the image is assured by proper installation; if there is a defilement, purity is regained by pouring over the image the five bovine purifiers—milk, curds, clarified butter, cow urine, and cow dung—with appropriate mantras. The image must of course be made of proper materials, that is, of stone, metal, or wood. Images which are worn out, torn, burned, desecrated, or dilapidated are restored through elaborate forms of ceremonial repair and reinstallation.

Purity of the things offered requires that certain things must be procured by the conscientious worshiper himself: the grass, the flowers, the river water, and the fuel for the fire. If not gathered by the worshiper himself, he must be sure that they have been properly gathered and prepared. The flowers must be freshly plucked, except in the case of the lotus, and they must not have fallen to the ground. Similar conventions hold good in the case of the tulasī leaf which is essential in the worship of Vishṇu, while the restrictions in the case of the vilva leaf are not so stringent.

Purity of the mantras requires that the proper mantra be repeated, that it be pronounced correctly, and that it be done with the proper mental attitude of understanding and belief.

Purity of the mind is related primarily to internal worship and is attained through yogic disciplines. In worship it is guaranteed by the rite called "The Obstruction of Obstacles," which is performed by waving the hand around the head while reciting non-Vedic mantras, thus assuring that all superhuman agencies obstructing concentration are driven out.

MENTAL ACTS IN WORSHIP

Physical and verbal effort in worship are completed by mental effort which takes the form of Vedic study and yogic practices.

Study of the Scriptures

The study of the scriptures, especially in the case of non-Vedic readings, is a part of the act of worship which is not just a scriptural obligation, but is an obligation sanctioned by society. The most frequently read sections of the scriptures are the Vedic Saṁhitās, extracts from the Upanishads, the Harivaṁśa which comes at the end of the Mahābhārata, the Rāmāyaṇa, the Bhāgavata Purāṇa, the Bhagavad Gītā, the One Thousand Names of the Mother, the One Thousand Names of Vishṇu, the Prayers of Śiva, the mystic prayer to the Sun God in the bigger Purāṇic form, and the prayer to the Divine

Mother. These and other similar sacred writings are often read at scheduled times throughout the year. For instance, the prayer to the Mother is read in full on the eighth, ninth, and fourteenth days of both fortnights of the lunar month by a devout Hindu; frequently, the Bhagavad Gītā is read in full on the eleventh and twelfth days of the month. The reading from the scriptures and the recitation of hymns and prayers gratify the Lord whose image form represents his worldly personality, a treasured property to be attentively served.

Yogic Practices

Mental effort as used in worship before the image, and in prolonged meditation exercises at other times, has been outlined in the Bhagavad Gītā and systematized in the writings on yoga by Patañjali. The practice of yoga is outlined under eight heads: the abstentions, obligations, postures, breath control, abstraction, concentration, meditation, and absorption. The abstentions are from violence, lying, theft, satisfaction of the senses, and acceptance of gifts. The obligations are to cleanliness, contentment, ascetic practices, study of the scriptures, and contemplation of the Lord.

The postures are worked out in detail, designed to control the body and to make it possible to remain motionless in worship and meditation for long periods of time without bodily distractions. Breath control, *prāṇāyāma,* which must be learned from a guru, calms and controls the body and contributes to the attainment of supersensuous states. Abstraction, concentration, and meditation are the means of mental effort by which the worshiper fixes the senses and mind on the one Reality; they are the intense mental effort of worship for which the devotee must be prepared by long and careful instruction from a guru. Before the worshiper is successful in this endeavor to become one with the Spirit, certain visions like that of mist, nebulous smoke, a lightning flash, and a sort of moonlight radiance are experienced. By means of control established through yogic disciplines, he makes himself secure from the disabilities of old age, disease, and even death, as well as the disabilities bequeathed to him from his previous birth. His body is rejuvenated, and, charged with the fire of yoga, he becomes proof against all temptations.

Vows

Vows are also an important part of the religious practices of the Hindus, though they are forms of ascetic rigor and are less prevalent. At present they are observed more among the womenfolk than among men. For instance, a woman might pray for some blessing, such as the health of her child, and in return take a vow that for six successive years she will fast on the sixth day of the bright fortnight every month, the fast becoming more rigorous every year until it culminates in total abstinence from food on that day during the sixth year. Many such vows are observed regularly throughout the year, or made in times of crisis.

RELIGIOUS PRACTICES IN THE HOME

Morning

The daily religious practices in the home begin before dawn, in the last eighth of the night. The devout Hindu rises from his bed, repeats the name of the Lord, offers obeisance in his mind to his guru, and recites the morning remembrance prayer in which he resolves to do the day's work under the guidance of the Lord: "I am the Lord in no wise different from Him, the Brahman, suffering from no disabilities such as affliction and anguish. I am existence-knowledge-bliss, ever free. O Lord of the world, all intelligence, the paramount deity, the spouse of Lakshmī, O Vishṇu, waking in the early morning I shall comply with the responsibilities of my mundane existence. I am cognizant of dharma, though I have no inclination toward it—I know its reverse but I am not averse thereto. O Lord, Hṛishīkeśa, dominating my sensuous entity, with Thee in my heart's cavity, as I am commissioned, so shall I act."

He then answers nature's call, observes strictly the rules of personal cleanliness, takes his morning bath, and binds the tuft of hair, śikhā, as he recites the Gāyatrī mantra. The morning worship is then performed, either on the river bank or in the pūjā room. He sits, facing the east, and sips water, purifying himself with a sprinkling of water, sprinkles water around where he is sitting, practices breath control, and then invokes the deity by nyāsa, the touching of the limbs. He repeats prayers for condoning lapses, meditates on the Sun, and facing the sun repeats the Gāyatrī a fixed number of times (ten, eighteen, twenty-eight, one hundred and eight, one thousand, or whatever is his custom). He then dismisses the deity with a short water offering, followed by the repetition of the first verses of the first three Saṁhitā Vedas. Then he offers water again, and finishes with obeisance. If he is fatherless, he makes an offering of water, sometimes with sesame seeds added, to the forefathers.

Midday

The second or midday prayers may be done any time after sunrise and must be done before taking food. The ceremony should be preceded by a visit to the guru if possible, and a look at an auspicious person such as a swāmī. This worship is performed in the pūjā room before the shrine. The deity is anointed to the accompaniment of the appropriate mantras; then the worshiper meditates on the deity. The offerings to the Lord are then made, including flowers, scent, incense, light, and food, both cooked and uncooked. Chips of wood are then offered to fire, with appropriate mantras. That is followed by offerings to groups of deities who are thought of as the same as the multiple-formed Lord. Food is offered to animals, and to guests, and the pūjā is ended.

The best time for reading the scriptures is after the pūjā. The offering of food to animals may be done by giving a few mouthfuls to cows, which are considered to be the mothers of the three worlds. The giving of food to the guest is done in some form or other, especially where there is an installed family deity. The satisfaction resulting from feeding a Brāhman and a guest is cherished in Hindu homes and is frequently mentioned in literature, ancient and medieval. No meal of any form can be taken in the household before the sālagrāma or family deity is offered food—an obligation on the family which at least one member, though not necessarily the same person every day, must perform.

During the day, mantras to secure the favor of the Lord are recited every now and then, and the various names of the Lord are frequently on the lips of the devout.

Evening

A similar, but shorter procedure is followed in the evening. The worshiper sips water, cleanses himself with water, sprinkles water around him as he sits facing the west or northwest, and practices breath control. He recites, then, the prayer for condoning lapses, and meditates on the Lord. After placing the deity on the six limbs, the Gāyatrī is repeated again, as in the morning; then he performs the act of sending away the deity. That is followed by a short water offering, a short recital of the three verses from the Vedas, an offering of water to the Sun, and a farewell mantra. In the pūjā room, the final worship of the deity is performed by waving lights, water, flowers, tulasī leaves, and similar symbols before the sālagrāma or deity and offering food. The sālagrāma or image is then retired for the night. After that ceremony, the evening meal may be taken, the day's duties are over, and one is allowed to retire after entrusting himself to the care of the Lord who is remembered at that time as Padmanābha, the Lord with Brahmā born of his navel of lotus.

The Five Daily Obligations

Thus does the orthodox Hindu meet his five daily obligations. The offering to the gods is accomplished by placing bits of wood sprinkled with clarified butter in the sacred fire, or by substituting other offerings in the pūjā provided they have been sprinkled with clarified butter. The offerings to the Seers are accomplished by the reading from the Vedas, or by the repetition of the first verses of the three Vedas. The offering to the forefathers is accomplished through the water offering. The offering to lower animals is generally done after midday; the offering to guests has come to include the giving of alms to the poor, and is done regularly by the devout.

The steps in daily worship have a definite order which varies according to the Vedic branch followed by the worshiper. The morning worship is and has been interpreted as sun worship pure and simple. The five primordial elements, earth, water, fire, wind, and ether constitute the five basic elements in worship; the worshiper is earth, the deity is ether, japa is wind, the fire offering is fire, and the water offering is water.

This program of daily practices would appear to be an elaborate one, but there have been in use short cuts practiced by a considerable section of the people. There are persons, not many, who perform their worship by the simple muttering of the Gāyatrī, generally one hundred and eight times. There is a well-known story of a Brāhman whose daily practices consisted only of the repetition of the Gāyatrī, and who had lapses of all kinds in his conduct. For several successive days while he was at the river at irregular times to take his bath he was disturbed by a washerwoman who came every day just when he did and washed her clothes nearby, scattering water all over his body. As this entails uncleanness, the Brāhman protested resentfully. One day, being irritated beyond endurance, the Brāhman took her to task and asked her the reason for her vexatious interference, and she disclosed herself as the Goddess of Gāyatrī, ever attending on him and cleansing him of all his sins of omission and commission because of his regularity in repeating the Gāyatrī.

Modern life has brought in its train a host of complications which make pressing demands on time; moreover, times are out of joint. Economic distress has hit many and the regular daily worship of the family image is being curtailed. Again, it is held that in the case of an undivided family, worship is not required of each member, one worship of the family deity or images being sufficient. One redeeming feature in the matter of daily practices has been the underlying emphasis on the satisfaction of the Lord, free from any hankering after rewards. The Lord is Lord of all and for all, beneficial, and one who is easily pleased.

Rites for the Forefathers

The religious observances in the home include, in addition to the daily worship, the ceremonial rites for the forefathers, and the sacraments. The ceremonial rite for the deceased ancestors, known as śrāddha, is performed by all Hindus except advanced sannyāsins and women. It consists of an offering to the deceased father, grandfather, and great-grandfather, and to the deceased mother, grandmother, and great-grandmother. It is offered only after the father or mother is dead. In its simplest form, it is a water offering; in its longer form it consists of offerings of seats to the fathers, and of cloth, of cooked rice balls covered with sesame and honey, and of cereals and seasonal fruits; prayers are offered for their welfare, terminating with water offerings to those who were burned with fire and those who were not, to friends and to nonfriends, of this life or of other lives.

It is a social and a religious responsibility to perform the rites for one's forefathers. The sins of omission and commission of the parents are visited on their children, and it is believed that the proper performance of the household rites, including the śrāddha, is insurance against them. For one year after death the father is moving in the air, not yet admitted to the class of the forefathers, so during that year there is a special śrāddha to be performed once a month. At the end of the first year there is a ceremony which makes the deceased father a full-fledged forefather, called a *pitṛi,* admitting him to the assembly of the forefathers. Special merit is attached to the performance of the śrāddha at Gayā, Allahabad, and Kurukshetra. Śrāddhas on special occasions such as eclipses and visits to a pilgrimage center, and those done with raw rice and new barley, are observed as a matter of routine by all devout Hindus. The annual śrāddhas to one's parents and grandparents are obligatory and are observed on the death anniversary, calculated according to the lunar calendar.

One who has not perpetuated himself by having children is considered to be cursed because he will be deprived after death of the śrāddha offerings. Stories are told of confirmed celibates who had to enter the householder's life because they were troubled at the thought of having no one to offer śrāddha to them and to their ancestors. For instance, the sage Chyavana could not refute the arguments of his forefathers who appeared to him in dreams and asked him repeatedly to marry and beget children so that the śrāddha ceremonies might be perpetuated, and he acceded in extreme old age. So also, the sage Jaratkāru late in life married Manasā the serpent deity and begot the host of offspring known as Nāgas.

The Sacraments

The sacraments most frequently observed today are those for birth, initiation, marriage, and death. The natal ceremony should be performed as soon as the child is born, but is usually done later along with other sacraments before initiation. It is performed by the father or the nearest male relative. The tongue of the newborn babe is rubbed with clarified butter, honey, sometimes also with powdered gold dust, an operation which has health value. Vedic mantras are repeated, praying for long life, intelligence, diligence, and concentration, but for no ordinary worldly gain.

The initiation, which is the key ceremony, is performed within the time limits assigned, eight to sixteen years from conception for a Brāhman, eleven to twenty-two years for a Kshatriya, twelve to twenty-four years for a Vaiśya. The twice-born boy is shaved and bathed, puts on garments newly dyed with red chalk, a waist girdle of sacred grass, a deerskin, and is provided with a staff. He is brought before the teacher, the āchārya, and offers a handful of water and looks at the sun at the bidding of his āchārya, who recites Vedic mantras and prays for his vitality and strength. He is given his first lesson in offering fire, in reading the Gāyatrī mantra, and in the nature of the vows which he must perform as a student. This done, he begs his first alms (usually food) from his mother or elder sister and offers them to his āchārya, who takes his share and allows him to cook the remainder for himself.

The marriage ceremony entails the worship of the bridegroom in the pūjā fashion by the father of the bride, or the nearest male relative if the father is dead or disabled, followed by consecration done by the women of the bride's family. The next step is the giving of the bride, with ornaments and presents for the groom, at which time the genealogy of both is recited up to the third generation. The groom accepts the hand of the bride and a fire offering is performed. Then comes the Seven Steps, the most important part of the ceremony, in which the bride and groom take seven steps around the fire, or go around the fire seven times. That is followed by pointing out the fixed star if it is at night, or by the putting of the bride's foot on the stone as a symbol of constancy, and the bride is asked to regard her husband as of herself in body and mind. The ceremonies are preceded by the formula of good intent, the auspicious śrāddha, and the worship of Gaṇeśa the remover of obstacles, and concluded by a prayer for peace, using Vedic mantras.

The final sacrament is performed at death. It is recommended that the dying man be taken to the bank of a sacred river to die, if that is possible. As soon as possible after death the body should be carried to the sacred cremation ground. Under no circumstances should the corpse be carried or touched by any but caste men, nor should the cremation be delayed for hours. As a preliminary to the cremation ceremony there should be rites of expiation, especially for bad diseases, accompanied by the gift of a cow (that which ferries safely to the next world), for which it is customary to substitute a standard gift of coins and gifts to Brāhmans. The corpse is washed, clothed in new garments, sprinkled with ghee, and laid on the pyre facing southward. In the meantime rice is cooked at the cremation ground and offered, half being previously thrown away. The Vedic mantra for driving away evil spirits is recited and the food is offered to the dead. Then the eldest son, or the next nearest male relative, goes around the pyre three or seven times with his right hand toward the corpse reciting the mantra "I apply fire to all limbs of this person, who, willingly or unwillingly, might have committed lapses and is now under the clutches of death—a person attended with virtue and vice, greed and ignorance. May he attain to shining regions." He then applies the torch to the pyre.

At the close of the cremation, seven chips of wood are thrown into the fire, followed by circumambulation; jets of water are then poured over the ashes by the party, one after another; some of the bones are thrown into the river or collected to be taken to a sacred river if there is none in the vicinity. A short water offering is made by each member of the party. The party remains near the cremation ground until sunset if the ceremony was held in the daytime, or until sunrise if it was at night, and then returns home with the youngest preceding and the rest following in order of their age.

During the period of defilement following a death a ball of rice in water and milk is to be offered every day by the person entitled to do it; at the end of the period of defilement there is a śrāddha for the recently deceased. The monthly śrāddhas follow, and at the end of the lunar year there is the śrāddha by which the dead man is admitted to the company of the forefathers.

Other Ceremonies in the Home

Another ceremony usually performed in the home is the appeasing ceremony, which is meant to avert evils indicated by an unfavorable conjunction of the planets, or by evil omens or calamities. It involves offerings of tulasī leaves with appropriate mantras, the reading of certain passages from the scriptures, with ten, eighteen, twenty-eight, one hundred and eight, and even a thousand repetitions and prostrations, according to the gravity of the situation.

Birthdays of the male members of the family are generally celebrated with the worship of Mother Shashṭhī; the Seer Mārkaṇḍeya and the seven longlived ones, including Hanumān, are worshiped and new garments are worn. There is also a semi-religious ceremony when brothers are entertained and fed by their sisters, and presents are given; and cows are worshiped on one day each year, when they are fed delicacies and decorated with vermilion powder and flowers.

In all domestic rites the times must be auspicious as indicated by the almanac or the astrologer, and the fire offering is the most important item. The fire worshiped is regarded differently in different sacraments, as vigorous in the natal ceremony, pure in the ceremony for the first taking of cooked food, the knower of everything in the ceremony of investiture with the sacred thread, and as the joiner in the case of marriage. Each of these special rites is accompanied by the welcoming and feeding of Brāhmans and by a feast for relatives and friends.

RELIGIOUS PRACTICES IN THE TEMPLE

In addition to the worship in the home, the religious disposition of man has spread itself to the world around him, to the temple and the pilgrimage. It is impossible to think of an Indian village without a shrine—it is an amenity which has been given priority of consideration in the selection of one's home from time immemorial. Because of the role of water in religious practices, shrines have been erected on river banks whenever possible. Where there is no river, big tanks serve the same purpose of purifying the worshiper through a dip in the water. Associated with shrines and temples there are pavilions where are held discourses on religion, readings from the scriptures, especially the Purāṇas, and musical entertainments of a religious nature. The wayside shrines help people no less than wayside inns and taverns, and house village deities which receive worship from the local people as well as from the pilgrim.

The institution of temples which are of more than local importance can be explained in many ways. From the earliest times the status and worth of deities were conceived on the model of kings among men, and as the kings built great palaces for themselves a demand arose for similar great temples. Sometimes a temple was built to house the relics of a saintly person belonging to one of the sects; at other times the temple grew up in connection with one of the monastic orders. Many great temples have grown up at places made sacred by legend.

Through the centuries, the technical skill and artistic creativity of the Hindus have been revealed in a genius for architecture which has created temples of singular felicity. Broadly speaking, a temple compound is made up of a pyramidal gateway, a terrace, a courtyard with a metallic bell hung high above it, the temple building proper with an inner shrine, and within that the most sacred inner room where the chief image is kept. The larger temples usually have a high wall surrounding the courtyard, a big tank near the temple, a kitchen, and a tapering spire. The sacred inner room where the image is kept is usually small and not well lighted; it is the cave in which the deity is lying, symbolic of the heart of the devotee. The tapering spire is meant to represent the upward ascent of the spirit of the devotee to the vicinity of the Lord who is poised above everything.

Daily Ceremonies in the Temple

There is a regular daily schedule in temple worship which is followed as strictly as the schedule is followed in the worship of the family deity in the home. It begins with the auspicious lamp ceremony at the last eighth of the night when the deity is awakened with sweet, solemn music and the recitation of scriptural prayers. The awakening ceremony is followed by the bathing ceremony an hour or so after sunrise; in Śiva shrines it is the liṅga which is bathed; for the other deities, a substitute which is often hidden from public view is bathed, or the ceremony is performed with the sālagrāma or the yantra. After the bath comes the anointing ceremony when sandal paste is offered profusely, and then the deity is worshiped with japa of appropriate mantras for some time. At midday the image is screened from public view and offered cooked food, followed by a fire offering if the Vedic code of worship is insisted on. After that the deity enjoys the midday rest and should not be disturbed, though this is not always possible at big temples where pilgrims come at all times and occasionally interrupt the rest for an anointing and decorating ceremony.

In the afternoon, before sunset, refreshment is offered to the deity in big temples—at Pūri, the deity is offered refreshment or food fifty-two times during the day! At dusk, the lamp ceremony is performed elaborately, followed by the offering of food for the night. The day ends with the lying down ceremony; after another elaborate lamp ceremony, the god is dressed in right royal fashion with beautiful clothes, flowers, and vilva leaves, and put to rest for the night.

In the daily worship in the temple the ceremonial stages of consecration, invocation, and sending away are dispensed with because the image is permanently installed. In Śiva worship, no cooked food is offered; in other temples care is taken to see that the food offered to the deity is in no way inferior to that which a well-to-do person in the locality takes for himself. Regularly, hymns and prayers are read during the day, especially during the early hours of the morning and during the midday and evening worship. Only priests who are versed in Vedic studies may perform the bathing and fire ceremonies; ordinary worship with japa is done by officiating priests who are next in rank to the chief priests; prayers in Sanskrit are recited by one group of priests, while decorating and anointing are done by other priests who in some temples may even be non-Brāhmans.

Care of the Temple Image

Much of the attention in the service in temples is concentrated on the image, for the care of the image is considered to be a religous obligation. From the time of the awakening of the deity with auspicious music and the lamp ceremony until the lying down ceremony at night, these teams of devout technicians and experts perform the daily duties to which they have been assigned. The anointing with sandal paste, especially in Śiva temples, is an admirable operation performed with exemplary patience. On special days there are fire offerings and sprinkling ceremonies on a grand scale. The placing of the golden sacred thread, particularly on important occasions, the putting on of the silken apparel in the case of Vishṇu and Śakti images, the lamp ceremony when done at nightfall before retiring—all these are spectacular demonstrations. Thousands of pilgrims flock to have a look at the form of the Lord on such occasions when it is royally attired, for it is really an achievement in the art of decoration with flowers, clothes, and jewels: a lovely figure, kingly and saintly.

The pilgrims who come to the temple offer flowers, scents, special cooked foods, garlands, ornaments, and sometimes they sacrifice animals, as at Kālighāt in Calcutta. They provide lighted lamps at the threshold to the inner sacred room, and attain special merit by arranging for the repetition of mantras and the reading of the scriptures. Going around the temple, always with the right side toward the deity, or prostrating one's self all around the temple or the courtyard is frequently done to appease the deity or to fulfill a vow. Providing for the singing of kīrtanas and bhajanas or the production of religious dramas is a popular means of adoring the deity.

PILGRIMAGES

The religious nature of the Hindu mind has directed that wandering instinct which is rooted in man's very blood into the institution of pilgrimages, considered as an essential part of religion. On a pilgrimage one gets away from the routine life and the economic hindrances which often deaden and impede religious practices, and as he walks with others realizing at every step the sincerity of the cry of the pilgrim, "All glory to the All-comprehensive Lord," he comes to see what a place god-mindedness occupies in life. As he worships before the Lord at Banaras, or Bālāji the Lord at Tirupati, or the Great Mother at Conjeeveram, the pilgrim comes to see that all are equal before the Lord, in whatever form or place the deity may be worshiped. As the pilgrims from all over India mix together and worship at the great, ancient shrines, they come to know and cherish the fundamental unity of this land of Bhārata, made sacred in so many places by the presence of the Lord.

Pilgrimages to the shrines of India are undertaken for the completion of vows, for the appeasing of the deity in times of misfortunes, to gain prosperity and good fortune, and as simple acts of devotion to the Lord. Toward the end of life when people are expected to be more godly minded, when the pettiness of worldly life seems to fade away, they are more inclined to go on pilgrimages to sacred spots. After the death of a parent, the son longs for the opportunity to visit Gayā, Banaras, and Allahabad to perform there the ceremonial rites for his father or mother. And at the time of the great festivals, when thousands of pilgrims gather to witness the ceremonies, there is a strong urge for the devout Hindu to join them.

Sacred Pilgrimage Places

Each section of the country has its favorite places of pilgrimage to which hundreds of pilgrims come daily, and thousands upon thousands on special occasions. Special sanctity is attached to the four great abodes of the Lord, Badarīnāth in the Himālayas in the north, Dwārakā in the west, Rāmeśwaram in the south, and Pūri in the east. Pilgrimages to the seven holy sites are highly prized: to Conjeeveram, Dwārakā, Ayodhyā, Mathurā, Hardwar, Banaras, and Ujjain. Conjeeveram, the city of golden temples, is the stronghold of the worship of the Mother in southern India; the temple to the Mother there is built in the form of a yantra. Dwārakā is the site of the kingdom ruled by Kṛishṇa and the place from which He left the world at the end of His embodiment recorded in the Mahābhārata. Ayodhyā, near Lucknow, is sacred to the memory of Rāma. Mathurā, and nearby Vrindāban, are cherished as the location of the nativity and youthful achievements of the Lord Kṛishṇa. Hardwar is the gateway to Śiva, the Lord of the Mountains, and is the place where the Ganges comes down to the plains from the Himālayas. Banaras has been the most sacred place of salvation in the belief of the Hindu from earliest times; those who die there by the Ganges are taken at once to the heavenly regions.

Ujjain, one of the seven holy sites, is also one of the twelve jyotirliṅgas, the perennial phallic forms of Śiva, which are especially sacred pilgrimage sites. There are also fifty-one pilgrimage places, called pīṭhas (footrests), dedicated to the Divine Mother as marking the places where her different limbs fell when her body was severed by Vishṇu's wheel at the time when Śiva was wandering grieving through the world carrying the dead body of his wife. They are found from Kashmir and Nepal in the Himālayas to Conjeeveram in the south; Kālighāt at Calcutta and Lalitā at Allahabad are famous pīṭhas.

Pilgrimages are also made to āśramas, hermitages where saints noted for their holy lives and learned instruction live, and to maṭhs where groups of swāmīs live and study. Hilltops difficult of access, where austerity and religious practices are enjoined, are the objects of pilgrimages. The seven holy rivers of India are especially sacred pilgrimage places, with the greatest sanctity attached to the places where two rivers join, or where a river enters the sea. Bathing in those rivers and in the sea at such places as Cape Comorin or Rāmeśwaram cleanses the pilgrim of his sins and gives him a sense of union with his fellow beings and their creator.

Some ancient sites are no longer the objects of pilgrimages, though still considered sacred, such as the Kailāsa temple in Ellora, the Sun temple at Kōṇārak near Pūri, and the seven pagodas in Mahābalipuram not far from Madras. Other ancient temples which had been abandoned for centuries have recently been restored and have again become the goal of the pilgrim, such as the temple at Somnath.

Special Occasions for Pilgrimages

Great throngs of pilgrims gather for special festivals such as the car festival at Pūrī when Jagannātha is pulled through the streets on a great car so heavy that it requires hundreds and hundreds of devotees to move it. Another great gathering takes place at the marriage festival of the Mother at the Mīnākshī temple at Madurai. One of the most joyous of the occasions which attract pilgrims is the ceremony of placing the sacred thread on the deity, generally Vishṇu or Śiva, which is of the nature of royal festivities in which a king is in a holiday mood, putting on his best garments and ornaments, and going out for a short trip to see his subjects. But the largest gatherings of all come at the great melas held every twelve years at Hardwar, Allahabad, Ujjain, and Nasik. It is estimated that more than a million devotees will be present at the largest of these melas.

Whether on pilgrimages or not, there are numerous special occasions for worship in the temple. Every deity has a seasonal rest, a lying down period lasting half the year, in addition to the daily rest from about 11:30 to 4:00 o'clock, and there is a ceremony for the lying down and for the waking. During that period the deity is sleeping, but the image is not considered to be asleep. Then there is the swinging ceremony for Vishṇu, a big holiday accompanied with the sprinkling of the devotees with colored water and powders. And many temples have temple cars, or boats in their temple tanks, on which the deity is taken for a holiday ride. All these are occasions for special ceremonies and festivities at the temple.

Birthdays, too, are celebrated; not only the birthdays of the gods, but of such saints as Vyāsa, Kapila, Śaṅkara, Rāmānuja, and Chaitanya. In modern times we have followed that pattern set by the orthodox Hindus of old and have included the birth anniversaries of such great men as Rāmakṛishṇa Paramahaṁsa and Mahātmā Gāndhi.

There are special days for each deity honored by the devout Hindu, filling the calendar with holidays which relieve life of its humdrum character and make the days solemn and sacred through the fulfilment of religious obligations. The fourteenth lunar day is sacred to Śiva, and the fourteenth day (dark fortnight) of the month of Māgha is especially sacred as Śivarātri. The story is told of a certain hunter from Banaras who was unable to get home at night and had to spend the night of the fourteenth reclining on a branch of a vilva tree. As luck would have it, a leaf fell and, besprinkled with the dew of the night, it touched a Śiva liṅga at the foot of the tree. Śiva was highly pleased, and this one act performed unconsciously secured for the hunter great merit which the heavenly judge Yama had to admit.

There are many special days for Vishṇu as Vishṇu, and also as Kṛishṇa and as Rāma. The nativity of Kṛishṇa is celebrated on the eighth day of the dark fortnight in Bhādrapada (August-September), and it has special sanctity when it comes at the time of the constellation Rohiṇī; then Kṛishṇa, together with his adopted parents, are worshiped with eclat. The auspicious time which saw the birth of Rāma is celebrated on the ninth day of Chaitra (March-April), when Rāma is worshiped along with Sītā, Lakshmaṇa, and his parents. In these ceremonies, while punctilious care concerning the details of ritual is insisted upon, the primary concern is to think of how the deity born on that day helps by his incarnation or his actions, a concern which is aided by reading from the Purāṇas.

Śakti is worshiped in many forms, as Sarasvatī, Lakshmī, Durgā, and Kālī, in particular. Sarasvatī is worshiped in the spring by teachers and students. The mode of worship of Lakshmī follows a prescribed date and place and there are no less than four or five occasions during the year when she is solemnly adored.. Devout people often worship Kālī on the night of every new moon. The Durgā-pūjā is an elaborate festival lasting nine nights and observed all over the land, beginning on the first lunar day in the bright fortnight of Āśvina (September-October). Another festival observed all over India is Diwali, when at dusk on the night of the new moon of Kārttika (October-November), worship is celebrated with lights in the homes and the temples.

Thus are the days, and many of the nights, filled with observances which help to keep the devout Hindu god-minded.

VARIATIONS IN RELIGIOUS PRACTICES

There are, of course, many variations in the practices throughout the land, of which perhaps the most noticeable are those based on Tāntric rather than Vedic practices. There are also variations as to the times and places for the performance of religious rites, variations due to cult differences and folk practices, and there are special concessions made for the diseased, for women, for Śūdras, and for sannyāsins.

Tāntric and Vedic Variations

Tāntric religious practices are based on the large body of scriptures known as the Tantras, practical writings designed to show the way to follow the theoretical teachings in the Vedas. One of the Tamil saints illustrates this practical concern by pointing out that if one wants some ghee (clarified butter) he does not get it by walking around a cow and chanting "O ghee, come unto me." He must milk the cow, churn the milk, and then clarify the butter. The Tantras deal with the procedures by which man can use ritualistic worship, the mantra, yantra, and yoga as means to the realization of the Supreme Being.

Variations based on a code of scriptural authority are at least a thousand years old, as is evident from the following passage from the Bhāgavata Purāṇa (XI.27):

"Vedic, Tāntric, and mixed, threefold is my worship. One may follow his wishes in choosing any of the forms. A twice-born may worship me, his Lord, through devotion, with materials, in an image, on the raised ground, on fire, in the sun, in water, or in his heart. After finishing the morning prayer sanctioned by the Veda he is to offer worship with his mind firmly fixed. Mobile or immobile, both types of images serve as his shrine or my abode by installation, with this difference, that there is no invocation and no sending away in immobile ones. The sincere devotee worships me with well-arranged offerings on images in case he has a fancy for the fruits of worship. If he has no such, he may perform with the things he can procure.

"For him who worships in the heart, his attitude of reverence is what matters. The daily bath and ornaments I like in case I am worshiped in images, the placing of the deity and his accessories in proper parts of the body is what pleases me if worship be on the raised ground. Oblation with clarified butter, if worship is done with fire, I prefer; an arghya" [an offering of rice, flowers, shoots of soft juicy grass, leaves, and water, sprinkled with sandal paste] "in case it be in the sun is what pleases me; and offerings of water if it be on water, delight me . . .

"With that [mental image of the Lord] created by meditation, and made his own, placed on the body of the image, the devotee worships with invocation duly done. With offerings of arghya he should adore Durgā, Gaṇeśa, Vyāsa, Vishṇu, the gurus, and that in their proper places, facing them in the assigned directions. After chanting, glorifying my name, dancing and gesticulating and recounting my achievements, he should for a moment be absorbed in me. With hymns old, and also common ones, he should bow down prostrating himself at my feet and asking pardon of me, saying, 'O Lord, protect me, who have resorted to you as my succor.' With flowers from the offerings on his head he should send the effulgence in him back to the Light and Spirit."

Tāntric initiation differs from the Vedic in that it is for all, male and female, the twice-born and the Śūdra, the householder and the monk, and entails the introduction of a spirit force that is held to exercise a profound influence through the guru. In the simpler form of initiation for the householder, the guru puts particular emphasis on the sixfold nyāsa, performs the fire offering in the Tāntric manner, sprinkles holy water, and recites appropriate mantras; he finishes by delivering secretly into the ears of the disciple the crucial mantra and charges him to repeat it as his daily prayer and to remember it in crises faced by him and his family.

A more elaborate initiation is reserved for one who seeks to attain perfection of spiritual excellence through the mental disciplines, for in his case the mental predispositions and routes have to be adjusted and this is a highly difficult affair. The full-fledged ablution which can come only to the highest aspirant assures him full amnesty from earthly worries, and even makes him capable of performing miracles. Tradition, both written and oral, describes the high spiritual powers possessed by such persons.

The Tāntric form of worship is more elaborate and systematized than the Vedic, and very particular about technicalities. The invocation, vivication of the image, and sending away are all necessary, to which is added salutation with the eight limbs: the knees, the legs, the hands, the chest, the mind, the head, the speech, and the look; ending with a complete prostration before the image. Going around the image, with the right side toward the image, is also a necessary part of worship, thereby making the worshiper realize every moment the presence of the deity. The Tāntric manner indulges in niceties in the matter of the placing of the vessel filled with water and besmeared and anointed, and in the drawing of mystic designs with colored rice flour. A professedly devout Tāntrika begins his pūjā with the worship of his guru, male or female, generally with five offerings including japa and with farewell at the end, often using wooden sandals, a picture, or a photograph as symbols of the guru. The Tāntric form of daily worship should be performed only by those who have been initiated.

The Śaiva Tāntric worship limits the bodily purification to the five upper parts of the body above the navel, for it considers the lower part of the body to be unclean. Those parts associated with speech-and-mind worship are the heart, the throat, the palate, the region between the eyebrows, and the head. The worshiper surrounds his body with a line of water, imagining it to be a wall of fire, and with his hands placed properly in his lap merges his spirit with that of the deity. The whole external world is drowned by the threefold scheduled process of breath control, the taking in, the holding, and the giving out of the breath. With this newly formed body he purges the ordinary body of dross; in this stage this vicious double is burned away by the "fire arrow," that is, the waving of the right hand around the head, and snapping of the fingers. Finally, with the spiritual body pure and shining, the worshiper installs the deity in himself. This is an extremely difficult operation depending as much on concentration as on facility in practice, and degenerates in most cases into a mere formality.

An alternative form of Tāntric worship is to imagine a tree of knowledge in one's lotus-heart, a tree whose root is dharma and whose trunk is knowledge, and whose eight petals are the virtues and their opposites; one then places the inner spirit in a line of contact with the Supreme Being through the sushumṇā vein, the spiritual channel or artery through which the breath passes connecting the individual with the Lord. The sushumṇā vein starts in the spinal column and goes out at the top of the head. The deity is then meditated upon as being placed in the heart, in the head, in the tuft of hair on top of the head, in the protecting armor (a mudrā of crossed arms across the chest as if God protects one in that way), in the three eyes (one in the forehead) suggestive of insight and wisdom, and on the palms.

The Tantras associate merit in worship with the attainment of three particular attitudes, animal, manly, and godly, in ascending order. One who performs worship in a routine way without regard for his spiritual affiliation is an animal. One who fixes his mind on one deity, leaving out the rest, belongs to the manly type; while he who regards everything as only differing forms of the same deity is a godly man.

An extreme form of Tantra, popularly called the left-handed Tantra, has come in for much censure for practices which border on intemperance and vulgarity. Although such rites have an esoteric and mystic meaning, aspirants who choose to follow these practices in the midst of temptations and risks stand, as it were, on a razor's edge. That this way is not for the ordinary aspirants is evident from its concern in worship with the three forbidden things: wine, meat, and copulation, even though their substitutes in practice are coconut water or milk, ginger, and intensive sixfold nyāsa. The mudrās used in this form of worship represent the five forbidden things: wine, meat, cereals representing the sensual addictions, copulation, and fish. The left-handed Tantra seeks to show detachment from these forbidden things.

Yogic Disciplines of Tantra

The code of worship elaborated in the Tantras depends to a considerable extent on the disciplines of yoga for its practical effectiveness. A careful consideration of these forms of yoga and their practical utilization cannot but arrest the attention of every discerning student of religious practices. Yoga, both in its Tāntric and non-Tāntric forms, is based on an underlying mysticism which conceives of the identity of man and the Lord. It is therefore in the fitness of things that worship is basically a matter of yogic disciplines, disciplines which enable man to attain union of the essential self with the Supreme Being which is its true self.

The Tantras have elaborated the eightfold yogic disciplines from a standpoint of practical utility, recognizing four distinct types of yoga: mantra yoga, haṭha yoga, laya yoga, and rāja yoga. In *mantra yoga,* worship and devotion predominate; in it the disciplines are adjusted to the emotional temperament and intellectual abilities of the worshiper, directing his devotion to his chosen deity as a disciple approaches a guru. He may approach as an attendant, as Hanumān approaches Rāma, or affectionately as Mother Yaśodā approached Kṛishṇa, or as a friend as Arjuna approached the Lord, or as the beloved as

Rādhā approached Kṛishṇa. In the second type, *haṭha yoga,* the aspirant tends to resort to risky practices of physical disciplines, such as breath control and special postures, which must be attempted under the close supervision of a guru. This type of yoga can be adapted to the leisure moments of one who is engaged in worldly economic pursuits, but is risky.

Laya yoga rests on the effectiveness of practices which bring about the merging of the spirit through the annihilation of the personality of the worshiper. *Rāja yoga,* the king among yogic methods, aims at self-realization but by methods somewhat easier than those used in laya yoga. Those who live god-centered lives preach and practice rāja yoga. It culminates in *samādhi,* absorption in the Divine, but it is attainable only when all the considerations and formalities of worship have been duly fulfilled and when internal worship has substituted itself for the formal and external requirements of worship.

The way of mantra yoga or haṭha yoga is for those who follow their routine duties, the way of injunctions, acting mechanically; the way of laya yoga or rāja yoga is for those who are advanced in worship. In all four types of yoga, much depends on the help received from the guru who is instrumental in inviting the attention of the Lord and in mediating for His favor and grace.

Variations Due to Time and Place

In addition to the Tāntric variations in religious practices, the variations in time and place are readily discovered. The day set aside for Sarasvatī in Bengal is the day for the worship of Kāma, the god of love in other parts of the country. Many such variations might be cited. The auspicious times for bathing in the Ganges are different from those set aside for the Godāvarī, the Narmadā, and the Brahmaputra rivers. In Bengal, when the sun is in the sign of Leo, the times are inauspicious, while in other parts of the country the times are inauspicious when Jupiter is in the sign of Leo. Calves are worshiped in entirely different months in northern and southern

India. Animals are offered in worship in Bengal, but rarely offered in other parts of the country. Durgā-pūjā may be an elaborate procedure covering a month in one place, while in others it may be a fortnight, nine days, three days, or only one day long.

Cult Variations

The cult of the worshiper is a very important factor in determining the differences in the details of religious practices. The Śaiva has his preferences for the phallic form as an abstract representation of the Lord and would even go to the extent of worshiping other deities in a clay liṅga. The Vaishṇava takes to the sālagrāma, and a Śākta to a yantra. Vilva leaf is taboo to certain sections of the Vaishṇavas, and is completely forbidden in the worship of Sūrya. Tulasī leaf is not offered to a Śakti, for they say that the Mother is put out of temper by the very smell of a tulasī leaf. The dūrvā with the inner shoots removed is for Śiva and the forefathers, while the inner shoots must be left on for Vishṇu and other deities.

In the matter of worship of deities, different sects assess differently the value of japa, fire offerings, meditation, and prayers, the more extreme views tending to extol the efficacy of one item to the exclusion of the rest. We have Vaishṇava and Śākta sects which have a fancy for japa, some of them regarding the chanting of the names of the Lord as the essential part of worship. Some sects attach considerable importance to prayers and protective hymns. In rather recent times, the Ārya Samāj has held that meditation and the fire offering are the only eligible forms, while the Brāhmo Samāj chooses meditation and sometimes the kīrtana, the singing of devotional hymns. Others use meditation and prayers and hymns in the local dialects as their means of worship.

In general it may be said that the service aspect has been emphasized more by the Vaishṇavas, the yogic disciplines by the Śaivas, and the practical details as worked out in the Tantras by the Śāktas. Many such variations have grown up in the different cults through the centuries.

Variations Due to Folk Religion

Folk religion accounts for a considerable number of popular observances which are sanctioned by custom. Serpent worship is of great antiquity, and has had adherents even among high-class people in areas where poisonous reptiles abound. In serpent worship Manasā and her serpent brood are appeased with offerings of worship, including milk. Śītalā the goddess of smallpox is worshiped in spring and summer, and at the time of illness the method of worship includes surrounding the patient with neem leaves, which modern research has shown to serve as a nonirritant prophylactic. Shashṭhī, the Mother-Sixth, is worshiped on the sixth day after birth as the protectress of children; sometimes she is worshiped with Kārttikeya as her husband, she being considered as his Divine Army. For the artisan class the guardian deity is Viśvakarman the divine carpenter. A peculiar and popular folk deity is Satyā-Nārāyaṇa, who is worshiped once every month at dusk with elaborate offerings including his favorite delicacy made with sugar, flour, milk, and banana. He has been metamorphosed from his medieval form of Satyapīr, the combination Muslim and Hindu deity, and is now considered to be the great Nārāyaṇa. Trees also are worshiped in many ways; for example, the damanaka tree which is associated with spring worship and especially with Kāma, the god of love and sport; town-bred as well as country folk offer the blossoms of the damanaka tree to Kāma, of the aśoka tree to Śiva, and twigs and blossoms of the mango to Sarasvatī.

Concessions for the Diseased

In addition to all the variations in religious practices which have been discussed, there are special concessions made for the diseased, for women, for Śūdras, and for sannyāsins. Distressed, diseased, or displaced persons cannot apply themselves heart and soul to religious performances. Certain concessions in rigor of diet and the length of a fast or vow become inevitable, and in the case of those who have been displaced from their homes certain lapses are regularized and certain irregularities are condoned. In extreme difficulty, a proxy is allowed, generally a priest or a member of the family. The poor perform their daily religious practices with as much as they can afford in the way of offerings. The ill, for instance, may substitute the mental bath for bathing in the river or tank.

Religious Practices of Women

There are, however, certain fundamental disabilities, such as those relating to women. Their sphere of religious observances has been restricted by the Hindu religious code from very old times, for rigor in practice as well as a proper understanding of the mantras to be repeated can hardly be expected of women. The Hindu woman is nothing more than an accessory and passive participator in her husband's religious practices. For her, the five daily obligations and the sacraments are simplified and modified; Vedic mantras are taboo for a woman, and thus the Vedic course of daily worship is no part of her religious routine. Her daily religious course is made up of Tāntric worship if she has been initiated, and includes especially the intensive japa of the mantra of her chosen deity, the midday pūjā with the Vedic mantras omitted or with Purāṇic mantras substituted, and a profusion of non-Vedic prayers, often in the vernacular. The one sacrament in her life is marriage. In temple worship women are not allowed to touch images, though there is a concession made in the case of Śiva images that were installed in the remote past.

Woman has been and is the never failing ministering angel to the family for the upkeep of the worship of the deity and the sālagrāma. Many of the attendant practices, the preparation of materials, the cooking of food, and the cleansing of utensils used in worship are her responsibility. She worships Śiva and the clay Śiva liṅga daily if she chooses, takes her ceremonial bath, and gives gifts and observes vows. Her life is no less regulated than that of the male members of the family and she, when she is the mistress of the family, has to look to the comforts of every member of the family as a religious duty; she can take her food only after all the members have taken theirs and the guests have been hospitably served.

The distinctive religious practices for a woman are the vows. Vows entail abstention from food and ascetic rigor on certain days, and on the days preceding and following them, for an approved number of years. For instance, a woman might vow that if her husband or child recovers from an illness she will not eat, or will refrain from eating certain foods, on certain days for a fixed number of months or years. There are special vows for the female sex, such as the vow of Sāvitrī, which is the worship of the husband through the worship of Sāvitrī, and the vow to her Lord Satyavat, and to Yama the Lord of Death. When the time comes for the completion of a vow, gifts are given to Brāhmans, and a feast is held for relatives and friends. Women also give gifts at the end of the solar months and at other particular times when special merit accrues, offering them first to the gods and then giving them to Brāhmans.

The Practices of the Śūdras

There are different religious practices for Śūdras (the caste not included among the twice-born) and those who are considered to have become Śūdras owing to general lapses and nonobservances which have continued for at least three generations. Their code is similar to that of women, with whom they are classed as laboring under certain disabilities. Special rules concerning food apply to the Śūdras; there are prohibitions concerning the preparation of food for the family, concerning methods of cooking food, and strict limitations concerning the persons with whom food may be eaten. For the daily religious practices they must follow the Tāntric mode of worship and a curtailed pūjā program, and all other observances must be done for them by the priests. As in the case of women, sacraments with the exception of marriage are performed without mantras, or with the Vedic mantras left out.

The fundamental characteristic of the Śūdra is service to the deities and to the Brāhmans in a spirit of sincerity and devotion. Śūdras may read from the Upanishads, the Mahābhārata, and the Purāṇas, but not from the Vedic Saṁhitās. For śrāddhas, no cooked food can be offered to the forefathers. In the funeral rites are included extra mantras imploring moral support and intellectual guidance of the twice-born. In modern times the invidious distinction in theory which necessitated stringent prohibitions is becoming more and more softened so that Śūdras are now being allowed all practical facilities for their spiritual betterment.

In spite of such disabilities and handicaps, the Śūdras have a legacy of great achievements. The practice of giving one's weight in money, gems, or jewels has been commended and practiced among Śūdras. Many of the services of public utility such as planting trees by the roadside, erection of hospitals and pilgrimage hostels and monasteries, owe their origin to them. Many of the temples of all cults have been built by them. Pilgrimages have been widely popular with Śūdras, as have been the practices of chanting the name of the Lord, and japa. There have been great religious teachers among the Śūdras who preached and practiced their faith and were held in high honor. Peculiar types of service to the temple deities, such as anointment with sandal paste and placing ornaments on the body of the deity, have been their privilege, and like the makers of chariots and the architects of Vedic times they have held a coveted position, and even been styled as temple priests. Kabīr and Tukārām have had great influence on esoteric worship, and they both were Śūdras.

The Practices of the Sannyāsins

The sannyāsins form an important class which has exercised enormous influence on the people of India, strengthening their religious tendencies and increasing their participation in religious practices. Almost all the great religious reformers, Buddha, Rāmānuja, Śaṅkara, Madhva, Nimbārka, and Chaitanya were sannyāsins.

They are divided into four types, in ascending spiritual order. The first type is the novice who must do his practices under instruction from his guru and in his guru's presence. The second level is for the sannyāsin who has advanced a bit more and can take pilgrimages as a part of his training. A sannyāsin on the third level is fairly far advanced in spiritual merit and is above all rules and regulations. The highest level is the paramahaṁsa, to whom all beings are equal and who has realized the Supreme Essence in himself. The great Śaṅkarāchārya and his successors in the four monasteries which he founded were paramahaṁsas, as was the great Rāmakṛishṇa in modern times.

A working knowledge of the eightfold discipline of yoga is conferred on the novice in all orders of sannyāsins. There is a rightful insistence that an ideal sannyāsin must have the six assets: pacification of the senses, active self-restraint, complete cessation of sense activity, endurance, habitual concentration, and perfected faith. Sannyāsins of the first two levels are given latitude in the following of formal religious practices, and at the last two levels they are free to omit all practices and devote their attention to internal worship which leads to perfect isolation and final absorption in the Divine Essence. Most sannyāsins bathe on ceremonial occasions, and all of them participate in the bathing at the time of the great melas, such as those at Hardwar and Allahabad, for the melas were originated by the sannyāsins. When a sannyāsin chooses to worship in a temple, he is given ungrudging priority by the devotees. Even among the highest type, the Śaṅkarāchāryas, we have sannyāsins of highest spiritual status who have never refrained from the most elaborate and exacting religious performances.

As to the daily practices, breath control is their greatest strength; the offerings to their forefathers are omitted, for they must disclaim kinship with them as well as with the living. The guru, Vyāsa, Śiva, and Vishṇu are properly worshiped often and elaborately. They shave once a year, and may have permanent residence during the four months of the rainy season. Most sannyāsins go on pilgrimages, though that is not obligatory since the greatest pilgrimage is the purification and improvement of one's self. They are wedded to perpetual poverty, free from desires for rewards, and diligent in their cultivation of detachment from the world. The difficulties of detachment are shown in the story of the saintly king Bharata who out of compassion for a young doe became involved in worldly life so much that his religious propensities met with a setback and he had to be born as a deer in the next life. He was purified by the asceticism of his past life and through the association with sages was restored to his own self again. As an example of the possibilities of spiritual attainment, the sannyāsins have been one of the greatest sources of religious inspiration in India through the ages.

Such, in brief outline, are the practices by which the devout Hindu fills his days, weeks, and years, as he moves along this worldly path toward his ultimate goal of union with the Supreme Being, confronted with the guidance given in the scriptures and calling out, "I remember that; that I attend on."

Chapter 6

HINDU RELIGIOUS THOUGHT

by SATIS CHANDRA CHATTERJEE

By Hindu religious thought is meant the body of ideas, beliefs, and theories which underlie the religious emotions, activities, and institutions of the Hindus.

These religious ideas do not constitute a single and simple system of thought, for Hinduism as a religion was not founded by one prophet, nor by one incarnation of God,[1] nor is it derived from the teachings of any one sage. Hinduism is based on the varied religious and moral experiences and insights of many ancient, medieval, and modern Indian sages and Seers, saints, devotees, and reformers, giving rise to a variety of religious ideas and practices which form the basis of different types of religious life.

Although the basic spiritual experiences are different, they are complementary, giving rise to types of religion which are not really antagonistic to one another. They are different ways of approach to the same goal, meant for different classes of people occupying different levels of spiritual development or having different tastes, aptitudes, and temperaments. Thus Hindu religious thought is a complex but unified body of many different religious theories.

[1] In this chapter the word 'God' with capital *G* does not refer to any minor deity but means the Personal Being (called Īśvara, Parameśvara, Paramātmā, Purushottama, Maheśvara, Saguṇa Brahman, etc.) who is the one ultimate reality and is the creator, preserver, destroyer, and moral governor of the world. God in this sense is almost the same Being as God in Christian theology and, generally speaking, in western philosophy. There is only this difference: God in Christianity is not the destroyer of the world, and God in Hinduism is not the creator of individual selves and other eternal entities. But the relation of dependence in which the world and selves stand to God is the same in both. *S.C.C.*

Broadly speaking, there are twelve chief types of religious thought in Hinduism. All of them are orthodox in the sense that they accept the authority of the Vedas, but not all of them are theistic in the accepted sense of the word, since some of them do not believe in God as the creator and moral governor of the world, who has a personal relation to man. There are still others which cannot be properly characterized as theistic because to all intents and purposes they really transcend theism. Hence, the chief systems of Hindu religious thought may be conveniently presented under three general heads: Nontheistic, Theistic, and Supertheistic.

NONTHEISTIC SYSTEMS

Hinduism as a religion is centered not so much in the belief in God, as in faith in the reality of spirit and the spiritual order of the world. All systems of Hindu religious thought believe that the self [2] of man is a spiritual reality which passes from one life to another, from the past to the present and the future, and that the history of the world is guided and governed by the moral law of karma; but there are at least two systems of religious thought in Hinduism which do not believe in God as the Supreme Person who is the creator and moral governor of the world. It is true that they lend themselves easily to a theistic interpretation, and that some of their followers have given them a theistic interpretation even though that interpretation is called in question by competent scholars. So we propose to call them nontheistic instead of atheistic or antitheistic. These are the Sāṅkhya and the Mīmāṁsā Systems of religiophilosophical

[2] In Hinduism the individual self (called ātman) is an immaterial or spiritual reality which, being eternal, is not created by God. It is conceived either as pure consciousness or as essentially conscious, or as having the quality of consciousness when related to a living body. As an immaterial reality, however, it is the same as the soul in the Christian sense. In Hindu religion and Indian philosophy the words 'soul' and 'self' mean the same thing and are used as synonyms. *S.C.C.*

thought. *Sāṅkhya,* which means "Number" or "Number of Principles," is followed by a very limited circle; it has, for instance, only one āśrama in Bengal. *Mīmāṁsā,* which means "Rational, Critical Study," is followed in the sacrifices but not in the scholastic sense as an exclusive system. We shall here consider them separately in view of their marked differences in form and spirit.

SĀṄKHYA AS A RATIONALISTIC RELIGION WITHOUT GOD

The Sāṅkhya philosophy, attributed by tradition to the Sage Kapila, is a system of dualistic realism which is the basis of a religion without belief in God. For it, there are two ultimate realities which exist independently of each other; a plurality of selves (purusha) on the one hand and infinite matter (prakṛiti) on the other. The self, purusha, is pure consciousness without any activity in it, while primal matter, prakṛiti, is unlimited energy and activity but has no consciousness or intelligence in it. Therefore neither of them can by itself produce the world system. The evolution of an orderly universe requires the guidance of cosmic energy by some consciousness. The process of the world's evolution is started by the contact between self, or purusha, and primal matter, or prakṛiti. It is through such contact that unconscious prakṛiti becomes, as it were, conscious and intelligent and evolves the whole world of objects, including gross physical things, the five physical elements, the five sense organs (sight, hearing, touch, smell, taste), the five motor organs (speech, apprehension, movement, excretion, reproduction), the mind, the intellect, and the ego (the I, or ahaṁkāra).

Prakṛiti is made up of three subtle elements called guṇas. The sattva element is of the nature of pleasure and is light and illuminating; the rajas element is of the nature of pain and is mobile and stimulating; the third element, tamas, is of the nature of indifference and is heavy and enveloping. These three elements of prakṛiti enter into the constitution of all things and beings of the world in different proportions and make them different in nature and character. A man in whom the element of sattva predominates tends to be bright in intellect and pure in mind; another in whom rajas predominates is always active and energetic; while a man who has a predominance of tamas in him is habitually lazy and confused in his mind.

Man is a complex being in whom we find a self to exist in intimate relation with a psychophysical organism. Although the self of a man thus stands related to a body, there is nothing in its intrinsic nature which makes it liable to birth as an embodied being in this world. In its real nature the self is the immortal spirit which is distinct from the body and the senses, and from the mind, the intellect, and the ego. It is really above the whole world of objects and transcends even prakṛiti—the ultimate material ground of the world. But because of its association with a certain body and the predominance of the elements of rajas and tamas in the constitution of that body, the self confuses itself with the body and seems to become identified with it. With this it becomes liable to all the affections and afflictions of the mind-body, and to birth and death in the world with all their attendant sorrows and sufferings. This means bondage for the self of a man—a self that is intrinsically pure and free, immortal and immaterial.

The aim of Sāṅkhya religion is the liberation of man's self from bondage to the body and the material world. To help man attain this end, it recommends the path of rational discrimination between self and the material world including man's body, mind, intellect, and the ego. The root cause of man's bondage being the false identification of his self with the body, what is absolutely necessary for liberation is the light of true knowledge about the self. It is not faith in and worship of God that is to save man's self from the ills and evils of its present existence. We cannot strictly prove the existence of God as the creator of the world and the savior of man's self. It is man himself who is responsible for his bondage because it is his ignorance about the reality of the self that has caused it. So it lies in man's power to liberate himself by means of a penetrating insight into, and a clear realization of, the nature of his self.

For common sense, the self of a man is his body with the quality or function of consciousness. So also some philosophers hold that the mind, as a series of conscious states, or the ego, as the knower of things and the doer of actions, is the self. But for the Sāṅkhya, body, mind, and the ego are all products of unconscious matter or prakṛiti, and are themselves unconscious. They become apparently conscious and intelligent when the light of the self's consciousness is reflected in them. We are apt to take the reflection of the self in these objects as the self itself and so speak of the body, the mind, or the ego as the self, just as one is apt to think of the reflection of the moon on the dancing waves as moving when it is the water that moves, not the moon. It is sheer ignorance to think that the self is identical with the mind-body or the ego. They are all objects of consciousness and so distinct from and other than the self which is consciousness itself.

If by such rational and critical study of experience we can discriminate the self from all that is not-self, we shall attain to the knowledge that the self is a hyperphysical, transcendent reality which is above body and mind and above birth and death, sin and suffering. This saving knowledge has to be attained through control of the passions, purification of the body and mind, and the practice of meditation and concentration. These will be elaborated in the discussion of the Yoga System. But it should be noted here that this knowledge is not mere intellectual understanding of the truth about the self as something distinct from the body and the mind. It is a direct experience and clear realization of the truth that the self is the unborn and undying spirit which is above the mind-body complex and the individual ego. For the Sāṅkhya, it is a clear and steady vision of this truth that dispels the gloom of ignorance and liberates the self of man once for all.

In conclusion it should be noted that some interpreters of the Sāṅkhya give a theistic form to the system. They hold that the existence of God as possessed of creative activity cannot be admitted, for there can be no activity in the self. Yet we must believe in God as the eternally perfect spirit who is the witness of the world and who by his mere presence moves and guides prakṛiti to act and evolve the world. He is the unmoved mover of the world and the unaffected, eternal witness of the world panorama.

MĪMĀṀSĀ AS A RELIGION OF RITUALISM

The Mīmāṁsā philosophy, founded by Jaimini, is one of the orthodox systems which is directly based on the Vedas and emphasizes their ritualistic aspect. It builds up a system of thought to justify and help the continuation of the Vedic rites and rituals. The Vedas are valued by the Mīmāṁsā, not because they are the work of God or of any person, but because they are the impersonal source of commandments to perform the sacrificial rites. It even holds that the sole use of the Vedas lies in directing rituals and that if any part of them does not contain such direction but gives information about the existence of anything it is useless, unless it can be shown that it is indirectly connected with some commandment. The Mīmāṁsā philosophy may thus be called ritualistic pragmatism, for according to it Vedic knowledge is valuable for ritualistic activity.

The Mīmāṁsā metaphysics is pluralistic realism. It believes in the reality of many independent things and beings in the world. For it, reality is a complex whole made up of such entities as physical things, atoms, selves, heaven, hell, and the deities to whom sacrifices are to be performed according to the Vedic injunctions. The world of nature is composed of living bodies wherein the self reaps the consequences of its past deeds, of the sensory and motor organs which are the instruments of feeling those consequences, and of the objects of sense perception which constitute the fruits to be enjoyed or suffered. The selves are permanent, eternal substances, and so also are the material elements of which the physical world is composed. The formation of the world is due to the operation of the law of karma. No necessity is felt for admitting the existence of God to explain the origin of the world. The law of karma is autonomous and it independently regulates the atoms to form just that kind of world in which the self may reap the moral consequences of all its past actions.

The self is an eternal, infinite substance which is conscious and is related to a real body in a real world. But consciousness is not the essence of the self. It is an adventitious quality which the self acquires when it is related to a mind and the mind is related to external objects through the senses. The self does not die with the body, but passes from one body to another to be able to reap the fruits of its past actions. All the deeds done by a man generate in his self a certain unperceived potency which persists even when the actions have ceased, and produces their fruits at the proper time and place. This is how a sacrifice performed here and now will bear fruit after a long time (say, after this life, in heaven). There are as many selves as there are individuals. It is ignorance that makes the self liable to birth and death, that is, bondage to the world through the body. But every self can attain liberation by means of knowledge and the performance of obligatory duties in the right spirit.

According to the Mīmāṁsā, religion, or dharma, consists in the performance of the sacrificial rites enjoined by the eternal Vedas, not in the belief in and worship of God. In its anxiety to secure the supreme place for the Vedas, the Mīmāṁsā could not believe in God, lest He should become superior or at least equal in authority to the Vedas. The Vedas embody not so much eternal truths as eternal injunctions or laws which enjoin the performance of rites and rituals. They supply the standard of moral judgment as to what is right and what is wrong. Morality and religion both consist of obedience to the Vedic commandments.

In the Vedic Age sacrifices performed by the Vedic sages and their descendants were meant to please different deities in order to win some favor or avert some ill. But the Mīmāṁsā is so much interested in the ceremonial details of the rituals as to forget the gods who gradually recede and fade into mere grammatical designations. They are no longer looked upon as living spirits but merely as objects of the act of offering oblations at a sacrifice. The primary object of performing a sacrifice is not to please God or gods. Nor is it purification of the self or moral improvement. Rituals are to be performed just because the Vedas command us to perform them. It is true that some of these rituals are to be performed in order to enjoy heaven in a future life or to obtain worldly benefits in this life, but there are some of them which must be performed daily or occasionally simply because they are enjoined by the Vedas. There the Mīmāṁsā religion reaches, through a thoroughgoing ritualism, the noble conception of "duty for duty's sake," without any ulterior motive.

In the early Mīmāṁsā, the highest good of human life and activity appears to have been the attainment of heaven or a state in which there is unalloyed happiness. Life in heaven is regarded as the usual end of the performance of rituals in strict accordance with the Vedic injunctions. Gradually, however, the followers of Mīmāṁsā realized that the performance of actions, good or bad, if directed by the desire for enjoyment of objects, causes rebirth and consequent misery. So instead of heaven, liberation is taken in the later Mīmāṁsā as the highest end of religion.

When a man understands that worldly pleasures are more or less mingled with pain, he ceases to run after them, tries to control his passions, and desists from forbidden actions, as well as actions with motives of future enjoyment. Thus being free from all passions and desires which impel life from one state to another, the chance of his future birth and bondage is removed. By the disinterested performance of obligatory duties and knowledge of the self, all the effects of his past actions are also worn out and exhausted. After this life such a person, being free from all the bonds that bind the self to the world, is never born again. He is thus liberated from birth and death, and from all sin and suffering.

The state of liberation, according to the later Mīmāṁsā as also for the Sāṅkhya, is not a state of happiness or bliss, but only one of complete cessation of painful experience. The liberated self, being dissociated from the body and the senses, cannot have any consciousness. As such, it can have no experience, either of pleasure or of pain. So liberation is a state in which the self abides in its intrinsic nature as pure substance beyond the reach of pleasure and pain.

In modern times the Mīmāṁsā religion has undergone considerable change in the Hindu society. It is no longer followed as a self-complete and self-sufficient religious path. The Vedic ceremonies and sacrifices, which continue to be performed in different parts of India in varying scales, are performed, not for their own sake, but for the propitiation of gods and goddesses or of the Supreme God. The Vedic faith in the living presence of God or the deities in the place of worship, which was lost in the heyday of Mīmāṁsā thought, seems to be now revived and to form an important part of the Mīmāṁsā religion.

THEISTIC SCHOOLS

Many of the Hindu systems of thought are theistic in the sense that they believe in a personal God who has created a real world of things and beings, and who has moral relations with mankind. But we do not find the same type of theism in all of them. Thus, while some orthodox systems of Hinduism combine the theistic faith with a pluralistic view of the universe, one of them at least is professedly dualistic and some others are obviously monistic. Hence we have three types of theism in Hinduism: pluralistic, dualistic, and monistic. We shall now consider them one by one.

PLURALISTIC THEISM—THE NYĀYA-VAIŚESHIKA THEORY

In Indian theism the idea of God's creation of the world out of nothing is absent. Here it is believed either that God created the world out of Himself or that He created it out of pre-existing materials. Some systems of Hindu religious thought hold that there are many such uncreated and independent things and beings out of which God formed and fashioned the world system. While God is one, the ultimate realities of the world are many. Thus these systems combine a pluralistic view of reality with a theistic faith in One God. As such, they may be characterized as pluralistic theism. This type of theism is represented by the Nyāya, Vaiśeshika, and Yoga Systems of Hindu thought. Of these, the Nyāya and the Vaiśeshika are allied systems and will here be considered together.

Nyāya, which may be translated as "theory of inference," or that which "leads from premise to conclusion," is not followed today as a school of religious practices, but more as a system of logic. *Vaiśeshika,* which means "study of ultimate particulars," is accepted more as a cosmological system than as a religious system complete in itself.

The Nyāya-Vaiśeshika philosophy, like many of the other Indian systems, aims at the liberation of the individual self from bondage through a right knowledge of reality. According to it, reality is a complex system of many independent and eternal entities like the four kinds of atoms of earth, water, fire, and air, and like ether, space, time, minds, and selves. There are two kinds of selves, the Supreme Self which is the creator, sustainer, and destroyer of the world, and individual selves which are different in different bodies and quite distinct from the body and the mind.

God and the World

God as the Infinite Self cannot, of course, be perceived by our senses but His existence is known through a number of rational arguments. There is first the cosmological argument. The world, as we know it, is a series of things and events, each of which is caused by certain antecedent conditions. Just as any part of the world, so the world as a whole is of the nature of an effect and, therefore, requires a cause to explain its origin and continued existence. Neither matter nor individual selves can be the ultimate or first cause of the world. A cause must be a conscious and an intelligent power that can select and combine the necessary materials for the production of a definite effect. Since the effect here is the infinite universe, the first cause thereof must be an infinitely wise and powerful being. That is, He must be God, and none but God.

Second, we have the moral argument. That there is a moral order of the world, or that there is any morality in the world, implies that the joys and sorrows of our life are in accordance with our moral deserts. This merit and demerit of our actions brings about the happy and unhappy experiences which we have in our lives. The stock of merit and demerit accruing from our good and bad actions is an unseen power which accounts for the differences in our lot in this world; but the stock of moral deserts, being unconscious and unintelligent, cannot lead to the proper moral consequences without the guidance of some intelligent being. The individual selves who are governed by this moral law cannot be expected to govern and control it. Hence there must be a supremely wise and intelligent person under whose guidance the moral law operates and makes proper moral adjustments. This person is the Supreme Being, God, the moral governor of the world.

Third, we have the argument from the authoritativeness of

the Vedas. According to some Nyāya-Vaiśeshikas, the authority of the Vedas is derived from the supreme authority of their author, just as the authoritativeness of the sciences is derived from the scientists who founded them. No human being can be the author of the Vedas, for the supersensible realities and principles related in the Vedas cannot be objects of the knowledge of any ordinary individual. Hence the author of the Vedas must be God, the Supreme Person who has a direct knowledge of all objects, past, present, and future; finite, infinite, and infinitesimal; sensible and supersensible.

Last, the testimony of the scriptures also proves the existence of God, the Supreme Being. The Hindu scriptures, such as the Vedas, Upanishads, and Bhagavad Gītā, bear unmistakable testimony to the reality of God. Scriptural testimony is the best evidence for the belief in supersensible realities like God, self, and immortality, for these can neither be perceived by our senses nor convincingly proved by any argument based on sense experience. They are to be apprehended through some sort of supersensuous, spiritual experiences. The scriptures embody the direct spiritual experiences of saints, sages, and Seers relating to moral, religious, and spiritual matters. We cannot reasonably doubt their honesty and the veracity of their statements. As such, the scriptures constitute a valid source of our belief in the existence of God.

God is the eternal and infinite spirit who is not limited by this world of nature and individual selves, since it is related to Him as a body to the self which resides in it. He possesses to the full all perfections and is omnipotent, omniscient, majestic, all-glorious, infinitely beautiful and wise, and perfectly free from attachment. God is the Supreme Self, the eternal, infinite self who first creates, then maintains, and finally destroys the world.

The creation of the world means the ordering of the eternal entities of atoms, space, time, ether, minds, and individual selves which co-exist with God, into a moral system in which individual selves enjoy and suffer the consequences of their actions and all physical objects serve as means to the moral and spiritual ends of our lives. Since the process of creation always has reference to the stock of merit or demerit acquired by individual selves in a previous world, the process of creation and destruction is beginningless and we cannot speak of a first creation of the world. When God wills to create a world, by His mere thought there appears the embryo of a world out of the atoms of fire and earth. God animates that vast embryo with the World Soul (Brahmā) who is entrusted with the work of creation in its concrete details and with proper adjustment between virtue and happiness, vice and misery.

God is also the moral governor of the world of living beings, including ourselves. Like a wise and benevolent father He directs all human beings to do such actions and experience such consequences as are consistent with their past conduct. Man is not absolutely free in his actions, rather he is relatively free and has to act under the guidance of the Divine Being who dispenses the fruits of his actions and is the supreme arbiter of his joys and sorrows. The order of the world is, on the whole, a moral order in which the life and destiny of all individual selves are governed both by physical laws and by the moral law of karma which ensures that every man must have his just dues according to his deserts.

The created world runs its course for many years, but it cannot exist for all time to come. Creation is followed by the destruction of the world. The periods of creation and destruction of one world system make one complete cycle (called a *kalpa*) which has been repeating itself eternally. The theory of cycles or recurring periods of creation and destruction is accepted by all systems of Hindu religious thought. When in the course of time the World Soul, Brahmā, gives up his body like other selves, there arises in the Divine Being the will to destroy the world. Then the creative function of the unseen moral deserts of individual selves ceases and they begin to operate for the dissolution and destruction of the world. When the dissolution is complete, the eternal entities of ether, space, time, minds, and selves with their stocks of merit and demerit continue to exist, but are at rest until God wills to create afresh.

The Individual Self and its Liberation

In the Nyāya-Vaiśeshika philosophy, the self is a unique, eternal, infinite, and indestructible substance because it is not limited to time, space, and causality. The self is different and distinct from the body, the senses, the mind, and the stream of consciousness. The body being by itself unconscious and unintelligent cannot take the place of the self. The senses cannot explain the functions of memory, imagination, and thinking, which belong to the self. The mind is, according to the Nyāya-Vaiśeshika, an atomic substance and an internal sense. If it were the self and the qualities of pleasure and pain belonged to it, we could not have any internal perception of them, for they would be as imperceptible as an atom. So we must admit that the self is a reality which is distinct from the body, mind, and the senses. It is a conscious substance and not, as the Advaita Vedānta holds, of the stuff or essence of consciousness.

Although consciousness belongs to the self as an attribute, it is not an essential and inseparable attribute of it. The self has the quality of consciousness when it is related to the mind, and the mind is related to the senses, and the senses come in contact with external objects. Otherwise, there would be no consciousness in the self.

For the individual self the highest good of life is liberation from bondage to the flesh, a state of complete and absolute cessation of all pain and misery. So long as the self is associated with a body it is impossible for it to be completely free from pain because the sense organs of the body cannot possibly avoid contact with unpleasant objects. Hence liberation is to be attained through complete dissociation of the self from the body. This happens when the self gives up its present body at death and there is no chance of its being born in any other body. The Nyāya-Vaiśeshika thus does not admit the possibility of man's attaining liberation in this life and in this world.

With the end of all connection with the body, the liberated self ceases to have painful or pleasurable experiences, nay more, it ceases to have any experiences or consciousness at all. It exists as a pure substance which has no experience or consciousness of anything. Liberation is thus a negative state of freedom from pain and not a positive experience of bliss or happiness. It is the condition of undisturbed peace and not of supreme bliss as it is conceived to be in the Vedānta.

To attain liberation one must realize the self as a transcendent reality which is distinct from the mind and the body. For this purpose a man should first receive scriptural instructions about the self. Then he should reflect on them and firmly establish the knowledge of the self by means of reasoning. Finally, he must meditate on the self in conformity with the methods of yoga practice. With the realization of the self in this way, all wrong notions about it are removed and he ceases to think of himself as the body or the mind. Such a man is no longer moved to action by the base passions and propensities of his animal nature, nor is he affected by other actions which are done by him with no desire for fruits. All his past deeds being exhausted by producing their proper consequences in this life, the individual has to undergo no more birth in this world. The stoppage of rebirth means the final cessation of the self's connection with the body and, therefore, of all pain and suffering. And this is liberation—the highest end of man's life.

PLURALISTIC THEISM—YOGA AS A RELIGION OF SPIRITUAL PRACTICES

Yoga as a philosophy combines the dualistic realism of the Sāṅkhya with a theistic faith in God. It accepts most of the metaphysics of the Sāṅkhya with its theory of a plurality of selves (purusha) on the one hand, and unconscious primal matter (prakṛiti) and its products on the other. God is the perfect spirit who is eternal, all-pervading, omnipotent, and omniscient. He is completely and eternally free from all actions and afflictions, and their effects and impressions. As such, He is distinguished from all other selves.

It is a highly controversial question among contemporary philosophers as to the way in which God brings about the association or dissociation between purusha and prakṛiti. One school holds that God merely removes all obstacles to the free working of the purposes of prakṛiti. More consistent with the theistic position of Yoga philosophy is the statement that God as the Supreme Self brings about the association or dissociation between purusha and prakṛiti in so far as the moral deserts of individual selves require the evolution or dissolution of the world. Purusha and prakṛiti being independent realities, they are not naturally associated with nor dissociated from each other. It is God who effects their association and dissociation for the creation and destruction of the world.

The special interest of Yoga as a religion is in the method of concentration (yoga), which is considered by it to be the sure means of attaining liberation. The individual self is in bondage so long as it confuses itself with the body, the mind, and the ego. In truth, the self is pure and eternal consciousness which is distinct from the whole world of objects including the mind, the intellect, and the ego. To realize this truth a man must restrain all bodily and mental functions and yet have that pure consciousness which is the self itself. This will convince him of the reality of the self as the transcendent spirit. When he has a clear and steady realization of the self as such, he becomes free from all affections and afflictions of the body and the mind. That is, he is liberated from sin and suffering, from birth and death.

Yoga as religion is a practical method of attaining liberation through self-realization. The word *yoga* means the cessation of all mental functions or modifications. The aim of yoga is to prevent the self from identifying itself with mental modifications, but this is not possible so long as the mental modifications are there and the self has not realized its distinction from them all. Hence some way of effecting the cessation of all mental modifications is necessary in order that the self may abide in itself as pure, self-shining consciousness. This is accomplished by the eight steps in the practice of yoga which are generally accepted by all schools of religious thought in Hinduism.

1. It is almost a truism to say that a man cannot realize spiritual truths so long as his mind is tainted with impurities and his intellect is vitiated by evil thoughts. Hence the first step in the practice of yoga is self-restraint or self-control, which is gained through (*a*) abstention from injury to any life, (*b*) truthfulness in thought, word, and deed, (*c*) nonstealing, (*d*) continence, and (*e*) nonacceptance of unnecesary gifts from other persons.

2. The second step in yoga is self-culture in order that the spiritual aspirant may cultivate good habits which will purify him. It consists in (*a*) purification of the body by washing, taking pure food, and similar practices; and purification of the mind by cultivating good sentiments and noble attitudes; (*b*) contentment; (*c*) penance and austerity; (*d*) study of sacred books; and (*e*) constant contemplation of God.

3. The next step is the adoption of suitable and steady postures for meditation. There are various postures of the body described in the Yoga System, all of which can be properly learned only under the guidance of experts. Of these, the lotus posture is most popular. In it one must sit erect with the left foot turned up and placed upon the right thigh and the right foot similarly placed on the left thigh, and with the two hands placed upon their respective knees, the thumb and the index finger touching each other at their ends. These postures are necessary for the health of the body and the concentration of the mind. They are effective ways by which the body can be

kept partially free from diseases and all the limbs can be brought under control and prevented from producing disturbances in the mind.

4. Then come certain breathing exercises which conduce to steadiness of the body and the mind. These consist in deep inspiration, retention of breath, and expiration with measured durations in the proportions of one to four and four to two time units respectively. The practice of breath control enables one to suspend breathing for a long time and thereby prolong the state of concentration, but the details of the process must be learned from experts.

5. The fifth discipline consists in restraint of the senses. Here one is to turn his senses from distracting sights and sounds, and make them follow the lead of the mind itself. It requires strong determination and long practice to control one's senses with success; but when a man gains mastery over his senses in this way, he rises above the ordinary distractions of life and can concentrate his mind steadily on the proper objects.

6. The next stage is steady attention to a desired object. It consists in fixing the mind and holding it on some desired object like the midpoint between the eyebrows, the images of gods, or the moon. The ability to keep one's attention steadily fixed on some object is the test of fitness for entering into the next higher stage of yoga.

7. The next step is meditation on the object of attention. It is just the even and continuous flow of thought all around the object of attention. When sufficiently prolonged, meditation enables the mind to penetrate into the object of thought and grasp its reality. Thus meditation reveals the reality of the contemplated object to the mind of one who is well advanced on the path of yoga.

8. The last stage in the practice of yoga is perfect concentration of the mind on the object of attention and meditation (samādhi). In it the mind is so deeply absorbed in the object that it loses itself in it and has no awareness of itself. At the

preceding stage of meditation the act and the object of thought remain distinct. But here the act of meditation is not separately known; it takes on the form of the object and loses itself, as it were. So here, only the object of thought remains shining in the mind, and one does not even know that there is a process of thought in the mind. This state of perfectly concentrated thought is known as the trance of meditation, or as conscious concentration, in so far as there is in it a distinct consciousness of the object of meditation.

A spiritual aspirant should practice yoga with its eightfold disciplines for a sufficiently long time and with a sufficiently determined will. He is then in a position to attain yoga perfectly, to attain the cessation of all mental modifications. This is the trance of perfect absorption in which, all mental modifications being restrained, nothing is known or thought of by the mind. Yet it is not a state of unconsciousness. Rather, it is that superconscious state of concentration in which all mental states and appearances of objects are negated, and there are no ripples in the placid surface of the mind. In this state the self abides in its own essence as pure consciousness, enjoying the still vision of self-shining existence.

He who realizes the self as this transphysical and supermental reality, as the transcendent spirit, rises above the whole world of objects and ceases to be affected and afflicted by the ordinary joys and sorrows of life. With this he reaches the final goal of life, liberation from all pain and suffering.

THE DUALISTIC THEISM OF MADHVA (DVAITA)

Madhvāchārya was a Vaishṇava thinker who lived in southern India in the thirteenth century and developed a system of dualistic theism out of the teachings of the Upanishads and the Vedānta. For him, there are two ultimate categories of reality, the absolute which is independent of everything else, and the relative which is completely dependent on the absolute. God, or Brahman, is the Absolute Reality and is the same as Lord Vishṇu. Individual selves and material objects are all relative realities, dependent on God. They are absolutely distinct and different from one another. The differences between them are of five kinds, of which each is absolute. These differences are between God and selves, God and material objects, one individual self and another, selves and material objects, and one material object and another. Madhva's religious thought thus combines dualism with theism and is a system of dualistic theism. (*Dvaita*—"philosophy of the two".) There are many followers of Madhva in India today, especially in the south.

God and the World

God is the Supreme Person who is called Nārāyaṇa, Vishṇu, Hari, and many other names. We cannot know Him through our unaided thought and reason. The belief in God must be based on the teachings of the scriptures, all of which aim at revealing the existence and nature of God. From them we know that God is the absolutely independent Being who is free from all imperfections, and possesses all good and glorious qualities in unlimited extent. He is of the essence of self-revealing consciousness and bliss, and has such attributes as infinite power and infinite mercy. Brahman or God is existence-consciousness-bliss (sat-chit-ānanda) incarnate and as such lives in His heavenly abode with His consort, Lakshmī, who is the personification of His power. He manifests Himself in various forms and through all the incarnations (avatāra) in the world.

He is the Lord of all beings and the creator, preserver, and destroyer of all things. He is the highest of all, since there is nothing like Him nor greater than He in the universe. It is He who controls all things, gives us the light of all knowledge, and also obscures it at times. It is He who leads us from life to life in bondage and it is He who helps us attain final deliverance. He is the Lord even of the gods and the sole ruling and controlling power of the universe.

God creates the world, not out of Himself, but out of the primal matter called prakṛiti which is an eternal and unconscious substance. God is not the material cause of the world, He is only its efficient cause. It is under His control and guidance that prakṛiti, the material cause, evolves the world of physical objects. The order of evolution of the world is much the same as in the Sāṅkhya, but here the three guṇas of sattva, rajas, and tamas are not regarded as the constituents of prakṛiti; they are its first products or evolutes.

Prakṛiti is not anything unreal and illusory like māyā. It is a real and an eternal entity which is the object of God's knowledge and creative activity. God Himself maintains the reality of the material world and its absolute distinction from Him, but God so controls and guides prakṛiti from within that it evolves into an orderly world in which individual selves may live and act and realize their moral destiny. Thus God is not outside the world, although He is quite different from it and is not embodied in it. Being eternally perfect, He has no end of His own which He wants to realize through the world's evolution. The history of the world is the revelation of God's perfection and of man's progressive self-realization.

Individual Selves and Their Liberation

Individual selves are finite and eternal entities, and also conscious and active subjects. They are infinitely small, infinite in number, and fundamentally different from one another. Selves are neither created by God nor do they form the body of God, but they are absolutely dependent on Him. Each individual self has its own imperfections, such as ignorance and suffering; although they are different from God, they possess in limited degree the qualities of knowledge and bliss in common with God. Such resemblance, however, does not mean identity of essence between God and the individual self, for the self which is always dependent on God can never be identical with Him. Just as a servant cannot be identical with his master, so the individual self can never become identical with God. It is sheer ignorance and folly to think that the finite self is ever identical with God who is the infinite and absolute self.

Even when the individual self is liberated, it does not become identical with the essence of God. The liberated self closely approximates and resembles God in the qualities of knowledge and bliss; it becomes similar, but not identical. Even in the state of liberation, the individual self's knowledge and bliss are finite and limited as compared with those of God which are infinite and unlimited. The knowledge and bliss attained by individual selves are in each case appropriate to their intrinsic merits, so that the distinction between one self and another is maintained even in the state of liberation.

There are three classes of selves, of which the first includes those that are always free, the second includes those that were once in bondage but are now liberated, and the third includes those that are still in bondage. Of the selves in bondage, those who are pure in nature, with sattva predominating, will be liberated; those who are of an intensely passionate temperament, with rajas predominating, will always wander from life to life in this world; and those who are grossly vicious in their nature, with tamas predominating, are doomed permanently to a miserable life in hell.

For an individual self liberation from bondage to the world (moksha) is the highest end of life. While such other ends of life as wealth and enjoyment are temporal, liberation is eternal and imperishable. The root cause of man's bondage is ignorance about his self and Brahman, so the first step in the attainment of liberation is the acquisition of true knowledge about Brahman and the self. A man should know that God is the omnipotent, omniscient, and all-merciful ruler of the world. He must have a clear realization of the Lord's infinite and unparalleled greatness and goodness. He should always think of himself as completely dependent on the Lord and never as identical with Him. It is the constant consciousness of his dependence on, and not the false notion of identity with, Brahman that can save man's self and liberate him from bondage.

Knowledge of the truth about God and the self is not, however, a sufficient condition of salvation. There can be no liberation for man without the grace of the Lord. What is, therefore, more important than knowledge is man's sincere devotion to and pure love of the Lord. To develop and maintain this essential religious attitude, a man ought to keep himself constantly engaged in the service and worship of God. He should devote his body and mind, his thought and speech to the cause of goodness and truth, and to the study of the holy scriptures. All this pleases God most, for God Himself is truth and goodness. Being thus pleased, God gives His grace to the man who loves Him as his dearest. Just with this does the man stand liberated from all bonds which bind the soul to the world. He leaves this body and this world at death, and lives for ever in the presence of God, enjoying the eternal bliss of communion with Him.

MONISTIC THEISM—THE QUALIFIED MONISM OF RĀMĀNUJA (VIŚISHṬĀDVAITA)

Rāmānuja, who lived about two centuries before Madhva, was also a Vaishṇava philosopher who attempted to synthesize Vaishṇavism with the Vedānta, but he developed a monistic system of religious thought out of it. He favored neither the dualistic philosophy which was later taught by Madhva nor the unqualified monism which Śaṅkara had taught two centuries earlier. For him, Brahman or God is not absolutely different from the individual self and the material world as the dualists believed, nor is He absolutely and unqualifiedly identical with the self as the followers of Śaṅkara believe. Rather, Rāmānuja said that Brahman as Absolute is really embodied in the self and the world, and there is identity between Brahman as absolute and Brahman as embodied. Brahman is the only absolute and independent reality which pervades the whole world. Material objects and individual selves are not independent realities, but are grounded in and dependent on Brahman, the Supreme Being. They are organically related to the Supreme Being and form the body of the Lord. Brahman is, therefore, not an unqualified and indeterminate reality, but a determinate and qualified being. He is both the independent, absolute reality and the embodied self of the world. Since Rāmānuja thus admits the identity of Brahman as qualified by two different forms or characters, his system is called qualified monism (*Viśishṭādvaita*—"one ultimate as qualified"). There are many followers of this position today, more than of the dualistic school of Madhva, and both in northern and southern India.

Brahman and the World

Brahman, according to Rāmānuja, is the absolute reality which includes within itself matter and finite spirits as its integral parts. He is the only reality in the sense that there is nothing outside or independent of Him, nothing either similar or dissimilar to Him. Brahman is thus free from all external distinctions between Himself and anything outside which is like or unlike Him. But Brahman possesses internal distinctions in so far as there are within Him conscious selves and unconscious matter which can be mutually distinguished. God as absolute contains within Himself material objects as well as finite selves as His internal parts or qualifying attributes. The Absolute One thus contains the many and is qualified by the many. Rāmānuja's Brahman is not a distinctionless unity which excludes plurality. Rather, He is a unity qualified by the many. This is another reason why his system is known as qualified monism.

Brahman is possessed of an infinite number of infinitely good qualities such as omnipotence, omniscience, benevolence. Therefore, Brahman is not qualityless, but is possessed of qualities. He does not, however, possess any bad or immoral quality. He creates, maintains, and withdraws the world, according to the moral exigencies of individual selves. The world is a real creation of Brahman out of eternal matter which exists within Him. Matter is the source of all material objects and as such is called prakṛiti or the material ground of the world. As in the Sāṅkhya, so here, prakṛiti is regarded as an unconscious and uncreated reality. But unlike the Sāṅkhya, Rāmānuja holds that it is a part of Brahman and controlled by Him, just as the human body is controlled from within by the human self.

During the state of dissolution, matter remains in Brahman in a latent, subtle, and undifferentiated form. Brahman creates the world of diverse objects out of subtle matter in accordance with the deeds (karma) of the selves in a previous world. It is Brahman's wonderful creative power that impels matter to evolve the world of objects. Matter is first transformed into the three subtle elements of fire, water, and earth. Gradually, the subtle elements become mixed up in different proportions and produce all gross objects which we perceive in the material world. The creation of the world is a real fact and not an illusory appearance, as Śaṅkara would say. The created world is as real as Brahman but it is dependent on Brahman and cannot exist apart from Him.

Brahman is sometimes described as the wielder of a magical power (māyā), not because the world is unreal and illusory like a magical show, but because His power of creation is as wonderful as that of a magician. Rāmānuja, therefore, holds that creation is a real act of Brahman, the Supreme Being, and that the world exists in and is controlled by Him. The Supreme Being is the immanent principle of the world as well as of selves. They are sustained and controlled by Him, and entirely subserve His purposes. Brahman with the world and individual selves is an organic whole. He is the Supreme Person who is at the same time transcendent to and immanent in the world and individual selves.

The Self and Its Bondage and Liberation

By the self Rāmānuja means the embodied self. The self, which exists eternally, is infinitely small and therefore is capable of penetrating into every material substance. It is not made, but it has a real body which is made of matter; like matter, the self is a part of Brahman and so cannot be infinite. Consciousness is not an accidental quality of the self, dependent on its connection with the body. It is an essential quality of the self and it remains under all conditions. In deep sleep and even in the state of liberation, when the self is altogether disembodied, the self remains conscious of itself as "I am." The self is, therefore, identified by Rāmānuja with what we mean by the word *I* or *ego*.

The relation between the individual self and Brahman is one of identity as well as difference. It is unthinkable that the self which is finite can be identical with Brahman in every respect. But at the same time the self cannot be totally different from Brahman, since it is a part of Him and is pervaded by Him. Brahman is the inner controller of all selves and all material objects. Hence between the self and Brahman there is identity as between a part and the whole, or between a quality and its substance. But it is not an unqualified or absolute identity between exactly identical terms, which is a meaningless tautology. It is an identity between two different forms of the same reality. A man is considered to remain the same person in his youth and old age. The identity of the man means the identity of his self in two different forms or bodily conditions. Similarly, the identity of the self with Brahman means identity between two different forms of the same reality, namely, Brahman as the creator of the universe and as existing in the form of man. It is, therefore, an identity qualified by difference, which is another reason for calling Rāmānuja's philosophy qualified monism.

Bondage of the self to the body is due to ignorance, which consists in the identification of the self with the body. As the effect of such ignorance, the self thinks of itself as the body and seems to enjoy pleasure or suffer pain as the body does. Ignorance is thus the egoism in man which leads him to identify the self with the not-self, and enjoy or suffer in life accordingly.

Liberation from bondage must be sought through religious work and philosophical knowledge. A man should perform the different obligatory rites enjoined by the Vedas according to his caste and station in life. These should be performed all his life as obligations without any desire for a reward, such as heaven. Disinterested performance of such duties destroys the accumulated effects of the past deeds which stand in the way of knowledge. Then, a man should study the Mīmāṁsā philosophy and thereby realize that the sacrificial rites cannot lead to any permanent good and cannot help him attain salvation. This persuades him to the study of the Vedānta. From the Vedānta he learns that Brahman is the almighty creator, sustainer, and controller of all things and beings, and that his self is not identical with the body, but is really a part of Brahman who controls it from within. He learns also that liberation can be attained, not by mere "study and reasoning," but only if Brahman is pleased to choose him for liberation.

The knowledge imparted by the Vedānta is not mere verbal knowledge of the scriptural texts. It is that real knowledge which consists in a steady, constant remembrance of Brahman, the Supreme Self. This is variously described as meditation, prayer, and devotion. Constant meditation on the Supreme Self as the dearest object of love should be practiced, along with the performance of the obligatory rituals. Intense remembrance of Brahman, or devotion thus practiced, ultimately matures into an immediate knowledge or direct experience of Brahman. This, therefore, is the final means of liberation.

This brings about the destruction of all ignorance and effects of past deeds (karmas) by which the self is bound to the body. Therefore, the self which realizes Brahman is liberated from the body for ever, without any chance of rebirth.

We should remember, however, that liberation cannot be attained simply by human efforts. Brahman, the Supreme Being, pleased by devotion and complete self-surrender, helps the devotee to attain perfect knowledge by removing obstacles. He gives His grace and lifts from bondage the man who flings himself at the mercy of the Supreme Being and constantly remembers Him as the only object of love. Absolute self-surrender to God, coupled with complete faith in His mercy and power, is sometimes regarded by Rāmānuja as alone sufficient to lead at once to liberation.

Liberation does not mean the self's identification with Brahman. Even when liberated, the self does not become identical with Brahman, but remains distinct from Him. The liberated self having pure consciousness, untainted by any imperfection, becomes, in this respect, similar to Brahman. Free from ignorance and bondage of every kind, its enjoys the bliss of complete communion with Brahman.

MONISTIC THEISM OF THE ŚAIVAS

Śaivism is a popular school of religion within the fold of Hinduism. Although it is a sectarian school, it does not depart from the dominant monistic trend of Hindu religious and philosophical thought. Each of the two main systems of religious thought in Śaivism is theistic in the sense that it admits a personal God, and also is monistic in so far as it holds that God is the only Ultimate Reality and that other realities are in some sense or other identical with God or God's creative power. The Siddhānta school of Śaiva philosophy has flourished in southern India and has many followers today (*Siddhānta*—"established doctrines"). The other school of Śaiva philosophy flourished in Kashmir in northern India and is sometimes called the Kashmir School of Śaivism; as a separate school it has a limited number of followers today. It is known as the *Pratyabhijñā* (recognition) school of Śaiva philosophy.

The Śaiva-Siddhānta

According to this system, there are three categories of reality: God or the Lord, the self, and matter. The Lord, who is here called Śiva, is the eternally self-manifest and independent reality. The Lord is different in nature from the self which is conscious but dependent, and from matter which is unconscious. The Lord is an omnipotent, omnipresent, and omniscient Being, because He is the first cause of the world, and the inmost self of all beings. The world being an ordered whole of parts is of the nature of an effect which must have been produced by a supremely intelligent and powerful Being. As the omniscient supreme ruler and moral governor of the world, He has full knowledge of all the elements in the constitution of the world and of all the activities in the history of living beings. The Lord is the eternal, free, and perfect spirit, with none of the impurities and imperfections which enter into the life of individual selves.

God, the Lord, is formless in Himself, but assumes various forms out of love for His devotees who find it impossible to worship Him as formless Being. He has no physical body made of bones and flesh, but His body is made of conscious force and energy. He creates the world with this body of energy in accordance with the merits and demerits of individual souls. The Lord acts through His Śakti, which is personified conscious energy. In relation to the World, the Lord (Śiva) performs the functions of creation, preservation, and destruction, and in relation to selves He has the two functions of obscuring their intellects when they go astray and giving them His grace when they want to be liberated.

Selves are conscious agents, not transitory and finite or atomic entities as some philosophers suppose. Since they are not limited by time and space, selves are eternal and infinite. It is wrong to identify the self with the body or to say that there is only one self in all bodies, for there are as many selves as there are bodies. Consciousness and activity are intrinsic to the self, and it is divine since in liberation it has, like the Lord, eternal knowledge and infinite activity; its conscious and intelligent activities are a participation in the nature of the divine. But because of the fetters of the material world, the self seems to lose its divinity and suffer in life in this world.

Matter constitutes the fetters of the self. It is unconscious and eternal like the Sāṅkhya prakṛiti, although its connection with any particular self is temporary. There are four kinds of matter: the impure, the overpowering, force generated by actions, and māyā or the cosmic energy. The first, impure matter, conceals the self's infinity and activity and produces the false notions of its finiteness and inactivity. The second, overpowering energy, is the energy of Śiva Himself which is a fetter of the self in so far as it obscures the self's intelligence. The third, karma, or the force generated by actions, is the stock of merit and demerit which arises out of the actions done by the self for personal ends and causes its rebirth into the world. Māyā is the cosmic energy of the Divine which manifests the whole world at creation and withdraws it at dissolution. It is the material cause of the world.

The self is in bondage when it comes under the sway of matter, so for liberation it is necessary to break the fetters of matter. The means to liberation is spiritual initiation, and this depends on knowledge of reality, performance of religious duties, practice of yoga, and righteous conduct. But above all, it is the grace of Śiva that leads man to liberation. The liberated self becomes free from bondage of every kind and attains identity of essence with Śiva, being in possession of the Divine consciousness and the Divine will.

The Pratyabhijñā System

The Pratyabhijñā System is more explicitly monistic than the Śaiva-Siddhānta. It looks upon God or the Supreme Lord, called Maheśvara, as the absolute reality which is both different and nondifferent from the world, and considers the individual self to be really identical with the Supreme Lord. The Supreme Lord creates the world by His mere will and not through the aid of any unconscious material cause like prakṛiti. Creation is the Supreme Lord's manifestation of Himself to Himself, like a reflection of God in a mirror which also is God Himself. The individual self is none other than the Supreme Lord in so far as the Supreme Lord has given His all to it, namely, His free will, His independence, and His absoluteness. Only in its ignorance as an embodied being of this world does the self forget its divine nature and complain of its weakness, smallness, and sinfulness.

God is the Supreme Self who is eternally free, self-manifest, and blissful in nature. He is both immanent and transcendent in relation to the world of many things and conscious beings. There is nothing to limit His absolute freedom, inexhaustible bliss, and universal manifestation; He is present in everything and is manifested everywhere in the universe. Eternal self-consciousness, infinite joy and activity belong to the essence of His being. The self of man knows all things through its identity with the Supreme Self, for He is the only knower of the world. He manifests all things in and by the light of His eternal consciousness.

In reality, God is without plurality or difference, since He transcends all limitations of space and time, form and figure. His consciousness is of the nature of creative power and is eternally self-manifest. His activity consists in the free creation of the universe. It is the expression of the infinite delight which He is and wishes us to have. The Supreme Lord is also the highest good for man. A man who is rich in the wealth of devotion to God asks nothing more; but he who is poor in this has nothing else to seek.

The individual self as a conscious and active principle is verily identical with the Supreme Lord. It has, like God, both consciousness and activity belonging to its essence. The identity of the soul with the Supreme Lord is established by the fact that it has the capacity to know the whole universe and the freedom to do all acts, both of which are divine characteristics. But although the self is intrinsically free and divine, it becomes liable to limitation and bondage through māyā or ignorance. In its ignorance the self thinks of itself as different from the Supreme Lord and of other things as different from itself. Hence the best way to deliver man from bondage is to make him recognize his identity with the Supreme Lord. It is the clear recognition (pratyabhijñā) of his self as the same as the Supreme Being who is described as the highest Lord in the scriptures that leads man to liberation.

The liberated self no longer considers itself to be different from and opposed to other things and beings. He becomes one with, or rather finds himself as identical with, the whole universe. No strife troubles him, no jealousy demeans him, and no conflict rends him. He lives in peace and amity with all. Being in possession of the highest good in human life, he does not hanker after worldly goods. With the realization of God, he realizes all ends, and acts in the world with no other end in view than the good of mankind.

In the Pratyabhijñā System we find a type of religious thought which, although theistic on the face of it, is more properly characterized as supertheistic. Its central creed of the identity of the self with God and of God's difference and non-difference from the world takes it beyond the limits of a strictly theistic faith and brings it in line with the supertheistic schools which come next.

SUPERTHEISTIC SCHOOLS

There are some systems of Hindu religious thought which, although allied to theism, cannot be accurately called theistic. The essence of theism lies in the belief in a personal God who stands in a personal relation to man through ties of friendship and love. Such a relationship requires that the persons related have a distinct reality and individuality of their own, and yet intercommunicate. If any of these marks be absent, we cannot speak of a personal relation between God and man, and consequently of theism.

Now in Hinduism there are certain religious systems in which God is conceived as both personal and impersonal and as either identical with man and the world or both identical with and different from them. Whether such a view is or is not justifiable is an open question, but that it is not theistic in the accepted sense of the word will have to be admitted. At the same time, these systems are neither opposed to nor subversive of theism. Rather, they represent a higher level of religious experience from which theism is found to be more rational than atheism. We may even say that in practical life they make a man more deeply religious than an ordinary theist. So we here propose to call them supertheistic.

THE MONISM OF ŚAṄKARA (ADVAITA)

The monism of Śaṅkara is based on his interpretation of the Vedānta. It is an absolutistic interpretation as distinguished from the later theistic interpretations of Madhva and Rāmānuja. *Advaita* ("one ultimate," or "not-two") is the most popular system of faith and philosophy in India today and has been gaining ground in the West as well.

Brahman and the World

According to Śaṅkara, Brahman is the Absolute Reality and there is no other reality but Brahman. Brahman is pure existence, consciousness, and bliss (sat-chit-ānanda). These, however, are not His qualities or characteristics, but His essence. He is pure existence-consciousness-bliss as one identical essence without any distinction or difference. Brahman is really devoid of all qualities and distinctions within Him or outside Him. Brahman does not really create any world. The world which we perceive is the product of Brahman's magical power called māyā. Māyā as a power of Brahman is indistinguishable from Brahman, just as the burning power of fire is from the fire itself. It is by this that Brahman, the Great Magician, conjures up the world show. The appearance of the world is taken as real by the ignorant, but the wise who can see through it find nothing but Brahman, the only reality behind this illusory show. So for the wise the world appearance is not real and Brahman is not the bearer of this illusion-producing power.

Śaṅkara goes further and asserts that from the purely philosophical or transcendental standpoint, Brahman cannot be described at all and is, therefore, perfectly indeterminate or characterless. The description of Brahman even as existence-consciousness-bliss cannot directly convey the idea of Brahman, for it only serves to direct the mind toward Brahman by denying of Him nonexistence, unconsciousness, and misery. Brahman in this transcendent aspect is called by Śaṅkara *Paraṁbrahma,* the Supreme God or the Absolute.

But the Absolute may also be conceived from the ordinary practical standpoint as distinguished from the philosophical or the transcendental. From this standpoint the world is believed to be real and the Absolute is considered to be the creator, the sustainer, and the destroyer of the world and therefore as an omnipotent and omniscient Being. The Absolute in this aspect is called Īśvara by Śaṅkara. He is the God of religion and the object of worship. This description of the Absolute as the creator of the world is true only so long as the world appearance is regarded as real, and it gives us not His essence but an accidental description of Him. Those who believe in the world show think of the Absolute through this show and call Him its creator, but for those wise few who know that the world is a mere show, there is neither any real world nor any real creator, just as for the man who sees through the magician's trick there is neither any magic nor any magician.

The distinction between the higher and the lower aspect of Brahman helps us to understand how Brahman can be both in the world and beyond it, that is to say, both immanent and transcendent. The world, so long as it appears, is in Brahman, the only reality, just as the snake conjured out of the rope is nowhere else except in the rope. But Brahman is not affected by the imperfections of the world, just as the rope is not affected by any illusory characteristics of the snake.

Śaṅkara's conception of the Absolute as Paraṁbrahma or perfectly indeterminate and attributeless Being differs from that of the God of religion who is possessed of the highest attributes and is an object of worship, but from this one should not think that it is antireligious or atheistic. If by God we mean the Supreme Reality, then Śaṅkara's view is certainly not atheism, but rather the perfection of the theistic faith. Whereas atheism believes only in the world and not at all in God, and ordinary theism believes in both the world and God, Śaṅkara, as an absolute monist, believes only in the Absolute. For him, the Absolute is the only reality. Such a view makes the most of the Absolute and marks the highest extension of the religious emotion where love of Brahman becomes all-absorbing, suffering neither the ego nor the world. If this type of faith is to be distinguished from ordinary theistic belief in a personal God, we should call it supertheism, not atheism.

The Self and Its Bondage and Liberation

Śaṅkara believes in unqualified monism and rejects all distinctions between objects and objects, the subject and the object, the self and Brahman as unreal and illusory. For him the self of man is really identical with Brahman. Man is apparently composed of the body, the mind, and the self. But the body and the mind are like other material objects, merely appearances. When this is realized, the reality that remains is the self, which is nothing other than Brahman.

In the ordinary waking state a man thinks of himself as identical with the mind-body. When he sleeps and dreams he is conscious of objects as images which arise from memory impressions. He then appears as a limited subject or knower opposed to certain objects. In deep, dreamless sleep a man ceases to have any ideas of objects, and in the absence of objects he ceases to be a subject or knower as well. Even then his consciousness does not cease, for how otherwise could he remember at all on waking that he had such a state or that he had a sound sleep? There is, therefore, in the state of dreamless sleep pure consciousness free from the limitations of the body and the affections of the senses and the mind. Thus the self in its intrinsic nature is pure, blissful, and unlimited consciousness. As such, the self of man is identical with Brahman, who is pure consciousness and bliss.

Owing to ignorance, which is beginningless, the self erroneously associates and identifies itself with the body. This means bondage for the self. In this state it forgets that it is really divine and behaves like a finite, limited, and miserable creature. It thinks of itself as an isolated ego or individual opposed to other individuals, as having its own interests and purposes, which are in conflict with those of other selves. But the ego is not the real self of man; it is an apparent limitation of the self through its association with a particular body and mind. In truth, there is identity between a man's real self and Brahman and, therefore, between one self and other selves, since Brahman is present in them all.

Liberation from bondage is attained through the realization of the self's identity with Brahman. The identity is a real fact from the very beginning, only it has been forgotten for the time being and must be recognized. The means to liberation, according to Śaṅkara, is the study of the Vedānta under a teacher who has himself realized Brahman. The performance of religious rites and duties or the study of Mīmāṁsā is not essential for this study. What is indispensable, however, is fourfold culture of the mind, namely, discrimination between things eternal and things temporal, freedom from attachment to worldly objects, control of the senses and the mind, and an ardent desire for liberation.

With such training of the mind and body, one should begin to study the Vedānta with a competent teacher. The method of study consists in the threefold process of listening to the teacher's instructions, understanding the instructions through reasoning until all doubts are removed and conviction is generated, and constant meditation on the truths thus accepted. When all wrong beliefs thus become removed and belief in the truths of the Vedānta becomes steady and permanent, the pupil is told by the teacher, *"Tat tvam asi"* ("That art thou," or "thou art Brahman"). He begins then to contemplate this truth steadfastly, until at last he has an immediate realization of the truth in the form, " I am Brahman." With this the false notion of distinction between the self and Brahman disappears and bondage goes along with it. Liberation (mukti or moksha) is thus attained.

It is possible for a man to live and act in the world even on the attainment of liberation. The body of the liberated self may continue for some time because it is the product of karmas which have already begun to bear their effects. But he never again identifies himself with the body and he is not deceived by the world which still appears before him. He has no desire for the world's objects and is, therefore, not affected by the world's misery. He is in the world and yet out of it. This conception of liberation is known as *jīvanmukti,* the liberation of one while he is alive. The liberated self is no longer swayed by the ordinary passions and impulses of life, he feels no urge for selfish actions meant to serve his personal ends. Renouncing all worldly desires, he lives in perfect peace and amity with the rest of the world and acts for the liberation of all selves who are still in bondage. The life of the liberated man is a worthy ideal for all societies and communities.

Liberation is not merely the absence of all misery that arises from the illusory sense of distinction between the self and Brahman. It is a state of positive bliss, because Brahman is bliss and liberation is realization of identity with Brahman. The liberated self attains the life divine, and lives and acts for the good of mankind.

THE NATURAL DUALISTIC MONISM OF NIMBĀRKA (DVAITĀDVAITA)

Nimbārka was a Vaishṇava thinker who, in his interpretation of the Vedānta Sūtra, attempted to synthesize dualistic theism (dvaita) with unqualified monism (advaita). Thus he built up a system of religious thought which is known as dualistic monism (*dvaitādvaita*, "dual-nondual"). This religious-philosophical position has a limited number of followers in India in modern times, chiefly in northern India.

For Nimbārka there are three categories of reality: the Supreme Self (Īśvara), the individual self (jīva), and the world (jagat). God, the Supreme Self, is both dual and nondual, and both different and nondifferent from the individual self and the world. This character of the Supreme Self is natural and intrinsic to Him and it can be supported by reason. Hence this system is called natural or rational Dualistic Monism.

God (Īśvara), according to Nimbārka, is the Supreme Self who by His very nature is both different and nondifferent from everything and is called Vāsudeva or Kṛishṇa. He is the omniscient being in whom the past, present, and future of the world are eternally manifest and existent. As such, there is no room for any change in the Supreme Self, and no distinction of subject, object, and process of knowledge in Him. In this aspect the Supreme Self is called attributeless and actionless Brahman. But the Supreme Self is also the omnipotent creator, sustainer, and destroyer of the world. Omnipotence is a natural and eternal character of the Supreme Self, therefore activity or power belongs to His essence and makes Him the Godhead. Apart from this power of creation, the Supreme Being would not be the Supreme Spirit.

The Supreme Being is both the material and the efficient cause of the world. The world of nature and selves is made up of finite parts of which the Supreme Being is the whole. It is the Supreme Being who manifests them by His will to be many and to have communion with the many. He is the universal and all-pervasive spirit who regulates all things of the world and controls all selves from within. He is the ground and support of all things and beings. The whole world and all selves live, move, and have their being in Him. In these aspects the Supreme Being is regarded as possessing infinite powers and infinite attributes. There is really no contradiction between the qualified and the unqualified aspects of the Supreme Being, for as the subject of attributes He is different from and transcendent to them, and as the ground and support of the attributes He is also nondifferent from and immanent in them. He is thus both qualified and qualityless, different and nondifferent from the self and the world. The Supreme Self has four forms (such as Kṛishṇa) and appears as various incarnations under different conditions.

The world is unconscious, finite, limited, and imperfect; it is real and eternal and is included within the Supreme Being as a finite part. It exists as a subtle power of the Supreme Being before creation, is manifested by the Supreme Being during creation, and becomes unmanifest in the Supreme Being on dissolution, which means that it is never unreal or nonexistent. The world as an unconscious reality is of three kinds: the supernatural such as the abode of the Supreme Being, the natural which is the product of prakṛiti or primal matter, and the temporal. The world, which is the manifestation of the objective and unconscious energy of the Supreme Being, is a real transformation and creation of the Supreme Being without in any way affecting His supreme perfection. The Supreme Being as the cause transcends the world which is an effect of His creative activity. He is also immanent in the world in so far as He is the material and efficient cause of the world and is thus manifested in it. The relation between the Supreme Being and the world is, therefore, one of difference and nondifference at the same time.

The individual selves are eternal, conscious, finite, infinitely small, and infinite in number. An individual self is of the essence of consciousness, and yet it is a knower or subject of consciousness, an active agent, and an enjoyer of pleasures and pain. The self is quite distinct from the body, the senses, and the mind. As a knower it is the ego or the "I" which knows, acts, and enjoys or suffers the consequences of its actions. It is an infinitesimal part of the Supreme Being and is completely dependent on Him. The self resembles the Supreme Being in that its being is of the essence of consciousness; it is the finite manifestation of the Supreme Being's infinite, conscious energy. As such, it is not absolutely different from the Supreme Being, but while the Supreme Being is the infinite and all-pervading Self who controls everything else, the self is finite, limited, and controlled and guided by the Supreme Being. So far, it is different from the Supreme Being. Thus the relation between the Supreme Being and the self is one of simultaneous difference and nondifference.

Although the self is really an integral part of the Supreme Being and is essentially divine, in its ignorance it considers itself and the world (which is also a part of the Supreme Being) to be separate from and independent of Him. In consequence it gets entangled in the meshes of its selfish activities (karma). This means bondage for the self and leads to its repeated birth and death in this world with their inevitable sorrows and suffering.

Deliverance from bondage is to come from the realization that the Supreme Self is the Lord of all and the abode of all. The way to attain this realization is through deep devotion (bhakti) and complete resignation to the Supreme Being. As means thereof, the spiritual aspirant should perform the duties enjoined by the scriptures in a disinterested spirit. He should also meditate on the self and the world as the form and manifestation of the Supreme Being (Kṛishṇa), and constantly contemplate Him as the omnipotent, omniscient, and transcendent spirit. It is in this way that the self realizes its unity with the divine and becomes free from bondage and suffering.

THE SUPRARATIONAL DUALISTIC MONISM OF CHAITANYA (ACHINTYA-BHEDĀBHEDA)

Śrī Chaitanya, the great Vaishṇava reformer of Bengal, laid the foundations of a system of religious thought now known as a system of dualistic monism which cannot be grasped by logical thought (*achintya-bhedābheda,* "inconceivable duality and non-duality"). It has in modern times a fairly large following in upper India, especially Bengal. Other Vaishṇava religious thinkers who followed Śrī Chaitanya elaborated the system in contrast with the other schools of the Vedānta. It is closely allied to the Dvaitādvaita of Nimbārka, but has certain distinctive features of its own which we shall especially note here.

According to this system, there is one ultimate reality and that is Vishṇu, the personal God of love and grace. God is the supreme, self-conscious, and absolute reality. He is the eternal consciousness and infinite bliss which Sṛī Kṛishṇa is. There is no independent thing similar or dissimilar to Him from which He can be distinguished, nor is there any distinction within Him. He is pure, self-manifest consciousness, possessed of the highest qualities and powers, but not devoid of attributes and activities. There are in Him three ultimate powers: the essential or internal power which is the energy of pure consciousness, the intermediate or self-creative power which is the subjective energy manifesting selves, and the external or world-creative power which is the objective energy creating the natural world. God as possessed of such inconceivable powers exists eternally as He is in Himself and His celestial abode, and in the world of selves and the world of physical nature.

The divine consciousness crystallizes itself in the person of Śrī Kṛishṇa, the Lord of all. The Advaita conception of Brahman as pure passive consciousness is imperfect, and the yogi's idea of the Supreme Self as completely detached from the world is incomplete. It is the Bhāgavata conception of God Vishṇu as the Supreme Person that is perfect and complete.

God's energy is both the material and the efficient cause of the world. The natural world is a real and eternal creation of God, a real transformation of God's world-creative energy. As arising out of the divine will or energy, it cannot but be real, but since it is subject to change it is therefore impermanent—but it is never totally destroyed. At dissolution, it persists in God in an unmanifested subtle form and is consequently invisible.

The individual selves are conscious and atomic entities. They are real transformations of the self-creative energy of God and are integral parts of the divine being. As they are revelations of the divine energy which stands midway between God and the world, selves are higher than nature and can transcend it. They participate in the subjective consciousness of God, though not in the divine consciousness itself. The self has in it the power of self-determination, but in the exercise of this power it is conditioned by and dependent on God. The self is similar to God in its gifts of consciousness and self-determination, but being a finite, limited, and dependent part of God it is also different from Him. So the relation between God and the self, as also between God and the world, is one of difference as well as nondifference (*bhedābheda*).

The same relation continues even in liberation, so the self never becomes identical with God. Just as the sun's rays are nondifferent from the sun in point of luminosity and also different from it in being but parts of the sun, so the selves are both different and nondifferent from God. How God stands in such contradictory relations to the self and the world, we cannot understand by means of our thought and reason. It is something inconceivable by thought and incomprehensible by reason, but that God really has in Him such inconceivable powers we must believe on the authority of the scriptures.

Selves are of two classes, the liberated and the fettered. Those who turn Godward and are always devoted to Him are liberated, and those whose minds are directed outward and are attached to the world are in bondage. Liberation from bondage is attained primarily through devotion to God (*bhakti*). For this liberation one should always meditate on God, recite His name in company with great, religious souls, and enjoy the bliss that lies in the sacred name of his chosen deity. The outcome of all this is the fervent love of the Supreme Lord that breaks all the fetters of man and helps him attain the highest goal of human life, that is, the Lord Kṛishṇa.

THE PURE MONISM OF VALLABHA (ŚUDDHĀDVAITA)

Vallabha was a Brāhman of southern India who migrated to the north during the fifteenth century A.D. He developed another Vaishṇava school of the Vedānta, free from the belief that māyā is an inscrutable power which conceals the reality of Brahman and projects the unreal appearance of a world of many things and beings. According to him, the world of nature and individual selves (*jīvas*) is not created by Brahman through any magical power like māyā as was supposed by Śaṅkara. Brahman in His pure being and as uncontaminated by anything—like māyā—is manifested as the world of jīvas and physical things. Hence the school of religious thought developed by Vallabha is called pure monism (*Śuddhādvaita,* pure nondualism).

Brahman is the absolute, independent reality. He is of the essence of existence (*sat*), consciousness (*chit*) and bliss (*ānanda*), and has many good and great qualities. The Upanishadic texts which declare that He has no qualities mean only that He has not the ordinary human qualities. He is the highest being, who, when qualified by action only, is the presiding deity of sacrifices and is to be propitiated by ritualistic works. As qualified by wisdom, He is Brahman, and can be approached through philosophic knowledge as taught by the Upanishads. He requires no physical body for His activity. Yet He appears in physical forms to favor His devotees who love to see Him. As endowed with the qualities of wisdom and action, He is thus personified as Śrī Kṛishṇa.

Brahman creates the world by His pure will, and not with the help of any second principle like māyā, for that would contradict His absolute, independent existence. The creation of the world means just the manifestation of His being as the world of matter, time, and selves (prakṛiti, kāla, and jīvas). These are real and eternal existences as being but manifestations of the divine life and existence. The inanimate world and individual selves are natural emanations from Brahman, and are subtly of the same essence as Brahman, just as the rays of light emanating from the sun are essentially the same light as the sun.

Brahman is both the material and the efficient cause of the world, since He is the substance which constitutes it and the energy or power of will which brings it into existence. He, however, does not undergo any change or transformation in manifesting Himself as the world. There is a manifestation of His power or will in different degrees in the objects of the world, but no loss or mutation of His essential nature. The infinite in giving birth to the finite does not lose any part of His infinite essence or existence.

The material world with its living and nonliving objects is an emanation in which the existence aspect of Brahman is manifested and the consciousness and bliss aspects are suppressed. The world is, therefore, real and eternal. It has its being in Brahman and has no separate existence of its own. The world is in essence one with Brahman. Creation and destruction of the world mean only the manifestation and nonmanifestation of Brahman in the form of a system of many things and beings in space. The world being real is never completely annihilated. When destroyed, it is dissolved into Brahman and remains nonmanifest in Him.

Individual selves (jīvas) are finite manifestations of Brahman. In them the divine qualities of existence and consciousness are manifested, but that of bliss is suppressed. Jīvas are infinitely small entities. They are atomic in size and are parts of Brahman. Being parts of the divine life, they are in essence one with Brahman and inseparable from Him. He is the whole of which they are the parts and they are partakers of His essence. As such, there is no real difference between Brahman and the individual self. The self is both an agent who acts and an enjoyer who reaps the consequences of his actions. Though atomic, the self (jīva) pervades the whole body in which it exists, by its quality of consciousness, just as the fragrance of a piece of sandalwood fills the room in which it is.

The individual self is not differentiated from Brahman by the separative force of ignorance (*avidya*). The individual is really one with Brahman, with only the quality of bliss rendered unmanifest. There are three kinds of selves. First, there are the pure selves in whom the divine qualities are not obscured by the force of ignorance. Second, there are the mundane selves who are entangled in the meshes of ignorance and pass through birth and death because of their false identification with the mind-body organism. Finally, we have the liberated selves in whom all ignorance has been destroyed by the knowledge of truth and for whom the bonds of worldly life have been broken.

Ignorance of the truth about Brahman, the world, and the self, is the cause of the individual's bondage to the world, that is, to the wheel of birth and death. While the individual selves and the inanimate world are really manifestations of Brahman and are in essence one with Him, it is sheer ignorance to think that there are so many independent realities. In his ignorance the individual thinks of himself as an independent being living in a world of independent things. He also thinks of himself as the body and the mind, and as subject to birth and death like them. While the world is real as a part of Brahman, it is unreal as an objective and independent system of many things and beings. It is ignorance of this truth that constitutes man's bondage and is at the root of all the ills and evils from which he suffers in life in this world.

Devotion to Brahman in the sense of unshakeable and supreme love is the only means of emancipation from bondage. There is no other way to it. Of course, such devotion should be preceded by an insight into the truth and an understanding of His glory and greatness. But man cannot attain to such devotion by his unaided efforts. It is to be gained through the grace of the Supreme Being, which is received by those who are pure in heart. A firm faith in Brahman destroys all sins of man and renders him perfectly pure. Such a pure soul receives the grace of Brahman and, free from bondage, lives in His celestial abode in eternal loving service to Him.

THE SUPERPERSONALISM OF THE BHAGAVAD GĪTĀ (ĪŚVARA-VĀDA)

In the Bhagavad Gītā we have a type of religious thought which may be said to be a monumental synthesis of the main trends of religiophilosophical thought in the epic period of Indian history. It gives us the quintessence of the Upanishadic philosophy as that is vitalized by the touch of the emotional and active elements of the religious life. The cold, colorless, and perfectly indeterminate absolute which we find in some Upanishadic texts becomes a living and loving God in the Bhagavad Gītā, although His absoluteness is not altogether lost.

The dualism of spirit and matter (purusha and prakṛiti) which is almost inexplicable in the Sāṅkhya thought is happily ended in the Bhagavad Gītā. The conflict of religions with their apparently exclusive views and ways of life finds reconciliation in its catholic spirit and comprehensive religious outlook. Although the interpretations of the Bhagavad Gītā may vary, it is in modern times cherished all over India as one of the most widely read of the Hindu scriptures.

In the Bhagavad Gītā God is regarded as the Supreme Self in whom there are two aspects, the transcendent and the immanent, the impersonal and the personal, or the unqualified and the qualified. The Supreme Self in His transcendent aspect is the immutable, indeterminate, unapproachable, and uncharacterizable absolute. He is the absolutely formless and attributeless Brahman of the Advaita Vedānta. In His immanent aspect the Supreme Self is a personal Being and is possessed of the highest attributes. He is manifested as the world of mutable things and immutable selves. But as combining these two aspects, the Supreme Self transcends the world of nature and of selves and stands higher than even the immutable Brahman.

If we keep in view these two aspects of the Supreme Self, we shall be in a better position to understand the apparently conflicting statements regarding His nature found in the Gītā. The Supreme Self is the creator, sustainer, and destroyer of the world. He creates the world out of Himself, not out of nothing. He has a lower nature which is manifested as the material world including mind, intellect, and the ego. He has a higher nature which constitutes the world of individual selves. The Supreme Self is thus the origin and end of the whole universe. Higher than the Supreme Self there is nothing.

All things and beings are centered in the Supreme Self like beads on a string. He pervades the whole world and is in the heart of all beings as their inner ruler and guide. He is the moral governor of the world and the dispenser of the fruits of our actions. He is also the final resting ground, guide, friend, and savior of the world. The world is but the manifest form of the Supreme Self. Everything great and glorious in the universe is a special manifestation of the Supreme Self. The Supreme Self also incarnates Himself in the world and shares the joys and sorrows of men in the fullness of His self-communicative love and sportive, playful activity (*līlā*).

Although the Supreme Self is and does all these things in one aspect of Him, yet from another He is none of these things and does nothing. He is the eternal, immutable, and transcendent reality in which there is no change, mutation, or activity. He neither acts nor induces other selves to act and enjoy or suffer the consequences of their actions. He is above the whole world of matter (prakṛiti) with its qualities of sattva, rajas, and tamas, which overpower other selves and blind their vision. It is the ignorant who think of the one, absolute reality as changed into the many and the mundane. Although He pervades the world and everything is in Him, yet He transcends them all and there is nothing in Him. Such is the mystery of the Divine life that it supports and sustains all beings and yet is not in them, just as the mighty air moves in the all-pervading space and yet leaves it unaffected.

The world of nature exists as a part of the Supreme Self and is dependent on and controlled by Him. It is constituted by the lower nature of the Supreme Self which consists of the eight elements of earth, water, fire, air, ether or space, mind, intellect, and ego. It is vitalized and sustained by the Supreme Self's higher nature, which is manifested in individual selves (jīvas). The world is evolved by these two aspects of God's nature, selves and matter.

The order of evolution is much the same as in the Sāṅkhya, but here self (purusha) and matter (prakṛiti) are but parts of the Supreme Self, not independent and ultimate principles.

The Supreme Self is the inspiring Spirit who infuses life and light into the womb of nature (prakṛiti). He is the Father and nature is the matrix of the world. As such, the world is neither the mechanical product of matter nor the illusory projection of māyā or magical power. It is a real and rational creation by the Supreme Self's natural and intelligent powers.

Individual selves (jīvas) are conscious, eternal, and infinite realities. They are the expressions of the higher conscious nature of the Supreme Self and form integral parts of the Divine life. They are not subject to birth and death, change and mutation, disintegration and destruction. They are above space, time, and causality, and are quite distinct from the mind, the senses, and the body. Just as a man casts off a worn-out garment and puts on a new one, so the self passes from a decaying body and enters into a growing one. Birth and death are but different stages in the life of the self, just as boyhood, youth, and old age are stages in the life of a man.

The self is really divine and transcends the whole of nature. It is the Supreme Self who is present in man's body as the witnessing and unmoving self. The self is not the limited ego in us which performs various acts and enjoys or suffers the consequences thereof. All activity belongs to nature or prakṛiti. It is only when the self is deluded by and identified with the ego that it thinks itself to be an agent, a doer, a sufferer, or an enjoyer. This means bondage and a consequent life of suffering for the self in this world. The self that is in bondage is liable to sin and suffering, birth and death.

Liberation from bondage is the highest end of the individual self. Liberation is attained through self-realization, that is, realization of the self as essentially pure and divine, as distinct from nature and her qualities, the three guṇas. It is the realization of the Supreme Self as well, for the Supreme Self is the self in us. As means to the realization of the Self, or God, the Bhagavad Gītā recommends the four paths of meditation, knowledge, action, and devotion.

Meditation is the way of self-realization through deep concentration of attention, steadied like an unflickering flame, on the self. The preparations necessary for this are purification of the body, regulation of life and its habits, control of mind and the senses, continence, and detachment. With such preparation one is to meditate on the self in a quiet and secluded place and with a determined will. Such calm and continued meditation leads to a clear realization of the self as a transphysical and supermental reality.

Knowledge as a way of self-realization consists in the direct experience of the Supreme Self as the ultimate reality and of the self as essentially identical with the Supreme Self. It requires faith in the Supreme Self, devotion to truth, and self-control to acquire a direct knowledge of ultimate reality. It requires also an inquisitive mind, a devotion and service to a teacher who has himself realized the Supreme Self. With the proper training of one's intellect, emotion, and will, one is to receive instructions from the wise and enlightened teacher. By constant reflection and continued meditation on the truths thus received one realizes that the Supreme Self is the self in us and beyond us, that He creates the world by His free will, and that He incarnates Himself out of love for man. With this realization, man finds himself in the Supreme Self and the same Supreme Self in all beings from the highest to the lowest. He lives in perfect peace with all other beings, finds in him the bliss that the Supreme Self is, and devotes himself to the service of humanity as the manifestation of divinity. Thus the Gītā does not approve of inactivity even on the part of those who are liberated.

Action as a method of self-realization consists in the disinterested performance of one's own duties according to one's station in life. One should do the duties assigned to him by his nature and his social status, but he should not act with any selfish motive of gain to himself. Rather, he should offer the fruits of his actions to the Supreme Self and do them in the spirit of service to the Supreme Self. He should also be free from the sense of egoism in relation to these actions. All actions, he should know, are due not to the self, but to nature (prakṛiti). His self is the standing witness of all activities, but not the body, nor the mind, nor the ego concerned in them. The disinterested performance of one's duties thus enables one to realize the self as the free, transcendent spirit.

Devotion to the Supreme Self (bhakti) is a comparatively easy method of self-realization. It is open to all, high and low, educated and illiterate. It consists in sincere love of the Supreme Self and devoted service to Him. Here we are just to give up all pride, shed all fears, and forget all restraint or reluctance to approach the Supreme Self and take shelter in Him as the highest Lord. We are constantly to remember Him, meditate on Him, and serve and worship Him. One who is thus devoted to the Supreme Self, heart and soul, and is resigned to Him in all humility and meekness, receives His grace and overcomes the lure of the world of māyā or nature. The Supreme Self gives him that enlightenment of the intellect by which he realizes the Divine and enjoys the bliss of communion with Him.

These are the broad paths to liberation as laid down in the Bhagavad Gītā. They are not exclusive but interrelated, and all of them lead to the same goal of liberation. We may follow one or the other according to our taste, temperament, and character, and reach the same goal, which is the Supreme Self. The Gītā leaves us in no doubt that the Supreme Self hears our prayer in whatever language we may say it, He accepts our worship in whatever form we may offer it, and comes within our sight in whatever direction we may seek His light. The synthetic outlook and catholic spirit of Hinduism are seen at their best in the religion of the Bhagavad Gītā.

THE SPIRITUAL DYNAMISM OF TANTRA (ŚAKTI-VĀDA)

The Tantras are reckoned among the ancient scriptures of the Hindus and are sometimes given a place of importance equal to that of the Vedas. They are written in the form of a discussion between Śiva and His spouse Pārvatī—the two fundamental principles of their philosophy. Some scholars trace their origin to the Vedas, while others treat them as independent of the Vedas and even as superior to them. The Tantras are mainly concerned with the practical side of religion, that is, religious practices and observances, so they are sometimes known as the *Śākta Āgamas,* the manuals of the worship of Śakti—the Divine Mother or the Supreme Godhead. But there is also a theory or philosophy in them which is very rich and high, although at present it is well-nigh forgotten.

The religious thought of the Tantra is another instance of a synthetic religious philosophy which tries to reconcile different religions and different philosophies. For it, there is really no antagonism between the monism of Advaita Vedānta and the dualism of Dvaita Vedānta. The latter is the steppingstone to the former, for the monistic truth is to be reached through the dualistic world. Thus it harmonizes Advaita with Dvaita Vedānta. Its sole purpose is to give liberation to the individual self by a method in which monistic truth is reached through the world of duality. The Tantra also helps to make up the quarrel between different religious sects by its solemn declaration that different sects worship only different forms of the one Supreme God.

The Supreme God is conceived in the Tantra as one, universal spiritual power (śakti) and is called the Divine Mother (Devī). The Divine Mother is variously named as Kālī, Tārā, Durgā, Chaṇḍikā, and so on. Of Her own free will and for the purpose of creation She divided Herself into the dual aspects of male and female. Of these, Śiva is the male principle and the supreme cosmic consciousness (purusha) and Śakti is the female principle and the supreme primordial energy (prakṛiti). Śiva and Śakti again are each divided according to whether they are with or without attributes. The supreme attributeless Śakti is full of luster; so also is the supreme attributeless Śiva. As attributeless self-shining Śakti She is of the essence of Brahman and is above the world of māyā or of objects. In Her state with attributes, She gives birth to Brahmā the creator, Vishṇu the preserver, and Maheśvara the destroyer of the world. It is with this attribute of māyā that She gives birth to the three worlds, consisting of moving and unmoving things.

This creative power of the Divine Mother has as its substance the three guṇas of *sattva* (balance or wisdom), *rajas* (activity or restlessness), and *tamas* (inertia or dullness), and it constitutes the vast and variegated world of objects. Again, with Her conscious energy She appears in the world as individual and embodied selves (jīvas). Although the cosmic consciousness and primordial energy are in their real nature free from attachment, as embodied selves they are under the influence of the Divine Mother who charms the world and the selves. Hence it is that the jīvas perform the vast world play and remain absorbed in it.

The Divine Mother pervades the whole world, giving birth to all things from the highest to the lowest and manifesting Her majesty both as mind and as matter. That is the way in which She plays the cosmic game. Mind and matter are not two diametrically opposed substances, of which one is conscious and the other is unconscious; rather, they are the forms in which the same divine energy figures in its playful cosmic activity. As such, they are held like two children in the embrace of the same Mother.

Śiva and Śakti, the supreme male and female principles, are inseparably connected. One does not exist independent of the other. United with Śakti, the cosmic consciousness becomes Śiva; and united with Śiva, the supreme primordial energy becomes Śakti. Apart from Śakti, the supreme self is a corpse; and apart from Śiva, the supreme primordial energy is blind force. Śiva and Śakti thus inseparably connected and covered up by māyā are called the Supreme Self by the Yogin and the Supreme God by the Vedāntin. Brahman is not actionless and attributeless pure consciousness; it is, rather, the supreme, spiritual power which is both moving and motionless, both with and without attributes. In short, the Divine Mother with Her two inseparable aspects of Śiva and Śakti, of motionlessness and motion, is the true Supreme God (Paraṁbrahma).

The world of material things and living beings is the manifestation of the energy of the Supreme God, that is, the Divine Mother. It reveals the wealth of the śakti or omnipotence of the Mother of the universe. The whole universe is but the reflection of the Mother in the bosom of māyā. It is as if the Divine Mother sees Her own face in the mirror of māyā and plays with Her children the great cosmic game. The world is thus in its own way as real as the Supreme God whose play, or līlā, it is. There is no other reason for the appearance of a world of things and beings out of the Supreme God than the free, sportive, playful will of the Supreme God. It pleases the Mother to create a world only for the joy of creation, just as it pleases a man to play a game only for the sake of enjoyment. Again, just as the player in the joy of play takes assumed things and conditions as real, but has no real connection with them, so the Divine Mother plays the worldly game but has no real connection with it.

The substance of the world is Śiva and Śakti, that is, the cosmic consciousness (purusha) and cosmic energy (prakṛiti). Out of the union between the two arises every thing and being of the world. The drama of the world is the play of the one on the bosom of the other. It has neither a beginning nor an end. In concrete imagery, it is the eternal dance of Kālī, the cosmic energy, on the eternal breast of Śiva, the cosmic consciousness.

It is not, as some people thought, the dance of blind atoms in empty space.

Individual selves (jīvas) are created by that power of the Divine Mother in which the element of rajas predominates; they are preserved by that in which sattva predominates; and they are destroyed by that in which tamas predominates. The jīvas have no independence in the matter of either their creation or dissolution for these are due to the force of the will of the Divine Mother, who creates and destroys the world by Her will. The jīvas cannot change the physical order of the world which proceeds from the will of the Divine Mother nor can they afford to ignore the world in their present state because, if they are to know the Mother of the Universe, they must know Her through the display of Her power in the world.

Individual selves are thus the children of the Divine Mother, and live, move, and have their being in Her; but under the spell of the Divine Māyā, they forget their Mother and live in separation from Her. With this they come under bondage to the world and live a life of sin and misery. Deliverance from bondage is to be attained through knowledge of Śakti as the Supreme deity and the Mother of the three worlds. But it is sheer folly to think that the truth about the Divine Mother can be known by mere logical reasoning or metaphysical thinking. To know this truth one must go through a long course of spiritual training (sādhana) extending over many lives. Customs, principles, rules and regulations, spiritual practices, worship, mantras and Tantras are all required in order to know the truth about the Divine Mother. One must also place one's self under the guidance of a qualified spiritual preceptor (guru) for attaining success in spiritual life. Above all, one should be resigned to the will of the Divine Mother and receive Her grace.

Such success in the spiritual life means the realization of the Divine Mother as the spiritual power (śakti) which pervades every thing and every being, every atom and molecule of the universe. One who realizes this supreme truth is no longer bound by māyā to mundane life. He lives and moves in the world, and yet remains unsoiled in the mud of worldly actions. The same Divine Mother who once caused his bondage now liberates him and stands before him as the Divine Mother with māyā as Her great power. Free from all lust and greed, fear and dread, craving and caprice, he lives forever in peace and bliss. He who in the state of bondage was a mere jīva attains in liberation the status of Śiva—the Great God.

. . . . .

This brief survey of Hindu religious thought shows the catholic and comprehensive spirit of Hinduism as a religion. Instead of forcing all religious souls to move through the same religious groove, Hinduism as a religion lays down different paths for different men, according to their different abilities and aptitudes. At the same time, it recognizes the essential unity of different religions as being but so many approaches to the same goal, freedom from sin and misery. As such, Hinduism may with some justification be called a universal religion.

PART II

Selections From Hindu Sacred Writings

Chapter 7

INTRODUCTION TO THE HINDU SCRIPTURES

by V. Raghavan

The primary scriptures of Hinduism are the Vedas, containing knowledge which has been handed down from the most ancient times, knowledge which does not owe its origin to man. The source of the Vedas is only God, the divine fountainhead of all knowledge. God revealed the Vedas to the Primary Creator, Brahmā, and through him the earliest sages and their pupils, the "See-ers," saw the eternally existing Vedas. The various names by which they are known make clear that they are ancient knowledge, revealed to men, "that which was heard," "that which rules authoritatively over mankind."

There are three main divisions of the Vedas: Saṁhitās, Brāhmaṇas, and Upanishads. The Saṁhitās form the core of the Vedas; in fact, the word *Veda* is often used to refer only to this section of prayers, hymns, and sacred formulae which are the basis of later elaborations in the scriptures. The Brāhmaṇas are a discussion and elucidation of the meanings, significances, purposes, occasions, and effects of the passages in the Saṁhitās. The Upanishads are the philosophic and mystical elaboration of the truths first revealed to the Seers and recorded in the Saṁhitās.

In addition to the Vedas there is a large body of authoritative writings known as *Smṛiti* (what is remembered) of the traditions which go back to the Vedas. These writings cover ritual, rules of conduct, commentaries, sagas, and digests of earlier writings. The most important are the Dharma Śāstras (such as the Laws of Manu), the Purāṇas (such as the Bhāgavata Purāṇa), and the epics (the Rāmāyaṇa and the Mahābhārata which includes the Bhagavad Gītā). The systematic expositions of the Vedas, called Darśanas, and the sectarian writings known as the Āgamas are included as part of the Hindu scriptures. The popular hymns of saints and teachers are also part of the sacred literature of the Hindus.

The Saṁhitās of the Vedas are made up of hymns and utterances called mantras, verses which have been revealed to intense thought and intuition and have the power of saving the soul of the one who cherishes them. The Vedic Seer (Ṛishi) was indeed a self-conscious poet who knew that speech is a divine gift. This speech he sifted and refined in his mind as flour in a sieve and out of this he fashioned an excellent hymn which, as a vehicle for the God whom he adored, he compared to a well-fitted chariot; this speech revealed itself to the Seer even as a loving wife reveals her charms and graces to her lord. Thus the Vedas are the perfect expression of what has been seen through intuitive perception.

ŚRŪTI—THAT WHICH WAS HEARD

The Vedas

There are four Vedas: Ṛigveda, Yajurveda, Sāmaveda, and Atharvaveda. The Ṛigveda is a body of hymns to be recited, gathered in sections according to the deities praised and the families of Seers who "saw" them. The Yajurveda is concerned with Vedic sacrifices, many of which are no longer offered in their original form. The Sāmaveda is a musical rendering of the Ṛigveda. The hymns of the Atharvaveda are of greater social interest, a large part of them dealing with the affairs of daily life.

In the Ṛigveda itself, the development of thought toward monotheism, abstract deities, and the praising of a divinity without assigning it any name show that in the earlier part of the Veda there was a philosophic tendency. A notable instance is in the very first book of the Ṛigveda, where one finds the well-known affirmation that "Truth is one, and the wise call it by different names," which is as emphatic a declaration of the one Truth as any that the Upanishads make.

The Ṛigvedic hymns are also notable for the richness of the devotional moods with which the devotee approaches his favorite deity, a devotion which was expressed in poetry far more striking than any in the best of the later hymnal literature. Thus the Vedic poets approached their gods not only as friends, as sons to their fathers, as servants to their masters, but also as the lover to the beloved.

The mystic potency pertaining to the mere text of the Vedas has been recognized from the earliest times; thinkers such as those in the Mīmāṁsā school emphasized the text itself and those in the school of grammar developed the philosophy of an indestructible ultimate sound substratum for the universe and held that the world of things was an emanation from the word of the Veda. Absolute sanctity attaches to the correctness of accents in pronouncing the words of the Vedas and any flaw in pronunciation may be attended with a change of meaning, and with demerit and sin.

The Yajurveda is concerned with sacrificial ritual, and is current chiefly in two recensions, the White (or *Śukla*) Yajurveda since it is a collection of pure mantras, and the Dark (or *Kṛishṇa*) Yajurveda because this collection includes sacrificial formulae such as those found in the later Brāhmaṇas.

The Sāmaveda is the oldest form of Indian music, and the source of the later musical tradition; a mysticism of Sāman singing is developed more fully in the Upanishads, and all later musical practices are based on the belief that the art of music is an aid to meditative practices and salvation.

The Atharvaveda is made up of hymns for procuring expiations for sins and for appeasing the gods, imprecations and rites for harming enemies, hymns for securing welfare in agriculture, trade, and other activities, and for creating love, concord, and understanding between husband and wife, father and son, teacher and students.

THE BRĀHMAṆAS AND UPANISHADS

The Brāhmaṇas elaborated the earlier Vedic writings by selecting a passage, praising its merits, and condemning the opposite which should be avoided. This kind of treatment of the hymns led to the development of some of the scientific disciplines and mythology and made the Brāhmaṇas the forerunners of the Upanishads. It was the speculative and inquisitive spirit of the Brāhmaṇas that led to the conception of the Brahman as the Ultimate Absolute which is the one basis of the universe, and began giving a higher interpretation and esoteric significance to many aspects of ritual and sacrifice, transforming them into meditative exercises. The Brāhmaṇas evolved the interpretative scheme, regularly used later in the Upanishads, according to which things are understood in three aspects: divine, natural, and subjective. Here started the subjective shift of emphasis which eventually led to the plumbing of the Self, and the esoteric interpretation of the teachings of the Seers, or Ṛishis.

The latter part of the Brāhmaṇas is called the Forest Books (*Āraṇyaka*), meaning the books meditated upon in the isolation of the forest. The concluding portions of the Āraṇyaka are the definitely philosophical writings called the Upanishads, or Vedānta. *Upanishad* means sitting near and receiving secret teachings; *Vedānta* means not only the end of the Vedas, but also the highest peak of Vedic knowledge. There are varying lists of the Upanishads, formally enumerated as one hundred and eight, but actually there are many more; only ten or a dozen of them are of major importance.

SMṚITI—THAT WHICH IS REMEMBERED

The Vedas, that is, the Saṁhitā, Brāhmaṇa, and Upanishad writings, are known as the *Śruti* (that which was heard). All authoritative writings outside the Vedas are comprehensively referred to as *Smṛiti* (that which is remembered). These Smṛiti are generally listed under five headings: *Vedāṅgas,* or the limbs of the Vedas; *Dharma Śāstras,* which include codes of laws, commentaries and digests and manuals; *Nibandhas,* rituals and domestic rites; Purāṇas; and the epics. Associated with these are the *Āgamas* or sectarian scriptures and the *Darśanas,* or six schools of philosophy.

The Vedāṅgas

The *Vedāṅgas* deal with phonetics, grammar, etymology, prosody, astronomy, and ritual codes which serve as handbooks for sacrifices. Four supplementary Vedas deal with Āyurveda medicine emphasizing prevention and the use of mental, moral, and spiritual aids for cures; with military science, calling for peaceful negotiations first, and only when unavoidable allowing warfare under a code of righteous fighting; with music as an art of great spiritual effectiveness; and with politics, which must always be subject to morality. A third class of writings in brief formulae are concerned again with grammar, meter, chanting, creation of sacrificial altars, and sacrificial and domestic rites. There are also metrical indices enumerating the meters, the gods, and the Seers who first heard the hymns: for no use of a hymn is considered to be in proper form if it does not take note of its meter, deity and Seer.

The Dharma Śāstras

The Dharma Śāstras are concerned with conduct, the way of righteousness, dealing even with personal hygiene, manners and polite behavior, morality, the administration of the state and justice, the seeking of spiritual salvation, and the duties which must be performed in carrying out domestic rituals and sacraments. The Laws of Manu are the most important statement of the way of dharma. Manu was a patriarch and great spiritual teacher who fixed Indian conduct for all time. According to the Veda itself, "What Manu says is medicine"

The Nibandhas

Later there grew up digests and manuals, called Nibandhas, which were codifications of Vedic laws and encyclopedic discussions of all aspects of conduct, even including such topics as gifts, pilgrimages, vows, worship, auspicious features of the human body, and descriptions of articles of utility. They deal with all the rituals to be performed from the time of conception to the death of the individual. In later times, popular instruction in the rules of conduct was taken over by the epics and Purāṇas, which devoted extensive attention to the topics dealt with in the Dharma Śāstras.

The Purāṇas

The Purāṇas and epics are the scriptures of popular Hinduism, a living literature which has been the subject matter for minstrels and story tellers who have kept the teachings and legends of the Vedas before the common people. The Purāṇas developed as a reinforcement and amplification of the Vedic teachings, dealing with the stories of creation, periodic dissolution and recreation of the world, giving the histories and genealogies of the gods, sages, and forefathers, and recording the history of the dynasties which ruled on the earth. As these stories and legends concerning the earlier kings, heroes, sages, and orders of divine and semidivine beings increased, they became a separate class of literature enjoying status equal to the Vedas.

The Purāṇas form the largest part of the writings in Sanskrit, a most voluminous and bewildering mass usually listed as eighteen major and eighteen minor Purāṇas, but although the number is constant, the names and texts vary considerably. They have been expanded to include the teachings of the different schools of philosophy, and stories of special interest to the different sects; they deal at great length with the different pilgrimage places, with vows and austerities, gifts, temples and images, caste, the duties of the devotee, and the responsibilities of rulers. They have become an encyclopedia of Hinduism, a popular handbook of knowledge, the source of as complete and liberal education as it is possible for the busy member of society to get, for many of them include also brief accounts of precious stones, poisons, perfumes and medicine, astrology, omens, architecture, dharma, the arts, grammar, lexicography, poetics, drama, agriculture, physiognomy.

The most popular of the Purāṇas is the Bhāgavata which glorifies Vishṇu. Retelling the old stories with new force, it breathes a new intellectual spirit, giving original turns to the ideas found in the earlier texts and expressing them with a rare pointedness. It brought about a synthesis of knowledge and devotion and inspired fresh devotional movements which continue today. Similar to the Bhāgavata in importance is the Sūta Saṁhitā, devoted to Śiva. It describes elaborately the worship of Śiva, the path of knowledge and yoga in general, and special spiritual exercises to be followed by Śaivas. Its exposition of the Advaita philosophy is fuller than that of the other Purāṇas and it is said to have been read many times by Śaṅkara before he wrote his famous Advaitic commentaries.

The Epics

The two great epics of Hinduism are the Rāmāyaṇa and the Mahābhārata, which constitute the greatest books of popular Hinduism. There is hardly a Hindu who has not heard the stories and teachings of these epics from childhood, imbibing them, as it were, with his mother's milk. The treatment was more literary and the authorship more definite than in the Purāṇas, but the epics sought to fulfill the same role in popular religious education, incorporating as much as possible of the Purāṇic accounts of creation, cosmography, dharma, and stories of heroes, sages, and gods. They are also a mine of wise sayings which guide the masses in all departments of life's activities.

The Rāmāyaṇa tells the story of how the Lord Vishṇu, as Rāma, makes himself the embodiment of righteousness and puts down Rāvaṇa the king of demons, who had prostituted all his powers in oppressing the world and gratifying his vicious lust. The epic illustrates ideals which ought to prevail in personal, domestic, social and public life, ideals of brotherhood, friendship, kingship, and above all, ideals of chastity on the part of women and sexual morality on the part of men. The ideals of kingship are summed up in the concept of Rāmarājya in which none injures another and the king himself is but the regent of righteousness and truth. It was the vision of Rāmarājya that animated the Father of the nation in modern times, Mahātmā Gāndhi, in India's struggle for freedom.

From this epic has come one of the most popular devotional movements of India; Rāma is worshiped as God Himself and Sītā, his wife, as the Goddess. The very name Rāma has become a mantra and a solace to millions of hearts. There is hardly a language in India which does not have its own Rāmāyaṇa, and the epic has cast its spell over the neighboring peoples of Cambodia, Siam, Ceylon, and the East Indian Islands. In the original Rāmāyaṇa written by Vālmīki there is the statement that the Rāmāyaṇa story and the fame of Vālmīki would last so long as hills stand and rivers flow on earth. Never was a truer prophecy or claim ever made in the literary world!

The Mahābhārata is larger in its sweep. If the Rāmāyaṇa appeals to one's heart, the Mahābhārata appeals to the mind; it sets less store by poetic grace, but is more direct and intellectual. While the Rāmāyaṇa melts us with the pathos of Sītā, the Mahābhārata uses the very pathos of the pyrrhic victory of the great battle for the development of detachment from the transient goods of life, for the attainment of peace of the Self. The stories of ideal Indian womanhood which the nation cherishes are here, and the hero Yudhishṭhira for whom there was no enemy, and the grandfather Bhīshma who sacrificed his youth for his father—these stand out as beacons before the people. At the heart of the Mahābhārata is the Bhagavad Gītā, regarded by many as the greatest of all the Hindu scriptures, summarizing in its teachings the best of Indian devotional and intellectual writings.

Vyāsa, the author of the Mahābhārata, was a contemporary of the characters of his poem, an elder related to the family. The epic says that he was none other than God Nārāyaṇa (Vishṇu) himself; his personal name is Kṛishṇa. *Vyāsa* was a title meaning editor or arranger. He was one of those outstanding figures who appear at times of chaos to salvage the scattered treasures and re-erect the edifice. Thus he arranged all the Vedic literature as it is current now, set forth the aphorisms of the Vedāntic system of philosophy, and created the Purāṇic literature. All this literature was transmitted through his disciples, "one of formidable ears," as he is called, that is, one of prodigious learning gained through listening. If the Rāmāyaṇa is the first and foremost poem, the Mahābhārata is, as the saying goes, verily the fifth Veda.

The Darśanas

It was inevitable that various schools of interpretation of the Vedas would develop. There are six main schools, *Darśanas,* or intuitions of truth; these are collections of aphorisms to which have been attached later commentaries. They fall into three pairs: Nyāya and Vaiśeshika; Sāṅkhya and Yoga; Mīmāṁsā and Vedānta. All these schools agree that the Vedas are a record of spiritual experiences and truths seen by Seers, and the work of these systems of thought is to codify, interpret, and reinforce them with logical arguments. Logic divorced from the Vedas is repudiated; the mere pursuit of reason leads nowhere; even eminent logicians agree that reasoning occupies the second of three stages in the realization of Truth: (1) listening to it as set forth in the Vedas; (2) understanding it well through the use of reason so that it may not be shaken; (3) contemplation of it. In the Rāmāyaṇa, it is said that Sītā, separated from her husband Rāma and found in a most sorrowful state, was like knowledge rendered weak by not being linked to the Vedas. Thus the six systems of thought which developed were not mere intellectual pursuits, but visions directed toward the realization and experience of Truth.

Before undertaking a study of the Vedānta, the student must have attained a sense of values regarding things permanent and transient, an absence of desire for enjoyments of either this world or the heavenly regions, a state of quietude and self-control, and must have an anxiety to be liberated.

The Sectarian Scriptures

The sectarian scriptures, related chiefly to the three main sects of Śaivism, Vaishṇavism, and Śāktism, are known as the Āgamas or Tantras, the two names being used indiscriminately. Generally they are arranged in four parts, dealing with the philosophical beliefs, meditative exercises, the erection of temples and making of images, and their use in worship, and, finally, conduct. In addition to the Āgamas, there are many sectarian hymns written even in modern times, and in common devotional use today alongside of the hymns taken from Vedic and Purāṇic sources.

POPULAR USE OF THE SACRED WRITINGS

It is sometimes held that the Upanishads, popular theism, temple worship, and Tāntric rites have superseded the Vedas. It is true that Vedic sacrifices as such have gone out of vogue and today only a few of the minor ones are performed by stray individuals in nooks and corners of the country, but the Vedas have not ceased to be of utmost use and value. All domestic rites and sacraments are done with their Vedic mantras, all the Vedic hymns are adored and recited according to the significance attached to them in the later commentaries. Special collections of Vedic hymns and certain individual hymns are on the lips of all, every day, at home or in the temple. Adorations with oblations in fire attended by recitals of hymns, repeated hundreds, thousands, or tens of thousands of times, according to procedures laid down in the manuals, are performed widely and at great expense even today. These selections from the Vedas are memorized by many and are recited as frequently as the latter-day devotional hymns.

The literature of the Purāṇas has been alive and growing all through history and continues so even today. More than half of the public meetings announced in a busy modern city like Madras are concerned with expositions of the epics and Purāṇas. Just as in the old days there were bards, or minstrels, who recounted the stories of the epics and Purāṇas, so today there are men who retell the same materials and explain them to the people who gather to hear them in the temples, the homes, and the meeting places of India. Hardly a day passes in any city, town, or village without an epic or Purāṇa being read and expounded in the local language to large gatherings of people, young and old, of either sex, and of all classes of society. More than even the Mahābhārata, the texts which never weary the people, high and low, erudite and otherwise, are the epic of Rāmāyaṇa and the Bhāgavata Purāṇa. As a series of musical discourses, or as a recital and exposition by a gifted reciter of the Purāṇas in the temple, in the house of a leading citizen, or in a public place, the Rāmāyaṇa is a source of sustained enlightenment and enjoyment to the whole nation. Seven-day or nine-day or longer sessions of such expositions are as popular as political conferences or other gatherings of modern life.

The preamble to the Bhāgavata says that its reading in the days immediately following the death of a person liberates the spirit of the departed. When the heart is heavy with the sorrow of a great calamity, the reading of a Purāṇa is a source of comfort. The practice of one daily reading of a part of the scriptures is still in force; it may be the Rāmāyaṇa, which is the most popular text in this respect, or the Bhāgavata, or the Bhagavad Gītā, or some favorite hymn—one does not sit down for his food without first reading from the scriptures. There are special programs of reading the Rāmāyaṇa with due ceremonial resorted to in times of adversity or for general welfare and prosperity. The fifth book, which is especially sacred, is often read alone, one of the most efficacious programs for reading it being called the "seven cantos a day" scheme. Such is the pious faith in Rāma and his story that the devout often, when perplexed with personal or domestic problems, open to a page of the Rāmāyaṇa and look for guidance.

If the women of the country cherish the ideals of chastity like Sāvitrī and Sītā, if men aspire to standards of truthfulness like Hariśchandra, generosity like Karṇa, righteousness like Rāma and Yudhishṭhira, the ideal brotherhood such as that exemplified by Rāma and his brothers, and if the whole nation is animated by ideals of ahiṁsā and universal benevolence and the establishment of a moral order of government such as existed under Rāma, it is all the achievement of the epics, the Purāṇas, and their expounders.

All aspects of Indian life have been shaped for centuries, and are molded today by the devotion of the Indian people to the Vedas and to the commentaries and poetic expositions which have grown up around them. Truth, as revealed to the ancient Seers and recorded in the Vedas, and as interpreted through the ages by devout men in the Purāṇas, epics, Āgamas and Darśanas, has been the inspiration of Indian literature, music, painting, and sculpture, of Indian political and social ideals, and has pointed the way toward release, the highest goal of life.

VEDAS—SAṀHITĀS[1]

ṚIGVEDA

SWEETNESS AND MORAL ORDER

Sweet are the winds to him who desires for himself moral order; for him the rivers flow sweet; even so, may the herbs be sweet to us; may the night be sweet, as also the dawns; may the earthly region be sweet; may Heaven, our Father, be sweet to us; may the Sun be sweet to us and sweet may the kine be to us[2] (I.90.6-8).

FIRE

Fire is our wealth like inherited patrimony; helps us come of age; takes the best and pleasing course like the teaching of a learned teacher; like a gratified guest he is in the restful chamber; himself like a priest, he bestows a home on one who tends him. He who supports the whole world like the Sun, who sits down [amidst us] like a favorable and friendly prince, before whom we sit like sons in the father's dwelling, who is pure like a devoted wife (I.73).

THE ASYAVĀMĪYA

(This unusually long hymn, apparently miscellaneous in subject matter but clearly mystical and philosophical, has traditionally been taken as a philosophical hymn and has been expounded extensively in later writings. In the Laws of Manu

[1] Editor's note: With the exception of the selections from the Bhagavad Gītā, the translations and summaries which follow were made by Professor Raghavan. An attempt has been made to bring together those passages of the sacred writings of the Hindus which form the background of religious thought in India, and are in common use today. Of necessity, all this material is greatly condensed.

[2] This is a frequently recited hymn.

the hymn is mentioned as an expiation for heinous sins. It anticipates the Upanishads, and is quoted by them.)

Who saw that First when it was born? What is that unembodied that bears the embodied? From earth are breath and blood: wherefrom the Soul? Who went to the learned to ask this? Ignorant, I ask here the knowing sages of vision: not knowing, I [ask] for the sake of knowing. He props up these six worlds: what is that ONE in the form of the unborn? They call Him Indra, Mitra, Varuṇa, Agni, and even the fleet-winged celestial bird Garuḍa. The One Reality, the learned speak of in many ways (I.164).

The Gāyatrī

(*This prayer, named after its meter, is called Gāyatrī, which means "the savior of the singer." It is considered to be the mantra of all mantras, the most important mantra, repeated as many times as possible every day in the sandhyā worship at morning, noon, and night. It is the essence of the spiritual power that a Brāhman gains. It is imparted at the time of a young man's initiation, giving him his second spiritual birth into the company of the twice-born. The Vedas themselves describe it as the Mother of the Vedas. It is primarily a hymn to the Sun* (*Savitar*). *It has played a dominant part in the religious history of India, being interpreted differently by the followers of different paths of worship, and being adapted and imitated for other deities from Vedic times onward.*)

WE MEDITATE UPON THAT ADORABLE EFFULGENCE OF THE RESPLENDENT VIVIFIER, SAVITAR; MAY HE STIMULATE OUR INTELLECTS (III.62.10).

The Augmenter of Growth

(*This is a mantra for long life and warding off untimely death or fear of death. It is used as a death-conquering mantra, and its repetition, with or without offerings in fire, is always done on birthdays, during illness, or when some danger to life is feared.)*

We adore the fragrant Tryambaka, the augmenter of growth. May I be freed from death as a cucumber from its stalk, but not from immortality (VII.59.12).

WATERS

(Ablution, bathing in holy lakes, rivers, the sea, and water in which special sanctity is infused by the recitation of mantras, plays a prominent part in Hindu rites and conduct. In cosmogonic and mystic speculations, the Waters exercised great influence on the imagination of the Seers of the Vedas and Upanishads. The following verses are always recited when water is thus used for purification.)

O Waters! As you are the source of happiness, infuse strength into us, so that we have great and beautiful vision. That essence of yours which is most auspicious, make us share it here, O you who are like loving Mothers! Let us resort to you fully for that removal of evil, whereby you gratify us. Waters! You have verily created us! (X.9).

CREMATION

(The following is an important mantra among those recited at the time of cremation. It is recited as addressed to the dead person, as the corpse is being buried. It has reference to the beliefs concerning eschatology and rebirth.)

Let your eye go to the Sun; your life to the wind; by the meritorious acts that you have done, go to heaven, and then [for rebirth] to the earth again; or, resort to the Waters, if you feel at home there; remain in the herbs with the bodies you propose to take (X.16.3).

All Names of God

O Gods! All your names [and forms] are to be revered, saluted, and adored; all of you who have sprung from heaven, and earth, listen here to my invocation (X.63.2).

Marriage

(*Used in the marriage ceremonies.*)

I take hold of your hand for good fortune, so that with me, the husband, you may attain to old age; the solar deities give you to me for conducting domestic life. (*To the Two*): May you not be separated; may you reach your full years, sporting with sons and grandsons and delighting in your house. (*To the Bride*): Flourish thou, without fierce looks and without harming your husband, be good to animals, be of amiable mind and of great splendor; be the mother of heroes, be devoted to gods and the bringer of happiness; be propitious to our men and women and to our cattle. Bounteous Indra! Endow this bride with excellent sons and fortune; give her ten sons and make her husband the eleventh [i.e., the husband should always be attended with love and care as if he were the youngest child] (X.85).

The Hymn to the Supreme Being—The Purusha-sūkta

(*This hymn describes the Supreme Being and the Universe, setting forth the creation of the Universe out of the Supreme Being as a sacrifice. It presents an epitome of the essential ideas of Hinduism. It is one of the most popular hymns, forming an essential part of worship in the home and temple at the time of the bathing of the Image. The recital of this hymn is also prescribed for expiation of one of the five heinous sins.*)

Thousand-headed was the Supreme Being, thousand-eyed and thousand-footed. Covering the world all around, He yet exceeded it by a span. All this is the Supreme Being, what is past and what is in the future; He is the Lord of immortality as well as of that which grows by food [mortal creatures]. Such is His greatness, and even greater than that is this Supreme Being. A fourth of Him constitutes all beings; three fourths of Him is immortal and is in heaven. With His three fourths, this Supreme Being stood above, and one fourth of Him came here repeatedly; with that one fourth, He extended on all sides into the animate and the inanimate. Therefrom the Cosmic Egg was born and within it this Supreme Being; having been born, He stretched Himself further [as gods, man, and created beings], then created the earth and the bodies. When they [the gods] apportioned the Cosmic Being [thus], into how many parts did they make Him? What became of His mouth? What are said to be His two arms, His two thighs and two feet? His face became the Brāhman, His arms were made into the Kshatriya; he who is the Vaiśya is His thighs; from His feet was the Śūdra born. The moon was born from His mind, the sun from His eyes, from His mouth, Indra and fire, and from His own breath was wind born. From His navel there arose the sky, from His head the heaven, the earth from His feet, the quarters from His ear—thus they fashioned the worlds (X.90).

Sharing of Wealth and Food

Not hunger, but death have the gods given; and deaths come to him who eats [without giving to others]. The wealth of one who gives never decreases, the niggard has none to give him happiness. The mean-minded amasses food in vain; I tell [this] in truth; it is indeed his death; he who nourishes [with his offering] neither the god nor his friend, he who eats alone, gathers sin alone (X.117).

God Whose Form Is Not Determined

(This hymn refers to God in all His attributes but without calling Him by any name but Ka which means "someone.")

He who gives us the soul and strength, whose high command all the gods abide by, whose shadow is immortality and death, that Some One who is God, let us worship with oblation. By whom ether was made formidable and the earth firm, the sky and heaven were fixed, who measured the space in the sky, that Some One who is God, let us worship with oblation. He who brooded over with His might those waters which produced the creative potency and the sacrifice, He who is the one sovereign divinity over other Gods, that Some One who is God, let us worship with oblation (X.121).

The Goddess of Speech

(*Vāk, the all powerful Goddess of Speech, speaks here about her own supreme greatness, speaking as the knower of the Supreme Brahman, herself that Supreme Being, the source of everything. The Brāhmaṇas indicate that this hymn should be used when the student first approaches his teacher; it is recited as a ritual for infusing the student with intellectual power.*)

I am the Queen of the land, the bringer of treasures; I am the knower and the first among those to be propitiated with a sacrifice; the gods have placed me everywhere, in manifold forms, and immanent in everything. It is by me that one eats; he who sees, he who breathes, he who hears what has been said, does so by me; those who know me not, decline. O you who can hear! Listen to this that can be had by faith; I shall teach you. This that the gods as well as the men seek, I, of my own accord, shall tell you: Whomsoever I like, him I make formidable, him a Brāhman, a man of vision, a man of excellent intellect. It is I who blow like wind bringing into being all the worlds and transcending the heaven and the earth; so much am I by my greatness (X.125).

The Hymn of Creation

(*The Supreme Being is at once the author and deity of this hymn.*)

At that time there was neither nonexistence nor existence; neither the worlds nor the sky; nor anything that is beyond; what covered everything and where and for whose enjoyment? Was there water unfathomable and deep? Death was not, nor immortality there; no knowing of night or day; that One breathed without air, by its own strength; besides that, nothing did exist. Darkness there was, wrapped in front by darkness; undistinguished, all this was (one) water;[3] the incipient that lay covered by void, that One became creative by the power of its own contemplation. There came upon it, at first, desire which was the prime seed of the mind; men of vision, searching in their heart with their intellect found the nexus of the existent in the nonexistent. The [very] gods are later to this creative activity; then who knows wherefrom this came into being? Where this creation came from, whether one supported it or not, He who was supervising it from the highest heaven, He indeed knows; or He knows not! (X.129).

Concord

(*In modern times, these verses are frequently used by leaders in addresses to public assemblies.*)

Come together, speak in agreement, may your minds see alike, even as the gods of yore, in mutual agreement, took their offerings. May your deliberation be uniform, and uniform your conclusion; uniform your mind, and thoughts together; I utter forth a common prayer to you and a common oblation do I offer you. Your intention the same, your hearts the same, may your minds be the same so that there may be amongst you perfect unity (X.191.2-4).

[3] According to the Śatapatha Brāhmaṇa, this prime creation Water is *Vāk* or Speech, called *Āpas,* because of its all-pervasive nature (VI.1).

Hymn to the Goddess of Beauty and Prosperity (Śrī-sūkta)

(This hymn to the Goddess of Prosperity and Affluence, though it occurs in the Supplementary hymns to the Ṛigveda, enjoys wide popularity. It is not only repeated orally as a general prayer, but on occasions of reverses and ill-luck special rites are performed according to prescribed modes comprising the repeated recital of this hymn alone or with oblations in fire. The concept of Śrī, beauty, prosperity and richness, has influenced the Indian mind from earliest times; the image of Śrī is to be carved on the lintel of the door of every house, and even to this day the only all-Indian mode of address to a gentleman or lady is Śrīman or Śrīmati, "one endowed with Śrī.")

Invoke for me, O Fire, that Goddess of Fortune, who will not leave me, through whom I may gain gold, cow, horse, and men. The pleasing, the resplendent Goddess of Fortune, who is shining in this world in Her glory, and whom the gods resort to as the Goddess of Bounty, that Goddess of the Lotus, I seek as my refuge; may my misfortune perish. I seek you, O Goddess! I shall abolish the earlier born Misfortune in the form of hunger, thirst, and dirt; [O Goddess of Fortune] drive out from my home all ill-being and poverty. May we attain the Goddess who is the mind's desire, the intention and fulfilment of one's word, and is embodied in cattle and food; may that Goddess of Fortune and Fame come to me.

KṚISHṆA YAJURVEDA

A National Prayer

(This prayer is used when an assembly is gathering, it is also used at the feast in memory of the departed [śrāddha] along with many other mantras. It is a favorite with many modern scholars, writers, and public figures who consider it suitable for a national prayer.)

Among the Brāhmans, may the Brāhman be born with spiritual luster; in this country, may the king be born a warrior, a capable archer and chariot-fighter; may the cow be born a milch cow; the ox a good draught ox; the horse a fleet one; the damsel the object of the city's admiration; the fighter victorious; and the youth fit for the assembly; may a hero be born to the performer of the sacrifice; whenever we wish may the cloud rain; may our vegetation ripen with fruits; may there be for us acquisition and conserving [of prosperity] (VII.5.18.1).

Śiva Hymns (Śatarudrīya)

(This collection of hymns from various parts of the Veda is popularly called the Rudra—after their deity (Śiva). It is a sacred hymn in constant use, recited during worship in the home and temple when the image is bathed, used as an expiation for sins, and for attaining material and spiritual rewards. It is the source of the greatest mantra of the Śaivas, the famous Five-syllabled mantra "Namaḥ Śivāya" to which Śaivas attach the highest sanctity. In these hymns Śiva is described as being everything in the universe, every aspect of society and nature, bringing home to us the truth that in the high and the low, in all that exists, God should be contemplated in His all-comprehensive form. Only brief excerpts from the very long hymn are given here.)

O Rudra, that form of yours which is benevolent, not fearful, not manifesting the sinful, with that most beneficent form, you who extend happiness [to people] from your mountain abode, reveal yourself to us often. This Rudra of blue neck and red complexion, who glides aside, Him the shepherds saw, the servant maids that bring water saw, and indeed all the beings; may He make us happy.[4] Obeisance to the bright multicolored grass, Obeisance to the Lord of the pathways. Obeisance to

[4] This passage is often cited to emphasize that the Lord is accessible to the lowliest.

Him who lies amidst the tawny cattle, the tormentor. Obeisance to the Lord of food. Obeisance to the Lord of the forests, to the counselor at assemblies, to the merchant. Obeisance to the Lord of all strength. Obeisance to the sitting and lying, the sleeping and the waking, the standing and the running. Obeisance to the assemblies and leaders of assemblies. Obeisance to those of different kinds, obeisance to those of all kinds. Obeisance to the great and small. Obeisance to the carpenters and artisans, to potters and blacksmiths. Obeisance to the God who is benevolent as well as terrible, who destroys beings and is their protector as well. Obeisance to the small and the puny, to the big and the aged. Obeisance to Him who is to be lauded with hymns and who is also there where hymns do not reach. Obeisance to the redeemer, to the bringer of peace and happiness, to the producer of well-being and joy. Obeisance to Him who is auspicious and exceedingly so.[5] (VI.6).

ŚUKLA YAJURVEDA

Universal Sacrifice

(This hymn is used in a sacrifice done for the good of the whole universe. It is performed by one who realizes the universal presence of the Supreme Being. It is from this hymn that the Poet Tagore took a motto for his University: "into it the whole universe comes as into a single nest.")

That [the Prime Cause of the Universe] is itself the God Fire and Sun; That itself Wind and Moon; That itself is the Veda and Knowledge; those waters and the Creator are That. For Him there is no counterpart [or image], great indeed is His glory. The wise man sees that eternal thing in the recesses of his heart; into it the whole universe comes as into a single nest; there, all this universe is gathered [at dissolution] and is thrown out [at creation]; that all-pervading Being is woven into beings as the warp and woof (XXXII.1-12).

[5] Namaḥ Śivāya ca Śivatarāya ca—this is the sacred five syllable Śiva mantra.

The Hymn of Good Intent

(Placed on a par with the Purusha-sūkta and the Śatarudrīya, this hymn has been held in the Smṛitis to be of great value as an expiatory hymn.)

That Mind, the Divine, which when one is wakeful or asleep, reaches far, which is the far-reaching light of all lights [sense of all senses], may that Mind of mine be of good intent. By which the active and the wise perform the duties in sacrifice and intellectual activities, that which is the wonder-being inside the beings, may that Mind of mine be of beautiful intent. That which is knowledge and fortitude, that which is the immortal light within all beings, without which no act is done, may that Mind of mine be of auspicious resolve. That which directs men like a good charioteer, directing the horses with reins, that which is established in the heart, is immortal and swiftest, may that Mind of mine be of good intent (XXXIV).

ATHARVAVEDA

For Success in Trade

I urge Indra the merchant, may he come to us and be our forerunner; warding off the unpaying, the cutting beast, let that masterful Indra be a bringer of wealth to me. O Gods! That money with which, desiring more money, I carry on my bargains, let that multiply, never decrease. O Agni, with this oblation, do thou frustrate those who ruin my profit (III.16).

For Success in Agriculture

The foresighted fit the ploughs and severally the yokes, the thoughtful ones seeking the good will of the gods. Fit the plough, place the yokes, and in the prepared furrow here, sow the seed; O Gods, may the ears of grain be full for us, let the ripe [grain] come near the sickle. May the sharp-pointed, well-furrowing, smooth-handled plough throw up for us cattle and sheep, a yoked chariot-drawer [horse], and a plump lass (III.17).

VARUṆA

(*Superintendent of the Moral Order*)

The great superintendent of all this sees as if from nearby; whoever thinks he is going secretly, all that the gods know. He who stands or moves, he who walks crooked, he who moved hiding or desperately, that two, sitting together, conspire, as the third, him Varuṇa knows. Even he who may cross to the other side of the sky will not escape King Varuṇa; from heaven, his spies are patrolling this earth; with a thousand eyes, they scan through the earth (IV.16).

THE EARTH

Great truth, formidable moral order, vow, penance, spiritual knowledge, and sacrifice sustain the Earth; may that Earth, mistress of our past and future, afford us a wide world [for our life]. Without congestion, amidst men, She who has many heights, stretches, and level grounds, who bears herbs of manifold potency, may that Earth spread out and be rich for us. Let all the people milk Her with amity; O Earth, give me sweet words (XII.1).

PEACE

Peaceful be earth, peaceful ether, peaceful heaven, peaceful waters, peaceful herbs, peaceful trees. May All Gods bring me peace. May there be peace through these invocations of peace. With these invocations of peace which appease everything, I render peaceful whatever here is terrible, whatever here is cruel, whatever here is sinful. Let it become auspicious, let everything be beneficial to us (XIX.9).

VEDAS—BRĀHMAṆAS AND ĀRAṆYAKAS

PURIFICATORY MANTRAS

(Purification must be done as part of all rites and especially when there has been pollution. Water into which sanctity has been infused by recital of purificatory mantras is sprinkled on the person and all over the residence or temple, and the water is sipped. Two of the mantras used in the act of purification are given here.)

May the purifying mantras grant us this world as well as the other; may these divine mantras which the gods themselves have gathered for us make our desires prosper. May Indra purify me with the shining goddess of right policy; Soma, with well-being; Varuṇa, with prosperity; may the all-controlling King Yama purify me with his chastisements; may Fire purify me with invigoration (Taittirīya Brāhmaṇa I.4.8).

PROPITIATION OF THE SUN (SŪRYA-NAMASKĀRA)

(These mantras are recited for the special propitiation of the Sun, particularly on Sundays, birthdays, and at special religious functions, accompanied by prostrations to the Sun after each tenth mantra until one hundred and thirty-two prostrations have been done. These prostrations to the Sun have also been adapted for a course of physical exercises in modern times. This long hymn of glorification of the Sun also refers to the Waters, and Time as represented by the seasons, year, day, night, and the atmospheric phenomena of light, clouds, thunder and lightning. A few mantras are given from this long collection.)

O Gods, may we hear only auspicious things with our ears. O Gods worthy of our adoration, may we see only auspicious things with our eyes; with our limbs and bodies firm and singing your praises, may we attain the God-given length of life. The wonderful army of gods [to fight darkness] has risen, the eye of Mitra, Varuṇa, and Agni, pervading all over the heaven, earth and ether, the Sun who is the Soul of [all] that moves and stands [still]. We seek the cure and prevention of ills [that are and are to be] so that we may proceed to the sacrifice, proceed to the sacrificer. May there be divine well-being for us, well-being for men. May we have the healing medicine in the future [also]; blessing to our men, blessing to our animals. He who rises blazing, He rises taking the lives of all beings; O Sun, not of my offspring, not of my cattle, not of me do you take the life as you rise (Taittirīya Āraṇyaka I.1,7,9,14).

Purificatory Mantra

The falsehood that we have uttered with our mouth in our desire to earn our livelihood, from that, O All-Gods, being pleased with us, free us here (Taittirīya Āraṇyaka II.3.2).

Purificatory Mantra

The injury that we have caused to heaven and earth, mother or father, from that sin may the domestic Fire pull us out (Taittirīya Āraṇyaka II.6.8).

A Hundred Autumns

That benevolent Eye of the Gods [the Sun] that moves brightly in the East, may we be seeing it for a hundred autumns; [by the grace of that Sun] may we live for a hundred autumns, may we rejoice for a hundred autumns, may we enjoy for a hundred autumns, may we be for a hundred autumns, may we hear for a hundred autumns, may we speak for a hundred autumns, may we be unvanquished for a hundred autumns, may we be seeing the Sun for a long time (Taittirīya Āraṇyaka IV.42.32).

At the Time of Bath Early in the Morning

(This sin-effacing mantra is repeated at the time of the morning bath.)

I seek the Lord of Waters [Varuṇa] whose surface is golden; entreated by us, give me a ford [for bathing and purifying myself]; the food I have eaten at the house of bad people, the gift I have received from evil men, the sin I have committed with my mind, by word or deed; of all that may Indra, Varuṇa, Bṛihaspati, and Sun purify me again and again. The sin of overeating, overdrinking, and receiving [gifts] from people of violent ways, may King Varuṇa wipe it off with his hand. Let me thus, rid of evil, impurity, and sin become liberated, ascend to heaven, and attain the world of the Lord of creation (Taittirīya Āraṇyaka X.1).

Morning Prayer

(This is one of the preliminary prayers used in the daily worship every morning.)

Sun, Anger, and the deities presiding over Anger, save me from the sin committed through anger. What sin I did at night, by mind, word and hands, by feet, stomach, or the organ of sex, may the deity presiding over the night destroy it. Whatever remains in me as sin, that and my own Self [its doer] here, I am offering as an oblation in the light of the Sun, the source of immortality (Taittirīya Āraṇyaka X.35).

At a Feast

(This mantra is repeated when people sit down for a feast.)

Let the Supreme Being come to me, let the sweetest bliss come to me, may that sweetest bliss, which is the Supreme

Being come to me. O Supreme Lord of spiritual knowledge, of your offspring, I am a child dear to you. O you who terminate this nightmare of transmigratory life, stamp out all misery. O Lord of spiritual wisdom, my vital breaths which are thine, I offer as an oblation to you (Taittirīya Āraṇyaka X.48).

Desire Did It

(These mantras are recited at the time of the annual ceremony of Vedic study, and also as expiation for sins committed through lust or anger. A man who has committed wrong acts through the force of passion here fixes the responsibility on the two evils of desire and anger and by repetition of this truth tries to throw out of his being these two evils.)

Desire did it, Desire does it, I do not do it. Desire is the doer, I am not the doer. Desire is the agent, I am not the agent. O Desire, here, this oblation to you! Anger did, Anger does, I do not do. Anger is the doer, I am not the doer. Anger is the agent, I am not the agent. O Anger, here, this oblation to you! (Taittirīya Āraṇyaka X.41-42).

The Five Great Daily Sacrifices

Five are the great sacrifices; they are the great continuous sacrifices: the propitiation of all things created, of human beings, of the forefathers, of the gods, and of the sacred lore. Everyone should make offerings to all creatures; thereby one achieves the propitiation of all creatures. Every day one should make gifts, even if it be only with a cup of water: thus one achieves the propitiation of human beings. Every day one should, even if it be only with a cup of water, make offerings to his ancestors: thus one achieves the propitiation of the forefathers. Every day one should make offerings to the gods, even if it be only with sacred twigs (and fire): thus one achieves propitiation of the gods. Then, the propitiation of the sacred lore: learning of one's own Veda is that propitiation. Speech, mind, and intellect are the various utensils of this sacrifice; Truth is the final purificatory ceremony; heaven is the end. He who understands this and every day does his sacred study, gains three times the world that is gained by one who fills the whole world with wealth and gives it away. Hence, one should study his own sacred scriptures (Śukla Yajurveda, Śatapatha Brāhmaṇa XI.3).

Prapadādi Japa [1]

(This is a part of the mantra recited by followers of the Sāmaveda during the daily propitiation of Fire in the morning.)

Penance, Luster, Faith, Sense of Shame at doing wrong, Absence of Anger, Giving, Fortitude, Righteousness, Strength, Speech, Mind, Soul, the Supreme Brahman—all these I resort to, may they protect me. I seek that Supreme Being which is the form of the three worlds and OM (Sāmaveda, Mantra Brāhmaṇa II.4.5).

(The following mantra is recited by followers of Sāmaveda in the daily noontime sandhyā worship; after repeating the Gāyatrī, the worshiper looks at the Sun and recites this verse.)

May I be like the Sun in seeing; like Fire in luster; like Wind in power; like Soma in fragrance; like Lord Bṛihaspati in intellect; like the Aśvins [twin sons of the Sun] in beauty; like Indra-Agni in strength; may my portion be knowledge; may my enemy's portion be sin (Mantra Brāhmaṇa II.4.14).

(The following mantra is recited by followers of Sāmaveda in the daily morning and evening sandhyā worship, after the repetition of Gāyatrī.)

May I attain fame among Brāhmans, among Kings and among merchants; may I attain fame as a speaker of Truth;

[1] Expiation for nonobservance of fast and other ordained austerities.

may I attain the fame of famous acts.... O Sun! I have mounted for my well-being, the boat full and of excellent wings, without any hole, with a hundred oars and capable of taking me across; obeisance to the Sun! May I rise along with you who rise (Morning). Following you, may I also get firmly established (Evening) (Sāmaveda, Mantra Brāhmaṇa, II.5.9-16).

OM

The Supreme Being created Brahmā, the creator on the lotus. Having been created, that Brahmā began to think, "By which single syllable may I be able to enjoy all the desires, all the worlds, all the gods, all the Vedas, all the sacrifices, all the sounds, all the rewards, all the beings, stationary and moving?" He practiced self-control and saw this OM, of two syllables, of four morae,[2] the all-pervading, omnipresent, the eternally potent Brahman, the Brahman's own symbolic syllable, of which the presiding divinity is Brahman itself. With it, he enjoyed all the desires of all the worlds, all the gods, all the Vedas, all the sacrifices, all the sounds, all the rewards and all the beings stationary and moving.... Therefore, the Brāhman who, desiring whatever he wants, fasts three nights, sits on sacred grass facing east and keeps under control his tongue and repeats this imperishable OM, for him all objects are realized and all acts are successful (Atharvaveda, Gopatha Brāhmaṇa, I.16-22).

[2] Short syllables.

VEDAS—SUPPLEMENTARY MANTRAS

Marriage

(In addition to the mantras from the Ṛigveda, given above, the following mantras are regularly used in the marriage ceremony. The bride and groom take seven steps together as symbolic of the joint journey through life. This act is recognized in modern Hindu law as completing the sacrament of marriage. Following this act, the bride places her foot on a stone, symbolic of the stonelike firmness of her devotion. These mantras are addressed by the bridegroom to the bride.)

Having taken seven steps with me, become my friend; may we two, who have taken together these seven steps, become companions; may I have your friendship; may I not be separated from your friendship, nor you from mine. With utmost love to each other, gaining luster, with mutually amicable minds, and enjoying together our food and invigorating things, may we walk together and take our resolves together. May we make our minds united, of the same vows and the same thoughts. I am the words and you are the melody; I am the melody and you are the words. I am the heaven, you are the earth. I am the seed, you are the bearer. I am the thought, you are the word; I am the melody, you are the words. You act in accordance with me, so that we may attain a son, may attain prosperity and progeny. Come along with me, O lady of pleasing words. Step on this stone; be you as firm as the stone; stand up to the assailants, overcome the aggressors (Supplementary Mantra).

THE NEWBORN CHILD

(*When the father first takes the newborn child in his arms, he repeats this mantra.*)

From each limb of mine are you born; you are born especially from my heart; you are my own Self bearing the name "son"; may you live for a hundred autumns (Supplementary Mantra).

EATING

(*Eating is not to be indulged in as a mere physical act prompted by desire. He who eats alone has been condemned in a Ṛigveda mantra; one must try to find any guest in need of feeding before sitting down to his food. Before eating, an offering is made to all kinds of beings; the food is first offered to the Lord and what is eaten is His praśāda, that which He has been gracious enough to leave for us, the leavings of the Lord. The very act of eating is heightened into a rite of offering oblations to the fire of the five vital breaths in the body. First, the food is sanctified with preliminary mantras including the Gāyatrī. Just before this he rids himself of all evils by reciting a hymn, "May my anger go to the lion, my hunger to the wolf, my thirst to the desert, my laziness to the brick," and so on.*)

O God the Stimulator! Permit me. You, Truth, I sprinkle over with Righteousness. O Water, You are the immortal sheet, spread for the vital breaths. Concentrating on the vital breath, I make this oblation leading to immortality; let it be a good offering to the vital breath. Concentrating on the downward breath, I make this oblation leading to immortality; let it be a good offering to the downward breath. Concentrating on the pervasive breath, I make this offering leading to immortality; let it be a good offering to the pervasive breath. Concentrating on the upward breath, I make this oblation leading to immortality; let it be a good offering to the upward breath. Concentrating on the equalizing breath, I make this oblation leading to immortality; let it be a good offering to the equalizing breath. May my soul be concentrated on the Brahman for the attainment of immortality.

(After eating, water is to be sipped with the following mantra.)

O Water, You are the immortal covering (Supplementary Mantra).

VEDAS—UPANISHADS

(The most important Upanishads are: Īśā, Kena, Kaṭha, Praśna, Muṇḍaka, Māṇḍūkya, Aitareya, Taittirīya, Chāndogya, Bṛihadāraṇyaka, and Śvetāśvatara. Representative selections from several of these Upanishads are given below.)

ĪŚĀ (VĀSYA) UPANISHAD

Whatever moving there is in the world, all that is pervaded by the Lord; enjoy by renouncing that [world]; covet not anybody's wealth. He who sees all beings in his own Self, and his own Self in all beings, has thereby, no more loathing [for others]. When to the knowing man all beings are but his own Self, then for him who sees unity, what delusion is there and what sorrow? The face of the Truth is hidden with a golden plate; that, O Sun, the nourishing Lord! remove, so that I may realize the Truth (1.6,7,16).

KAṬHA UPANISHAD

(The Kaṭha covers the whole field of Vedānta, the nature of the Ultimate Being, and the path of Yoga. It begins with the story of the way in which the god Death (Yama) is made to unlock the secret of what happens after death.)

That state which all the Vedas reveal, all the penances bespeak, desiring which [men] observe austere life, that state I [Yama] shall give you in a nutshell: it is OM.

The knowing one [Self] is neither born nor does it die; it came from nowhere nor does it become anything; unborn, eternal, permanent, ancient, it is not killed when the body is killed. If the killer thinks of killing, and the killed thinks he is killed, both know not; this [Self] neither kills nor is it killed. Smaller than the small, greater than the great, the Self of this living being is laid in the cave of his heart; he that is rid of desires and dejections, sees the glory of the Self by the sublimation of the faculties.

The Self is not to be gained by teaching, intellect, or much learning. It is to be had only by him who seeks that Self [*or* it is to be had only by him whom the Self itself chooses]; to him this Self reveals its nature. No one who has not refrained from evil conduct, has not attained tranquillity, has not concentration of mind, has not a composed mind, can attain this Self by knowledge (I.2).

He who is ignorant, of uncontrolled mind and always impure —he does not reach that state [of the Self] and comes back to transmigratory existence. He who has knowledge, has controlled mind, and is always pure—he reaches that state after which he is not born again. He who has knowledge as his charioteer and has control over his mind, he reaches the end of the road; that is the all-pervading Lord's supreme abode (I.3.5,7-8).

I [Yama] shall expound to you this mysterious eternal Brahman and what, after death, the Self becomes. Some Selves enter a womb for taking a [new] body, others the static objects [trees, etc.], according to their acts, according to their knowledge. The Being who is awake in those asleep, fashioning one desired object after another, that is the [pure] light, that is the Brahman, that is called the Immortal; in it do all the worlds abide; that none transcends; this is, in truth, that. As the one fire, entering the world, assumes forms according to each form [that it burns] as the one wind, entering the world, assumes forms according to each form [it enters], so also the One that is the inner Self of all beings assumes forms according to each form that it enters and [at the same time] exists outside [that form] also. Just as the Sun, the eye of the whole world, is not contaminated with the external forms of [one's] vision, even so, the inner Self of all beings, being outside them, is not affected by the misery of the world (II.2.6-11).

His [the Brahman's] form is not within the range of the eye; none sees Him with his eye; with the heart, with the intellect, and with the mind [in proper concentration] is He made out; they who know this become immortal. When the five sense perceptions along with the mind come to a standstill, and the intellect too does not stir, that, they say, is the Supreme State (II.3.9-10).

MUṆḌAKA UPANISHAD

Flimsy boats are these in the form of sacrifices; the foolish who gloat over these as the highest good proceed again and again to old age and death. Imagining sacrifice and benefactions to be the highest, the stupid know not of the other [knowledge of Self] which is the highest good; after enjoying in heaven, where the fruits of good acts are enjoyed, they enter this [human] world or those inferior still [of animals, etc.]. But they who cultivate penance and faith in the forest, with tranquillity and knowledge, and living by alms, they, rid of impurity [of both good and bad acts], pass through the gates of the Sun to where that Immortal Being, the Imperishable Soul, is.

Seeing through the worlds accumulated through acts, he who is devoted to the Brahman, shall become detached; that which has not been caused cannot be had by an act; for knowing that, he should, the sacred twig in hand, approach a preceptor, learned in the Vedas and established in Brahman. To him who has thus approached, whose mind is completely rid of passion, and who is endowed with tranquillity, the knowing preceptor should impart in truth that knowledge of Brahman whereby he [the pupil] will understand the Truth, the Imperishable Being (I.2.7,10-13).

That which is effulgent, subtler than the subtle, in which all the world as well as its inhabitants are deposited—that is this Imperishable Brahman; it is the vital Breath; it is speech and mind; it is Truth and Immortality; know, my dear pupil, that is to be hit. Taking the great Upanishadic missile as the bow, you should fit thereon the arrow of pointed concentration; drawing it with the mind engrossed with the thought of the Brahman, hit, O dear pupil, that same unswerving target of Brahman. OM is the bow; one's Self is the arrow; the Brahman, it is said, is that target. One should shoot with all attention, and like the arrow, he will become one with it [the target, Brahman]. In whom the heaven, earth and ether [space] are woven, and mind too with all the breaths, that One alone, the Self, you understand; give up all other words; this is the causeway to the Immortal. Wherein, like spokes in a wheel's hub, are all veins gathered, there in the heart inside is moving this Being, who multiplies manifoldly; that Self, contemplate as OM; well be it with you in the journey to the shore that is beyond darkness (II.2.2-6).

By Truth and penance is this Self to be realized, by knowledge and constant self-control the form of bright light inside the body is seen by the recluse—aspirants who have become pure. *Truth alone triumphs,* not falsehood; the divine path to liberation has been laid with Truth, which the Seers who have no more desires tread, and wherein is also that supreme treasure to be gained by Truth.[1] (III.1.5-6).

Those who have, by the knowledge of Vedānta, conclusively understood its import (the Brahman), the recluse-aspirants who have, by the path of renunciation, burnished the luminous quality of the mind, they, at the time of the final fall of their

1 "Truth alone triumphs" has been adopted as the motto of the Government of India.

body, having become the Supreme Immortal, become liberated in the world that is Brahman.[2] (III.2.6).

Just as rivers running their course disappear into the sea, leaving off their name and form, even so the wise one, freed of name and form, reaches the Divine Being, higher than the high. Whoever knows that Supreme Brahman becomes Brahman itself; none who is not a knower of Brahman is born in his line; he crosses sorrow; he crosses sin; freed of the knots of heart, he becomes immortal (III.2.8-9).

MĀṆḌŪKYA UPANISHAD

(Of the Atharvaveda; studied together with a set of memorial verses in four sections (Kārikās) which the Advaitic tradition considers as the work of Śaṅkara's grand-preceptor Gauḍapāda, and other traditions consider partly or wholly as Upanishads. Here the basic prose text alone is presented.)

This OM is [the Syllable], the Imperishable; all this is but its elaborations; the past, the present, the future—all this is only OM; and that which is, transcending the three times, that too is but OM. All this [identified with OM] is Brahman; [3] and this Self is of four grades.[4] Of the waking state, with knowledge of external objects, consumer of gross objects—the physical man as such is the first grade. Of the dream state, perceiving within one's Self, of enjoyment devoid of gross objects—the luminous one of impressions is the second grade. That is deep sleep where the sleeping one does not fancy any desire and sees no dream. Of the state of deep sleep unified, one mass of pure knowledge, as if of the form of bliss and enjoying only bliss, and having the mind as the [sole] face—this one of Intel-

[2] This paragraph is always recited as welcome when sannyāsins arrive.

[3] This is the Mahāvākya (*Ayam ātmā Brahma*) of the Atharvaveda.

[4] Śaṅkara clarifies this by citing the simile of currency where a piece of major coin, say a rupee, has four quarter rupees, four grades of the same reality.

ligence is the third degree. This [Self resting in its own real state] is the All-powerful, the Omniscient and the Immanent Lord; this is the source of all, the beginning and end of all beings. Perceiving neither internally nor externally, nor even both ways, nor the one which is just consciousness; neither knowing nor nonknowing; the imperceptible, indescribable, unnamable, of the sole form of the consciousness of the one Self, the negation of the phenomenal world, *the Peaceful, the Happy, the One without a second* [*Śāntam Śivam Advaitam*] [5]—this they consider the fourth grade; that is the Self, that is the thing to be realized. This Self is, with respect to its indication by the mystic syllable, the OM; the grades of the Self are with reference to the morae of the OM; for the morae are its components, *A, U,* and *M.*[6] The Vaiśvānara [physical being] in the waking state is *A,* the first of OM [AUM], for the reason that both are widely pervasive, and the first. The Taijasa [luminous one of impressions] in the dreaming state is *U,* the second mora of AUM, by reason of eminence and facing either. The Intelligent one in the state of deep sleep is *M,* the third mora [of AUM], because of measuring and becoming one in the end. The unmeasured further part of OM [7] is the fourth grade, the indescribable, in which the phenomenal world has completely ceased, the happy, the One. Thus OM is the Self itself. He who knows thus enters the Supreme Self with his Self (I.1-12).

TAITTIRĪYA UPANISHAD

(The Taittirīya is so called after the school of that name belonging to the Kṛishṇa Yajurveda. The preliminary portion, which deals with the teacher, the pupil, and their relations and

[5] This is the famous main motto of Poet Tagore's University, which the Government of India, when it chartered the institution as a Union Government University, removed to the regret of many.

[6] OM is made up of the two vowels *A* and *U,* and the nasal *M.*

[7] OM is considered to have a subtle form extending beyond its three morae.

with the ideals of education, is widely quoted in modern times in convocation addresses to university graduates. The first book starts with phonetics and the phenomenon of coalescence between letters and words from which the Ṛishi starts his mystic speculations to help spiritual exercises.)

That Praṇava (OM) which is the head of the Veda, is of the form of the Universe, and was born [as essence] out of immortality from amidst the Vedas—may that all-powerful lord, Praṇava, gratify me with intellect. May I, O divine Praṇava, be the bearer of the spiritual wisdom that confers immortality. May my body be efficient; may my tongue be sweetest; may I hear [teachings] amply with my ears. O Praṇava, you are the treasure casket of the Brahman, covered with the lid of intellect; protect my learning.[8]

(In the following mantra, "Bhūḥ, Bhuvaḥ, Suvaḥ" are the names of the three worlds; these syllables are always prefixed to the Gāyatrī, and frequently repeated in any contemplation or ceremony. In them are all the worlds comprehended. They are given here for the internal meditation of Brahman.)

"Bhūḥ, Bhuvaḥ, Suvaḥ"—these are the three sacred names that are well known; over them a fourth is revealed by (sage) Māhāchamasya, namely, Mahaḥ. That is Brahman, that is the Self; limbs of it are the other gods.

[The artery sushumṇā starting from the heart passes through] the piece of flesh which hangs like a nipple in between the palates, reaches that place where the hairs have their roots, and therefrom pierces to the head and skull—that is the way to reach the Brahman. Reaching out that way, one utters "Bhūḥ" and pervades the world in the form of fire; utters "Bhuvaḥ"

[8] This mantra, together with oblation, is recited as a prayer for intellectual power and for Śrī, all-around enrichment.

and pervades the world in the form of wind; utters "Suvaḥ" and pervades the world in the form of the sun; and utters "Mahaḥ" and pervades the world in the form of the Brahman. [Thus established], one attains the kingdom of his Self; becomes the lord of mind, speech, eye, ear, and knowledge; and above that he becomes this, namely, the Brahman subtle like the ether, of the form of Truth, the garden where life sports, whose mind is bliss, who is rich in peace and is immortal (I.4-6).

OM signifies Brahman; because by OM is meant all this (I.8).

Righteousness and the practice of learning and teaching should be observed; Truth and practice of learning and teaching, Penance and the practice of learning and teaching, Self-control and the practice of learning and teaching, Quietude and the practice of learning and teaching, the Propitiation of the Fires and the practice of learning and teaching, the Propitiation of the guest and the practice of learning and teaching, the Attending to human affairs and the practice of learning and teaching, Progeny and the practice of learning and teaching are to be observed. The truth-speaking Rāthītara thinks that Truth [alone] need be observed; Pauruśishṭi who is always in penance thinks that penance [alone] need be observed; Nāka Maudgalya thinks that learning and teaching alone suffice; that is verily penance, that is verily penance (I.9).

The Vedic Convocation Address

Having imparted the Veda, the teacher instructs the pupil: Speak the truth; do your duty; do not neglect your study. After procuring for the teacher such fees as he desires, see that you do not snap the continuity of your family line. You should not swerve from truth; you should not swerve from duty; you should not neglect your welfare; you should not neglect prosperity; you should not neglect learning and teaching; you should not neglect the duties towards the gods and the ancestors. Adore your mother as god; adore your father as god; adore your teacher as god; adore the guest as god. Those actions of ours that were blameless, those you must follow, not the others; what good acts we have done, those you must cherish, not others. And those Brāhmans [Teachers] who are superior to us, them you should honor. You should give with faith; you should not give without faith; you should give with plenty, give with modesty, give with fear, give with due regard. Then, if you should have a doubt about a duty or conduct—conduct yourself there as is done by such Brāhmans as can deliberate well, are devoted to their duties on their own or others' behalf, are not severe, and are desirous of righteousness. Regarding then things that are prohibited, conduct yourself again as those Brāhmans of judgment, who are devoted to duty, mild and virtuous, do. This is the command, this the advice; this is the inner teaching of the Veda; this is the instruction; thus should one cherish; thus should this be observed.[9] (I.11).

Grades of Bliss

Now, this is an inquiry into bliss: suppose there is a youth, a youth of character, one educated, very quick, firm and strong, and has the whole world filled with wealth—that is one joy of man. A hundredfold of that human joy is the one joy of those men who have become *Gandharvas,*[10] as also the Brāhman of Vedic learning who is not a victim of desire; a hundred joys of human Gandharvas form the one joy of the divine Gandharvas, as also of the learned Brāhman not ruined by desire; a hundred joys of the divine Gandharvas form the one joy of the forefathers who are in a long enduring world, as also the learned Brāhman not beset by desire; a hundred of the joys of the forefathers in their long-standing worlds form one joy for the gods born in

[9] This mantra is frequently cited in modern times as an exhortation to teachers and students to devote themselves to teaching and learning.

[10] Singers and musicians who attend the banquets of the gods.

the ājāna-heaven,[11] as also for the desireless Vedic scholar; a hundred joys of the gods of the ājāna-heaven form one joy for the gods who have become so by the merit of their sacrificial acts, as also for the desireless Vedic scholar; a hundred joys of these gods of sacrificial acts form one joy for the real gods, as also for the passionless knower of the Veda; a hundred joys of the gods form one joy for Indra [their king], as also for the passionless knower of the Veda; a hundred joys of Indra form one joy for Bṛihaspati and a passionless student of the Veda; a hundred Bṛihaspati joys form one joy for the Creator and a passionless student of the Veda; a hundred joys of the Creator form the one of the Brahman and of the knower of the Veda who is free from desires. This [Brahman] in the individual and this in the Sun are one and the same; one that knows thus, turning away from this world, comprehends it as the self of the form of food, [then] comprehends it as the self of the form of life, [then] comprehends it as the self of the form of mind, [then] of the form of knowledge, [then] of the form of bliss. There is also this verse here: That from which, without reaching it, words return along with the mind, knowing that bliss of the Brahman, one is not afraid of anything. Him torments not the thought, "What good here did I fail to do? What evil did I do?" For him, who knows thus [the Self], both these [good and evil] alike please the Self; indeed both do please the Self for him who knows thus. This is the secret teaching (II.8-9).

That from which all these beings are born, that by which the born ones live, that which they reach in the end and enter into, that you learn as the Brahman (III.1).

CHĀNDOGYA UPANISHAD

(The Chāndogya, belonging to the Sāmaveda, is one of the two most important Upanishads, the other being the Bṛihadā-

[11] Reached by the performance of duties laid down by the Smṛitis.

raṇyaka; both are notable for the mystic meditative exercises which they impart. As an Upanishad of the Sāmaveda, Chāndogya devotes its first portion to the meditative exercises based on the chanting of Sāmans. The grammatical philosophers built up a system of thought according to which an imperishable substratum of sound was the Brahman and from it meaning and the objective world came forth. Its greatest classic expounder, Bhartṛihari, was a predecessor of Śaṅkara in the restoration of the place of the highest authority to the scriptures and in building up Advaitic ideas. For Bhartṛihari, OM is Brahman, but Śaṅkara differs from his interpretation, saying that OM is only the nearest name and symbol of the Brahman, and never Brahman itself. Elsewhere in the Upanishads, the high-flown descriptions of OM are to be taken, according to Śaṅkara, as due to this being the most proximate symbol of the Brahman; and it is as the highest symbol of the Brahman that it is recommended by the Upanishads again and again for worship.)

One should worship the syllable OM, the Udgītha; it is with OM that one begins to sing. Now to its exposition: of these beings, the earth is the essence; of the earth, water is the essence; of the waters, herbs are the essence; of the herbs, man is the essence; of man, speech is the essence; of speech, the hymn is the essence; of the hymn, the song is the essence; of the song, the Udgītha (OM) is the essence. This eighth, the Udgītha, is the inner essence of all essences, the ultimate, the most adorable. This syllable is one of permission; whatever one permits, OM does one say for that; this permission is verily fullness. By that OM does this sacrificial science of the three Vedas subsist; and by its greatness and essence does the sacrificial science of the three Vedas proceed. With this OM, both perform the sacrifice, he who knows it thus and he who does not know; different are knowledge and ignorance; and only that which is done with knowledge, faith, and understanding, of its inner significance is more efficacious. This is the full exposition of this syllable (OM) (I.1-3,8,9).

The creator contemplated intensely upon the worlds for extracting their essence; from the worlds so [heated] contemplated, the three-fold Vedic science [flowed out], and from it so contemplated, these imperishable syllables flowed out: "Bhūḥ, Bhuvaḥ, Suvaḥ." He contemplated on those syllables and from them so contemplated, the syllable OM flowed out. Just as all leaves are fastened to a stalk, even so all speech is fastened to the syllable OM. All this is only OM, all this is only OM (II.23.2-3).

The Gāyatrī is all this, whatever there is alive here; speech is Gāyatrī, for speech makes everything resound and saves everything. What is Gāyatrī is this earth; for on earth all that lives is established, and it does not exceed the earth. (III.12.1-2).

All this is verily Brahman, produced from it, absorbed into it and living by it; so should one meditate in tranquillity. Now, man is made of resolve; of what resolve he is in this world, that he becomes on his death; so he should make a resolve [to meditate on Brahman], absorbed in contemplation, embodied as it were in knowledge of the form of light, of true intentions, like ether in subtlety and all-pervasiveness, with the whole universe as his act, with everything become desirable to him, with every smell fragrant to him, with every taste relishable to him, comprehending all this, without a word, without a flurry.

"This my Self within my heart is subtler than a grain or subtler than barley, or subtler than mustard, or subtler than a canary seed, or subtler than even its core; and this Self within me is bigger than ether, bigger than heaven, bigger than [all] these worlds. That for which all acts are duties to be done, all things are desirable, all smells fragrant, all tastes delicious, that which comprehends all this, that which speaks no more and is no more flurried—this Self of mine within my heart is that Brahman. Departing from this world, I shall become that"—he who takes resolve like this and doubts it not [attains that state of the Brahman]. So doth Śāṇḍilya say, Śāṇḍilya (III.14).

The Sun has been taught as the Brahman; now the exposition of that. In the beginning there was the undistinguished; it became the distinguishable; it developed; it became the [primordial] egg; it lay for the duration of a year; then it burst; its two halves were of silver and gold. The silver one is earth; the golden one is heaven; the hard and soft membranes in the interior became mountains, and mist coupled with cloud; the veins became the rivers, fluid the sea. What was born there [out of the egg] was the Sun; as he arose, there arose shouts and hallelujas, and arose also all beings and all desires (III.19.1-3).

In the fifth oblation, the water poured is called "Purusha." Wrapped in the womb, the seed lies inside for ten or nine months or so and is born. Having been born, it lives as long as its [alloted] life extends; on death, it is to fire that people convey him for being taken to the world determined by his acts—the fire wherefrom he came here, wherefrom he was born (V.9.1-2).

Now, those householders who understand thus and those who practice in the forest faith and penance—they reach the flame; from flame, the day; from day, the bright fortnight; from the bright fortnight, those six months when the Sun goes north; from those months to the year; from the year to the Sun; from the Sun to the moon; from the moon to the lightning. There, a Person not human takes them to the Brahman. This is the path of the gods.

But those who, residing in the village, adore sacrificial and beneficial acts and generous gifts, they reach the smoke; from smoke, the night; from night, the dark fortnight; from the dark fortnight those six months when the Sun goes south. They do not proceed [from there] to the year. From the months they go to the world of the forefathers; from that world to the ether; from ether to the moon; this moon is King Soma, the food of the gods; [hence] the gods eat them [make them their playthings]. Abiding there till the end of the fruits of their acts, they return by the same path—this sky, from sky to air; having been air, they become smoke; having been smoke, they become vapor; having been vapor, they become cloud; having been cloud, they come down as rains; the rains are born as the grain and barley, herbs and trees, sesame and beans. Hence this is inescapable—whoever consumes food and scatters his seed is thereby born again.

Of these, they who have been men of good conduct, reach soon a good birth, of a Brāhman, a Kshatriya, or a Vaiśya; they who have been of bad conduct, soon do they attain bad births, of a horse or a pig.

Now, those mean creatures [who practice neither knowledge nor good acts], who go by neither of these paths: "Be born and be dead"—so do they go on revolving; this is the third state. Hence does the other world never become full; one should loathe that path.

There is also this verse here: "The stealer of gold, the drinker of liquor, one who betakes to his elder's bed, the murderer of a Brāhman and the fifth who is their associate."[12] But he who knows thus these five fires, though he associates with the above sinners, is not tarnished by the sin; pure, sanctified, he attains the world of merit, he who knows thus, he who indeed knows thus (V.10.1-9).

There was Śvetaketu Āruṇeya; to him his father (Āruṇi) said: "Did you ask of your teacher that teaching by which

[12] These are the five heinous sins.

even that which has not been known, becomes known?" "My Lord, what is that teaching?" asked Śvetaketu. The father said, "Just as with one lump of clay all that is of mud becomes known, the change being only a name, the product of speech, and the truth is that it is all clay. Even so, my dear, is that teaching." (VI.1.3-4).

"My dear! In the beginning, there was only this being, one and without a second. Some say here that in the beginning, there was this nonbeing, one and without another, and that from nonbeing being was born." The father continued: "My dear, how could this be? How can being come out of nonbeing? Therefore, my dear, being alone existed at first, one only, without a second. It reflected, 'Let me become many and be born.' It created light. Light thought, 'Let me become many and be born,' and produced waters. The waters thought, 'Let me become more and be born,' and produced food. The Supreme Deity thought, 'I shall enter these three divinities [of light, water, and food] with this life, namely, my own Self, and shall unfold names and forms' " (VI.2.1-4; 3.2).

Uddālaka Āruṇi told his son Śvetaketu, "By the offshoot of food, seek the root, water; by the offshoot of water, my dear, seek the root, fire; by the offshoot of fire, my dear, seek the root; the true Being. All these things, my dear, are rooted in this true Being, in it they abide, in it are they established. My dear, when this man departs from here, his speech becomes one with the mind, the mind with the life-breath, the life-breath in fire, the fire in the Supreme Deity. This true Being, this subtle source of the world, that is the soul of everything; that is Truth, that is the Self, THAT THOU ART, O Śvetaketu" [13] (VI.8.4,6,7).

"Just as, my dear son, honeybees produce honey, collect the

[13] "That Thou Art" is one of the four great basic texts of Upanishadic philosophy.

honey from diverse trees, and make it all one, and just as in that honey the essences do not have the distinct knowledge, 'I am the juice from this tree, I am the juice from this tree,' and so on, even so, my dear, all these beings, having become one with the one True Being, do not know that they have come into Him" (VI.9.1-2).

"Drop this salt into water and come to me tomorrow morning." Śvetaketu did accordingly. The father said, "Ah, the salt that you put in overnight, bring that." The son reflected and did not know [where it was]. The father said, "Ah, it has been dissolved; sip it at the top, how is it?" "It is saltish." "Sip it at the middle, how is it?" "Saltish." "Throw it away and come to me." He did accordingly, saying, "That salt remains all right there for ever." To him the father said, "But here in your body, my dear, you do not see the True Being; verily, here itself is it.

"My dear, just as one brings a man blindfolded from the Gāndhāra country and leaves him in a man-forsaken forest, and that man shouts to the east or north, south or west, 'I have been brought blindfolded and left blindfolded,' and then one removes the fold from his eyes, and tells him, 'This way lie the Gāndhāras, go in this direction,' and enquiring from village to village, that informed and intelligent man reaches the Gāndhāras, even so here, he who has a teacher knows. To one such, there is only so much delay as it takes for the release from the body; then he becomes one [with the True Being] [14] (VI.13-14).

"When one is happy, he performs his duty; in sorrow, one does not do [his duty]; it is in happiness that one does; happiness should be known. That which is without any limitation is happiness; there is no happiness in the finite; the infinite alone is happiness. When one sees nothing else, hears nothing

[14] The phrase, "he who has a teacher knows," is an axiomatic text of all sects of Hinduism; the mere self-taught book learning is of no use; only by direct imparting by a teacher, a guru, does knowledge or a mantra become effective.

else, is conscious of nothing else, that is the unlimited. When one sees another, hears another, is conscious of another, that is the limited. What is unlimited is immortal; what is limited is mortal." "My Lord, where is that unlimited established?" "In its own greatness, or rather not in any greatness. In the world cows and horses are said to be greatness, elephant and gold, servant and wife, cornfields and houses; I do not speak of a greatness like this in which one is established in another; but I speak of that which alone is below and above, behind and before, on the right and left; that alone is all this.

"Now this is taught as the I and nothing else; it is I that is below and above; it is I that is behind and before; it is I that is to the left and right; it is I that is all this. Then this is taught as the Self, nothing else. It is the Self that is below and above, behind and before, on the right and left; the Self is all this. He who sees like this, thinks like this, knows like this, becomes one who delights in the Self, sports in the Self, consorts with the Self, enjoys the Self; he becomes lord of himself; he moves as he pleases in all the worlds" (VII.22-25).

The words of the Creator (Prajāpati) about the Self both the gods and the demons heard of; they said, "Ah, we shall search for the Self, by finding which one attains all the worlds and all desires." Indra, of the gods, started out, and Virocana, of the demons. Independently, the two, sacred twig in hand, approached Prajāpati.

The two observed studentship for thirty-two years; Prajāpati [then] asked them, "Desiring what, have you been staying here?" They said, "That Self wherein all evil is destroyed, which is devoid of old age, death, and sorrow, hunger, and thirst, of true desires and resolves—that is to be sought, that is to be known, and he who searches for it and knows it obtains all the worlds and all desires. They are teaching these as your Lordship's words; desiring that Self, we have lived here [as students]."

Prajāpati told them, "The Person seen in the eye is the Self; this is immortal and fearless, this is Brahman." "Now, Lord, who is he, the Person [image] who appears on the waters or in the mirror [when one looks into them]?" [asked Indra and Virocana]. Prajāpati replied, "He alone is seen at all ends." Prajāpati told them, "Look into a dish of water and tell me if you do not understand the Self?" They looked into the dish of water. Prajāpati asked them, "What do you see?" They replied, "Lord, we see the whole of ourselves, our replica, to the very hairs and nails." Prajāpati told them, "Put on excellent ornaments and good dress and decorating yourself look into the dish of water." [They did so and] said, "Lord, just as we are ornamented and dressed well, decorated, even so are we in this dish of water, with excellent ornaments and dress, and decorated." Prajāpati said, "This is the Self; this is immortal and fearless, this is the Brahman." With their hearts at rest, the two departed.

Looking at the two, Prajāpati said, "Without grasping the Self, without searching and knowing it, these two are going. Gods or demons, they will take this as the teaching and will come to grief."

With heart at rest, Virocana went to the demons and taught them this teaching that the Self alone was to be adored and served and that by adoring and serving the Self, one attained both the worlds, this and the other. Therefore it is that even now they say of one who gives not, believes not, and offers no sacrifice, "Alas, he is a demon." This is the knowledge of the demons, they decorate the body of the dead with perfumes and flowers and food, dress and ornaments; with this they think they are winning the other world.

But without going to the gods, Indra thought about this danger: "Just as this person in the image becomes well ornamented and well dressed and decorated, even so he will become blind, squint, and maimed, when this body becomes blind in the eyes, squint in one eye and maimed in the limbs, and following the death of the body he will also die; I do not see anything to be enjoyed in this person of the image." So, with the sacred twig in hand, Indra came back to Prajāpati. Prajāpati told him, "Indra, with a heart at rest you went away with Virocana; now, desiring what have you come back?" [Indra told him the danger that he saw in the belief that the image-person is the Self.]

Prajāpati said, "Indra, so it is. But I shall expound to you again; live here for another thirty-two years." Indra lived there as a student for another thirty-two years. To him Prajāpati said, "This person who moves about in a dream in a good manner, he is the Self; he is immortal and free from fear, he is the Brahman."

With his heart at rest, Indra departed, but without going to the gods, he saw danger here too. "Even though this person of the dream does not become blind, or squint when this body becomes so, and is not affected by the defects of this body, yet these seem to affect him and haunt him. He appears to be conscious of pain, and even weeps as it were. I do not find here anything of joy."

With the sacred twig in hand, he came back to Prajāpati, underwent studentship for another thirty-two years, and then Prajāpati told him, "Where one sleeps completely, in full serenity, and knows no dream, that is the Self; it is immortal and fearless, it is the Brahman." With a heart at ease, Indra went away, but without going to the gods he saw the danger there, too. "Even he in deep sleep does not know himself as 'I am,' nor does he know these beings; he has become extinct; I do not find anything of joy here."

Again, sacred twig in hand, Indra came to Prajāpati and lived there for five more years. The years became one hundred and one, and then Prajāpati told him, "Indra, this body is mortal, caught by death. It is the place of stay for the immortal unbodied Self. Becoming embodied, the Self becomes caught up in the pleasant and the unpleasant; so long as it is in the embodied state, there is no overcoming of the pleasant and when it exists, dissociated from the body, the pleasant and unpleasant touch him not. That is the Person par excellence. It then goes about laughing, playing, and sporting with women or vehicles or kinsmen, never having in mind this body which is a product, or into which it had come. Like unto a horse or ox fitted to a carriage to be drawn is this Self [individual] joined to this body.

"Now, where the ether is marked by the eye, there the Self is in the eye, and eye itself is only the instrument of seeing. That which has the knowledge, 'I smell this,' is the Self, the nose is but the instrument of smelling. That which has the knowledge, 'I speak this,' is the Self, the tongue itself being the instrument of speaking. That which has the knowledge, 'I hear this,' is the Self, the ear itself being the instrument of hearing. That which has the knowledge, 'I think this,' is the Self, the mind is the divine eye. With this divine eye [of the mind] the Self sports seeing all these desires and those that are in the world of the Brahman.

"This Self the gods adore, and they therefore have all the worlds and all the desires. He who seeks that Self and understands it obtains all the worlds and all the desires." Thus said Prajāpati, indeed thus did he say (VIII.7-14).

This Brahmā told Prajāpati, Prajāpati to Manu, Manu to men; having learned the Vedas at the teacher's place, according to the rules laid down and in the leisure available after attending upon the teacher, having completed his study and having been discharged, one should settle down to family life in a holy place, continue his Vedic study, build up a body of virtuous men [sons and pupils], establish firmly all his senses in the Self, avoid hurt to other beings except where ordained—he who conducts himself like this to the end of his life attains the world of the Brahman, he never returns, indeed he returns not (VIII.15)

BṚIHADĀRAṆYAKA UPANISHAD

(The Bṛihadāraṇyaka, one of the two most important Upanishads, belongs to the Śukla Yajurveda as the closing part of the extensive Brāhmaṇa associated with that Veda. It opens with the interpretation of the inner meaning of the greatest of all the scripture-ordained acts, the horse-sacrifice, as a means of spiritual meditation. There follows a section dealing with the greatness of the mantra OM, dealt with in the Chāndogya Upanishad, closing with three mantras which, according to Śaṅkara, help one who repeats them to ascend to one's own divine Self. These mantras given here have become greatly popular in modern times and are widely cited as mottoes or recited as prayers.)

From evil lead me to good; from darkness lead me to light, from death lead me to Immortality (I.3).

There was the Brahman at the beginning; it knew itself as "I am the Brahman," therefore it became everything. Whoever among the gods understood this, became that Brahman; even so among the Seers, and among men. The Seer Vamadeva saw this and claimed, "I was Manu, I was the Sun." So, even now, he that knows this, "I am the Brahman," becomes all this. Even the gods are not powerful enough to undo him, for he becomes their Self [15] (I.10).

He created above what is still further superior, Righteousness. This Dharma is more formidable than formidable royalty. Therefore, there is nothing greater than Righteousness. Hence, a weak man hopes to vanquish a strong one through Righteousness as through the King. Righteousness is Truth, for he who speaks Truth is said to espouse Righteousness, and he espouses Truth; both are thus the same (I.4.14).

[15] "I am the Brahman" is one of the four basic Upanishadic texts.

Now the indication of this Person [Brahman] is "Not this, not this," for beyond saying "Not this, not this," there is nothing else possible. Then as to the name [of the Brahman], it is the "Truth beyond the truth." The faculties are the truth; of them, this is the truth (II.3.6).

Maitreyī said, "Worshipful Lord! If this whole world is filled with wealth for me, would I become immortal thereby?" "No," said Yājñavalkya [her husband], "just as the life of those that command ample resources, even so would your life be; but of immortality, there is no hope through wealth." Maitreyī said, "That by which I would not become immortal, what shall I do with that? What, my Lord, you know [of the means to immortality], tell me that alone." Yājñavalkya said, "Look here, it is not for the pleasure of the husband that the husband is dear [to one], but it is for the pleasure of [one's] Self that the husband is dear; it is for the pleasure of one's Self that the wife is dear; it is for the pleasure of one's Self that the sons are dear; it is for the pleasure of one's Self that wealth is dear; it is for the pleasure of one's Self that all things are dear. Maitreyī, by seeing the Self, hearing about it, thinking about it, and understanding it, all this becomes known" (II.4.2-5).

"Where there is, as it were, a duality, there one smells another, one sees another, one hears another, one speaks to another, one thinks of another, one knows another—but where, to one, everything was but the Self, there what shall he smell and by what? What shall he see and by what? What shall he hear and by what? Whom shall he address and with what? What shall he think and by what? What shall he know and by what? That by which he knows all this, whereby shall he know it? By what can this knower be known? This Self is the Lord of all beings, the King of all beings. Just as at the hub and the rim of the chariot wheel, all the spokes are fitted, even so are all beings, all gods, all worlds, all lives, all selves laid in this Self," said Yājñavalkya (II.4.14-15).

(Ushasta Chākrāyaṇa to Yājñavalkya), "That Brahman which is immediate and directly perceivable, the Self which is interior to everything—explain that to me." (Yājñavalkya), "This your Self is the innermost of everything." "Which is it, Yājñavalkya, the innermost of everything?" "You cannot see the seer of the eye itself; you cannot hear the hearer of the ear itself; you cannot think of the thinker of the mind; you cannot know the knower of the knowledge; this is your Self, innermost of everything; everything besides this is subject to suffering." Thereupon Ushasta Chākrāyaṇa became silent (III.4).

Then Gārgī Vācaknavī said, "Reverend Brāhmans, I shall ask this Yājñavalkya two questions and if he answers them, then none indeed among you can vanquish him in a discussion about Brahman." (They replied), "Ask, Gārgī." She said, "Yājñavalkya, what is it that they say is above the heavens, and below the earth and in between this heaven and earth, and is itself the past, the present, and the future? And in what is all this woven, warp and woof?" Yājñavalkya replied, "Gārgī, what they say is above heaven and below earth, and indeed in between those two and is itself the past, present, and future is the ether; it is in the ether that it is woven warp and woof." "In what is the ether woven, warp and woof?" He said, "Gārgī, that is what the Brāhmans call the Imperishable; not big, not small, not short, not long; neither glowing red nor moist, without shadow or darkness, neither air nor ether, not sticking, devoid of taste and smell, bereft of eye and ear, of speech and mind, of heat and breath, without entrance and measurement, without either an inside or an outside, neither does it eat anything nor does anything else eat it.

"Gārgī, in the reign of this Imperishable do the Sun and

moon stand, held to their duty; earth and heaven stand held to their places; the moments, hours, days and nights, fortnights and months, seasons and years, stand held to their courses; some rivers flow east from the white mountains and others west or other directions. At its command, O Gārgī, men praise the giver; the gods, the sacrifice, and the forefathers look to the offerings.

"Gārgī, he who without knowing this Imperishable, pours oblations in this world, sacrifices, practices penance for many thousands of years—all that of his comes to an end. He who, O Gārgī, without knowing this Imperishable departs from this world is miserable. He who, after knowing this, departs, is a Brāhman. This Imperishable, O Gārgī, is the unseen seer, the unheard listener, the thinker unthought of, and the unknown knower" (III.8.1,6-11).

Vidagdha Śākalya asked, "Yājñavalkya, how many are the gods?" Yājñavalkya replied, "Three, three hundred, three and three thousand." Śākalya said, "Well, how many are they really?" "Thirty-three." "Well, how many really?" "Six." "Well, how many really?" "Three." "Well, how many really?" "Two." "Well, how many really?" "One and a half." "Well, how many really?" "One." "Which is that one god?" "Life; they call it Brahman." "He whose abode is earth, sight, fire, light, mind—he who knows that Person, the ultimate abode of all Selves, he indeed is the knower, Yājña-valkya" (III.9).

"Yājñavalkya, which is the Self?" "That which is of the form of knowledge among the senses, the light within the heart, the all-filling Person, who, identifying Himself with the intellect, moves about both the worlds of sleep and waking, and appears to remain in contemplation or constant movement; taking to sleep, He transcends this world and all forms of death [that is, activities of the world]. In that state [of sleep] the person is self-illumined. That [the state of deep sleep] is the form of Self in which there is no desire, no taint of virtue and vice, no fear. Just as one hugged by his beloved lady is not conscious of anything outside or inside, even so is this person hugged by the Self in the state of the Intelligent not conscious of anything outside or inside (IV.3.7,9,21).

"When he departs, life following him departs; and following life, all senses depart. He has consciousness and it is with consciousness that he passes over. Him follow both his knowledge and acts and the impressions of previous existences. Just as a caterpillar, having reached the end of one blade of grass, taking hold of another support, draws itself to it, even so this Self, after kicking off this body and rendering it insentient, steps over to another resort and draws itself to it. Just as a goldsmith, taking a bit of gold, makes another newer and more beautiful form, even so, this Self, kicking off this body and rendering it insentient, takes another newer and more beautiful form—of the forefathers, Gandharvas, gods, Prajāpati, Brahmā, or of other beings" (IV.4.2-4).

The three offspring of Prajāpati, gods, men, and demons, underwent studentship under their father Prajāpati. Completing their studentship the gods said, "Give us, O blessed Lord, your teaching." Prajāpati told them this syllable, "Da," and asked "Did you understand?" They said, "We have understood. You said to us, 'Subdue yourselves.' " "Yes, you have understood." Then men asked him to give them his message. To them he spoke the syllable "Da," and asked if they had understood. They said, "We have understood. You said to us, 'Give.' " "Well, you have understood." Then the demons asked him to give them his message. He spoke to them the syllable "Da," and asked them if they had understood. They said, "We have understood. You said to us, 'Be compassionate.'" "Well, you have understood." This is what this heavenly voice, the thunder, goes on saying, "Da-Da-Da": "Be subdued, Give, Be compassionate." Therefore one should cultivate this triad, Self-control, Giving, and Compassion (V.2.1-3).

DHARMA ŚĀSTRAS

ĀPASTAMBA DHARMA SŪTRA

The teacher is called *āchārya* because the student gathers from him the dharmas. Never should [a student] think ill of him [the teacher], for the teacher gives him a [new] birth in knowledge, [and] that is the highest birth. Mother and father produce one's body only (I.1.14-18).

The student should be soft, subdued, controlled in senses, and shrinking from doing wrong; firm in his fortitude, not lazy, not irascible, not jealous. The student should neither indulge in self-praise nor run down others (I.3).

One should not observe the ordained duties with a worldly end in view, for, in the end, they bear no fruit. Just as when a mango is planted for the fruit, shade and fragrance also result, even so the ordained duty that is performed is attended by material gains. To the words of the hypocrite, the crook, the heretic, and the juvenile, one should react neither with hate nor deception. In all realms, one should conform to the conduct which enjoys the consistent sanction of the noble ones, those who are well disciplined, elders, self-possessed, free from avarice and vanity. Thus one gains both worlds (VII.20).

Now we shall enumerate the evils that scorch the bodily elements: anger, elation, indignation, avarice, delusion, vanity, enmity, speaking falsehood, overeating, traducing others, jealousy, passion, ill-feeling, lack of self-possession and of mental concentration—these are to be destroyed through yoga. Absence of anger, of elation, of indignation, of avarice, of delusion, and of vanity and enmity; speaking truth, moderation in eating, refraining from exposing others' weak points, freedom from jealousy, sharing one's good things with others, sacrifice, straightforwardness, softness, quietude, self-control, friendliness with all beings, absence of cruelty, contentment—these form approved conduct for men in all stations of life; observing them duly, one becomes universally benevolent (VIII.1).

Of that which is to be eaten by the householder, offerings to the gods and beings are to be done; these offerings are productive of heaven as well as nourishment. After these offerings, one should feed those to whom priority is due. First are to be fed the guests; and boys, aged men, invalids, and pregnant women. The husband and wife of the house should not turn away any who comes at eating time and asks for food. If food is not available, a place for rest, water for refreshing one's self, a reed mat to lay one's self on, and pleasing words entertaining the guest—these at least never fail in the houses of the good [1] (VIII.2).

Four are the stations of life, household life, studentship, life of the silent sage, and life in the forest. He who renounces life should go about without any sacrificial rite in fire, without a house, without any enjoyment, without seeking anybody's shelter, opening his mouth only for recital of sacred texts and mantras like OM, taking from the village only so much as will hold his soul and body together, and bereft of any act of this-worldly or other-worldly prospect (VIII.2).

GAUTAMA DHARMA SŪTRA

Apart from the forty sacraments, there are the eight qualities of the soul: compassion toward all beings, forbearance, absence of jealousy, purity, moderation, auspiciousness, dignified conduct of one's self and freedom from avarice. He who has re-

[1] India is a land of hospitality; this last verse may be found verbatim on everybody's lips.

ceived all the sacraments and does not have the eight personal qualities—he does not attain the world of Brahmā and oneness with Him. He who has only a few of the sacraments but has the eight personal qualities—he, however, attains to the world and identity with Brahmā (VIII).

The places [suitable for expiatory meditation are] all hills, all rivers, holy lakes, and waters, āśrama abodes of sages, cow-pen, and temple. Continence, truth-speaking, ablutions in the morning, noon, and evening, remaining in wet clothes, lying on bare ground and fasting are [expiatory] penances (XIX).

SUPPLEMENT TO THE GAUTAMA DHARMA SŪTRA—KRIYĀPĀDA

The Daily Routine

I shall then speak of the accepted conduct. From observance of accepted conduct one gains merit, wealth, happiness, and from the same, final liberation.

Arising in the last quarter of the night, with a composed mind, casting off sleep, holding evenly the vital and downgoing breaths, calling upon the Sun [in one's heart] and in the lotus blown open by the Sun, one should rest the swan of one's heart. Seeing [there] with a divine eye the divine Being, of a thumb's size, comprehending the higher and lower [Brahman] and of the form of light, remaining as much as possible [in that state] in the dawn and praising [that Supreme] manifoldly with hymns.

One should go out with his shoes toward a water reservoir, without treading on bones, excreta, urine, ash, or worms.[2] With a steadied mind, one should leave his things at a clean spot, go out far away from the roadway and answer the calls of nature in privacy. One should not answer calls of nature in the pre-

[2] As one treads on the ground one should address to Mother Earth the prayer saying, "Please forgive me treading upon you with my feet."

cincts of sages, temples, gardens, anthills, water, land with cultivated crops, lake, hill, stone, holes, in front of open sky and quarters, other's excreta, the moon, fire, the Sun, cows, Brāhmans, women; nor in shades of trees used for rest by travelers nor in ploughed field, road, or water.

Sitting without distraction and facing east, one should clean one's teeth with a green twig, cut evenly, with skin and nodes, astringent, bitter or sharp in taste, from a thorn tree or of a fragrant smell. One should throw away the twig with the recital of the prayer "O tree [twig], grant us longevity, strength, fame, lustre, progeny, cattle and wealth, sacred love, knowledge and intellect."

Before the [actual] sunrise, at [early] dawn itself, a bath in the sea, confluence of sea and river, lake, tank, and river destroys the heinous sins. From the midst of water one should gratify the gods, by offering of water, facing east; gratify the sages, facing north, and the forefathers, facing south. Coming out of the water, one should twist the wet cloth and discharge the water on the left with the words, "Those born in our line and clan who passed away without sons, let them take this water offered by me by the pressing of the wet cloth."

The mental bath is one that is secured by contemplating upon the all-pervasive Lord of the form of undiminished bliss and knowledge. By reason of exigencies of physical unfitness, and unsuitability of place and time, all kinds of baths are of equal efficacy. The mental bath is the highest. The mantra bath is prescribed when one is undergoing medical treatment, is ill, and when there is local commotion by reason of politics, thieves, etc. [preventing one from going out to a bathing-place].

When talk is unrestrained, the bath loses luster, the fire in which oblations are offered is deprived of prosperity, and while eating, death is hastened; therefore one should observe silence in these three acts [bathing, worshiping, eating].

When there is a river, one should not bathe in other waters; Gayā, Ganges, Kurukshetra, etc., are the holy places for special sacred baths, therefore one should remember them and thrice immerse himself in the water.[3] One should not splash the water with his feet nor enter water when he is full of dirt; one should not discharge blood, excreta, urine, spit, or semen into water.

With a steady mind, facing east, on a seat, one should, after washing his feet and palms, sip water twice and worship Sandhyā. Seated, one should practice control of the breath. Without Sandhyā worship one is always impure and unfit for all further rites. After control of the breath and sprinkling of water, one should stand facing the Sun, take water in both palms, sanctify it with the recital of Gāyatrī mantra, and offer it at the morning and evening twilight by throwing it up three times. One should repeat the Gāyatrī in meditation, facing east and up to the actual sight of the Sun in the morning; facing west and up to the rise of the stars in the evening. Ten repetitions of Gāyatrī destroy sins of the moment; a hundred, the sins of the day and night; and a thousand, those of a year.

After this, one should go home, then one should do the daily oblations in fire, and the different propitiations to sacred lore, gods and forefathers. Then, entering the room where the divine images are kept, and with the materials of worship ready, one should sit on a clean seat and worship god. Then one should salute the teachers, elders, and those learned in the Vedas. Until noon, one should attend to Vedic study, and after the midday worship of the Sun one should eat. The act of eating is similar to the propitiation of fire with oblations. One should not sleep or indulge in sex during daytime. Till evening, one should engage himself in the study of his school of philosophy, then one should perform the evening worship of Sandhyā.

THE LAWS OF MANU

(The Laws of Manu are recognized as the foremost code of sacred and civil conduct (dharma). Manu, man's first progeni-

[3] The verse generally recited for this is: "O Gaṅgā, Yamunā, Godāvarī, Sarasvatī, Narmadā, Sindhu, and Kāverī, come into the water I am bathing in."

tor, is praised thus in the Veda itself, "Whatever Manu said is medicine.")

The single syllable OM is the Supreme Brahman; control of breaths is the supreme penance; there is nothing higher than the Gāyatrī; better than silence is to speak of the truth. By mere repetition of a mantra a Brāhman attains spiritual success here; there is no doubt about this; he may or may not do other rites; the Brāhman is said to be he who is the friend of all.

Brāhmans are superior by knowledge, Kshatriyas by heroism, Vaiśyas by grain and money, and Śūdras by their very birth. The teaching of the good to beings should be done nonviolently; he who desires dharma should employ his words sweetly and finely. Even when harassed, one should not hit against another; that word of his at which another would shudder, that word which is against heaven, one should not utter.

From honors a Brāhman should always shrink as from poison; and humiliation he should always covet as he would nectar. The humiliated sleeps happily, wakes up happily, and moves about in this world happily; he who has inflicted the humiliation perishes (II).

Fathers, brothers, husbands, and brothers-in-law should honor the brides and deck them, if they desire welfare. Where women are honored, there the gods delight; where they are not honored, there all acts become fruitless.

(At the end of the śrāddha ceremony done for the propitiation of the forefathers, one should ask the forefathers): "May bounteous givers multiply in our families, may our own Vedic studies and progeny increase; let not faith go away from our house; and let us have much to give."[4] (III).

One should speak the truth and speak it pleasingly; should not speak the truth in an unpleasant manner nor should one

[4] An additional request made at this time is, "May we have ample food; may we get guests; let us have others to beg of us, and let us not beg of anybody."

speak untruth because it is pleasing; this is the eternal dharma.[5]

Whatever is dependent on others is misery; whatever rests on one's self is happiness; this in brief is the definition of happiness and misery.

Though one is entitled to receive gifts, one should avoid the occasions for them; for quickly is one's spiritual effulgence quenched by receiving gifts.

Having duly cleared his obligations to the great sages [by learning], to the ancestors [by progeny], and to the gods [by offerings], one should entrust everything to the son, and live betaking himself to an attitude of detachment. Alone and in seclusion, he should daily think about the good of his own soul (IV).

Without doing injury to living things, flesh cannot be had anywhere; and the killing of living beings is not conducive to heaven; hence eating of flesh should be avoided.

The wise get purified by forbearance, the wrongdoers by giving away, the secret sinners by silent repetition of mantras, the learned in the Vedas by penance. The limbs are cleansed by water, the mind by truthfulness, the soul by learning and penance, and intellect by knowledge.

The housewife should always be joyous, adept at domestic work, neat in her domestic wares, and restrained in expenses. The woman has no independent sacrifice to perform, no vow, no fasting; by serving her husband, she is honored in the heavens. On the death of her husband, the chaste wife, established in continence, reaches heaven, even if childless, like students who have practiced self-control. Controlled in mind, word, and body, she who does not transgress her lord, she attains the same heaven as her lord (V).

For that twice-born for whom there is not even an iota of fear for beings, for him who has detached himself from his

[5] This is one of the axiomatic verses of Hinduism.

body, there is no fear from any quarter. He should rejoice neither in death nor in life; like an employee at this appointed task, he should simply be looking forward to his time.

He should endure high-handed criticism; he should insult none. While yet in this body, he should not pick enmity with anyone; he should not return anger with anger; decried, he should say a good word.

He should observe the course of human beings as determined by the defect of actions: falling into hell and undergoing tortures in Yama's abode, separation from the dear, union with the undesirable, overpowered by old age, harassment by maladies, exit from the body, birth in a womb again, passage of the inner soul through thousands and tens of millions of wombs, the misery caused to embodied beings through vice; and the gain of imperishable happiness, happiness through virtue. He should also see by concentration the subtle nature of the Supreme Self.

Contentment, forbearance, self-control, abstaining from forcible talking, purity, sense control, intellectual pursuit, spiritual knowledge, truthfulness, freedom from anger—these ten constitute the definition of dharma (VI).

Nonviolence, truthfulness, nonstealing, purity, sense control—this, in brief, says Manu, is the dharma of all the four castes (X).

By not doing ordained duties, by doing condemned acts, and by addiction to objects of senses, it becomes necessary for man to undergo expiations. Brāhmancide, drinking wine, theft, betaking to an elder's wife, and association with those who are guilty of the above are said to be the five great sins. By public confession, repentance, penance, repetition of holy mantras, and by gifts, the sinner gets released from sin. That which is hard to get over, hard to get, hard to reach, hard to do, all that can be accomplished by penance: penance is hard to be overcome [by anything else] (XI).

YĀJÑAVALKYA SMṚITI

Fate and Effort

On fate and personal effort depend the success of an undertaking; of the two, fate is only the consolidated force of the personal exertion in the previous birth. Just as a chariot's progress is not to be had by a single wheel, even so, without personal exertion, fate [alone] does not bring success (XIII.349,351).

YOGA SŪTRAS OF PATAÑJALI

(The basic disciplines for the practice of yoga are contained in the Yoga Sūtras of Patañjali. They can be properly understood only under the instruction of an accomplished guru; these excerpts are given only as an indication of the practices set forth here.)

CONCENTRATION

Yoga is the control of the activities of the mind. Then [when the mind is rippleless] the Subject [Purusha] is in its own form. By practice and detachment are these activities of the mind to be suppressed. Concentration is [of the type called] conscious when there continue in it gross objects, subtle objects, the sense of blissfulness only, or that of mere existence. The other type is that in which impressions alone survive and which results from practice toward the state of cessation of the above-mentioned fourfold content.

Or [that concentration is achieved] by the contemplation of God. God is a special Being who is not vitiated by afflictions, works, fruits, or impressions thereof. He is the Teacher of even the earliest teachers, being unlimited by time. He is indicated by OM. The repetition of that OM and the contemplation of its import [that is, God] [are means of achieving concentration].

To a mind whose activities have died down, as unto a pure crystal, there happens absorption in and conformity with the cognizer, the means of cognition [senses] and their objects. The noncognitive condition is that in which the cognition of an object is shorn of its recollective aspects of name and form and as if void of content, shines in itself. When there is the clarity of the nondeliberative state, there comes the peace of the Soul.

There the mind becomes Truth-laden. On this state, too, being held in restraint, as there is restraint of everything, there arises the objectless Concentration (Samādhipāda).

Means

Penance, repetition of mantra, and the contemplation of God represent the active means of yoga. The active means are for the cultivation of concentration and attenuation of the afflictions. The afflictions are nescience, egoism, desire, dislike, and attachment. The activities consequent on these afflictions are to be eradicated by contemplation. These afflictions are the root of the impression of acts which are experienced in the present or the future birth. When the Causes [the afflictions] are operative, the acts fructify into forms of birth, life, and experiences. They are productive of either happiness or suffering according as they proceed from virtue or vice. To one of discrimination, everything is misery, because of the eventual painful culmination of all pleasure.

By the practice of the accessories of yoga, when the impurities [in the form of the afflictions] disappear, knowledge shines forth culminating in discriminative knowledge. The accessories are eight: restraint, observance, posture, breath control, withdrawal, concentration, contemplation, and absorption. The restraints are noninjury, truthfulness, nonstealing, continence, and nonpossession. These constitute a great vow when practiced without consideration of class, place, time, or occasion. The observances are cleanliness, contentment, penance, study or recital of mantra, and contemplation of God.

When one is established in noninjury, beings give up their mutual animosity in his presence. When one is established in truthfulness, the fruits of acts accrue to him. When one is established in nonstealing, all gems present themselves. When one is established in continence, energy is retained. When nonpossession is firmly established, there is the understanding of the how and wherefore of birth. By cleanliness, disgust at one's body and dissociation from others [seclusion] result; as also the refinement of the mind [by the elimination of rajas and tamas], pleasantness, one-pointedness, subjugation of senses, and fitness to have the vision of the Spirit.

From contentment highest happiness results; from penance, the annihilation of the impurity of afflictions and thereby the excellence of body and faculties. By recital of mantra, communion with one's favorite deity. By contemplation of God, the accomplishment of concentration. Posture is that in which one can continue for long and with ease. When posture is mastered, the pairs (heat-cold, etc.) do not assail.[1]

And while posture is firm, breath control is the regulation of inhaling and exhaling. The regulation of breath is exhaling, inhaling, and storing within; it is governed by place, time, and number, and by long and fine. A fourth form of the control of breath is storing up with attention on an external or internal object. By breath control, the afflictions that shroud the luminous quality get destroyed, and the mind becomes fit for steady contemplation. In withdrawal, the senses do not come into contact with their objects, and the mind takes its own form. Thereby supreme control of senses results (Sādhanapāda).

Powers

The fastening of the mind at a point in the body [navel, heart, nose-tip, head, etc.] is concentration. Contemplation is knowledge being solely engrossed there. That itself becomes absorption when as if void of itself, it is wholly of the form of the contemplated. These three together at a point are called samyama. By success there, results the effulgence of knowledge [2] (Vibhūtipāda).

[1] The yogic postures are dealt with in detail in the treatises on Haṭha yoga; there are eighty-four postures, of which five are said to be most important: Padma, Svastika, Bhadra, Vajra, and Vīra. The physical and psychological benefits of the yogic postures are now universally recognized.

[2] Then various occult powers gained by the successful practice of the different aspects of yoga are set forth. These powers or accomplishments (siddhis) are

Emancipation

When one does not expect any fruit even in contemplation, and has perfect discriminative knowledge, the absorption called the "dharma-raining cloud" results. At that stage, afflictions and actions cease. And by virtue of knowledge then being rid of all enshrouding dross, there is little to be known. And the qualities having fulfilled their role, the evolutionary series comes to an end. The emancipation of the Soul is the Seer's power established in its own innate nature (Kaivalyapāda).

of three kinds: (1) strength, freedom from thirst and hunger, firmness, etc., which are useful for the further practice of yoga itself; (2) the power to isolate or exteriorize the mind, conferring the accomplishment of the great disembodied state, the exercise of sensory faculties without the aid of their physical instruments, omniscience—which represent really successive stages of yogic perfection; (3) knowing one's own past and others' minds, entering others' bodies, going in air, etc. The last especially are not to be exhibited or abused, for Aphorism 37 says that these powers as such are really impediments to the attainment of the state of perfection.

THE RĀMĀYAṆA[1]

The Rāmāyaṇa tells the story of Rāma, the prince of Ayodhyā, as it was composed by the sage Vālmīki. Rāma was noble, dear to the whole world and equal toward all; he observed his own duty, that righteousness which was fitting for his nature and the time and place, and thereby protected those near him and the whole world, and dharma itself.

Brahmā, the creator, came to the sage Vālmīki, and commanded him to compose the story of Rāma, the embodiment of dharma, and gave to him the power to compose in poetry and to know all events, both public and private, concerning Rāma. "Not a word shall be false in your poem; compose the holy and beautiful story of Rāma in these same verses," said Brahmā and prophesied, "The fame of your Rāmāyaṇa will stand as long as hills stand and rivers flow on the surface of this earth."

The righteous sage then purified himself, sat facing eastward on the sacred grass, and in his yoga he saw it all, as clearly as a fruit on his palm. The venerable sage composed the story of the family of Raghu, of Rāma's great birth, his heroism, friendliness to all and truthful conduct, together with all the wonderful subsidiary stories.

In the city of Ayodhyā, there ruled the virtuous Daśaratha, almost a sage and a keeper of his word. The citizens under him were gay but righteous, learned, each contented with his possessions, and truthful. But the king had no son to continue his line, so he performed the great horse-sacrifice to gain sons.

[1] Editor's note: The *Rāmāyaṇa,* The *Mahābhārata,* and the *Bhāgavata Purāṇa* are retold here in a greatly condensed form designed to summarize the stories and teachings which have played an important part in shaping the beliefs and practices of Hinduism. Many well-known incidents have of necessity been omitted, others have been paraphrased, and others told or described in Professor Raghavan's own words.

Just as the gods were to receive his oblations they came to Brahmā and told him that because he had given boons to Rāvaṇa the demon they were being tormented by the demon and could not subdue him. Brahmā replied, "Rāvaṇa asked the boon that he should not be killed by any of the divine or semidivine beings and he forgot the men; he has therefore to be killed by a man." So the gods and Brahmā together asked Vishṇu to be born in the world to kill Rāvaṇa. "Choose Daśaratha, the victorious, generous, and sage-like king of Ayodhyā and to his three wives you be born as four sons; and kill Rāvaṇa." Vishṇu promised that he would go down, kill cruel Rāvaṇa and his men, and live in the world as the ruler of the earth. When Lord Vishṇu had thus become the sons of Daśaratha, Brahmā asked the gods to be born in the world of monkeys, with all their invincible valor, so that they might aid the Lord in the mission of his incarnation. Accordingly they became thousands upon thousands of powerful monkeys, with power to take any form they pleased, and spread themselves over the hills and forests.

The four sons of Daśaratha were Rāma, Bharata, and the twins Lakshmaṇa and Śatrughna. All of them were rich in natural endowments, but among them Rāma was supreme, a veritable god among beings; he had true valor and valor displayed in righteous cause; he became dear to the world like the pure moon. From childhood, Lakshmaṇa was always dear to Rāma, looking verily like his external breath, for without him Rāma would not sleep nor take food; wherever Rāma went Lakshmaṇa was always at the back, bow in hand guarding him. Similarly, Śatrughna was dear to Bharata.

When Rāma was not yet sixteen years old, the great sage Viśvāmitra came asking his help against the two demons who were interfering with his austerities and sacrifices by raining blood and flesh, polluting the altar. "The austerity I am in is such that I shall not show anger and curse them," he said to Daśaratha. "You must give me this young son of yours, Rāma, of true valor; protected by me, even as nectar by fire, he will be able to destroy the demons who disturb me; in fact, none but Rāma can kill them. I know Rāma as the great soul of unfailing prowess; permit ten days absence and grieve not."

Rāma traveled with Viśvāmitra, receiving from him instruction concerning the sages and the gods, hearing the story of his austerities, and the creation and the glory of Mother Gaṅgā, the great river. On the way, he killed the powerful demoness Tāṭakā who possessed the strength of a thousand elephants, and when they came to the abode of Viśvāmitra and the two demons attacked as the sage practiced his austerities, Rāma quickly killed one of them and flung the other far away. Then Rāma went on to visit King Janaka who had a wonderful divine bow of such strength that none among the gods or men had been able to lift or string it. The bow, Janaka said, was Śiva's own. "While I was leveling the sacrificial ground with a plough, there arose from earth this daughter of mine, Sītā; she is to be wed on a prize; suitors have to lift and string the bow before taking her; no king has so far succeeded in doing so; if this Rāma can do it, I shall give her to the son of Daśaratha." A hundred and fifty servants dragged the bow in a box on eight wheels. Lightly did Rāma take it at the center and string it; when he pulled it with an arrow, it broke with a terrific noise which shook the earth.

Then Sītā became Rāma's wife, her sister Ūrmilā was wed to Lakshmaṇa, and her two cousins were married to Bharata and Śatrughna, in one great wedding ceremony. Together they returned to Ayodhyā. With Sītā, Rāma enjoyed himself, his heart being wholly on her. Sītā was dear to him because she had been found for him by his parents and elders, and the love increased all the more by reason of her qualities and beauty. Rāma was always in Sītā's heart; whatever was innermost in their hearts, that heart spoke to heart in clear accents. Verily, with her, Rāma shone like Lord Vishṇu with Goddess Lakshmī.

All the four sons were indeed dear to the King, but Rāma

delighted Daśaratha most. He was superior in qualities over all—is he not the eternal Lord, Vishṇu, born among men at the instance of the gods for the killing of the demons? Incomparable in his qualities, Rāma was always of a composed nature; he talked softly, talked first, and talked with a smile. With exceeding valor, he was yet unelated; he spoke nothing false, honored the elders, learning from them whenever leisure was available. Attached to the people, and drawing their attachment, kind, controlled in anger, and sympathetic toward the suffering, he had the high notion of the duty of the Kshatriya to which he was born. He considered pure fame as equal to the great heavenly fruit; he indulged in nothing which did not contribute to welfare, had no taste for idle gossip; though in meeting argument with argument he was as gifted as the god of speech himself. He knew the time and place, and in the world he was the only one who weighed and understood a man's worth and yet continued to be ever good. He never felt miserable, was straightforward, and had memory and imagination. In worldly conventions and behavior he was trained and proficient; quiet in bearing, he did not disclose his mind and kept his deliberations confidential; gathered help, was effective in anger or satisfactions, and knew the time to give or withhold. He never got wrong ideas, never spoke foul words, was never lazy or careless. He knew the faults of himself and others, he judged well between man and man, and was adept in putting down or bringing up people. He knew the means of earning and the proper method of expenditure. Not only in the higher branches of knowledge, but in the miscellaneous accomplishments, too, he was qualified, and could enjoy himself without being indolent. He knew the recreational arts, knew also the proper place of everything. Free from intolerance, pride, or envy, he never insulted any being, but was not on that account soft enough to succumb to the force of circumstances. Rāma shone with these qualities as the sun with the rays, and Earth herself desired him as her Lord.

Daśaratha, in consultation with his ministers, desired to make Rāma the heir-apparent. Unfortunately, egged on by her hunchback maid Mantharā, Kaikeyī, Daśaratha's favorite wife, wanted her son, Bharata, crowned king, and on the coronation day she forced the King to fulfill two boons promised to her long ago by the King: the coronation of Bharata and the exile of Rāma for fourteen years. The King could not go back on his word. The loss of the kingdom did not reduce the excelling charm and grace of Rāma's countenance. As he gave up the kingdom and desired to leave for the forests, no untoward change was seen in him; he was as one high above all the world. The inner joy which was always his characteristic the heroic Rāma did not give up.

Lakshmaṇa was very angry at this turn in their affairs and sought to persuade his brother to take the kingdom by force, but Rāma pointed out, "I am not starting any new dharma; none ever comes to grief by acting up to his father's word. Father has made a promise and the word has to be kept. So, leave off this military mind; take to dharma, not to violence; follow my mind." Thus, finally, by Rāma's words was Lakshmaṇa pacified, but not until Rāma had consented to allow Lakshmaṇa to accompany him into the forest.

Then Rāma went to Sītā's apartments to tell her that he would not be crowned king that day, but was banished to the forests and must leave her. Her great love took the form of indignation and she replied, "Why do you speak lightly such funny things? My beloved lord, father, mother, brother, son, daughter-in-law, all enjoy their respective fortunes; the wife alone shares her husband's fortunes. Not father, sons, her own self, mother or friend, but the husband is the sole resort of a wife. If you have decided to go to the forests, I shall go in advance, clearing the path of thorns. High or low, whatever be the husband's state, his proximity is best for the wife. I shall gladly walk the difficult man-forsaken jungles, and thinking only of following my lord I shall enjoy the forest as much as the mansion. Even heaven will not appeal to me, no never, if it is without you." When poor Sītā broke down, streaming in tears, Rāma then embraced her, comforted her and said, "Divine Lady, even heaven will not be welcome to me at the cost of your grief; I can leave you only if I can leave off my fame. Come along, help me in my dharma, prepare for the forest."

Then, after a sad parting, Rāma, Sītā, and Lakshmaṇa set forth from their home. Gloom descended on the city; an ominous turn of planets was seen; there was no cooking in the houses, no business in the city; elephants dropped their feed, cows did not suckle their calves; and even a mother who was delivered of her first male child that day was not pleased. But Rāma, Sītā, and Lakshmaṇa went on, crossing the Ganges and the Jumna rivers.

A few days after Rāma left for the forest, King Daśaratha died of grief. The counselors immediately sent for Bharata to come home and assume the crown; but instead of being glad to become the ruler he was filled with rage against his mother who had conspired on his behalf, and as soon as he had performed the last rites for his father he set out to persuade Rāma to come back and be king. The meeting of the two was like that of the Sun and the Moon, of Venus and Jupiter in the heavens. With matted locks and mendicant robes, like himself, Bharata appeared to Rāma, as he lay there in front of him, like the Sun himself fallen from the skies. Rāma lifted him, embraced him, took him on his own lap and asked him about the welfare of his father and the kingdom. Rāma, Lakshmaṇa, and Sītā wept on hearing the news of Daśaratha's death, then went down to the river, bathed, and offered water and oblation to the spirit of their father.

When Bharata pleaded with Rāma to return and be crowned king, Rāma replied that Bharata was not to be blamed, that parents had a right to do as they pleased with their children, and that what his father had commanded, that he would do. Furthermore, when Daśaratha had married Bharata's mother, he had promised that the kingdom would go to her son; hence, Rāma insisted, Bharata must go back and rule if he wanted to save his father from hell. When Bharata begged further, Rāma replied, "The sea would transgress its shores, but not I the promise that father gave." Finally, Bharata was persuaded to take Rāma's sandals back to Ayodhyā as a symbol of Rāma's presence and to rule as regent for the fourteen years, living as a mendicant outside the city.

Rāma, Sītā, and Lakshmaṇa hoped to live quietly in the forest, but soon the demons, resenting his protection of the sages, attacked him with a force of fourteen thousand demons. Rāma brought upon himself intense anger for killing all the demons, emitted a frightful shout, and aimed at them the divine Gandharva missile, and the whole of that holocaust of fourteen thousand demons was destroyed by Rāma in but forty-eight minutes. That victory won for him the gratitude of the sages and the ecstatic embrace of Sītā, but it so enraged Rāvaṇa, the chief of the demons, that he resolved to kill Rāma. The demon Mārīca, who had seen Rāma, warned Rāvaṇa that he could "never vanquish Rāma in open battle; all the gods and demons put together cannot do away with Rāma. He can bring down the heavens, uplift the earth, flood the world, destroy creation, and bring it into being again." He suggested that rather than fighting Rāma, he should by stealth carry off Sītā, and then Rāma would give up his life because of his great love for her.

With the aid of Mārīca in the guise of a golden deer, the demon Rāvaṇa enticed both Rāma and Lakshmaṇa away from their hermitage for a moment, and in their absence seized Sītā and took her away in his magic chariot. Rāvaṇa sped across the sky carrying Sītā, who was crying and calling out to Rāma and Lakshmaṇa. As she was being taken along the sky by Rāvaṇa, she saw on the top of a mountain below five monkey-chiefs and to them she threw some ornaments, hoping that they would inform Rāma. Rāvaṇa flew on across the ocean to Laṅkā [Ceylon] where he put Sītā in his private garden under guard.

He made every effort to get her to yield to him, but she scorned even to talk directly to him. He finally left her saying that he gave her twelve months to come around and threatened that if she did not agree, cooks would prepare her for his breakfast.

Rāma and Lakshmaṇa were overcome with grief when they returned to their hermitage and found that Sītā had been stolen by a demon. They immediately set out in search of her, and guided by the animals of the forest that cast their eyes southward, they moved southward. Finally they were advised by Kabandha, a divine being in a temporary accursed state, "Rāma, you must take a friend now, for I see no way to your success except through a friend; Sugrīva, that chief of monkeys, is endowed with valor, a keeper of his word, modest, firm, intelligent, capable; he is your help in the search for Sītā; do not sorrow any more, go now and make him your friend before the holy fire. He can trace your Sītā who has been taken by Rāvaṇa to his place."

The two brothers accepted Kabandha's advice and sought Sugrīva, the monkey chief who was living in exile, driven from his kingdom by his brother Vāli. Through Rāma's aid, Sugrīva regained his kingdom, and in return promised to aid in the recovery of Sītā; but the rains set in and there was a delay of four months before they could set out to find her.

Sugrīva then called Hanumān, his vigilant minister, and had him assemble the myriads of monkeys in his armies. They came, in such numbers that they screened the light of the sky itself, running, jumping, and roaring, some of them as big as elephants. They were dispatched in all four directions to search for Sītā, and Hanumān was selected to go on the expedition to the south, for Sugrīva had full confidence that he would succeed in any mission entrusted to him. "There is no being equal to you; therefore you yourself see that Sītā is discovered. Only in you are strength, intelligence, sense of time and place, and the politic way of doing things." Rāma gave Hanumān his signet ring as a token of recognition to be shown to Sītā when he met her.

After many delays and discouragements, the band of monkeys who had gone to the south met an old eagle who told them that Sītā had been taken by Rāvaṇa to his place on the island of Laṅkā. They hurried to the seashore, but when they saw the great distance to be jumped to reach the island they were once more in despair, for none of them could fly that far and return. All this time Hanumāṇ sat silently, and finally the oldest in the party, the bear Jāmbavān, burst forth, "Hanumān, hero of the monkey world, great expert in all lores! Wherefore are you thus sitting silent and alone in a corner? Strength, intelligence, power, force, everything you have, and you do not know that. Let me tell you; you were begotten by the Wind-god himself, and when you were born, the Wind-god gave the boon that the son would be his own equal in flying. You alone can save us now. Therefore, go forth, O Hanumān, the whole monkey army is desirous of seeing your exploit. Rise up and take your strides, even as Vishṇu of yore, who measured the three worlds."

As these words fell on Hanumān's ears, power swelled forth in his person; his body attained magnitude. Hanumān himself gained now full consciousness of his innate power and cried, "I can now go round the ends of the earth, all the seas and the entire sky; I can dry up the ocean, tear up the earth and pound the mountains. I shall blow away clouds as I go. I shall find Sītā and bring her back." When Hanumān roared thus, his friends felt exhilarated and said, "With the grace of your elders, fly forth; our lives are in your hands; we shall be standing on one foot till you come back." Wondering if earth or mountain could stand his impact, Hanumān ascended the mountain from which he was to take his flight.[2]

The flight of two hundred and fifty miles to Laṅkā did not make Hanumān even draw a deep breath. He marveled at the

[2] Hanumān is widely worshiped today as an Immortal and the exemplar of true service and devotion to the Lord; and as a teacher.

size and beauty of the city and for a moment despaired of success when he saw its fortifications and armaments and thought of the terrible Rāvaṇa. Then he contracted himself to a cat's size, and slipped into the city after dark. First, he searched the harem, but he could not see anywhere among them that highborn lady who had been snatched away from Rāma and was firmly following the eternal path of virtue. He continued his search without success and became depressed; suddenly he saw a park which he had not searched. "Ah," he said, "I shall go there after saluting the gods." As he rose up with renewed enthusiasm, Hanumān uttered a prayer, "Obeisance to Rāma with Lakshmaṇa! Obeisance to that divine daughter of Janaka! Obeisance to all the gods." [3]

There in the park Hanumān saw a lady, clad in a soiled garment, surrounded by demoness guards, emaciated by fast, heaving, hard to be seen like the first digit of the waxing moon, like a flame enveloped in smoke, with suffering and penance, with tears and sighs, immersed in sorrow and thought, missing her beloved one and seeing all around only demonesses, like a fawn encircled by hounds. She was undoubtedly Sītā, though it took some time to recognize her in that state of suffering. "Ah, this Sītā!" thought Hanumān, "She does not see the demonesses nor the flowers and fruits of the trees; with her heart on only one, she is continuously seeing therein her Rāma: for the husband, indeed, is woman's ornament of ornaments." There under the tree, in the midst of the demonesses, was the irreproachable Sītā, like a star fallen, bedecked with virtue and devotion to her Lord. Looking at her who lay there like a neglected lyre, Hanumān wept and bowed to Rāma.

Then, singing softly of Rāma, he attracted Sītā's attention and disclosed himself as Rāma's messenger. He explained that Rāma's delay in coming was due to his failure to know her

[3] This prayer of Hanumān at the turning point of his search is included in the preliminary prayers with which devout readers of this epic begin its daily reading.

place of imprisonment and went on to reassure Sītā, "Owing to your separation, Rāma does not taste good food; he does not even brush aside flies, mosquitoes, or insects sitting on his body, so absorbed is his mind in thinking of you. He is always in deep thought and poignant sorrow, he has no sleep and if he dozes, he rises up suddenly uttering your sweet name. If he comes across any flower or fruit, or anything exceedingly charming, he sighs 'Ah, my beloved!', and begins to address you."

Hanumān could have carried Sītā on his back, but she refused because it would greatly detract from Rāma's glory and honor if Rāma did not rescue her himself, and besides, she could not, of herself, touch the body of another than her husband. So it was agreed that Hanumān would hurry to Rāma and bring him back to release Sītā at once, since at the end of two months Rāvaṇa would have his cooks dress her for his breakfast. Hanumān gave Sītā Rāma's signet ring and took for him her crest jewel.

Before leaving, however, Hanumān decided to show the demons something of the force they would have to contend with, so he destroyed all the grove of trees except the one under which Sītā sat, and when the demons came against him he took his full stature, lashed his tail, roared, plucked an iron rod from the arched gateway, and killed them all. Then, after killing several of Rāvaṇa's chieftains, he let himself be captured so he could meet and warn Rāvaṇa, and when the captors tied his tail with cotton rags, poured oil on it and set it afire, he broke away and roamed over the city setting fire to all the buildings. Then he quenched the fire on his tail in the ocean and hurried back to Rāma to tell him of the austerity and safety of the faithful Sītā.

Rāma was immensely pleased and embraced Hanumān. Then, because it was just noon, the sun was at meridian, and it was an auspicious moment which would bring victory, they set out at once toward the south. When they came to the seashore, they stopped to make their plans for crossing the sea to Laṅkā. As they rested there, the thought of Sītā disturbed Rāma intensely. He said, addressing the breeze blowing from across the water, "Blow from where my beloved is; having touched her, touch me also, and through you, let me have her touch."

In the meantime, at Laṅkā, Rāvaṇa called his counselors and asked for their advice as to the best way to overcome Rāma. Vibhīshaṇa, his younger brother, opposed a war, saying, "This violation of another's woman is infamous, detrimental to one's longevity, root of terrible loss and sinful; before Rāma tears Laṅkā to pieces, let Sītā be returned to him, O King, give up wrath which is the enemy of virtue and happiness. Seek righteousness whereby happiness and fame will increase; please, I beseech you, let Sītā be returned to him." And when Rāvaṇa reviled him, he went on, "Those whose time is up do not take wholesome advice. Easy is it to have men who always talk what is pleasing; hard is it to have one who can speak forth what is unpleasant but is wholesome." [4] Then Vibhīshaṇa left Laṅkā and flew over to where Rāma was and said to the monkeys who intercepted him, "Announce me quickly to that great soul, Rāma, the refuge of the whole world." [5] Hearing of Vibhīshaṇa's arrival, Rāma said, "I afford security to him who surrenders but once, and beseeches with the words, 'I am yours.' This is my vow. Bring him, Chief of Monkeys, I have given security. Let him be Vibhīshaṇa, let him be Rāvaṇa himself."

They then thought of the way to cross to Laṅkā, and after Rāma had spent three days in austerities and threatened to hurl the terrific divine missile Brahma-astra at the sea, the Lord of the seas came up, suggested that they should build a causeway, and offered to sustain that causeway. The monkey army brought huge trees and rocks and threw them into the sea; Hanumān flung hill after hill to be placed in the water, until

[4] This famous saying is known to almost everyone.

[5] This act of abandoning everything else and taking refuge in the Lord is a vital tenet of the sect of Śrīvaishṇavism which attaches great importance to this story of Vibhīshaṇa, as well as the following words of Rāma in which the Lord affords security to those who surrender and take refuge in him.

the causeway extended over two hundred and fifty miles and the sea looked like hair parted in the middle.[6]

Rāma, Lakshmaṇa, Sugrīva, Hanumān, and all their hosts of monkey warriors then crossed over to Laṅkā and the terrible battle with the armies of Rāvaṇa was fought. The losses were great on both sides, but one by one the great warriors who fought for Rāvaṇa were destroyed. At one point Indrajit, Rāvaṇa's son, making himself invisible through his magic powers, rained such a storm of arrows that Rāma and Lakshmaṇa lay sorely wounded on the battlefield, and hundreds of their monkey warriors were wounded or killed. To revive them, Hanumān was sent flying to the Himālayas to the mountain of herbs to get the four luminous herbs: the rejuvenator, the remover of broken particles of arms inside one's body, the restorer of complexion, and the joiner of broken limbs. The very smell of the herbs rid all the warriors of their wounds and the dead rose as if from sleep.

There followed a fierce battle in which Lakshmaṇa killed Indrajit, and the terrible fight in which Rāma destroyed Rāvaṇa. After using all his other weapons, finally Rāma took the dread Brahma-astra, the missile which originally Brahmā himself devised and gave to Indra, which was constituted of the energy of all beings. He uttered the Vedic mantra for its use and laid it on his bow string. The entire living world shuddered; earth quaked, and like inexorable Fate the Brahma-astra fell on Rāvaṇa's heart and came back to Rāma's quiver. Deprived of life, Rāvaṇa's body fell from the chariot with terrible force.

Over his body the beautiful favorite Queen Maṇḍodarī lamented, "You lie here, thus, you who gave ache to all the three worlds, vanquished the guardians of the world, shook Śiva himself and made all living beings cry in fear and pain. The saying

6 The modern Rāmeśwaram is the site of this causeway, a holy place for Hindus next in importance only to the Ganges; a bath in the sea there is a most efficacious expiation for sins.

is true that the tears of a chaste woman do not fall in vain; the curses of those violated by you have come true. When a warrior like you stooped to the cowardly act of stealing Sītā, it was clear that your misfortune had begun to fructify. Mad with your strength you never listened to those who spoke truth, and now has come this destruction of the demons as a result of ceaseless addiction to lust and passion."

The battle over, Rāma sent Hanumān to tell Sītā of their victory and to return with her message. When Hanumān returned with the word that Sītā desired to see him, Rāma immediately plunged into thought, tears brimmed in his eyes, and with deep and hot breath he asked Vibhīshaṇa to dress Sītā well and bring her before him. Dejection and indignation disturbed his joy; ominous indications of indifference to his wife were perceptible in Rāma, and Lakshmaṇa and Hanumān gathered that Rāma was dissatisfied with Sītā. For her part, as if melting into herself in shame, Sītā approached Rāma, just addressed him as 'Lord,' then shrouded her face in her garment and wept. The sight of her only increased Rāma's fury and he spoke to her very cruel words, "Know, Sītā, the effort of war was not taken by me on your behalf, but to clear my name and that of my family of disrepute; I am not able to stand your sight even as a man of sore eyes cannot stand a light. Therefore, go, with my leave, anywhere. I have no need for you, for what man of honor and high breeding will take back a woman who has lived in another's house?"

Sītā shrank within herself in shame, wept and spoke in broken tones, "I am not what you take me to be; believe me, I swear by my character. If Rāvaṇa's body had touched me when he carried me off, I am not to blame. What is in my control, that, my heart, is wholly in you. Yielding to anger alone, you behave like a man of the street." Then she ordered Lakshmaṇa to prepare a pyre, and when it was ready Sītā went around Rāma who was standing with a downcast face and approached the burning fire. Bowing to the gods, Sītā addressed

Fire, "If my heart has not swerved from Rāma, let Fire, witness of the world, protect me; if by act, thought, and word, I have not been unfaithful to Rāma, let Fire, witness of the world, protect me; if Sun, Wind, the Quarters, Moon, the Day, the two Twilights, the Night, Earth, and others know me as one of character, let Fire protect me." With these words, Sītā entered the fire.

Immediately, the Fire god rose up bearing Sītā and gave her to Rāma with the words, "There is no sin in Sītā; she has not been faithless to you by word, thought, or sight. Accept her. Do not speak a word: I command you." Rāma thought for a while and replied, "True Sītā is stainless, but if I take her without a purification, the good ones may remark that, young and passionate, Rāma simply took his wife who had been taken and kept by Rāvaṇa for a long time in his place. I too know her chastity and single-hearted devotion to me, but I allowed her to enter fire so that the world at large may believe in her chastity."

Then, their time of exile being completed, Rāma and Sītā returned to Ayodhyā where Bharata, living in a hermitage, continued as regent. They were received with great joy, Rāma was crowned king, and there he reigned long, performing many sacrifices.

In Rāma's reign [Rāmarājya] there was no wailing of widowed women, no fear of disease, thief, or other calamities; elders did not have to perform the obsequies of the younger ones; everyone was righteous, and thinking always of Rāma, refrained from injuring another; rains fell in proper times, vegetation put forth its fruits in season and out of season; and everyone was satisfied with his duties, the classes were contented and free from avarice.

. . . . .

This blessed first poem, composed of yore by Vālmīki, bestows fame and long life, and he who listens to it is freed from sin, gets sons like Rāma, Lakshmaṇa, and Bharata and crosses over all difficulties. In whatever house a copy of the poem is kept, there malignant spirits get appeased; by the worship and reading of this ancient story, Rāma, who is the eternal Lord Vishṇu, is pleased. Those who desire prosperity should listen to this epic-story which fosters good brotherhood, and promotes knowledge and happiness.

So did this story happen of old; well be it with you all; freely recite it; let the Lord's might increase. And they who write with devotion this epic of Rāma composed by the sage, or cause it to be written, take their place in heaven.[7]

[7] There is an epilogue, but religious readings and recitals of the epic always stop here.

THE MAHĀBHĀRATA

The Mahābhārata was composed by the Sage Vyāsa who set forth here the greatness of Lord Vāsudeva, the truthfulness of the Pāṇḍavas, and the evil conduct of the sons of Dhṛitarāshṭra. It is a treatise on the principles of material welfare, righteous conduct, emotional gratification, and spiritual realization. What is here is found elsewhere; what is not here is not to be found anywhere.

By virtue of his penance and spiritual discipline, Vyāsa arranged the eternal Vedas and then composed this holy epic, concentrating his mind and seeing the course of its development through the power of his virtue and knowledge. Poets cannot excel this epic poem; in fact, they will have to draw upon it for their own creative activity. It is verily the food of all writers. The Eternal Lord is sung of here; He is Truth and the Moral Order, the Supreme Brahman and the everlasting light. Truth and Immortality are the body of the Bhārata epic. It is called Mahābhārata because it is great (Mahat) and weighty (Bhāravat).

Although Dhṛitarāshṭra was the older son of the king of the Kuru race, since he was blind his brother Pāṇḍu was made king. Pāṇḍu had five sons, called the Pāṇḍavas: Yudhishṭhira the embodiment of dharma, or righteousness; Bhīma of terrible prowess; Arjuna, as powerful as Śiva and as pleasing as Vishṇu, and the twins Nakula and Sahadeva, of incomparable beauty.

Dhṛitarāshṭra had a hundred sons, but all of them were born in one mass which was put in a clarified-butter trough; out of that mass began to appear one after the other the hundred sons during the course of a hundred days. The first of them, Duryodhana, brayed like an ass as he came forth, and everybody advised his abandonment as he portended the annihilation of the whole race, but his father was too fond of his son to permit it.

The sons of Pāṇḍu and Dhṛitarāshṭra grew up together, but in all the sports of their boyhood the Pāṇḍavas outshone their cousins, leading to jealousy which continued all their lives. The rivalry which had grown up between them increased when the blind Dhṛitarāshṭra, who had become king after the death of Pāṇḍu, decided that Yudhishṭhira should be the heir-apparent. With his truthfulness and sympathy Yudhishṭhira had endeared himself to the subjects. Their teacher Droṇa told Arjuna, "The only person above you, I must now reveal to you, is Kṛishṇa, the Lord who makes and unmakes the world. He is the past, present, and future of the world; He is born as your cousin and will become your intimate friend and with you as His aid He shall fulfill the mission of this incarnation of His. Take your refuge in Him." Arjuna went forth, won battles and brought fame and booty. All this excited the jealousy of Duryodhana.

Duryodhana contrived to send the five brothers and their mother, Kuntī, on a pilgrimage and to have the house in which they stopped set afire, but they escaped in time; they disguised themselves as recluses and went to King Drupada's capital to compete in a contest for the hand of his beautiful daughter, Draupadī. To win her, the contestant had to be bend the bow and hit the target, but none of the suitors assembled there could do it. Duryodhana tried, but the impact of the bow flung him on his back. Then Arjuna came forward, made obeisance to Lord Śiva, thought of Kṛishṇa and took up the bow. In a moment, he strung it and shot the target; heavenly flowers fell on Arjuna, Draupadī walked forward, her face beaming even without a smile, her feet tremulous even without intoxication, her eyes eloquent without a word. The victorious brothers walked out of the arena with Draupadī.

Coming home, the Pāṇḍavas announced to their mother that they had secured some alms for the day, and as usual, the mother said that all five of them should share their gain, without knowing that the gain of the day was Draupadī. But Yudhishṭhira remembered that sage Vyāsa had told them, when he met them on their way to the contest, that they would secure a wife to be married by all of them together. Just then Kṛishṇa arrived and saluted their mother and congratulated his cousins on their acquisition of Draupadī, and Vyāsa came and revealed that the Pāṇḍavas and Draupadī were of divine origin; their marriage was then duly celebrated.

Duryodhana was even more jealous of the Pāṇḍavas when he saw their success in the contest and wished to do away with them, but Dhṛitarāshṭra's advisors counseled him to seek peace: "The Pāṇḍavas are as much kings as your sons are. The talk of vanquishing them is idle, for who can stand against the ambidextrous Arjuna, the terrible Bhīma, or even those twins? In the eldest Pāṇḍava you always find fortitude, kindness, forbearance, truthfulness, and valor, how can he be vanquished? And above all, there is Kṛishṇa: where Kṛishṇa is, there success is! Duryodhana is childish, unrighteous, and perverse; do not listen to his words." Dhṛitarāshṭra accepted their advice and called Yudhishṭhira and said, "My sons are evil-minded and haughty; let there be no more quarrel. You have half the kingdom and rule it."

With his brothers, the truthful Yudhishṭhira ruled the kingdom in righteousness. Yudhishṭhira pursued without any disproportion the three ends of human endeavor: virtues, desires, and material acquisitions—and looked verily like the fourth end of man, spiritual discipline, controlling the other three. The people delighted in him, his very sight made their eyes and hearts bloom. What he would consider beneficial if done unto himself, that Yudhishṭhira did; and never untruthful, unbearable, or unpleasant, the speech of the wise Yudhishṭhira was always attractive.

This success of his cousins made Duryodhana cry out in despair, "I am unable to stand this prosperity of my cousins; I burn within myself. What am I—neither a man nor a woman nor even any human being—I who put up with this rise of my rivals?" When he cried out thus to his uncle, Śakuni, the uncle advised that they should not attempt direct action against the Pāṇḍavas but should deprive them of their possessions by stratagem; he suggested that since Yudhishṭhira was fond of dice and was not good at gambling, he should be invited to a game of dice at which Duryodhana could win all his riches.

So Yudhishṭhira was invited to come to the court of Dhṛitarāshṭra and was goaded into playing the game of dice, being called by Fate and Time to this unfair contest. Yudhishṭhira offered as stake his ornaments, gems, gold, treasury, chariots and horses, servants, elephants, and lost them all. Then he staked his brothers one by one and finally bet his own self and lost. Then, goaded by Śakuni, Yudhishṭhira said, "This paragon of beauty, endowed with all qualities, this Draupadī I offer as stake," and on the next throw of the dice he lost her, too.

Duryodhana at once sent for Draupadī, had her dragged into the hall, and there his brother tried to disrobe her. Draupadī thought at this moment of trial of Lord Kṛishṇa, affectionate to those who take refuge in Him, "O Imperishable Lord armed with conch, discus, and mace, residing at Dwārakā, Govinda of lotus eyes! Protect me! I have taken refuge in you." Praying thus, Draupadī covered her face and wept. And lo! by the grace of the Lord, as he went on pulling her garment, the garment multiplied endlessly and amidst shouts of wonder, acclamation of Draupadī, and condemnation of the base attempt to disrobe her, he gave up the attempt.

At that time ominous portents were seen, jackals yelled, and asses brayed; this suddenly aroused Dhṛitarāshṭra and he reviled Duryodhana for dragging the lady into the hall and addressing foul words to her. The king then offered Draupadī whatever boons she might want. She asked only for the liberty of her five husbands, saying, "I do not want more; avarice destroys righteousness. My husbands have been freed and they shall look to the future welfare." And the Pāṇḍavas returned to their capital.

After they had gone, Duryodhana reproached his father for interfering in their plans to put down the Pāṇḍavas; he got Dhṛitarāshṭra to permit them to invite Yudhishṭhira to another game of dice, the wager this time being only this: whoever lost should go into exile in the forests for twelve years, then spend one year incognito and if found out during that one year, should go again into a twelve-year exile. The old king, wavering between righteousness and his weakness for his son, yielded.

Yudhishṭhira, because of his status, could not honorably refuse such an invitation and returned for this last game of dice where, again, he lost. Bark and deerskin replaced the garments of the Pāṇḍavas as they started their exile in the forests. Bhīma, Arjuna, and the twins vowed to return and kill Duryodhana and all his followers in battle. As the five brothers left with Draupadī, the streets were crowded with people who wept and wanted to accompany them. Yudhishṭhira succeeded in persuading most of the people to return, but was unable to shake off the numerous Brāhmans devoted to austere pursuits who accompanied him into the forest. He wondered how to maintain them since he had been deprived of everything, but he propitiated the Sun God and secured the miraculous vessel inexhaustible with which he could entertain any number of guests.

While they were in the forest, Arjuna did severe penance until Lord Śiva blessed him and gave him his divine missile which could be used to deliver the brothers from ignominy; the other gods, too, gave him their missiles.

When Yudhishṭhira sat brooding over his suffering, sage Bṛihadaśva consoled him by narrating the story of the sufferings of King Nala and Damayantī, and later the sage Mārkaṇḍeya narrated at length the story of Rāma and Sītā, and to console the brothers further concerning the sufferings of Draupadī, told them the story of the great Sāvitrī, whose love brought her husband back to life.

At the end of their twelve years of exile they disguised themselves as servants and courtiers in the palace of the king of Virāṭa and there they passed successfully the year of incognito life.

The Pāṇḍavas sent word to Duryodhana asking for the return of their half of the kingdom, but he preferred war to a fair settlement. When it became clear that there would be a war, both Arjuna and Duryodhana sought Kṛishṇa's aid; he promised to help them both; to Duryodhana he gave his huge army, and he agreed to drive Arjuna's chariot in the war. Huge armies began assembling on both sides, made up of the thousands of elephants, chariots, and footmen of their allies, with close relatives on both sides of the battle.

In an effort to avert the war, Yudhishṭhira sent a message to Duryodhana, "We have forgiven and forgotten the dishonor done to Draupadī and the exile imposed on us. Let us now have our share of the kingdom, turn your mind away from others' possessions; let there be peace and mutual good will. Give us at least a portion, just five villages for the five brothers. Duryodhana, we are ready for peace as well as war!" Then Kṛishṇa himself went to the Kaurava [Kuru] court and begged for peace, warning them that what they did not give now they would part with in death on the field of battle. When Duryodhana scorned the plea, and even plotted to capture and bind Kṛishṇa, the Lord laughed, sparks flashed forth from him like lightning, and he assumed his cosmic form, blinding everyone but those whom the Lord blessed with divine vision.

When Kṛishṇa returned to the Pāṇḍavas and reported the failure of his peace mission, the armies moved to the great battlefield at Kurukshetra. The blind old king, Dhṛitarāshṭra, seated himself with Sañjaya by his side to tell him what happened.

With Queen Draupadī's brother as the formal general, Arjuna led the hosts of the Pāṇḍavas. Duryodhana chose his uncle, Bhīshma, as the leader of the Kauravas. Bhīshma, whose mother was the Goddess Gaṅgā, had renounced his claim to the throne of the Kuru clan and had never married in order that he should have no sons to be rivals for the throne. He was renowned for his wisdom and virtue, had served as counselor to two generations of kings, and as teacher of both the Pāṇḍavas and Kauravas was loved and revered by all.

At the break of dawn, the blare of conchs, the beating of drums, the neighing of horses, the roaring of elephants, and the tumult of warriors rose everywhere. The chariots drew up on both sides and the sight of the golden standard of Bhīshma sent shivers through the Pāṇḍava hearts. "How are we to break through an army commanded by Bhīshma?" asked Yudhishṭhira. Arjuna replied, "Victors win not so much by strength and heroism as by truth and goodness. Let us eschew unrighteousness and fight without egoism. Where there is right, there victory is; where Kṛishṇa is, there victory is."

Strangely the same Arjuna who spoke with such faith and courage to his elder brother was unnerved when he came to the center of the two armies and had a full look at all the elders and brothers, teachers and kinsmen against whom he was expected to fight. It was when he laid down his bow and expressed his resolve not to fight that Kṛishṇa, his charioteer, gave him the instruction which is embodied in the great philosophical discourse of the Bhagavad Gītā.

Encouraged by Kṛishṇa, Arjuna took up his arms and the fight began with the Kurus and Pāṇḍavas falling upon each other as if possessed. Son did not recognize father, nor father his son; nephew and uncle saw not each other, nor friend his friend. So did the battle rage.

Under the leadership of Bhīshma the forces of the Pāṇḍavas were hard pressed and might have been overcome had it not been for Bhīshma's vow that he would not kill any of the five brothers. After ten days of slaughter, Bhīshma wearied of the fighting and decided to give up his life. His body was so full of arrows from Arjuna's bow that when he lay down he was supported in the air on arrowshafts, and there he lay on his bed of arrows until after the battle. He said, "I shall hold my life till the auspicious summer solstice when the Sun turns north; then shall I reach back to my original state, for my father has given me the boon of giving up life at my will." Contemplating on the highest, Bhīshma lay in yoga; both sides gathered around him and once more he urged that the fighting cease, but he was not heeded.

Then leader after leader of the Kaurava side fell, and finally Duryodhana himself was destroyed by Bhīma. Thus the bloody war drew to an end. Dhṛitarāshṭra, who had lost all his sons, then left for the battlefield, along with their mother and the other womenfolk of the palace, lamenting the loss of their menfolk with heart-rending wails. The last rites for the dead heroes were gone through, with the Pāṇḍavas joining in the offering of water libations.

The thought of his dead kinsmen depressed Yudhishṭhira so much that he repented having waged the war, wished his enemies had continued to follow their own ways, and that he and his brothers had gone on in the mendicant life. His brothers and Draupadī, aided by Kṛishṇa, corrected his attitude, praised the dignity and scope of service in the life of a householder and king, and induced him to enter the city and be crowned king. The citizens welcomed him with a chorus of praise.

After the coronation, Yudhishṭhira went to Kṛishṇa to express their gratitude for his help, but Kṛishṇa sat immersed in thought and replied not. When Yudhishṭhira questioned him about his silence, Kṛishṇa said, "Lying on the bed of arrows, Bhīshma thinks of me and my mind is gone to him, to that repository of all knowledge. When that great soul is no more, the world will be as if bereft of its moon. Approach him and ask him whatever is in your mind; the different branches of learning, the duties of men, the duties of kings, ask everything. After him, there will be a decline of knowledge."

Then the five Pāṇḍavas and Kṛishṇa and others went to Bhīshma and requested him to set forth the duties of men in all stages of life. Bhīshma saluted dharma and the Lord Kṛishṇa and began his discourses on every imaginable subject coming under the four ends of human endeavor: virtue, gain, desire, and salvation. With principles and illustrative stories, Bhīshma dealt with polity and kingly duty, the duties of the four classes of men and the stations of life, duties in abnormal times and the duties to be observed by one intent on spiritual salvation. He taught them hymns to Śiva and Vishṇu, the merits of fasting and bathing in holy waters and of repeating sacred mantras, and pointed out to them the evil of avarice, ignorance, and cruelty, and the good of self-control, penance, and truthfulness.

Finally the day of the summer solstice came. Bhīshma uttered a hymn to the Lord, and his last words to all of them were, "Strive for truth; be good." He then gave up his body by yoga and his Self went to heaven.

Under Yudhishṭhira's rule, timely rains fell, people suffered not from hunger or disease either physical or mental, and were not addicted to evil pursuits. Men or women, everyone was sweet-tongued, of straight mind and pure. All sounds and touch were exceedingly happy, tastes very sweet, forms beautiful and smells pleasing.

In the thirty-sixth year of his reign the evil portents made it clear to Yudhishṭhira that the time had come to leave the world. Having turned the kingdom over to his successors, he set out with his brothers and Draupadī to cross the Himālayas, ascend the Meru mountain, and reach heaven. They were all proceeding toward heaven by virtue of yoga when Draupadī slipped from that yoga and dropped by the way. "Why has this virtuous Draupadī fallen?" asked Bhīma. Yudhishṭhira replied, "She was partial to Arjuna," and passed on. After a while the scholarly Sahadeva fell and to Bhīma's question Yudhishṭhira replied that Sahadeva was proud of his intellect. Then Nakula fell; Yudhishṭhira said that Nakula thought that he had no equal in beauty. Arjuna then fell because of his high opinion of his own heroism; and Bhīma, too, because of his inordinate eating and boasting about his physical strength. Yudhishṭhira quietly moved on, accompanied only by his dog.

Indra then appeared with his chariot and asked Yudhishṭhira to get in it to be taken to the heavens. When Yudhishṭhira said that he did not want the heavens without his brothers, Indra promised that he would meet them there. Yudhishṭhira then asked permission to take his dog with him, but Indra protested that dogs had no place in heaven and that even their sight was pollution. Yudhishṭhira replied that even if it cost his own life, he would have not give up a being devoted to him. The dog then revealed itself as the god Dharma who was testing him again, as he had in the past. Dharma declared that even in heaven there was none equal to Yudhishṭhira and that in his own body Yudhishṭhira would attain the imperishable worlds.

The gods then led Yudhishṭhira to heaven where he found Draupadī and his brothers, and there he saw again the Lord Kṛishṇa who, at the end of his mission on earth, had entered into the eternal Lord Nārāyaṇa of whom he was an incarnation.

THE BHĀGAVATA

The Bhāgavata Purāṇa begins with a verse which puts the whole Vedānta in a nutshell: "Let us meditate on that Supreme Truth, which by its inherent light dispels illusion for all time, that material and efficient cause from which alone the creation, existence, and dissolution of the universe result, because such causal character is present in that only and not in objects like primordial matter; [let us meditate on the Lord] who is omniscient and self-luminous, who through his heart extended to the prime poet [Brahmā] the knowledge in the form of the Veda, about whose real nature the sages are in bewilderment, and in whom as the substratum there appears the essentially false threefold creation of elements, senses, and deities, even as the transfiguration of glare or glass into water."

The Bhāgavata begins where the Mahābhārata ends, seeking to correct what it considers to be the fault of a story which tells of gambling, dishonoring women, and a devastating war which ends in a pyrrhic victory, and neglects the emphasis on the glory of the Lord and devotion to him: "Renunciation without devotion to the Lord and action without dedication to Him are not good. However much your ultimate idea may be the inculcation of dharma, you ought not to have put to the people stories with loathsome themes and incidents. By nature addicted to the obvious pleasures of the senses, they revel in the doubtful material and miss the inner message." Thus the Sage Nārada urged Vyāsa, the author of the Mahābhārata, to concentrate on the pure glory of the Lord. Vyāsa then sat in contemplation in his hermitage, saw the Prime Being in his pure devoted heart, and composed this Purāṇa which allays the ills of man and constitutes the means of his attaining devotion to the Lord.

It tells the stories of the many incarnations and partial manifestations of the Lord and of many sages and heroes who revealed in their lives the three paths of dedicated acts, knowledge, and devotion. Of Dhurva [the prince who became the pole star], for instance, the story is told of how he learned from the Sage Nārada the supreme secret mantra "OM, obeisance to the Lord Vāsudeva," and after severe austerities attained the blessing of the Lord and was touched with the Lord's conch of knowledge. Whereupon he burst into a hymn of praise of the Lord: "He who, entering me, revives with his power my dormant speech, as indeed every other faculty of mine—to you that Lord, the Being endowed with all powers, I make this obeisance. It is by the intelligence that you have extended that this moribund world awoke to life. How can one, if grateful, forget your feet, the sole refuge for one's salvation?"

Of King Rantideva, who, himself dying of hunger, gave away the little that he had to eat to the hungry beggar with the words: "I do not want the great state attended by divine powers or even deliverance; establishing myself in the hearts of all beings, let me seek their suffering so that they may be rid of their misery."

The efficacy of reciting the Lord's Name is told in the story of Ajāmila, a fallen Brāhman who, just as he was dying, said the name of his youngest son, "Nārāyaṇa," which is the same as the name of Lord Vishṇu. When the emissaries of the god of Death came to take him, they were stopped by the attendants of Lord Vishṇu, who said, "Did you not hear him uttering the Lord's name, Nārāyaṇa, though involuntarily? This is the greatest expiation of sins, the utterance of the Lord's name whereby the Lord's memory is roused and sustained. Even if the Lord's name that is uttered is associated with another person, even though the utterance is in fun, a meaningless sound or in derision, whether it is with or without knowledge, it burns away all sins. A powerful medicine cures, even if it is taken accidentally; and a mantra too does, even if one does not understand its full efficacy." Thus Ajāmila was saved, the words of Vishṇu's attendants kindled his innate knowledge, and with poignant contrition of heart Ajāmila repaired to the Ganges and attained to the Lord through yoga.

Manifesting himself as Sage Kapila, the Lord taught: "Ignoring me who am permanently enshrined in all beings, man is making a mockery of idol worship. He who, in arrogance, hates me who am resident in another's body, sees difference, and is inimical, attains no peace; I, as enshrined within all, should be honored with charity, courtesy, and friendliness."

In addition to the many stories about the sages and heroes, the Bhāgavata tells of the minor incarnations of Vishṇu, and of such major ones as Boar, Man-lion, Tortoise, Dwarf, Fish, Rāma, Paraśurāma, and Kṛishṇa, and Kalkin of the future. As Boar, at the time of the creation of the world when a demon was holding the earth under the waters, he plunged into the waters, lifted up the earth with his tusk, and killed the demon who stood in his way.

The demons are fallen gods; they seek the path of opposition to the Lord only for their quicker salvation; they hate the Lord and court death at his hands, eventually to be saved by him. A brother of the demon killed by Lord Vishṇu in the Boar incarnation had obtained from Brahmā the boon that he could not be killed by gods, men, or animals, and thus when it became necessary to kill him in order to protect his son Prahlāda who was a devotee of God, Vishṇu took the form of a Man-lion, neither man nor beast, and killed him. Prahlāda then sang of the Lord the greatest of all the numberless hymns in the Bhāgavata; he said: "Sages practicing silent meditation in lonely forests care not for others; but leaving these brethren of mine, I do not want my lonely salvation."

As the war between the gods and the demons continued, the gods came to Lord Vishṇu for help. The Lord advised them, "Let the gods call off the fight and come to terms with the demons, for things are achieved not by agitation so much as by persuasion. Let the milk-ocean be churned, and the nectar secured from it will make you gods immortal. The first emanation will be poison, and then a number of precious things will arise. You should be neither afraid of the poison nor covetous of the precious things; above all, there should be no anger. Mount Mandara will be the churning rod, Serpent Vāsuki the rope, and myself your help." When they began to churn the milk-ocean with the mountain, it sank, and Lord Vishṇu assumed the form of a huge Wonder-tortoise and supported it on his back. When the ocean was thus churned, there arose the terrible poison before which the people and gods fled in fright, taking refuge under the ever-auspicious Lord Śiva. Śiva then brought the whole poison to His palm and swallowed it in His overflowing compassion; the poison could not harm Him but left a blue stain at His throat. Thus the stain caused by benevolent service is indeed an ornament to the good souls. When the nectar was obtained from the churning, it benefited only the gods because the gods worshiped the Lord and the demons did not.

Of all the incarnations of the Lord Vishṇu, the most complete and the most popular is that of Kṛishṇa. Earth was again overburdened with demons in the form of arrogant kings. Earth went to Brahmā and wept. Brahmā said, "In the house of Vasudeva, the Supreme Being Vāsudeva [Vishṇu] will be born; let the celestial damsels be born as cowherd lasses; let the sages be born as cows; let the serpent Śesha, who has an element of the Lord, be born as his elder brother. The Mystic Power of the Lord [Yogamāyā] will also be born for furthering the Lord's plan."

When Kaṁsa, ruler of Mathurā, learned that the eighth child of his sister Devakī would cause his death, he put Devakī and her husband Vasudeva in prison and as each son was born to them, Kaṁsa put him to death. The serpent Śesha became the seventh child in Devakī's womb, and before birth the Lord directed his Mystic Illusion [Yogamāyā] to transfer the child from Devakī's womb to Rohiṇī, a wife of Vasudeva in the cowherd village across the Jumna River, and then he himself became the eighth child of Vasudeva and Devakī.

Then came the blessed moment when the whole universe took an auspicious appearance; a mild fragrant breeze blew, the sky was bright, and the hearts of good men became tranquil and happy. At midnight, Lord Vishṇu, who lies indeed within the heart of everybody, appeared in the divine Devakī, like the full moon in the east. Vasudeva and Devakī first saw the Lord in His divine form, and then as a common baby who told them that if they were afraid of Kaṁsa they might take him to the cowherd village and bring back instead his own yogamāyā born there as a daughter of Nanda and Yaśodā. Vasudeva considered it more prudent to do so and, as he decided, the guards and others around fell miraculously asleep, the heavily locked doors opened, darkness gave way, a fine shower fell, the serpent Śesha bent over the child in protection, and the deep overflowing Jumna River parted her waters. Vasudeva quietly came with the divine child to where Nanda's wife was asleep with a female child by her side. There he exchanged the children and returned to the prison house, put the female child on Devakī's bed, and replaced the iron fetters on his feet. As soon as the guards announced the birth of the child, Kaṁsa ran to the prison, snatched the baby by the feet and flung her against a stone. The child, the divine Māyā, jumped into the sky, showed Herself as the Goddess with eight arms, equipped with all weapons, and said scornfully, "Fool, what is the use of your trying to kill me? He who is to be your death has been born somewhere. Victimize not poor Devakī and Vasudeva."

Kaṁsa then sent forth a demoness to go through the cities and villages devouring children. When she came to Nanda's village, the Lord knew of her arrival and pretended to be asleep. She took the boy on her lap and began to suckle him with her milk of poison but the Lord sucked up not only her breasts, he also sucked her very vital breaths, and her huge carcass fell in the village crashing many a tree. Thus did little Kṛishṇa account for many a demon emissary of Kaṁsa that came to kill him.

When Lord Kṛishṇa was born as their child, the cowherds knew no restraint to their joy and splashed each other with milk, curd, and butter. The child was named Kṛishṇa (The Dark One), on the advice of the priest, who said, "because the Lord who took different colors in the successive ages, white, red, and yellow, now took the dark color. As Vasudeva's son, he is also Vāsudeva, but really His names and forms are infinite; He shall bring you welfare and joy, and with His help you shall surmount all difficulties." And Rohiṇī's son was called Balarāma: Bala because of his exceeding strength and Rāma because of his attractive qualities.

As boys, the two brothers indulged in play and pranks, releasing calves, milking the cows, and stealing curds and butter. Once while all the boys were playing together some went to Yaśodā and reported that Kṛishṇa swallowed mud. The mother caught Kṛishṇa and enquired. "No, not I. Look here," said Kṛishṇa and opened his little mouth. And lo! What did Yaśodā see there! The entire Universe, static and moving, heaven and the quarters, the luminary bodies, the earth with all her continents, mountains, and seas! Yaśodā realized that the son she was fondling was none other than Hari, whom the Vedas and Upanishads and the paths of knowledge, action, and devotion were adoring. But the Lord drew over the mother again the veil of parental affection.

Once she was churning and Kṛishṇa could not be attended to and given his meal and in his peevishness the boy broke the churn and ate the butter. Yaśodā became angry and tried to catch Him whom even the minds of yogis, directed by penance, were unable to grasp. She seized a rope and tried to tie the Lord, one for whom there was no inside or outside, this side or that, front or back. She tied Him with a rope to a rock, but the rope was two inches too short; she joined another piece of rope, and again it was short by two inches. When every length that she could make was short by two inches and the poor mother was perspiring, Kṛishṇa submitted himself to the bondage.

Another time, Kṛishṇa went with his friends and the cows to the banks of the Jumna. The sun was hot, and afflicted with thirst they went to a pool of the river where the water was poisoned by the serpent Kāliya, and the cows and cowherdesses swooned on drinking the water. Kṛishṇa, who had come to rid the world of all evildoers, climbed a tree nearby and jumped into Kāliya's pool. Kāliya attacked Him with its lifted hood but the Lord jumped on the hood and danced. To witness His dance, the whole heavenly world gathered with its orchestra. Kṛishṇa grew in size until Kāliya could not bear the weight of the Lord's steps, each one of which brought blood out of its mouth. Finally the serpent prayed that it might be pardoned and Kṛishṇa left it, commanding that it leave the river immediately and betake itself to the sea.

Kṛishṇa went about in Vrindāban in a yellow silk garment, with a peacock feather on his head, bearing a garland of blossoms, playing his divine flute. The magic fell on the ears of the cowherd lasses who became jealous of the flute that drank the sweet breath from the jewel-like lips of the Lord: the very cows stood still, drinking the music of the Lord's flute with upturned ears; the calves stood ignoring their mother's udder and the grass. Perhaps the birds that sat on the boughs in silence listening to these strains were the sages themselves! The Jumna eddied all the more and appeared to stretch her arms of waves to clasp the tender feet of the Lord.

Winter arrived, the time when the Lord is the object of special worship. The maidens of the cowherd village observed the vow of worshiping the Mother, sustaining themselves only on the sacred food that they offered to the Goddess. Bathing at dawn in the Jumna they made images of the Goddess with the river sand and worshiped Her, praying to Her, "O Goddess, the Mystic Power of the Lord! Make Kṛishṇa our husband.

Obeisance to you." Clasping each other with their arms, they sang of Kṛishṇa as they went down to the Jumna to bathe. They left their garments on the shore and sported in the waters. To teach them the lesson that those in vows, especially, ought not to bathe like that without their garments on, the Lord gathered their garments and got up on a tree on the bank. As they had prayed that He should become their husband, He granted their wish. He said, "The love that is directed to me can hardly be the desire for sensual enjoyment, for it is burnt in the fire of devotion and knowledge. Burnt seeds sprout not. This vow of yours and adoration of the Mother will be fruitful. You shall sport with me these autumnal nights."

The Lord saw these autumnal nights fragrant with blown jasmine and took it into His head to sport, resorting to His Mystic Illusion [Yogamāyā]. Seeing the moon in its full orb, the Lord played most sweetly on His flute. The spell of those notes fell on the ears of the cowherd lasses [gopīs], and possessed as it were by Kṛishṇa, they came to where Kṛishṇa was. "Why have you come on this terrible night? Your kith and kin will search for you; go home and serve your lords like virtuous wives. It is not so much by physical proximity to Me as by hearing of Me or contemplating on Me or singing of Me that love for Me is developed," observed the Lord.

"Like souls desiring release have we sought you, abandoning everything. Speak not these cruel words, we are your devotees, accept us," replied the gopīs. The Lord listened to their moving words. Though one always delighting in His own self, the Lord, the Great Master of Yoga, smiled and in His compassion delighted the gopīs. With the garland of flowers, flute in hand, the Lord shone amidst them like the moon among the stars. Going down to the sands of the river, He sported with them.

Now pride took possession of the gopīs who had won Kṛishṇa's love. The Lord noticed their elation at their own fortune and, for purging their minds of its evil and purifying them, the Lord disappeared at that very spot. When the Lord was no longer to be seen, the gopīs joined together, and thinking of Him, speaking of Him, imitating His acts and becoming thus one with Him, they remained singing of Him and expecting His arrival. "Those who are your own, whose life-breaths are in you, are searching for you in every direction. You are the immanent witness inside all beings. It is to protect the world that at Brahmā's own request you have come." Singing thus and thirsting for Kṛishṇa's sight, the gopīs wept sweetly.

Then, with a smiling face, the most charming Lord presented Himself before them. As soon as He had come, they arose all at once, even as a body would rise up on the coming of life. They felt a relief such as people feel on getting at a man of wisdom. Surrounded by them Kṛishṇa shone like the Self surrounded by His powers. The Lord of Mystic Powers made Himself as many as the gopīs and placed Himself in between every pair of them. Locking His arms with theirs, the Lord began on the sands of the river His Rāsa Dance. The Lord of the Goddess of All Beauty sported thus with the lasses even as a child would play with his own reflections. The Lord who, as the Master, is within the gopīs as well as their husbands, has taken this body for sport.

Kaṁsa then resolved to overcome Kṛishna in a wrestling match, and sent Akrūra to invite him to the contest in the arena. Akrūra brought the two brothers to Kaṁsa, and on the way as he bathed in the Jumna River he was blessed with a vision of the heavenly form of the Lord, lying on the serpent couch. Akrūra praised the Lord, "By manifold paths and at the direction of manifold teachers, people worship you, the same, the sole Lord, who is of the form of all gods, and even as all streams flow to the same ocean, so do all paths come to you in the end." At Mathurā, Krishṇa and Balarāma came to the arena, overcame the wrestlers, killed Kaṁsa, released their parents from prison, and restored the kingdom to its rightful ruler.

Thereafter Kṛishṇa spent much of his time overcoming demons and evil-doers, helping righteous rulers, and carrying out his mission on earth. He participated in the great battle between the Kauravas and Pāṇḍavas recorded in the Mahābhārata, and ruled his own kingdom at Dwārakā. The Lord had rid the Earth of many demoniac kings such as Kaṁsa and Duryodhana. Power and affluence, as the Lord again and again pointed out, always corrupted men; it turned the head and led the successful to arrogance and the insulting of others. Therefore, the Lord said again and again that when He wanted to bless one, He stripped one bare.

After many years of such services, the time came for Kṛishṇa to leave this earth. Before leaving, he gave a spiritual discourse to his beloved cousin and companion, explaining the nature of a good man, "Compassionate, unharmful, and forbearing toward all, having Truth as his strength, free from all impurity, equal and helpful to all, with a mind not ruined by desires, subdued, mild, clean, unburdened by possessions, without craving, moderate in taking things in, quiet, firm, silent, and meditative; with a spirit surrendered to Me, careful, deep, and unperturbed, devoid of pride, honoring others, fit, friendly, merciful, endowed with imagination—such indeed is the nature of the good and pure soul."

The nature of the true devotees of the Lord (bhaktas) was then described by Him, "Giving up everything, and every other duty, they who worship Me alone, with no other purpose in view, are My best devotees. Adoration of My devotees and My symbols, service, singing of My praise, recital of My story, listening to such recital, thinking of Me, the sense of being My servant while collecting the goods of life, surrender to Me, freedom from pride and vanity, refraining from advertising what he has done—such are the features of a devotee of Mine who may attain Me through devotion and the service of the good and pure."

Of the three paths, the Lord said: "The path of knowledge is for those who are fed up with life; those that still have desires should pursue the path of sublimation through works; and for those who are neither completely indifferent nor too much attached, the devotional path bears fruit."

Finally the Yādavas, the people over whom Kṛishṇa had ruled, who had become proud of their power, were led into a fratricidal war in which they destroyed each other. Balarāma then sat on the seashore in yoga and left his mortal frame. The Lord sat similarly on the ground underneath a tree. From a distance a hunter mistook one of the red lotus-like feet of the Lord for an animal and shot at it. Under the pretext of this arrow shot at His feet, the Lord departed from the earth. The celestial beings rained flowers and sang, and the effulgence that was the Lord shot across the firmament like lightning.

THE BHAGAVAD GĪTĀ

(These selections from the Bhagavad Gītā were made by Professor V. Raghavan from the translation of Professor D. S. Sarma of Madras. The Bhagavad Gītā is part of Book VI of the Mahābhārata, the account of the discourse of the Lord Kṛishṇa on the battlefield when the Kurus were drawn up against the Pāṇḍavas and Arjuna decided not to fight. For the story of the setting of the Bhagavad Gītā see the summary of the Mahābhārata above. On one side the hosts were led by the five Pāṇḍava brothers: Yudhishṭhira, Arjuna (with Kṛishṇa as his charioteer), Bhīma, Nakula, and Sahadeva; the one hundred sons of Dhṛitarāshṭra on the other side were urged on by Duryodhana, the eldest, and led by Bhīshma and Droṇa, the beloved teachers of all the warriors on both sides. Dhṛitarāshṭra, who was blind, sat with Sañjaya who told him what happened. The Bhagavad Gītā is recorded as Sañjaya told it to the blind king of the Kurus.)

CHAPTER 1

Suddenly conchs and kettledrums, tabors and drums and horns blared forth; and the sound was tumultuous. Then stationed in their great chariot, to which white horses were yoked, Kṛishṇa and Arjuna blew their celestial conchs. And Arjuna, whose banner bore the crest of Hanumān, looked at the sons of Dhṛitarāshṭra drawn up in battle; and as the clash of weapons began, he took up his bow.

And, O King, he said these words to Kṛishṇa, "Draw up my chariot, O Kṛishṇa, between the two armies, and I will look on these men standing eager for battle and see with whom I must contend in the strife of war." Thus addressed by Arjuna, Kṛishṇa drew up the fine chariot, O Dhṛitarāshṭra, between the two armies. In front of Bhīshma, Droṇa, and all the chiefs he said, "Behold, O Arjuna, these Kurus assembled here."

Then saw Arjuna standing there fathers and grandfathers, teachers, uncles, brothers, sons, grandsons, and comrades; and also fathers-in-law and bosom friends in both the armies. When Arjuna looked on all these kinsmen thus arrayed, he was overcome with great compassion and said these words in sadness, "When I see these, my kinsmen, drawn up and eager for fight, O Kṛishṇa, my limbs give way, my mouth is parched, my body trembles, and my hair stands on end. I am not able to stand, my mind is reeling. And I see adverse omens, O Kṛishṇa, nor do I expect any good in slaying my kinsmen in the fight. I desire no victory, O Kṛishṇa, nor dominion nor pleasures. Of what use is the kingdom to us, O Kṛishṇa, or enjoyment or even life. Those for whose sake we desire kingship, delights, and pleasures are arrayed here in battle, risking their lives and riches. These I would not kill, though killed myself, O Kṛishṇa, even for the sovereignty of the three worlds, much less for this earth. What joy can be ours, O Kṛishṇa, when we have slain the sons of Dhṛitarāshṭra? For how can we be happy if we kill our own kindred, O Kṛishṇa? Alas! what a great sin we have resolved to commit in striving to slay our kinsmen through our greed for the pleasures of the kingdom! Far better would it be for me if the sons of Dhṛitarāshṭra, weapons in hand, should slay me in the battle while I remain unresisting and unarmed."

Having spoken thus on the field of battle, Arjuna sank down on the seat of his chariot and cast away his bow and arrow, his heart overwhelmed by grief.

CHAPTER 2

He was thus overcome with pity, his eyes were troubled and filled with tears, and he was much depressed.

Then Kṛishṇa said these words, "Whence has this loathsome feeling come upon thee, O Arjuna, in this crisis? It is ignoble, it is disgraceful, it debars thee from heaven. Do not yield to this weakness, O Arjuna, for it does not become thee. Shake off this base faintness of heart and stand up, O dreaded hero!"

Arjuna said, "How can I attack Bhīshma and Droṇa in battle with my arrows, O Kṛishṇa? Worthy of worship are they by me. It is better indeed to live as a beggar in this world without slaying these venerable teachers. My heart is stricken with the weakness of compassion; my mind is perplexed about my duty. And so I ask thee, tell me for certain which is better. Teach me, for I am thy pupil and have taken refuge in thee."

The Lord said, "Thou weepest for those whom thou shouldst not weep for, and yet thou speakest words that seem to be wise. Wise men weep neither for the dead nor for the living. Never was there a time when I did not exist, nor thou, nor these kings of men. Never will there be a time hereafter when any of us shall cease to be. As the soul in this body passes through childhood, youth, and old age, even so does it pass into another body. A wise man is not deluded by this. The senses in contact with their objects, O Arjuna, give rise to heat and cold, and pleasure and pain. They come and go, and do not last forever. Endure them, O Arjuna. The man who is not affected by these, O chief of men, and who remains the same in pleasure and pain, steadfast—he is fit for immortality.

"The unreal never is, the Real never is not; the conclusion about these two is well perceived by seers of Truth. Know that to be indestructible by which all this is pervaded. None can cause the destruction of this which is immutable. Transient are said to be these bodies of the eternal soul which is indestructible and incomprehensible. Therefore, fight, O Arjuna.

"He who thinks it [the eternal soul] slays, and he who thinks it is slain—neither of them knows it well. It neither slays nor is it slain. It is never born, it never dies, nor having once been does it again cease to be. Unborn, eternal, permanent, and primeval, it is not slain when the body is slain. He who knows that it is indestructible and eternal, and that it has neither birth nor change—how can that man slay anyone, O Arjuna, or causc anyone to slay?

"As a person casts off worn-out garments and puts on others that are new, so does the inner man cast off worn-out bodies and enter into others that are new. Weapons do not cleave him; fire does not harm him; water does not make him wet; nor does wind make him dry. He is eternal, all-pervasive, unchanging, and immovable. He is the same forever. Therefore, knowing him as such, thou shouldst not grieve for him.

"Even if thou holdest that he is frequently born and that he frequently dies—even then, O mighty Arjuna, thou shouldst not grieve. For whatever is born is sure to die, and whatever dies is sure to be born again. Therefore for what is inevitable thou shouldst not grieve. The soul that dwells in the bodies of all, O Arjuna, can never be slain. Therefore thou shouldst not grieve for any creature.

"Further, if thou shouldst regard thine own duty, thou shouldst not falter; for to a Kshatriya there is no higher good than a righteous war. But if thou wilt not wage this righteous war, thou wilt relinquish thy duty and thy honor, and wilt incur sin. If thou dost fall, thou wilt go to heaven; if thou dost win, thou wilt enjoy the earth. Therefore, arise, O Arjuna, having made up thy mind to fight. Pleasure and pain, gain and loss, victory and defeat—treat them alike and gird thyself for the fight. Thus wilt thou not incur sin.

"Fools who rejoice in the letter of the Veda say, 'There is nothing else but this.' Their souls are ridden with desire, and they long for a Paradise. They quote florid texts that give out rebirth as the reward of rituals and lay down various rites for the acquisition of pleasure and power. Therefore those that are attracted to pleasure and power are carried away by these words, and have not the resolute will of a steadfast mind. The Vedas treat of Nature's threefold disposition [the three guṇas]. But do thou transcend this, O Arjuna; be free from the pairs of opposites, be steadfast in purity, never care for possessions, but possess thy soul. As is the use of a pond in a place flooded with water everywhere, so is that of all the Vedas to a Brāhman who knows.

"Work alone art thou entitled to, and not to its fruit. So never work for rewards, nor yet desist from work. Work with an even mind, O Arjuna, having given up all attachment. Be of even mind in success and in failure. Evenness of mind is called yoga. Far inferior indeed is mere action, O Arjuna, to equanimity of mind. So take refuge in equanimity; miserable are they who work for results.

"A man of even mind puts away here both good and evil. Therefore strive for yoga. Yoga is skill in action. Sages of even mind, who give up the fruits of their actions, are freed from the bonds of birth, and go to the place where no ills exist. When thy mind has crossed the slough of delusion, thou wilt become indifferent to what has been learned and also to what is yet to be learned. When thy mind, which is distracted by the Vedic texts, rests steadfast and firm in spirit—then wilt thou gain true insight."

Arjuna said, "What is the mark of the man of steadfast wisdom, of steadfast spirit, O Kṛishṇa? How does the man of firm understanding speak, how does he sit, and how does he walk?"

"When a man puts away all the desires of his mind, O Arjuna, and when his spirit finds comfort in itself—then is he called a man of steadfast wisdom. He who is not perturbed in mind by adversity and has no eagerness amidst prosperity, he from whom desire, fear, and anger have fallen away—he is called a sage of firm understanding. He who has no attachments on any side, and who does not rejoice nor hate when he obtains good or evil—his wisdom is firmly set.

"When a man withdraws his senses from their object on every side, as a tortoise does its limbs, then is his wisdom firmly set. The objects of sense fall away from the embodied soul when it ceases to feed on them, but the taste for them is left behind. Even the taste falls away when the Supreme is seen. Though a man may ever strive, O Arjuna, and be ever so wise, his senses will rebel and carry off his mind by force. So he should control them all and remain steadfast and devoted to me; for he whose senses are under control—his wisdom is firmly set.

"When a man dwells in his mind on the objects of sense, he feels an attachment for them. Attachment gives rise to desire, and desire breeds anger. From anger comes delusion, from delusion the loss of recollection, from the loss of recollection the ruin of the understanding, and from the ruin of the understanding he perishes.

"But a man of disciplined mind, who moves among the objects of sense with his senses fully under his control, and free from love and hate—he attains to a clear vision. And in that clear vision there is an end of all sorrow; for the man of clear vision soon acquires a serene comprehension. When a man has no self-control, he can have no comprehension, nor can he have the power of contemplation. And without contemplation, he can have no peace; and when he has no peace, how can he be happy? When his mind runs after the roving senses, it carries off with it the understanding, as a gale carries away a ship upon the waters.

"Therefore, O mighty Arjuna, he whose senses are all withdrawn from their objects—his wisdom is firmly set. What is night for all beings is the time of waking for the disciplined soul; and what is the time of waking for all beings is night for the sage who sees. The man into whom all desires enter as the waters enter into the sea, which, though ever filled, remains within its bounds—such a man attains to peace, and not he who hugs his desires.

"The man who gives up all desires and goes about free from any longing, and bereft of the feeling of 'I' and 'mine'—he attains to peace. This is a divine state, O Arjuna. He who has reached it is deluded no longer, and he who is established in it even at the hour of death—he attains to the bliss of God."

CHAPTER 3

Arjuna said, "If thou holdest that true insight is superior to works, why dost thou urge me to do this horrible work, O Kṛishṇa?"

The Lord said, "In this world, a twofold way of life was taught of yore by me, O Arjuna—that of knowledge for men of contemplation, and that of works for men of action. No man can ever be free from a life of action by merely avoiding active work; and no man can ever reach perfection through mere renunciation. For no man can sit still even for a moment, but does some work. Everyone is driven to act, in spite of himself, by the impulses of nature. He who controls his organs of action, but continues to brood in his mind over the objects of sense—he deludes himself, and he is termed a hypocrite. But he who controls his senses along with the mind, O Arjuna, and directs his organs of action to work without attachment—he is indeed superior. Do thou thy allotted work, for to work is better than to desist from work. By desisting from work thou canst not even sustain thy body.

"This world is fettered by work unless it is done as a sacrifice. Therefore, O Arjuna, give up thy attachments and do thy work as a sacrifice. In the beginning it is along with sacrifice that the Creator created men and said, 'By this shall ye multiply, and this shall be the Cow which will yield unto you the milk of your desires. With this shall ye cherish the gods and the gods shall cherish you. For cherished by sacrifice the gods will bestow on you the pleasures ye desire. He is verily a thief who enjoys the things they give without giving them anything in return.'

"The good men who eat what is left over after a sacrifice are freed from all sins. But the wicked who prepare food for their own sake—verily they eat sin. From food are all creatures born; from rain is food produced; from the effects of sacrifice comes rain; and these effects spring from the acts of sacrifice. Know that the acts of sacrifice are taught in the Veda, and that the Veda springs from God. Therefore the Veda, which comprehends all, ever centers around the sacrifice.

"Thus was the wheel set in motion, and he who does not follow it, but takes delight in the senses and lives in sin—O Arjuna, he lives in vain. But the man who rejoices in the Spirit, who is content and satisfied with the Spirit alone—for him there is nothing for which he should work. He has nothing to gain by the things he has done or left undone in this world; nor has he to depend on any created being for any object of his. Therefore always without attachment do the work thou hast to do, for a man who does his work without attachment wins the Supreme.

"There is nothing in the three worlds, O Arjuna, for me to achieve, nor is there anything to gain which I have not gained. Yet I continue to work. For if I did not continue to work unwearied, O Arjuna, men all around would follow in my path. If I should cease to work, these worlds would perish; and I should cause confusion and destroy these people. As ignorant men act from attachment to their work, O Arjuna, so too should an enlightened man act, but without any attachment, so that he may maintain the order of the world. Let no enlightened man unsettle the minds of the ignorant who are attached to their work. Himself doing all works with faith he should make others do so as well.

"Surrender all thy works to me and fight—with thy mind in unison with the Spirit and free from every desire and trace of self, and all thy passion spent. Those who, full of faith, ever follow this teaching of mine and do not carp at it—they too are released from their works. But those who find fault with my teaching and do not act thereon—know that such senseless men, blind to all wisdom, are lost.

"Even the man who knows acts in accordance with his own nature. All beings follow their nature; what can repression do? Love and hatred are bound to arise towards the objects of each sense. But let no man come under the sway of these, for they are his enemies. Better is one's own dharma (law, path, righteousness, nature), though imperfectly carried out, than the dharma of another carried out perfectly. Better is death in going by one's own dharma, the dharma of another brings fear in its train."

Arjuna said, "But what impels a man to commit sin, O Kṛishṇa, in spite of himself and driven, as it were, by a force?"

The Blessed Lord said, "It is desire, it is wrath, which springs from passion. A monster of greed and sin—know that it is our enemy here. As a flame is enveloped by smoke, as a mirror by dust, and as an unborn babe by the womb, so is knowledge enveloped by ignorance. Enveloped is true knowledge, O Arjuna, by the insatiable fire of desire which is the constant foe of the wise. The senses, the mind, and the understanding are said to be its seat. Through these it veils knowledge and deludes the soul.

"Therefore, O Arjuna, control thy senses from the beginning and slay this foul destroyer of knowledge and experience. The senses are great, they say; the mind greater than the senses, and the understanding greater than the mind; but what is greater than the understanding is He. Therefore know Him who is higher than the understanding, control the lower self by the higher self, and kill the enemy, O Arjuna, who comes in the guise of desire, and who is hard to overcome."

CHAPTER 4

The Lord said, "Many a birth have I passed through, O Arjuna, and so hast thou. I know them all, but thou knowest not thine. Though I am unborn and my nature is eternal, and though I am the Lord of all creatures, I employ Nature which is my own, and take birth through my divine power. Whenever there is a decline of dharma, O Arjuna, and an outbreak of lawlessness, I incarnate myself. For the protection of the good, for the destruction of the wicked and for the establishment of dharma, I am born from age to age.

"He who knows aright my divine birth and works will never be born again when he leaves his body, but will come to me, O Arjuna. Freed from passion, fear, and anger, absorbed in me, seeking refuge in me, and purified by the fire of knowledge, many have become one with me. However men approach me, even so do I accept them; for on all sides whatever path they may choose is mine, O Arjuna.

"The four castes were created by me according to the division of aptitudes and works. Though I am their creator, know thou that I neither act nor change. Works do not defile me; nor do I long for their fruit. He who knows me thus is not bound by his works. Men of old who sought deliverance knew this and did their work. Therefore do thy work as the ancients did in former times.

"What is work, and what is no work—even the wise are perplexed here. I will tell thee what work is, so that thou mayst know and be freed from evil. One has to understand what work really is, and likewise what is wrong work and also what is no work. Hard to understand is the way of work. He who sees no work in work, and work in no work, he is wise among men, he is a yogi, and he has accomplished all his work.

"He whose undertakings are all devoid of desire and self-will, and whose works are burned up by the fire of knowledge—him the wise men call a sage. Giving up attachment to the fruit of works, always satisfied, and depending on none, he is ever engaged in work—and yet he does no work at all. Having no desires, bringing his mind and self under control, and giving up all possessions, he commits no sin since his work is of the body alone. Satisfied with whatever he gets, rising above both pleasure and pain, having no ill-will, and remaining the same in success and failure, he acts indeed, but he is not bound.

"The works of a man whose attachments are gone, who is free, and whose mind is well established in knowledge melt away entirely, being done as for a sacrifice. To him the offering is God, the oblation is God, and it is God that offers it in the fire of God. Thus does he realize God in his works, and he reaches Him alone. Some offer as sacrifice their hearing and other senses in the fires of restraint; while others offer sound and other objects of sense in the fires of their senses. Some likewise offer as sacrifice their riches or their austerities or their practices; while others of subdued minds and severe vows offer their learning and their knowledge. This world is not for him who makes no sacrifice, O Arjuna, much less the other. Thus many kinds of sacrifice are set forth as the means of reaching the Absolute. And they all spring from active work. Know them as such, and thou shalt be free.

"Knowledge as a sacrifice is superior to all material sacrifices, O Arjuna, for all works with no exception culminate in knowledge. Learn this by humble reverence, by enquiry, and by service. The wise who have seen the truth will teach this divine knowledge. When thou hast known it, thou wilt not err again as now, O Arjuna; for thou wilt see all things without exception in thyself and also in me. Even if thou art the most sinful of sinners thou wilt cross over all transgression by the raft of divine knowledge. As the fire which is kindled reduces all fuel to ashes, O Arjuna, so does the fire of knowledge reduce all works to ashes.

"There is no purifier on earth equal to divine knowledge. A man who becomes perfect in yoga finds it in himself in the course of time. He who is full of faith and zeal and who has subdued his senses obtains divine knowledge; and when he has obtained it, he soon gains supreme peace. But the man who is ignorant and has no faith and who always doubts goes to ruin. There is neither this world, nor the world beyond, nor happiness, for the man who always doubts.

"Works do not bind the man, O Arjuna, whom yoga prompts to selfless action and whose doubts are destroyed by divine knowledge, and who ever possesses his soul. Therefore having cut asunder with the sword of knowledge this doubt in thy heart which is born of ignorance, betake thyself to yoga and arise, O Arjuna."

CHAPTER 5

Arjuna said, "Thou praisest, O Kṛishṇa, the renunciation of works and also their selfless performance. Tell me for certain which is the better of the two."

The Lord said, "The renunciation of works and their selfless performance both lead to bliss. But of the two, the performance of works is better than their renunciation. He who neither hates nor desires should be known as one who has ever the spirit of renunciation; for he who is above such contraries, O mighty Arjuna, is easily freed from bondage. It is the simple and not the wise who speak of works and their renunciation as diverse ways. He who is firmly set on one reaches the end of both. The place which is reached by men of renunciation is reached by men of action also. He who sees that the way of renunciation and the way of works are one—he sees indeed.

"But to achieve renunciation is hard, O mighty Arjuna, for one who is not trained in selfless action; while the sage who is trained in selfless action reaches the Absolute in no time at all. He who is trained in selfless action and is pure in soul, who has conquered himself and subdued his senses—his self being the self of all creatures—he is undefiled, though he works. He who works without attachments, resigning his actions to God, is untouched by sin, as a lotus leaf by water. A selfless man who has renounced the fruit of his actions attains to a disciplined peace of mind. But the man who is not selfless is impelled by desire and is attached to the results of action and is therefore bound. The soul which has renounced all works with a discerning mind dwells at ease, self-subdued in the city of nine gates, neither working nor causing work to be done.

"Knowledge is veiled by ignorance, and mortals are thereby deluded. But for those in whom the ignorance is dispelled by knowledge the knowledge illumines the Supreme like the sun. Thinking of Him, at one with Him, abiding in Him, and delighting solely in Him, they reach a state from which there is no return, their sins being dispelled by their knowledge.

"Sages look upon all alike—whether it be a learned and lowly Brāhman or a cow or an elephant or even a dog or an outcaste. Those whose minds are thus set on equality have even here overcome their being. God is pure, and is the same in all, therefore are they established in God. He who knows God, and is established in Him, he who is undeluded and is firm of mind—he neither joys at what is pleasant nor is vexed at what is unpleasant. His soul being unattached to external objects, he finds the happiness that is in himself; he is in union with God, and he enjoys undying bliss.

"For the pleasures that arise from attachments are only sources of pain. They have a beginning and an end, O Arjuna, and no wise man delights in them. He who is able to resist the force of desire and anger even here before he quits his body—he is a yogi, he is a blessed man. The yogi who is happy within becomes divine, and attains to the beatitude of God.

"Those whose sins are destroyed and whose doubts are removed, whose minds are disciplined and who rejoice in the good of all beings—such holy men attain to the beatitude of God. Those who are free from desire and anger, and who have subdued their minds and realized themselves—around such austere men lies the beatitude of God.

"Shutting out all external objects, fixing the gaze of his eyes between his brows, and equalizing the inward and the outward breath moving in his nostrils, the sage who has controlled his senses, mind, understanding, and who has put away desire, fear, and anger, and who is ever bent on liberation—he is indeed ever liberated. And having known me who am the Recipient of all sacrifices and austerities, the Lord of all the worlds and the Friend of all creatures, he attains peace."

CHAPTER 6

The Lord said, "He who does the work he ought to do, and does not seek its fruit—he is a sannyāsin, and he is a yogi, not he who does no work and maintains no sacred fires. When a man has no attachment to the objects of sense nor to works, and when he has wholly renounced his will, he is said to have attained to yoga.

"He who has conquered himself is the friend of himself; but he who has not conquered himself is hostile to himself as a foe. The spirit of a man who has conquered himself and attained to serenity is steadfast in cold and heat, in pleasure and pain, and in honor and dishonor. He is said to be a steadfast yogi whose mind derives satisfaction from knowledge and experience, who having conquered his senses, never vacillates, and to whom a clod, a stone, and a piece of gold are the same. He who has equal regard for friends, companions, and foes, for those who are indifferent, for those who are impartial, for those who are hateful, for those who are related, and even for those who are righteous and those who are sinful—he stands supreme.

"A yogi should always try to concentrate his mind in absolute solitude, having retired to a secret place, and subdued his mind and body and got rid of his desires and possessions. Having in a clean place firmly fixed his seat neither too high nor too low, and having spread over it the sacred grass, and then a deer-skin, and then a cloth, he should practice yoga for his own purification, restraining his thoughts and senses, and bringing his mind to a point. Sitting firm he should hold his body, head, and neck erect and still, and gaze steadfastly on the point of his nose, without looking around. Serene and fearless, steadfast in the vow of celibacy, and subdued in mind, he should sit in yoga, thinking on me and intent on me alone.

"Keeping himself ever steadfast in this manner, the yogi of subdued mind attains to the peace which abides in me, and which leads to bliss. Yoga is not for him who eats too much, nor for him who eats too little. It is not for him, O Arjuna, who is given to too much sleep, nor for him who keeps vigil too long. But for the man who is temperate in his food and recreation, who is restrained in all his actions, and who is regulated in his sleep and vigil, yoga puts an end to all sorrow. When the disciplined mind of a man is established in the Spirit alone, free from the desire of any object—then he is said to possess concentration. 'As a lamp in a place sheltered from the wind does not flicker'—that is the figure employed of a yogi who, with a subdued mind, practices concentration of the Spirit.

"Renouncing entirely all the desires born of the imagination, and restraining with his mind all his senses on every side, a man should gain tranquillity little by little, and with a steadfast purpose concentrate his mind on the Spirit, and think of nothing else. Whatsoever makes the wavering and fickle mind wander away—it should be withdrawn from that and brought back to the control of the Spirit. For supreme happiness comes to the yogi whose mind is at rest, whose passions are composed, and who is pure and has become one with God.

"Thus making the soul ever steadfast the yogi whose sins have disappeared easily experiences the infinite joy of union with God. Steadfast in yoga he sees himself in all beings, and all beings in himself—he sees the same in all. He who sees me everywhere and sees everything in me—I am never lost to him, and he is never lost to me. The yogi who, having attained to oneness, worships me abiding in all beings—he lives in me, howsoever he leads his life. He who looks upon all as himself, in pleasure and in pain—he is considered, O Arjuna, a perfect yogi."

Arjuna said, "This yoga which thou hast declared to be evenness of mind, O Kṛishṇa—I do not see any steadfastness for it because of fickleness. For the mind is fickle, O Kṛishṇa, it is violent, powerful, and obstinate. To control it is as difficult, it seems to me, as to control the wind."

The Lord said, "Doubtless the mind is fickle and hard to curb, O mighty Arjuna, but by constant practice and by detachment it can be controlled. Yoga is hard to achieve, I agree, by a man who cannot control himself. But it can be achieved by a man who has controlled himself and who strives through proper means."

Arjuna said, "A man who has faith but who is not steadfast, and whose mind has fallen away from yoga, having failed to accomplish it—what way does he go, O Kṛishṇa? Does he not perish like a riven cloud, O Kṛishṇa, fallen from both, and without any hold, and bewildered in the way that leads to God?"

The Lord said, "Neither in this world nor in the next will he perish, O Arjuna. For a man who does good, my son, will never come to grief. The man who has fallen away from yoga goes to the regions of the righteous. Having lived there for unnumbered years, he is reborn in the house of the pure and prosperous. Or he is born in a family of yogis rich in wisdom. But a birth like this is hard to gain in this world. There he regains the understanding acquired in his former body, O Arjuna, and strives still further for perfection. By his former habit he is led on in spite of himself. Even a man who merely desires to know of yoga transcends the Vedic rule of works.

"But if a yogi strives with diligence, he is cleansed of all his sins, and becoming perfect through many births he reaches the Supreme State. A yogi is greater than a man of austerities, he is considered greater than even a man of knowledge, and greater also than a man devoted to works. Therefore do thou become a yogi, O Arjuna. And of all yogis, he who worships me with faith, his inmost dwelling in me—he is considered by me to be most attuned."

CHAPTER 7

The Lord said, "Hear thou, O Arjuna, how by fixing thy mind on me and taking refuge in me and practicing yoga, thou mayst without any doubt know me in full. Earth, water, fire, air, ether, mind, understanding, and self-consciousness—such is the eightfold division of my nature. This is my lower nature. My other and higher nature—know that to be the immanent spirit, O Arjuna, by which the universe is sustained. And know that all beings have their birth in these. I am the origin of all this world and its dissolution as well. There is nothing whatever that is higher than I am, O Arjuna; all this is strung on me as rows of gems on a string. I am the taste in the waters, O Arjuna; I am the light in the sun and the moon. I am the syllable OM in all the Vedas; I am the sound in ether and manliness in men. I am the pure fragrance in the earth and the brightness in the fire. I am the life in all creatures, and the austerity in ascetics. And whatever things there may be—good, passionate, or dull of nature—know thou they are all from me. I am not however in them, they are in me.

"Four types of righteous men worship me, O Arjuna—the man in distress, the man who wishes to learn, the man who has an object to gain, and the man who knows. Of these, the man who knows, who has his devotion centered in One, and who is ever attuned, is the best. For supremely dear am I to the man who knows, and he is dear to me."

CHAPTER 11

The Lord assumed the Divine Cosmic form and said, "I am the mighty world-destroying Time, which has begun to slay these men here. Even without thee all the warriors standing arrayed in hostile ranks shall die. Therefore, arise and win renown; subdue thy foes and enjoy a prosperous kingdom. By me they have been slain already. Be thou merely an instrument, O Arjuna."

Arjuna said, "Rightly, O Kṛishṇa, is the world moved to joy and love by glorifying Thee. The demons flee on all sides through fear, and hosts of Perfected Souls all bow down to Thee. And why should they not bow down to Thee, O mighty One, who art greater than all, being the Primal Cause even of Brahmā? Thou art the Father of the world—of all that move and all that do not move. Thou art the object of its worship and its greatest Teacher. Therefore I bow down and prostrate myself before Thee, adorable Lord, and seek Thy grace. I now feel composed in mind: I am myself again."

CHAPTER 12

Arjuna said, "Those devotees who, ever steadfast, thus worship Thee and those again who worship the Imperishable and the Unmanifested—which of these are better versed in yoga?"

The Lord said, "Those who have fixed their minds on me, and who, ever steadfast and possessed of supreme faith, worship me—them do I consider perfect in yoga. Having subdued all their senses, and being of even mind under all conditions and engaged in the good of all beings—they come to me indeed.

"The difficulty of those whose minds are set on the Unmanifested is greater, for the goal of the Unmanifested is hard for the embodied to reach. But those who consecrate all their actions to me and regard me as their dearest one, who meditate on me and worship me with single-hearted devotion—I save them full soon, O Arjuna, from death and the ocean of mortal life, their minds being ever set on me. Fix thy mind on me alone, let thy thoughts rest in me. And in me alone wilt thou live hereafter. Of this there is no doubt.

"If thou art not able to fix thy mind on me, O Arjuna, then seek to reach me by the practice of concentration. If thou art not able even to practice concentration of mind, then devote thyself to my service. For even by doing service to me thou canst reach perfection. If thou art not able to do even this, then give up the fruit of all action, seeking refuge in devotion to me with thy mind subdued. For knowledge is better than the practice of concentration, and meditation is better than knowledge, and renunciation of the fruit of action is even better than meditation, for close on renunciation follows peace.

"He who never hates any being and is kindly and compassionate, who is free from the feeling of 'I' and 'Mine,' and who looks upon pleasure and pain alike, and has forbearance; he who is ever content and is steady in contemplation, who is self-restrained and is of firm conviction, and who has consecrated his mind and understanding to me—dear to me is the man who is thus devoted. He by whom the world is not harassed and who is not harassed by the world, he who is free from joy and anger, fear and anxiety—he is dear to me. He who has no wants, who is pure and prompt, unconcerned and untroubled, and who is selfless in his enterprises—dear to me is the man who is thus devoted to me.

"He who neither joys nor hates, neither grieves nor wants, and who has renounced both good and evil—dear to me is the man who is thus devoted. He who is alike to foe and friend and through good and ill repute, who is alike in cold and heat and in pleasure and pain, and who is free from attachments—he who is alike in praise and dispraise, who is silent and satisfied with whatever he has, who has no home and is firm of mind—dear to me is the man thus devoted.

"And they who have faith and follow this righteous way of everlasting life thus set forth, and regard me as Supreme—exceedingly dear to me are they who are thus devoted."

CHAPTER 13

The Lord said, "Modesty, sincerity, nonviolence, patience, and uprightness; service to the teacher, purity, steadfastness, and self-control; indifference toward the objects of senses; self-effacement, and the perception of the evil of birth, death, old age, sickness, and pain; detachment and freedom from identification with children, wife, and home; and constant evenness of mind in the midst of agreeable and disagreeable events; unswerving devotion to me through constant meditation, resort to solitude, and aversion to society; steadfastness in the knowledge of the Spirit, and an insight into the object of the knowledge of Truth—this is declared to be true knowledge, and all that is contrary to it is not knowledge."

CHAPTER 16

The Lord said, "Fearlessness, purity of heart, steadfastness in knowledge and devotion; almsgiving, self-control, and sacrifice; study of the scriptures, austerity and uprightness; nonviolence, truth, freedom from anger; renunciation, tranquillity, aversion to slander; compassion to living beings, freedom from covetousness, gentleness, modesty, and steadfastness; courage, patience, fortitude, purity, and freedom from malice and overweening conceit—these belong to him who is born to the heritage of the gods, O Arjuna.

"Hypocrisy, arrogance, and self-conceit; wrath, rudeness, and ignorance—these belong, O Arjuna, to him who is born to the heritage of the devils. The heritage of the gods is said to make for deliverance, and that of the devils for bondage. Possessed by self-conceit, power and pride, and also by lust and wrath, these traducers hate me in the bodies of others and in their own. These cruel haters, the vilest of men, these sinners I always hurl down into the wombs of devils in the cycles of births and deaths. Three are the gateways of this hell leading to the ruin of the soul—lust, wrath, and greed. Therefore let man renounce these three."

CHAPTER 18

The Lord said, "Fix thy mind on me, be devoted to me, sacrifice to me, prostrate thyself before me, so shalt thou come to me. I promise thee truly, for thou art dear to me.

"Surrendering all duties come to me alone for shelter. Do not grieve; for I will release thee from all sin.[1]

"Has this been heard by thee, O Arjuna, with undivided attention? Has thy delusion, born of ignorance, been dispelled?"

Arjuna said, "My delusion is gone. I have come to myself by Thy grace, O Kṛishṇa. I stand free from doubt. I will act according to Thy word."

[1] This call of God to the devotee to surrender unto Him is held to be of utmost importance by the Śrīvaishṇavas.

PRAYERS

(The growth of devotional cults, the institution of temples, and the worship of different forms of deities served as the background for the production of an extensive hymnal literature in Sanskrit and the regional languages of India. Every devotee, according to his favorite deity and author, learns by heart and repeats some hymns every day, whether he prays at home or at the temple. The recital of the epics and the Purāṇas and the singing of these hymns have kept lit the flame of devotion and piety in the hearts of the masses and helped them maintain their keen sensibility to higher values. The masses have been illiterate, but they have never been uncultured; all through Indian history we see that, just as the waters of the high Himālayas have always flowed down to the plains, even so the spiritual culture has spread to the lowest levels of society. In addition to the hymns quoted here, characteristic examples of hymns in everyday use, and of the correct chanting of the Vedas, are given in a collection recorded by Folkways Records as a supplement to this volume.)

The Heart of the Sun

(The Sun has been worshiped from Vedic times as the object of meditation in many spiritual exercises. The best known of the hymns to the Sun is the one taken from the Rāmāyaṇa, imparted to Rāma during the battle with the demon Rāvaṇa. A portion of the hymn is given here.)

Adore the Sun rising with all His rays, receiving the obeisance of gods and demons, the shining maker of light. Effulgent home of the rays, He is indeed the embodiment of all gods; He, in fact, protects with His rays all the gods and demons and worlds.

He who with His rays consumes, produces, propels; who traverses the skies like a bird, shines like gold, makes the days and is the golden seminator [of the universe]. The hot, tawny disk, He burns everything and is indeed death; He is also the universal creator, greatly effulgent, loving and the source of all good. He is the master who destroys and makes again the world; with His rays He draws, heals, and rains. Singing of His glory in calamities and difficulties, in lonely forests and fright one does not come to grief, O Rāghava! With concentration, worship this God of gods, the Lord of the world; by repeating this hymn thrice, you will succeed in battles.

The Thousand Names of Lord Vishṇu

(Of hymns to Vishṇu, that which is on everybody's lips is the Thousand Names of the Lord, taken from the discourses of Bhīshma in the Mahābhārata. Hymns on the names of the Lord are recited as a means of salvation, being the easiest means and the best suited for the present age when higher spiritual qualifications are difficult of attainment. The repetition of the names helps to recall to mind the presence of the Lord, His infinite excellences and exploits, and enables one to become wholly absorbed in Him.)

The Universe, the Pervasive, the Sacrifice, the Lord of the past, present, and future, the Creator of beings, their Sustainer, Existence, the In-dweller of beings, and the Well-wisher of beings; the Pure Being, the Supreme Being, the Supreme God of the liberated, the Undiminishing, the Spirit, the Onlooker, the Knower of the body, the Unswerving; the Yoga and the Leader among those that know the Yoga, Himself Matter, Spirit, and God, the Supreme Being who incarnated as the Man-lion, who has rays of light as hair, and possesses the Goddess of Fortune; the All, the Destroyer, the Beneficent Śiva, the Steadfast, the primary Source of beings, the Undiminishing Repository; One who manifests Himself as He pleases, the Benefactor, the Protector, One who takes a superior kind of birth, the Capable, the Lord. . . . He who bears the Conch, the Sword, the Discus, the Bow, the Mace, the Discus-armed, the Unperturbed, He who will use anything as a weapon to strike with.

Thus these thousand names of the Lord, the Great Keśava who is fit to be sung about, have been completely told. He who listens to this or recites it daily shall not come to grief here or in the hereafter.

The Mother

(From the hymns of the great Śrī Saṅkarāchārya)

O Mother! Let whatever I articulate be your prayer; let all my manual craft be the mystic gestures of your worship, let all my movement be your devotional circumambulation; let everything that I eat or drink be oblation offered to you; let my lying down be prostration to you; let all my happy experience be in the spirit of offering myself to you; whatever I do, let it be a synonym of your service.

Hymn to Śiva

(From Pushpadanta's Mahimnas-stava)

For men who, by reason of the variety of their tastes, tread diverse paths—the three Vedas, Sāṅkhya, Yoga, Śaivism, and Vaishṇavism—and claim that among the different paths one is superior and another wholesome, You [Śiva] are the one goal to be reached even as the ocean is for all waters.

All Sects Worship But the One Truth

(Typical of India's toleration, this prayer has gained wide vogue in modern times.)

He whom the Śaivas adore as Śiva [the Auspicious], the Vedāntins as the Absolute, the Buddhists as Buddha [the Enlightened], the Logicians, adepts in demonstrative proofs, as the author of the world, those devoted to Jainism as the Arhat [the Worthy], the Mīmāṁsakas as ordained duty—may that Hari, the Lord of the three worlds, extend to you the desired fruit.

Benediction

(*This prayer is used at the end of all public recitals of the epics.*)

May there be welfare for the people; may rulers follow the righteous path and protect the world; may there always be good to cows and Brāhmans; may the entire universe be happy.

Appendix

BIBLIOGRAPHY

BOUQUET, A. C. *Hinduism.* New York: Hutchinson's University Library, 1948.

A brief, modern exposition of Hinduism, one of the series on World Religions, published as an introductory study for the general reader.

BROWN, PERCY. *Indian Architecture.* Bombay: D. B. Taraporevala Sons & Co., Ltd., 1942.

A popular account of Hindu and Buddhist architecture in India.

BROWN, W. NORMAN (ed.). *India, Pakistan, Ceylon.* Ithaca, N.Y.: Cornell University Press, 1950.

Concise, authoritative articles on the history and culture of the Middle East, providing excellent background for the study of contemporary Hinduism.

CHATTERJEE, SATIS CHANDRA. *The Fundamentals of Hinduism.* Calcutta: Das Gupta & Co., 1950.

A brief, introductory, philosophical study of Hinduism, well written and easily understandable by western students.

CHATTERJEE, SATIS CHANDRA, and DUTTA, D. M. *An Introduction to Indian Philosophy.* Calcutta: University of Calcutta, 1950.

One of the clearest expositions of Indian philosophy.

FARQUHAR, J. N. *An Outline of the Religious Literature of India.* London: Oxford University Press, 1920.

A mine of information making this an indispensable book for students of Indian religious literature. Although some of the author's conclusions may be questioned by Hindus, it gives information not available elsewhere.

GANDHI, M. K. *Autobiography—The Story of My Experiments with Truth.* Washington, D.C.: Public Affairs Press, 1948.

A revealing picture of the attitudes of a devout Hindu.

GANDHI, M. K. *Hindu Dharma.* Ahmedabad: Navajivan Publishing House, 1950.

Gandhi's writings dealing with religion, edited by Bharatan Kumarappa.

GARRATT, G. T. (ed.). *The Legacy of India.* London: Oxford University Press, 1937.

Short, introductory essays giving background information useful for the study of Hinduism.

HIRIYANNA, M. *The Essentials of Indian Philosophy.* London: George Allen & Unwin Ltd., 1949.

A simpler and shorter edition of the author's *Outlines of Indian Philosophy,* designed for the general reader.

HIRIYANNA, M. *Outlines of Indian Philosophy.* New York: The Macmillan Co., 1932.

A clear, concise, and complete study of Indian philosophy, one of the best available, done by one of the great Hindu scholars of this generation.

HUME, ROBERT ERNEST. *The Thirteen Principal Upanishads.* London: Oxford University Press, 1934.

The introduction, as well as the translation, make this a valuable book for the study of Hinduism.

MONIER-WILLIAMS, M. *Hinduism.* Calcutta: Susil Gupta (India) Ltd., 1951.

First published in 1877, this study of Hinduism is still useful, full of information which is not readily available elsewhere.

NIKHILANANDA, SWAMI. *The Bhagavad Gita.* New York: Ramakrishna-Vivekananda Center, 1944.

A translation with an introduction and notes which make this the most useful edition of the Gita for those who would understand it from the Hindu point of view.

NIKHILANANDA, SWAMI. *The Gospel of Sri Ramakrishna.* New York: Ramakrishna-Vivekananda Center, 1942.

The conversations of Sri Ramakrishna with his disciples, devotees, and visitors; one of the best available books presenting the religious attitudes of contemporary Hinduism.

NIKHILANANDA, SWAMI. *The Upanishads.* New York: Harper & Bros., 1949.

Two volumes of a projected six-volume translation of the Upanishads have been published, with introductions and full notes which make these sacred writings much more understandable for the western reader.

NIRVEDANANDA, SWAMI. *Hinduism at a Glance.* Vidyamandira, Dhakuria, Bengal: S. Mandel, 1946.

A brief, introductory exposition of Hinduism, written by a devout

Hindu, designed for the Indian or westerner who knows little about the religion.

POPLEY, H. A. *The Music of India.* Calcutta: Y.M.C.A. Publishing House, 1950.

An introduction to Indian music which can be readily understood by the layman.

RADHAKRISHNAN, S. *The Bhagavadgita.* New York: Harper & Bros., 1948.

A translation with the Sanskrit text transliterated and an illuminating introduction and notes.

RADHAKRISHNAN, S. *The Hindu View of Life.* New York: The Macmillan Co., 1931.

Four lectures outlining the beliefs of Hinduism; a popular book which has been translated into many languages as a standard introduction to Hinduism.

RADHAKRISHNAN, S. *Indian Philosophy,* 2 vols. London: George Allen & Unwin, Ltd., 1948.

A full authoritative exposition of the philosophies of India, by India's most famous scholar and philosopher.

RADHAKRISHNAN, S. (ed.). *History of Philosophy: Eastern and Western,* 2 vols. London: George Allen & Unwin, Ltd., 1952.

This work was sponsored by the Government of India and edited by S. Radhakrishnan, A. R. Wadia, D. M. Datta, and Humayun Kabir. Over sixty scholars from India, China, and Europe have contributed articles which outline clearly the chief philosophical positions of the world. Volume I includes brief articles on the leading philosophical schools of India, written by men of recognized competence.

RAGHAVAN, V. *Prayers, Praises and Psalms.* Madras: G. A. Natesan & Co., 1938.

Translation of the hymns and prayers which are in common use among Hindus.

RAJAGOPALACHARI, C. *Mahabharata.* New Delhi: The Hindustan Times, 1950.

A readable retelling of the Mahabharata epic, closely following the form and spirit of the original.

RAWLINSON, H. G. *India, A Short Cultural History.* New York: Frederick A. Praeger, Inc., 1952.

A short, informative history of the cultural development of India, with many useful illustrations.

SARMA, D. S. *The Prince of Ayodhya.* Madras: Sri Ramakrishna Math, 1946.

The story of the epic Ramayana, told in a narrative style which retains the spirit of the original.

SARMA, D. S. *The Renaissance of Hinduism.* Banaras: Banaras Hindu University, 1944.

Biographical studies of the leaders who have made outstanding contributions to Hinduism in the nineteenth and twentieth centuries.

SARMA, D. S. *What is Hinduism?* Madras: The Madras Law Journal Office, 1945.

An illuminating introductory exposition of Hinduism, designed for the general reader.

THOMAS, P. *Epics, Myths and Legends of India.* Bombay: D. B. Taraporevala Sons & Co., Ltd., n.d.

A popular, generally sympathetic discussion of Hindu myths, gods, and customs. Contains much interesting material not generally available.

THOMAS, P. *Hindu Religion, Customs, and Manners.* Bombay: D. B. Taraporevala Sons & Co., Ltd., n.d.

A popular, generally sympathetic account of Indian religions, customs, ceremonies, literature, music, and arts; full of interesting details.

ZIMMER, HEINRICH. *Myths and Symbols in Indian Art and Civilization.* New York: Pantheon Books, Inc., 1947.

An outstanding study of the meaning of the symbols of Hinduism; of great help to western readers who seek to understand Hinduism.

ZIMMER, HEINRICH. *Philosophies of India.* New York: Pantheon Books Inc., 1951.

Dr. Zimmer's posthumous papers on the philosophies of India, edited by Joseph Campbell, give the perceptive insights of a great scholar.

GLOSSARY

(Editor's Note: These definitions are given in the form approved by the writers of this book—although not all the writers agree entirely with the wording in every definition.)

āchārya—the spiritual teacher, so called because he puts into practice his teachings and guides the pupil along the spiritual path.

adhikāra—spiritual competence; the idea that religious teaching should be graded according to the competence of the pupil.

advaita—monism; different forms of this doctrine are current in Hindu philosophy, the most famous being that of the absolute monism of Śaṅkara.

Āgamas—scriptures of certain later Hindu sects, mainly Tāntric.

Agni—god of Fire, guardian of the southeast quarter of the compass.

Agrahāyaṇa—one of the twelve lunar months (November-December).

ahiṁsā—nonviolent spirit in defense of Truth; harmlessness; noninjury to beings and things in thought, word, or deed; the vow of noninjury to life.

Ālvārs—medieval mystical Vaishṇava poets of southern India.

Apsaras—celestial damsels, courtesans of the heavens.

Āraṇyaka—The Forest Books, the Vedic writings coming between the Brāhmaṇas and the Upanishads.

arghya—an offering used in worship in the home and temple, consisting of grain, flowers, leaves, grass, and water.

Arjuna—one of the five Paṇḍava brothers in the Mahābhārata story; noted for his skill in archery.

artha—wealth, worldly prosperity; regarded as one of the four ends of man.

Ārya Samāj—modern Hindu organization which seeks to persuade Hindus to return to the Vedas.

Āshāḍha—one of the twelve lunar months (June-July).

āśrama—a hermitage where men noted for their holiness and learning live; also one of the four stages of the ideal life.

āśramadharma—the body of rules of conduct, duties, and obligations relating to the four stages in the personal life of a Hindu.

Asuras—demons, the enemies of gods.

Āśvina—one of the twelve lunar months (September-October).

Asyavāmīya—a long philosophical hymn in the Ṛigveda (I.164) beginning with the words "asya vām."

Atharvaveda—the fourth Saṁhitā of the Veda, dealing with the affairs of daily life, and incidentally with charms and incantations that ensure safety and immunity from evil and mishaps.

ātman—the Self; the Universal Spirit approached from the subjective side.

avatāra—the descending of god into the world in different forms in order to correct the growing evils in the world; an incarnation.

avidyā—original ignorance, the cause of the illusion that the true Self is identical with the body and the senses and is different from the Supreme Being; the illusion that the phenomenal world is essentially real.

Āyurveda—the system of medicine growing out of the Atharvaveda and first outlined in the auxiliaries of the Vedas.

Balarāma—Kṛishṇa's elder brother, born to Rohiṇī in the cowherd village.

bāṇaliṅga—a stone found in the Narmadā river and used as a symbol for Śiva.

Bhādrapada—one of the twelve lunar months (August-September).

Bhagavad Gītā—the discourse between Kṛishṇa and Arjuna on the field of battle, retold in the Mahābhārata.

bhāgavata—devotee of Vishṇu, an ardent bhakta.

Bhāgavata Purāṇa—the story of Vishṇu's incarnations, especially of the incarnation as Lord Kṛishṇa.

bhajana—a song of devotional love.

bhakta—a devotee, one who worships the Lord with fervent love.

bhakti—devotion, fervent love of God.

bhakti yoga—path leading to union with God through self-forgetting love and devotion.

Bharata—Rāma's brother.

Bhīma—one of the five Pāṇḍava brothers in the Mahābhārata story; noted for his strength.

Bhīshma—the grand-uncle of the Pāṇḍavas and Kauravas in the Mahābhārata; the embodiment of continence, unselfishness, loyalty, and wisdom.

Brahmā—the primary creator, first member of the Hindu Triad, or Trinity.

Brahman—the Ultimate Absolute which is the sole basis of the universe; the Supreme Being; Ultimate Reality.

Brāhman—the first of the four Hindu castes; a priest, a man of knowledge.

Brāhmaṇas—part of the Veda consisting of discussion and elucidation of the Vedic mantras, mainly from the ritualistic point of view.

Brahmaputra—a sacred river flowing from the Himālayas to the plains of eastern India.

Brāhmo Samāj—modern Hindu organization seeking reforms in Hinduism.

Chaitanya—leader of a Vaishṇavite devotional movement centering around Kṛishṇa, and founder of a philosophical school known as dualistic monism.

Chaitra—one of the twelve lunar months (March-April).

Chaṇḍikā—another name for Durgā.

darśanas—a school of philosophy or a view of life connected with or inspired by the Upanishads; doctrines prescribed in any system of philosophy or religion.

Daśarā—also called Durgā-pūjā; the major autumn festival at which Śakti in one of her forms is worshiped.

Daśaratha—Rāma's father.

Devakī—Kṛishṇa's mother.

dharma—righteousness, duty, law; the path which a man should follow in accordance with his nature and his station in life; one of the four ends of man.

Dharma Śāstras—part of the sacred writings, dealing with rules of conduct, morality, and social law.

Dhṛitarāshṭra—blind ruler of the Kuru clan in the Mahābhārata.

Draupadī—wife of the five Pāṇḍava brothers.

Droṇa—one of the elder statesmen and a famous warrior-teacher of the clan of the Kurus, in the Mahābhārata.

Durgā—female goddess, the divine Śakti, in the form of a goddess; the Divine Mother.

dūrvā—a species of grass used in the ceremonial worship of the deities.

Duryodhana—eldest son of Dhṛitarāshṭra, leader of the Kauravas against the Pāṇḍavas in the Mahābhārata.

dvaita—philosophical school of dualistic theism developed by Madhva.

dvaitādvaita—literally, 'dual-nondual'; philosophical system of dualistic monism founded by Nimbārka.

Gaṇapati—another name for Gaṇeśa.

Gaṇeśa—the god with the elephant head, son of Śiva and Pārvatī; mainly celebrated as the remover of obstacles.

Gaṅgā—the goddess representing the river Ganges.

Ganges—the most sacred of the rivers of India.

Garuḍa—the vehicle of Vishṇu, also known as Suparna the Vedic sun-bird.

Gāyatrī—famous Vedic prayer to the Sun, used in daily worship.

ghee—clarified butter, made by melting butter and pouring off the liquid, clarified portion, which is the ghee.

Godāvarī—one of the seven sacred rivers of India.

gopī—cowherd girl from the cowherd village where Kṛishṇa lived; devotee of Kṛishṇa.

guṇas—the three subtle elements which make up primal matter (prakṛiti).

guru—the teacher; the spiritual preceptor who has himself attained spiritual insight.

Hanumān—the monkey hero who helped Rāma recover Sītā; a deified devotee of Rāma; sometimes called Mahāvīra, the Great Hero.

Hara—another name for Śiva.

Hari—another name for Vishṇu.

Hariśchandra—hero in a Mahābhārata story, famous for keeping his word at any cost.

Harivaṁśa—appendix to the Mahābhārata, primarily concerned with stories about Kṛishṇa.

haṭha yoga—one of the four types of yoga, based on postures and control of the physical processes in the human body.

Indra—the most prominent Vedic god of the Heavens; guardian of the east quarter of the compass; later superseded by Vishṇu and Śiva.

Indus—one of the seven sacred rivers of India, also called Sindhu.

ishṭa-devatā—the chosen deity, the deity which best satisfies the devotee and becomes the primary object of his devotion.

Īśvara—the personal god.

Jagannātha—the image of Kṛishṇa in the temple at Puri.

japa—the repetition of a mantra or a name or names of a god.

jīva—the individual embodied soul.

jīvanmukta—the Self which has realized its oneness with Brahman while still in its human body.

jīvanmukti—the state of the jīvanmukta.

jñāna—transcendent knowledge of the Supreme Being.

jñāna yoga—doctrine concerning liberation through transcendent knowledge of the Supreme Being.

Jumna—one of the seven sacred rivers of India, also called Yamuna.

Jyeshṭha—one of the twelve lunar months (May-June).

Kabīr—late medieval mystic who tried to combine some of the religious teachings of the Muslims and Hindus.

Kālī—female goddess, Śakti, in the form of the Divine Mother.

Kalkin—the tenth incarnation of Vishṇu, yet to come (held by some to be now current).

kalpa—aeon, the period including the creation and the dissolution of one universe; and auxiliary part of the Vedas.

kāma—used in various meanings: love, erotic pleasure, enjoyment, the ordinary pleasures of life, the pleasures of the senses; one of the four ends of man.

Kāma—the god of love.

Kaṁsa—ruler of Mathurā who tried to kill Kṛishṇa at the time of his birth.

Kanyā-kumārī—the virgin goddess in the shrine at Cape Comorin.

Kapila—the founder of the Sāṅkhya system of philosophy.

karma—literally, action; the law of causation applied to the moral realm showing that all actions have inevitable moral consequences in this life or the next; sometimes used in the sense of the effect of past deeds, or the stock of merit or demerit arising from past deeds which causes rebirth.

karma yoga—doctrine concerning liberation through disinterested service, through the selfless performance of one's duties.

Kārttika—one of the twelve lunar months (October-November).

Kārttikeya—the warrior god, commander of the Divine Army, the son of Śiva and Pārvatī; also called Skanda, Kumāra, or Subrahmaṇya.

Kauravas—descendants of Kuru, the one hundred sons of Dhṛitarāshṭra; cousins and opponents of the five Pāṇḍava brothers in the Mahābhārata story.

Kāverī (Cauvery)—one of the seven sacred rivers of India.

kīrtana—a song of devotional love.

Kṛishṇa—an avatāra of Vishṇu, sometimes worshiped as Vishṇu himself.

Kshatriya—the ruling and warrior caste, the second of the four Hindu castes.

Kubera—the god of wealth; the guardian of the north quarter of the compass.

Kuru—the clan to which belonged the parties involved in the war described in the Mahābhārata.

Kurukshetra—the sacred battlefield where the Mahābhārata war was fought.

kuśa—a species of grass essential for domestic rites and ceremonies.

Lakshmaṇa—beloved brother and constant companion of Rāma.

Lakshmī—goddess of wealth and good fortune; wife of Vishṇu, mother of Kāma.

Laṅkā—home of the demon Rāvaṇa who carried Sītā away from Rāma; generally identified with Ceylon.

laya yoga—one of the four types of yoga, it seeks to merge the spirit of the worshiper in the Ultimate Reality.

līlā—the free, sportive, playful will of God.

liṅga—literally, "indicating symbol" of Śiva; shaped somewhat like a post, regarded as an abstract symbol of Śiva.

Madhva—thirteenth-century philosopher who developed the school of dualistic theism (dvaita).

Māgha—one of the twelve lunar months (January-February).

Mahābhārata—one of the two great epics of India; tells the story of the struggle between the Pāṇḍavas and Kauravas.

Mahādeva—Śiva, the Great God.

Mahākāla—Śiva, the Great God of Time Eternal.

Mahamāya—the goddess of illusion, an aspect of Durgā.

Maheśvara—Śiva, the Great God.

Manasā—the snake goddess, mother of the Nāgas, sister of the serpent god, Ananta.

maṇḍala—mystic symbols made on the ground usually with powders of five different colors; worshiped by the initiated as representing any of the deities.

mantra—a syllable, word, or verse which has been revealed to a Seer in meditation; an embodiment in sound of a deity.

mantra yoga—one of the four types of yoga in which worship and devotion predominate.

Manu—the patriarch and Seer who outlined the rules of conduct for Hinduism.

maṭh—a monastery where groups of ascetics live and study.

māyā—from the human point of view, māyā is illusion producing ignorance; from the point of view of the creator, it is the will or energy to create the appearance of the world; the illusion by which the One Absolute appears as many; cosmic energy; the material cause of the world.

mela—religious gathering, attended by hundreds of thousands of pilgrims; held periodically at Hardwar, Allahabad, Ujjain, Nasik, and other pilgrimage places.

Mīmāṁsā—philosophical school emphasizing the authority of the Vedas; one of the six classical schools of philosophy.

moksha—liberation, or release, from the bondage of finite existence; one of the four ends of man.

mudrā—a mystic and symbolic gesture of the hands and fingers.

Nāga—snake deity.

Nānak—founder of Sikhism, the religion of the Sikhs.

Nandi—sacred bull, vehicle of Śiva.

Nārāyaṇa—another name for Vishṇu.

Narmadā—one of the seven sacred rivers of India.

Naṭarāja—Śiva dancing, symbolizing the cosmic processes.

Nāyanārs—medieval, mystical, Śaiva poets of southern India.

Nibandhas—writings popular since about the ninth century A.D., mainly dealing with rituals, domestic rites, and social law.

Nimbārka—Vaishṇava teacher of the philosophical system of dvaitādvaita.

Nirṛiti—ancient deity of darkness and evil, the guardian of the southwest quarter of the compass.

nyāsa—the act of placing the deity or deities in the body by symbolically touching the forehead, upper arm, chest, and thighs, signifying the identification of the worshiper with the deity or deities he worships.

Nyāya—one of the six classical schools of philosophy, pluralistic and theistic, mainly known for its system of logic.

OM—the most sacred mantra of the Vedas; it stands for both the personal and impersonal God.

Padmanābha—another name for Vishṇu, the Lord with Brahmā born of his navel of lotus.

Pāṇḍavas—the five sons of Pāṇḍu, victorious in the battle in the Mahābhārata: Yudhishṭhira, Arjuna, Bhīma, Nakula, and Sahadeva.

paṇḍit—a learned man, a scholar; also, a title sometimes used for Brāhmans.

Pāṇḍu—brother of Dhṛitarāshṭra, father of the five Pāṇḍava brothers.

paramahaṁsa—the fourth, and highest, stage in the development of a sannyāsin, in which union with the Ultimate Reality has been attained.

Paraṁbrahma—the Supreme God.

Paraśurāma—Rāma with an axe in his hand, the incarnation of Vishṇu as a Brāhman chastising the Kshatriyas.

Pārvatī—the daughter of the Himālaya Mountain, wife of Śiva.

Patañjali—author of the Yoga Sūtras setting forth the system of yogic disciplines.

paṭṭa—stone or metal plaque with figures of the chosen deity carved on it.

Pausha—one of the twelve lunar months (December-January).

Phālguna—one of the twelve lunar months (February-March).

pitṛi—deceased forefather, dwelling in the heavenly regions.

Prajāpati—the creator, progenitor of men, often represented as a great teacher; later identified with Brahmā.

prakṛiti—the ultimate material cause of the universe; unconscious primal matter; ultimate cosmic energy.

prāṇāyāma—breath control; used in daily meditations, and as part of the yogic disciplines; consists of breathing in, holding the breath, and breathing out, in a rhythmic manner.

Pratyabhijñā—monistic, theistic system of philosophy associated with the Śaivism of Kashmir.

pūjā—worship of an image of any deity.

Purāṇas—ancient texts giving popular stories and legends about gods and heroes, often embodying the teachings of Hinduism.

purusha—the principle of consciousness as opposed to prakṛiti, or matter; sometimes used in the sense of the plurality of selves in the universe.

Rādhā—the celebrated gopī, or cowherdess, who was Kṛishṇa's favorite of all his female devotees; regarded as Kṛishṇa's Śakti.

Rāhu—ascending node of the moon, sometimes considered to be a planet and considered to be a demon causing eclipses.

rajas—one of the three guṇas; the element which is of the nature of pain, is active and stimulating; restless, energetic.

rāja yoga—one of the four types of yoga; discipline by which the god-centered devotee attains control of body and mind and spirit, and attains self-realization.

Rākshasas—semidivine beings, demons.

Rāma—hero of the epic Rāmāyaṇa; worshiped as a god, the incarnation of Vishṇu.

Rāmakṛishṇa—Bengali religious mystic and teacher who died in 1886; guru of Swami Vivekānanda, the founder of the Rāmakṛishṇa Mission, and now worshiped as an avatāra.

Rāmānandis—followers of Rāmānanda, leader of the devotees who worship Rāma as the Supreme Being.

Rāmānuja—eleventh-century philosopher, teacher of the philosophical system of qualified monism (Viśishṭādvaita).

Rāmarājya—political ideal in which the ruler is the embodiment of truth and righteousness and the ruled are happy and prosperous.

Rāmāyaṇa—epic telling the story of Vishṇu's incarnation as Rāma.

Rāvaṇa—the king of demons who was slain by Rāma; the story is told in the Rāmāyaṇa.

Ṛigveda—basic hymns, mantras, of the Vedas; the first and foremost Saṁhitā Veda; mainly consisting of hymns addressed to various gods.

Ṛishi—Seer, sage, a "see-er" of truths recorded in the Vedas.

ṛita—the natural and moral order in the universe; cosmic law.

Rohiṇī—Mother of Balarāma.

Rudra—Vedic god later identified with Śiva.

sādhana—a course of spiritual teaching or discipline.

sādhu—a general term applied to all holy men.

Śaiva—a devotee of Śiva; pertaining to the worship of Śiva.

Śaiva-Siddhānta—theistic philosophical school of the devotees of Śiva in southern India.

Śaivism—one of the three chief sects in Hinduism, centering in the worship of Śiva.

Śākta—worshiper of the Divine Mother in one of her forms.

Śakti—personified conscious energy; the Divine Mother; female creative power.

Śāktism—one of the three chief sects in Hinduism, worshipers of the Divine Mother.

sālagrāma—small, rounded stones used in worship as symbolizing the living presence of Vishṇu.

samādhi—the final stage in yogic discipline; perfect concentration of the mind on the object of meditation.

Sāmaveda—one of the four Vedas, consisting mostly of musical renderings of mantras of the Ṛigveda.

Saṁhitās—the first portion of the Vedas consisting of collections of the mantras; the core of the Vedic literature.

saṁsāra—the impermanent world into which the individual souls are born; life of phenomenal experiences; the passing of individual souls from one life to another; family.

saṁskāra—the innate tendencies of the individual.

sandhyā—"twilight"; the morning, noon, and evening prayers of the twice-born.

Śaṅkara—famous philosopher, the greatest exponent of the Advaita school of philosophy; about the eighth century A.D.

Sāṅkhya—one of the six darśanas, or classical schools of philosophy; dualistic, realistic.

sannyāsin—a person who has renounced the world and entered the fourth and last stage of human life.

Sarasvatī—goddess of learning and knowledge; often described as the wife of Brahmā; also the name of one of the seven sacred rivers of India.

sat-chit-ānanda—existence, consciousness, bliss; which constitutes the Absolute.

sattva—one of the three guṇas; the element which is of the nature of pleasure and purity; is light and illuminating; harmony, balance, wisdom.

Satyapīr—late medieval deity; combining Hindu and Muslim ideas.

Savitar—the Sun.

Sāvitrī—the heroine in a Mahābhārata story who won her husband from the god of death through her devotion; also the goddess of Gāyatrī.

Śesha—great serpent who symbolizes Time, on whose coils Vishṇu rests on the ocean before creation.

Shashṭhī—the Mother Goddess, worshiped popularly as the protector of children.

śikhā—short lock of hair worn on the top of the head by a devout Hindu, marking the orifice of the spirit, and sometimes thought of as indicating a resolve to face life unmoved by circumstances.

Sītā—wife of Rāma, who is the hero of the Rāmāyaṇa.

Śītalā—goddess of smallpox.

Śiva—the third member of the Hindu Triad, or Trinity, worshiped by the Śaivas.

Śivarātri—special festival for the worship of Śiva, held generally on the fourteenth lunar day (dark fortnight) of Māgha (January-February).

Smārtas—sect of devotees who follow the ancient Smṛitis and who worship equally the Śaiva, Vaishṇava, and Śakti deities.

Smṛiti—literally "that which is remembered," texts written on the basis of the Vedas, mainly dealing with religious practices, domestic rites, and social law.

Soma—the moon; also a kind of creeping vine; also, the juice of that creeper used as an intoxicating drink in the Vedic age.

śrāddha—ceremony in memory of one's dead ancestors.

Śrāvaṇa—one of the twelve lunar months (July-August).

Śrī—another name for Lakshmī, goddess of beauty and prosperity; also mode of address meaning beauty, prosperity, and richness.

Śrī Yantra—the mystic diagram used especially in Śakti worship in temples.

Śrīraṅgam—famous Vaishṇava shrine and pilgrimage center in southern India.

Śruti—literally, "that which was heard," the revealed scriptures usually identified with the Vedas.

Subrahmaṇya—another name for Kārttikeya, the warrior god.

Śūdra—lowest of the four Hindu castes, engaged in labor and service.

Śukla Yajurveda—white Yajurveda, a version of the Yajurveda in which mantras and sacrificial formulas are given separately.

Sūrya—the Sun god.

sushumṇā vein—the spinal channel through which, according to the Tāntric teaching, the spiritual power passes at the time of Realization; the sushumṇā vein starts in the spinal column and goes out at the top of the head.

Sūta Saṁhitā—devotional Purāṇa similar to the Bhāgavata Purāṇa, but devoted to Śiva; popular with Śaivas.

sūtra—an aphorism; a thread of suggestive words or phrases; compact mnemonic phrases summarizing religious and philosophical instruction.

swāmī—an initiated member of a religious order, and one who has renounced the world.

tamas—one of the three guṇas; the element which is of the nature of indifference and inertia, and is heavy, dull, or lazy.

Tantras—esoteric writings on Hinduism outlining spiritual disciplines related generally to the Divine Mother, Śakti.

Tārā—one of the Śākta goddesses; one of the two wives of Bṛihaspati.

tilaka—sectarian marks made with clay, ashes, or sandal paste; usually placed on the forehead; they are made differently for different sects, for instance, horizontal for Śaiva, vertical for Vaishṇava.

Tryambaka—another name for Śiva, with three eyes.

tulasī—a sacred plant; tulasī leaves are used for the ceremonial worship of Vishṇu.

Umā—another name of Pārvatī, daughter of the Himālaya mountain, wife of Śiva.

Upanishads—ancient philosophic and mystical elaboration of the truths of the Veda; the quintessence of Vedic spiritual speculations.

vāhana—that which carries a god, the mount of the god; usually translated "vehicle"; the animal associated with a particular deity.

Vaiśākha—one of the twelve lunar months (April-May).

Vaiśeshika—one of the six darśanas or classical schools of philosophy; pluralistic, theistic.

Vaishṇava—one of the three main sects; worshipers of Vishṇu or one of his incarnations.

Vaiśya—the third of the four Hindu castes, engaged in agriculture and commerce.

Vāk—goddess of speech.

Vālmīki—author of the Rāmāyaṇa.

Varāhamihira—famous astrologer and natural scientist of the sixth century A.D.

varṇadharma—the duties and obligations of the four social orders; also used in the sense of the body of rules governing the caste system.

Varuṇa—god of the sea, of the waters; guardian of the west quarter of the compass.

Vāsudeva—another name for Kṛishṇa.

Vāyu—the wind god; guardian of the northwest quarter of the compass.

Vedāṅgas—the six limbs of the Veda, the six auxiliary branches of instruction supplementing the Vedas.

Vedānta—literally, "the end of the Veda," name given to the highest teaching of the Upanishads and sometimes to the philosophical sūtras based on them; also a system of philosophy based on those writings.

Vedas—primary scriptures of Hinduism

vilva—a sacred tree; the leaves of the vilva (or bel) tree are used for the ceremonial worship of Śiva and Śakti.

Vishṇu—the second member of the Hindu Triad, or Trinity; worshiped by the Vaishṇavas.

Viśishṭādvaita—system of philosophy taught by Rāmānuja; qualified monism.

Vyāsa—author of the Mahābhārata.

Yajurveda—one of the four Vedas, concerned mainly with Vedic sacrifices.

Yakshas—spirits dwelling in trees and woods.

Yama—the god of death; guardian of the south quarter of the compass.

yantra—metal plaque with mystic diagrams inscribed on its surface, used as an object of worship.

Yaśodā—Kṛishṇa's foster mother who brought him up in the cowherd village.

yoga—literally, "union" (with God), or a path leading to that union; a method of concentration as a means of liberation; the cessation of all mental functions.

Yogamāyā—the mystic power of the Lord.

yogi—one who seeks union with the Supreme Being by means of the disciplines of yoga.

Yudhishṭhira—eldest of the five Pāṇḍava brothers in the Mahābhārata.

INDEX

Names of deities are given only once, under: Deities, names.
Names of pilgrimage places are given only once, under: Pilgrimage places.
Names of sacred writings, and selections from them, are given only once, under: Scriptures, *by title*. Selections are indicated by boldface type.